Dangerous Instrument

BRIDGING THE GAP

Series Editors
Goldgeier James
Jentleson Bruce
Steven Weber

Adaptation under Fire:
How Militaries Change in Wartime
David Barno and Nora Bensahel

The Long Game:
China's Grand Strategy to Displace American Order
Rush Doshi

Cyber Persistence Theory:
Redefining National Security in Cyberspace
Michael P. Fischerkeller, Emily O. Goldman, and Richard J. Harknett

War and Chance:
Assessing Uncertainty in International Politics
Jeffrey A. Friedman

Delta Democracy:
Pathways to Incremental Civic Revolution in Egypt and Beyond
Catherine E. Herrold

The Logic of American Nuclear Strategy:
Why Strategic Superiority Matters
Matthew Kroenig

Planning to Fail:
The US Wars in Vietnam, Iraq, and Afghanistan
James H. Lebovic

A Small State's Guide to Influence in World Politics
Tom Long

Delaying Doomsday:
The Politics of Nuclear Reversal
Rupal N. Mehta

Dangerous Instrument

Political Polarization and US Civil-Military Relations

MICHAEL A. ROBINSON

OXFORD
UNIVERSITY PRESS

Oxford University Press is a department of the University of Oxford.
It furthers the University's objective of excellence in research, scholarship,
and education by publishing worldwide. Oxford is a registered trade mark of
Oxford University Press in the UK and certain other countries.

Published in the US of America by Oxford University Press
198 Madison Avenue, New York, NY 10016, US of America.

Cataloging-in-Publication data is on file at Library of Congress

ISBN 978–0–19–761156–2 (pbk.)
ISBN 978–0–19–761155–5 (hbk.)

DOI: 10.1093/oso/9780197611562.001.0001
DOI: 10.1093/oso/9780197611555.001.0001

For my Jojo

For my Jojo

CONTENTS

CONTENTS

ACKNOWLEDGMENTS

This book is the result of years of effort, brought into being only through the support and generosity of so many from whom I have been fortunate enough to learn. It is in this spirit that I offer the deepest gratitude to those who made this work possible, through their mentorship, instruction, and attention. It should be mentioned first the gratitude I hold for the support of my friends and family, without whom I would not be where I am. From this group, including my childhood friends back home, the love of my life, my close comrades in Army service, and my colleagues in the academic world came immeasurable inspiration and encouragement. Most of all I want to thank my mother, my father, and my brother, for the love and support that they have given me my entire life.

This project would not have happened without the teachers I have had along the way, both in and out of the classroom. For the formative influence they had on this project and my own academic aspirations, I offer special thanks to my Stanford doctoral committee members Mike Tomz, Scott Sagan, Kenneth Schultz, and Amy Zegart. I also wish to thank those who provided much-needed advice at critical points in the project's research design development, including Adam Bonica and Paul Sniderman. The collective patience and expertise of this incredible group of scholars is evident not only in the project that became this book, but in demonstrating to me the qualities of truly great teachers. In this spirit, I also offer the deepest of thanks to my colleagues, my outstanding graduate school cohortmates, and my "CMR-ades" in the civil-military relations scholarly community whose professional support and critical eye were integral to this project over the years.

Further, I owe a particular debt of thanks to the wonderful mentors in my career, from whose generosity, care, and attention I have benefited immensely. Chief among these are the leaders at the United States Military Academy Department of Social Sciences—Colonel Suzanne Nielsen, Colonel (ret.)

Tania Chacho, Lieutenant Colonel Heidi Demarest, and Dr. Rob Person—
who granted me the opportunity to go to graduate school, gave me the honor
of teaching in front of cadets, and supported my continued efforts to think and
write about the issues of the day, including the development of this book. Their
counsel and encouragement speak not only to their character as mentors, but to
the amazing culture they have created at SOSH, a true gem amidst both academia
and the military enterprise.

To the ranks of these indispensable mentors I add several civil-military relations experts whose support and advice made this book possible. I thank Risa
Brooks and Heidi Urben, both peerless scholars and mentors, whose generosity
and advice at every step of the process kept this work (and its author) grounded.
I also wish to thank Kori Schake, a two-time teacher of mine reaching back to
my salad days as a cadet at West Point, who not only advised this project on
committee but provided constant encouragement for its success. It would not
be hyperbole to state that without them, this book would never have happened.

Finally, I want to thank those whose advocacy helped bring this project into
being, including Peter Feaver, whose long-standing encouragement to junior
scholars made this book a reality. I also want to thank Bruce Jentleson, Holly
Mitchell, David McBride, Alexcee Bechthold, Thomas Deva, and the entire editorial team at Oxford University Press. I am similarly grateful for the constructive
feedback and counsel of the anonymous reviewers whose critiques helped make
this a better product.

To these individuals—and to the many more too countless to name—I offer
my thanks, in the hopes that the insights and prescriptions herein prove of value
to military leaders, civilian officials, scholars, analysts, and the American citizen.

*The views expressed are those of the author and do not reflect the official policy or
position of the Department of the Army, the US Military Academy, the Department
of State, the Department of Defense or any part of the US government.*

LIST OF ILLUSTRATIONS

LIST OF TABLES

*"...the Army...is a **dangerous instrument** to play with..."*
George Washington, a letter a Alexander Hamilton, April 4, 1783

Introduction

How do you politicize a military? At a glance, the answer in the American case may be just as Ernest Hemingway suggested one goes bankrupt: "gradually, then suddenly."[1] Indeed, both long-unfolding and recent trends are evident in the precarious future of American democratic traditions, reflecting a general loss of trust in their governing institutions. At the top, low confidence in bureaucratic and federal agencies has crystallized as partisan identity increasingly shapes perceptions of government performance. Among the public, cultural animosity and interpersonal tribalism have sharpened as that same partisanship alienates individuals from each other. The state of hyper-polarization that has invaded nearly every aspect of American political life has brought with it the threat of "politicizing" institutions that have traditionally remained outside the skirmishes of partisan politics. Even casual observers of politics are likely aware of the problem posed by such politicization. The maintenance of fair law enforcement establishments, independent court systems, and credible scientific communities—to name a few—relies on an institutional credibility that sets them apart from mere secondary partisan battlefields. The focus of this book concerns the struggle for non-partisanship among America's most favored institution: the military.

This analysis of partisan polarization and the civil-military relationship comes at a critical juncture, as concerns over the erosion of democratic institutions and advancing authoritarianism worldwide have ignited debate over the future of American governance. Some of the most popular books of the day bear names like *How Democracies Die, How Civil Wars Start,* and *Twilight of Democracy,* while the United States has experienced a noticeable decline across numerous metrics of democratic quality adopted by political scientists.[2] Surveys of the American public reveal sharp divides over matters of objective fact, the growing influence of mis- and disinformation sources, and a creeping normalization of political violence in line with partisan identity.[3] Amidst this backdrop is the American military, both a reliable bastion of public esteem and one increasingly immersed in unprecedented partisan political waters.

Dangerous Instrument: Political Polarization and US Civil-Military Relations. Michael A. Robinson,
Oxford University Press. © Oxford University Press 2023. DOI: 10.1093/oso/9780197611555.003.0001

The modern relationship between the American public and its military is complicated. In the span of fifty years, the military has gone from its nadir of public confidence following the Vietnam War to a seemingly untouchable post-9/11 level of prestige. But this reversal of fortune for the military's image has occurred alongside a shrinking understanding amongst the public of the military and veterans. Citizens consistently register high confidence in the military institution despite organizational mismanagement, ethical scandals, and two decades of frustrated stalemates abroad.[4] This same confidence, it should be noted, far outstrips the public's impression of the representative institutions in government that characterize American democracy.[5] A cursory glance at such patterns might lead one to suspect that the military enjoys an unassailable insulation from politicization amidst rising partisan polarization. In short, that despite the tangible effects of politicizing behavior on public regard for the courts, mass media, or law enforcement, the armed forces possess some ineffable quality. One of the central contentions of this book is that this assumption is deeply flawed.

While not the specific focus of this study, the nature of public confidence in the military is an important pattern in understanding the dynamics of military politicization today. Many scholars and policy-makers have steadily observed these trends at the surface level, seeing high public confidence in the military as evidence of strong civil-military relations or even as an example for other institutions to follow. But these patterns—subjects of increasing concern in civil-military affairs—aren't happening in a vacuum. The political environment in which they exist reflects different normative sensibilities, media environments, and governing philosophies than those that existed in the foundational years of civil-military theory. Perhaps more troublingly, an increasing deference to the military amongst many Americans has run concurrently with spiking dissatisfaction with democratic governance, acute partisan polarization, and growing acceptance of illiberal political norms. As developed democracies in many areas of the world struggle to hold back a tide of anti-democratic political activity, the United States continues to imbue most of its trust in its least democratic institution.

When observed against such a backdrop, Americans' relationship to the military has far different implications. Despite long-held norms against their inclusion in partisan politics, military figures are more present in that sphere than at any time in modern history, whether intentionally or unintentionally. Retired military officers have crossed into this arena as regular political appointees, popular policy commentators, and outright partisan rabblerousers. Even active-duty servicemembers have found themselves drawn into partisan fights, not only as instruments of policy, but totems of institutional credibility. As polarization degrades the traditional firewall that has kept professional institutions like the military out of partisan politics, the result is an environment ripe for politicization.

The purpose of this book is to gain new insights into the state of civil-military relations in a time where partisan polarization, selective media exposure, democratic backsliding, and military politicization have taken on new proportions and higher stakes. The seemingly positive pattern of confidence in the military institution over time may instead mask a more negative trend of political tribalism and illiberal norms, with potentially deleterious effects to American democracy. What do we mean by "politicization" and what are the ways in which this idea can manifest? With whom does the military have credibility, and why? What are the *limits* of that credibility, and how does this reflect the depths of polarization? What are the implications of such deference to the armed forces on the future of democratic governance? Using data-driven analysis of experimental and observational information about the American public, this book offers a humble contribution to answering each of these questions, concluding with recommendations for policy-makers and national security professionals on how best to curtail the negative effects of politicization on civil-military affairs.

A Persistent Dilemma

In the tradition of developed democracies, the structural arrangements that govern how civilian leaders interact with their militaries all seek to address a common dilemma: how to house a martial institution like the armed forces within a liberal democracy without either failing at their respective functions. The mandate of the military—to fight and win wars—and its important possession of the means of force within the state requires a civil-military architecture capable of reconciling its existence with a free society that places a premium on non-violent conflict resolution. This challenge, which civil-military scholar Peter Feaver refers to as the civil-military "problematique," has elicited a variety of theoretical solutions and prescriptions over time.[6] How can the military perform its own role as institutional security guarantor without threatening the larger framework of liberal democratic governance?

Many civil-military frameworks have been strongly influenced by the prescriptions of political scientist Samuel Huntington in his 1957 treatise *The Soldier and the State* in which he outlined two architectural plans for civil-military co-existence, the most favored being the concept of "objective civilian control."[7] This arrangement, devised on a "division of labor" between civilians and the military, envisions both in respective spheres of responsibility. The former articulates broad strategic goals and political objectives, while the latter tends to the execution of policy on the battlefield. The American military's own organizational ethic seemingly reflects the aspirations of objective control and Huntington's assertion that civilian leaders can maintain both liberal political values and a competent military establishment by compartmentalizing the latter into a profession that is politically "sterile and neutral."[8] Despite its many anachronisms and lack of fit within the modern national security environment, even this basic arrangement requires a credible military institution composed of reliable experts in the training and implementation of the force. Therefore, a cornerstone of this classical civil-military theory is a prohibition against partisan activity by the military, a tradition that successive scholars would deem essential to the maintenance of a stable solution to the "problematique."[9]

This school of thought obliges the removal of the military from the partisan political sphere in order to satisfy both a "functional" imperative for the armed forces to win wars, as well as a "societal" imperative to prevent threats to liberal governance.[10] This is not only a normative measure, but a pragmatic policy, ensuring both a stable democratic regime and a unified command structure effective in wartime. As a result, institutionalized control of the military by civilian political leaders is commonly seen as a mainstay requirement of true democratic governance. This concept of *objective control* has informed the study of civil-military relations for decades and has strongly influenced the American military's professional education and organizational ethos.[11] This does not mean, as we will observe, that objective control's purist vision for civil-military relations is either sound or realistic. For example, this theoretical firewall between the military and "politics" not only applied to overt displays of partisan affiliation, but to any involvement in the political roots of policy more broadly. Many scholars, such as Risa Brooks, have since expressed skepticism at this extreme interpretation of the "apolitical norm," as a hyper-aversion to "politics" that could prevent military officers from performing their job effectively.[12] Eliot Cohen similarly argues that military and political leaders operate in a common, if "unequal" dialogue regarding security affairs given civilian control of the process. As such, political elites are better served by involving themselves directly in the military "sphere" rather than outsourcing its management to military elites.[13] Despite its influence, it is objective control's blindness to the actual intersections of partisan politics and military affairs that demands additional scrutiny.

In this sense, it is *Soldier and the State*'s own (if ill-favored) inverse concept of *subjective control* that may prove more important in understanding military politicization today. While the "separate spheres" approach of objective control sought to solve the problematique through professionalization and independence of activity, subjective control captured efforts to directly influence the normative values of the military itself. Civil-military scholars such as Morris Janowitz offered a similar observation that military and civilian responsibilities in security decision-making are not so easily subjected to a clean division of labor and that the American political system is in fact designed to accommodate a military voice in policy-making.[14] Instead, this *convergence* idea assumes that "it is inevitable that the military will come to resemble a political pressure group," such that the only meaningful insurance for the preservation of liberal values and civilian control is for the larger society to more directly shape the character of the military institution.[15] Recent American and comparative political trends have even encouraged some scholars to re-examine the utility of subjective control's application in the US case.[16] While the institutionalized guardrails of objective control are depicted as protections against a politicized military, the integrative tenets of subjective control (and similar sociological approaches to civil-military relations) take such politicization as table stakes. In this school of thought the military is inevitably entwined with partisan politics: the best that liberal-minded civilian politicians can do is bring the military into line with civilian political values.

Understanding these different accounts of the military's relationship with both civilian leaders and the mass public is even more significant today given the contemporary challenges faced by democratic governments. The classical theorists have informed much of our understanding of civil-military relations, particularly in the American context, offering seemingly contradictory accounts of the most favorable methods by which the civilian political elite can constrain the military in society. The key thread that connects them is a common concern regarding a military institution captured by specific partisan interests such that it cannot be trusted to live peaceably alongside a democratic society. If objective control more cleanly separates the military from politics, it may prove naive to the actual nexus between them. Similarly, if subjective control accepts some baseline politicization of the military as given, its prescription to have civilian leaders shape the institution's character may assume too much about those same civilians' political incentives. In either case, the conflation of the military and partisan political institutions not only poses a potential challenge to the functionality of the armed forces, but to the stability of democratic governance more broadly.[17] These frameworks will inform much of the subsequent analysis of this work, as we assess the causes and consequences of politicization and how these classical ideas can help us make sense of them.

While models of civil-military architecture vary, the proscription against "political" activity by the military has been a centerpiece of professional educa-tion and organizational ethics for the modern officer corps. One of the principal contributions of this book will be to examine how recent political trends have affected the extent to which this norm persists and the different ways in which politicization of the military can manifest. The twin patterns of high public trust in the military and deepening partisan polarization amongst that same public have resulted in an environment where politicization of institutions like the military is more likely. A politicized institution, as defined by Alice Hunt Friend, "exercises loyalty to a single political party and/or consistently advocates for and defends partisan political positions and fortunes."[18] Heidi Urben discusses the challenge of politicization as a function of political activity by the institution or its representatives, namely, whether the armed forces are too partisan in composition, too vocal in speech, or too resistant to civilian control.[19] These are helpful foundations for understanding this idea of politicization: by these categorizations, both existing civil-military relations thought and the more intuitive requirements of democracy demand that the military not only avoid being politicized by partisan organizations, but refrain from politicizing itself.

Indeed, this conceptualization of politicizing behavior is essential to the succeeding chapters' analysis on its many manifestations. When individuals hear that an issue or institution is being "politicized," the reflexive assumption is often that the item under dispute is being used for partisan political gain against some perceived normative prohibition or expectation. For example, when major events shake the public consciousness, any resulting discussion of the policy implications or sources of culpability may be seen as "politicizing" the issue if the proposal redounds to the benefit of one party's political agenda over another.[20] Politicized domains, therefore, are typically ones in which no bipartisan consensus exists, leaving room for repurposing issue areas, key individuals, or even whole institutions for the benefit of partisan political advantage.[21] With regards to the military, traditional norms against its use as a partisan implement—or self-advancement as one—reflect the belief among many civil-military scholars that a non-partisan military is a public good and to use it as a partisan instrument "politicizes" an otherwise objective institution.

However, an important distinction will inform the use of "politicization" as a term in this book, in an effort to provide clearer criteria for its sources and consequences. As Jim Golby notes, political science offers an opportunity to provide such clarity as opposed to less precise or amorphous employment of the concept.[22] Civilian leaders in charge of military activities nearly always represent some partisan interest, whether as appointees or as private citizens who harbor some political sensibilities closer to one party or the other. When it comes to the military, organizational oversight, administrative reform, and employment at home and abroad fall into the hands of these same individuals. In addition, the military may reform organizational practices or engage in decision-making that reflects a non-partisan desire to improve its own functionality in warfighting or administrative management. Are these politicizing acts? In both cases, politicization can still occur because of the distorting effects of partisanship amongst the public. One of the effects of polarization in American politics, as we will see, is the increasing number of issue domains over which there is no bipartisan consensus. The more "partisan" issues there are, the higher the probability that actions taken by any actor—whether military or civilian, intentional or incidental—will have a politicizing effect. This can occur from purposeful partisan behavior taken by civilian politicians or military officers as well as actions taken in good faith by these same figures in accordance with the legal bounds of their respective offices.

Therefore, this book envisions military politicization as any activity taken by military or civilian actors that not only moves the armed forces closer to advocacy of (or opposition to) a specific political party, but creates the *perception* that this is the case. This likely expands the universe of cases that have some politicizing effect on the military, from executive-level employment of the force, to Congressional activity, to more overt examples of using the military for partisan gain. To be sure, the most noticeable instances of politicizing behavior often occur when key actors step outside their prescribed roles. Military leaders engaging in partisan advocacy or civilian leaders leveraging the military in legally dubious ways certainly fit this bill. But politicization, as we will uncover, can occur without intention and without any actors deviating from Constitutionally envisioned roles. Politicization may therefore be just as much a function of observable effect as purposeful motive. It is this distinction that will inform our understanding of how high public confidence in the military and declining cross-partisan consensus both contribute to several categories of politicization.

Chapter 2 will outline a basic typology of politicizing behaviors based on this definition, acknowledging the importance of three major players in civil-military relations: the public, the military itself, and the major political parties. From this constellation of bodies—and their relative position to one another in a perceived ideological space—we will identify four patterns of politicization from the perspective of the observing public. *Active* and *passive* politicization occur when the "moving" actor is the military; specifically, when the military engages in behavior that either moves the institution closer to party "capture," or creates the impression of the same. Active politicization indentifies when this happens due to the purposeful agency of the military itself, while passive politicization identifies when the behavior was ordered or contrived by civilian leaders instead. Of particular importance to these categories is an understanding of the military as a broad community that also includes retired servicemembers, who, though no longer in uniform, represent the institution to the public.

The last two categories address when political bodies re-position *around* the military, creating the illusion of movement. *Relative* politicization occurs when the parties themselves move along the ideological spectrum, leaving the public observer with the impression that the military is now "closer" or "farther away" from one party or another despite a lack of tangible action. By contrast, *aspect* politicization occurs with the opposite: due to media consumption, responses to political rhetoric, or preference shifts, individual observers themselves move along the ideological range, gaining a new (if often incorrect) perspective of the military's position. In total, this *parallax* model of politicization recognizes the importance of relative position for these bodies in the political space, the prospect of illusory movement, and the significance of perspective, all of which are likely shaped by partisan sensibilities.

As this book will detail, these manifestations of politicization pose powerful challenges to the non-partisan norm on which so much of civil-military theory is based. To the scholarly thinkers reviewed here, keeping the military out of partisan political battles has manifest utility: preventing the institution from becoming an advocate for a single political platform or "captured" by a specific political party. Applied to the contemporary environment, this central normative claim fails to account for new political realities. Perhaps more pointedly, it relies on a critical—if potentially flawed—assumption that the public broadly embraces a non-partisan military as a desirable and politically necessary fixture of government. Instead, this assumption's chief obstacle comes in the defining characteristic of the modern political landscape: partisan polarization.

Polarization and the Civil-Military Relationship

Partisan polarization significantly complicates the idealized image of civil-military relations that classical theorists offer. Some of the most important contributions of the succeeding chapters will be to reveal the damaging effects of political tribalism on preserving not only the "politically sterile and neutral" military that Huntington envisioned, but the maintenance of well-functioning democratic governance. Stripping the state's institution for the management of violence of its objectivity has manifestly dangerous implications, made more likely in an environment where the military is increasingly tugged into unfamiliar waters. To be sure, some of the most dire instances of military politicization outside the Unites States have resulted in its institutional capture by domestic partisan factions or its weaponization as an oppressive apparatus. However, even short of the extreme scenarios of brutal state-directed repression or coups d'etat, a loss of military credibility can erode this traditional notion of civil-military relations in a variety of ways.

Through the use of various survey instruments and observational data analysis techniques, this book will probe public attitudes about the military institution, particularly from the vantage offered through the public's partisan identity. From the way individuals consume media to their preconceptions about the armed forces, this effort will provide new insights into the nature of public confidence in its military. It will also attempt to offer recommendations in which military leaders and policy-makers can address the challenges that polarization-driven military politicization poses to the civil-military relationship. First, this trend threatens to compromise the general credibility of the military institution. As indicated in this introduction, the prospect of a military seen as an extension of one political party could collapse public trust in the institution and hamstring its ability to perform its primary function: fighting and winning wars. Given the high level of public trust that the military enjoys with the public, hyper-partisanship makes using military voices for political gain more tempting and potentially lucrative. This can politicize the institution from without, by making the military a prop for partisan opportunism, and from within, by incentivizing partisan activity by representatives of the military institution.

Second, polarization over the quality of the military institution threatens the continued ability of the military to perform its principal function as national security guarantor. A side effect of the tribalism described above is a tendency among specific partisans to view the military as an extension of their own domestic political identity rather than merely an agent of government. Partisan political sensibilities can result in a reticence to criticize or interrogate military decision-making on the battlefield, even amidst failure and frustration, because of the fear of poor "optics." As a result of the desire to insulate the military from criticism, the public is unlikely to learn the lessons of failed foreign policy ventures and are more likely to repeat them in the future. A military institution perceived as hostile to the interests of a large swath of Americans is also unlikely to be attractive for recruitment in an all-volunteer force, degrading its ability to maintain suitable readiness. Failing to internally manage ethnic or political divides within the force could in turn lead to a less effective military, as research by Jason Lyall has shown.[23] Additionally, absorbing the military into existing partisan superstructures would not only result in less objective policy abroad, but could result in ham-handed or neglectful management of organizational issues as well, from matters of gender and race equality in promotion to curtailing sexual assault.

Finally, politicization of the civil-military relationship threatens the long-term stability of democratic governance. The inclusion of the military insti-tution in overtly partisan enterprises not only chips away at the credibility of the armed forces more broadly, but more pointedly increases the likelihood of eroding cherished liberal political norms in the process. Polling of the American public continues to unearth latent attitudes over the acceptability of military or technocratic rule, a result of both frustration with democratic process and deference to the military institution.[24] Investigation into the turbulent tran-sition of power during the 2020 election has revealed the extent to which military entities were targeted as potential instruments of partisan activity.[25] Perhaps just as troubling are recent escalations in partisan political violence that reflect not only sharpening divides in the public, but include military veter-ans or servicemembers themselves.[26] Political polarization threatens to intensify these trends, further complicating the relationship between the American public and their armed forces. In each of these cases, partisan polarization risks compromising a key tenet of stable civil-military relations, by weakening the military's own credibility, it's relationship to civilians, and its place within democratic society.

Politicizing the Military Institution

Polarization first threatens to degrade the civil-military relationship by compromising a credible voice—the military's—for partisan political gain. The influence of political or social elites in shaping public attitudes has been well documented. Experts in political science and social psychology researchers argue that the heuristic offered by such elite voices can offer the shortcut necessary for individuals to achieve reasoned opinions without expending the cognitive resources necessary for expert-level knowledge.[27] This process may be more essential to understanding political sensibilities among the public than before. As Amy Zegart notes, the signal offered by credible actors in a crowded information space is even more important in a contemporary environment where "the volume of data is exploding, and yet credible information is harder to find."[28]

The credibility of such information sources factor prominently in how individuals form preferences about policy. Political psychology speaks to the role played by political and social elites in shaping the public's preferences on policy, because individuals frequently seek the short-cut provided by such "elite cues" as a cognitively efficient means for achieving an informed opinion.[29] The influence of various elite communities—such as partisan leaders, media outlets, policy experts, and international institutions—have proven important shaping forces on public attitudes towards political choices.[30] One of several contributions of this book is extending analysis of how perceptibly credible actors can influence public policy choices by including the most trusted institution in US society: the armed forces.

However, politicization risks stripping the military of credibility with the public because it strikes at the perception that it is competent and transparent. Scholarship on political messaging has found that one consistent dimension of credibility is *knowledgeability* or *expertise* on an issue under debate.[31] Sources that have highly localized subject matter expertise should speak more authoritatively on issues regarding that knowledge base. Another dimension of credibility established by the existing literature is *trustworthiness*. Elites who share ideological or partisan inclinations with a "like-minded" audience are more likely to be seen as credible by that same audience.[32] However, individual-level partisanship can complicate both of these characteristics. Though political alignment may create a perception of trustworthiness, it can similarly result in a biased rejection of contrary information, even if that information is credible.[33] Though expertise in a specialized area of policy may imbue non-partisan elites with a degree of influence, this effect is conditional on the underlying level of partisan polarization about the issue itself.[34]

By these measures, the military should prove to be a potentially influential institution in the political information space, possessing both general trust from the public and localized subject matter expertise. Chapter 3 will use original survey experimentation to observe how military cues are indeed quite effective in shaping public attitudes on issues like foreign policy, even in the face of contradictory information or cuing. However, the normative proscriptions against the *use* of that voice in politics is one of the load-bearing elements of that same trust: the military "cue" is powerful because it is (at least ostensibly) prohibited. But the environment engendered by partisan polarization threatens to draw that voice into partisan politics more by lowering its cost and creating perverse incentives. If the public's aversion to partisan activity by military figures weakens—or even turns to encouragement—there is little reason to suspect that traditional norms against such behavior will endure. The result of such politicizing forces could collapse any image of the military as a fair dealer, with potentially deleterious consequences for civil-military relations.

The military's enviable position as trustworthy among nearly all political and social institutions in US society could not only be jeopardized, but could signal the end of one of the last threads of public confidence to government. The perception that military leaders were espousing inaccurate, misleading, or partisan-driven operational information or priorities was part of a general loss in governmental confidence following the war in Vietnam.[35] Recent political flashpoints involving the deployment of military servicemembers into the country's own streets have brought this concern home, as retired officers and civil-military scholars offered concerns over the implications of a military perceived to be a partisan implement, rather than an objective security guarantor for the nation.[36] The placement of military elites in increasingly partisan political positions could lead to a general shift in perceptions of the institution's reliability, as the line between the partisan political and military realms blurs.

Hampering Military Effectiveness

Weakening the distinction between the partisan and the military among the public may not only influence the latter's organizational credibility, but its effectiveness as national security provider. First, hyper-partisanship can blind the public's ability to clearly learn the lessons of failed foreign policy ventures by refusing to fully interrogate military performance. As we will find in Chapters 4 and 5 of this book, partisan identity and its associated media diets can strongly influence how individuals draw conclusions about the military's performance. Recent polling in Kori Schake and Jim Mattis's 2016 book *Warriors and Citizens* on this subject suggests that civilian leaders carry more responsibility than the military for a lack of decisive victory in foreign wars.[37] As Kenneth Schultz argues, allowing partisan considerations to override an objective evaluation of the merits of foreign policy could contribute to broader polarization effects that "impede the country's collective ability to learn and adapt from foreign policy."[38] If an institutional preference for the military is closely aligned with partisan identity, then polarization over military interventions can prevent a clear-eyed assessment of failure.

Second, the erosion of the normative firewall between the military and partisan politics risks more frequent forays by military actors into that sphere of activity, damaging the credibility of the expert advice they owe civilian leaders. Casting the veracity of military information into doubt jeopardizes not only its esteem with the public, but the level of trust it enjoys from civilian leaders during wartime, where such military counsel is essential to informed decision-making. As we will find, representatives of the military institution do not necessarily have to be in uniform to be influential in public perception of the armed forces on the whole. Remarking on the military's seemingly immovable trust with the public, former Chairman of the Joint Chiefs of Staff Martin Dempsey remarked in 2011 that, "maybe if I knew what it would take to screw it up, I could avoid it."[39] Subsequent analysis in this book will suggest the magnitude of this question and its broad applicability to understanding the interplay between political parties, mass media, the public, active-duty servicemembers, and retired military officials. An increasingly vocal retired military elite could create friction with serving members of the active force, who rely considerably on the credibility of their military counsel when advising civilian leaders on the proper courses of action in foreign and security policy.

Such activity among the retired military elite risks jeopardizing the reliability of advice given by uniformed officers ostensibly representative of the same institution. This prospect is potentially problematic for forming coherent policy; retired Army Lieutenant General David Barno argues that "[c]ivilians will now be asking, 'is the J.C.S. a Democrat or Republican?' and men and women in uniform will begin to wonder whether some day they can become the secretary of defense, or national security adviser."[40] The negative externalities of such behavior are heightened in that the retired community draws on the same pool of credibility as their active-duty counterparts, while repeated use of that shared resource may in fact deplete it.[41] In response to retired senior officers speaking at both major party conventions during the 2016 presidential campaign, former Chairman Dempsey stated that "[t]hey were introduced as generals. As generals, they have an obligation to uphold our apolitical traditions. They have made the task of their successors—who continue to serve in uniform and are accountable for our security—more complicated."[42] Such an environment could compromise the integrity of military advice, if civilian leaders are given reason to worry that serving officers are weighing prospects of a political afterlife to their careers when offering it.

Finally, military politicization can harm security planning by having the opposite effect on the military voice: not by compromising it, but by elevating that same military advice over more holistic viewpoints on the use of force. The public's high esteem for the military as an institution makes it a tempting partisan political implement for civilian leaders seeking to lend credibility to policy; however, this can result in undue delegation of important civilian-led processes to military leaders, degrading civilian control of the military. As Polina Beliakova argues, this "erosion by deference" can result in compromising the military's nonpartisan image as it is continually dragged into policy leadership roles, as well as limiting appreciation of non-military instruments of power.[43] Furthermore, this level of deference taken to an extreme can lead to over-reliance on the concept of "best military advice" and deprive civilian leaders of the ability to shape policy considerate of—rather than dependent on—technical counsel.[44] Jim Golby and Mara Karlin similarly offer that this line of thinking can subvert civilian preferences in favor of military input.[45] Not only does this have deleterious consequences on the creation of smart, adaptive policy incorporating numerous perspectives, but to the preservation of an important pillar of democratic governance: civilian control of the military.

Eroding Democratic Governance

The polarization of institutional confidence and politicization of the military pose three direct challenges to liberal norms of democratic governance. First, while public trust in institutions is indeed a desirable goal in democratic society, the military's singular status as both most-trusted and least-democratic institution is potentially troublesome. At the user level, this seeming asymmetry can have poor effects on the management of the military directly, including a culture of weak civilian oversight. For example, former Army officer and Obama administration official Andrew Exum contends this issue has become so acute that veterans themselves should campaign for public office and make a concerted effort to ensure that the military is "brought down a peg or two" in the public's esteem by challenging active-duty officers from the chairs of committee hearings.[46] Indeed, one of the recommendations of this book is for the public to more clearly evaluate their military's performance apart from conceptions of patriotism or partisanship. However, this does little to correct more large-scale problems incumbent to the public's simultaneous trust in the military and loss thereof in actual representative institutions. The military's recent involvement in the backdrop of decidedly partisan flashpoints, such as electoral politics, the January 6 insurrection, and the protests following the murder of George Floyd represent type cases in which trust in the military has proven a tenuous commodity.[47] Military officials would seemingly benefit most from a concerted campaign to distance the institution from partisan co-optation or rhetoric; however, as we will see, this possibility may not always be within the organization's control. The public's continued deference to military figures, absent a similar level of trust in key institutions of representative democracy, risks engendering a continued partisan incentive for politicization and an erosion of liberal political norms.

Second, cracks within democratic institutions are more likely to widen because norms about political activity by the military and military elites are far weaker than many scholars and policy-makers identify. Another empirical contribution of this book finds that while military actors who engage in traditionally taboo partisan activity can expect to lose credibility with the broad public compared to their non-partisan counterparts, they can also gain a dedicated and ideologically coherent partisan base for doing so. In Chapter 6, we will find that retired military officers who engage in partisan politics can expect a loss in perceptions of their expertise and trustworthiness—but only from those on the other side of the partisan aisle. Co-partisans to retired officers speaking out in the partisan space do not sanction, and may even reward, such behavior. Data-driven analysis of the social media follower networks of prominent military officers confirms this trend, where military elites with regular appearances on partisan news outlets can actually elicit audiences that are even more partisan than those garnered by elected politicians. The result is not only an intensification of the politicization that many fear, but clear evidence of a public that is detached from traditional civil-military norms. This trend is more troubling alongside similar shifts among developed democracies toward illiberal political practices.[48] Taken together, a public less desirous of a non-partisan military and a military less willing to commit to non-partisanship are both manifestly damaging to democratic governance that relies on both.

Finally, politicization of the military risks compromising its capacity to effectively perform its assigned functions in defense of democratic governance. The military institution and its representative elites are increasingly being called upon to perform political functions not previously conceived by civil-military scholars. While not unique to any administration, partisan leaders have more recently sought out military elite involvement in government as a way to "borrow" national security credentials from a credible source or to publicly advocate for budgetary or strategic interests.[49] Civil-military scholars have pointed to highly partisan speeches and appeals to the military as a conservative constituency as evidence that military politicization can occur *to* the institution just as well as *by* the institution. Conversely, many activists have come to view the military and its retired elites as a power-checking institution with an opportunity to constrain executive power or as a repository for the ideals of liberal democracy that could resist an "authoritarian model" of governance.[50] These patterns represent a slow normalization of politicizing activity that, taken to an extreme, could include the incorporation of the military into extra-constitutional activities outside the bounds of liberal governance.[51]

Plan of the Book

This book is divided into six subsequent chapters that provide the empirical diagnoses of and possible remedies to the state of civil-military relations amidst partisan polarization in the United States. Chapter 2 will provide a broad theoretical context by outlining two concurrent trends—Americans' increasing esteem for the military and surging polarization from one another—and how the convergence of these patterns has created an environment where concerns over politicization are far more pressing than in years past. Here I outline that military politicization, the belief that the armed forces are moving toward or against the orbit of a single political party, is likely to manifest in one of four forms. The *active* form, where members of the military take measures that create the impression of the institution moving closer to a partisan establishment; the *passive* form, where the military is instead moved into such positions by external actors; the *relative* form where shifting political parties in the ideological backdrop create the illusion of movement by the military; and the *aspect* form, where an ideologically mobile public views a generally fixed military differently. This parallax model of politicization will help us to understand the ways in which civil-military relations has been affected by the surrounding polarized environment.

Chapter 3 will examine the potential influence of the military voice by exploring the power of military elites to use their public esteem in the pursuit of shaping attitudes about policy. If politicization poses a challenge to stable civil-military relations, it is necessary to first ascertain whether the military voice is even one worth co-opting. Using the results of original survey experimentation placing presidential and military cues in a competitive environment, the chapter finds that not only are military voices deemed highly credible by the public and potent even when co-partisan presidents issue contradictory cues, but that retired officers may be even more effective in this effort than their active-duty counterparts. This will set the stage for understanding how the credibility military figures enjoy make the armed forces a vulnerable target for politicization. Using examples from the Bush and Obama administrations, this section illustrates how this form of *active* politicization can manifest in practice over the wars in Iraq and Afghanistan.

Chapter 4 expands on this finding, exploring how partisanship interacts with this public confidence in the military and attempts to explain the widening partisan "gap" over trust in the armed forces. Partisan subgroups have steadily split on impressions about trust in the military, a trend masked by high aggregate trust over the public as a whole. As this research effort will show, partisans acquire and respond to new information on military behavior—particularly negative performance—in very different ways. This chapter employs a data-driven approach to analyze media reporting on the military over time. With the "surge" period in the Iraq War as a central case, this chapter uses unsupervised machine learning techniques and text-as-data topic modeling to highlight how partisan identity widened this understanding of the military's credibility during a critical period of war reporting. In particular, conservative-friendly media outlets were far less likely to report frequently on negative events from the worst year of the Iraq War, characterized by stalemate and heavy losses. This pattern holds for reporting on organizational scandals and ethical malpractice, even under Democratic presidencies. Using examples from other high-profile military reporting periods, this section depicts how media and third-party information about the military facilitates *aspect* politicization, directly changing the public's views about the hostility of the military to partisan "in-group" preferences.

Chapter 5 further probes the partisan gap on military confidence: if some partisans are less likely to receive negative information, what happens when they are confronted with it? If politicization and polarization pose a threat to the standing that the armed forces have generally, as many civil-military theorists claim, this should be clear when directly exposed to negative information about the institution. Using the results of a second original survey experiment, this section instead finds that while Democrats and Independents negatively re-assess their impressions of the military in light of knowledge about battlefield failures and scandals, Republicans—who are likely to see the military as part of their political identity group—are unmoved. Partisans drawing such different conclusions about the reliability and quality of the military institution can con-tribute to downstream politicization as political elites leverage these perceptions for credibility with the public. Using examples scholars have analyzed from the Trump administration, the end of this chapter illustrates how this climate leads to both *passive* and *relative* forms of politicization. The first can emerge when partisan leaders believe the military to be a valuable political instrument and engage in behaviors designed to co-opt its policies, symbols, and credibility for partisan political gain. The second becomes more likely when party leaders adopt ideologically extreme positions, exposing the "daylight" between that party and the military institution.

Chapter 6 attempts to investigate the notion that civil-military norms among the public may be much weaker than previously contemplated, particularly with concerns to military politicization. Using the results of a third original survey experiment, this section finds that partisans don't principally sanction retired military officers for engaging in partisan politics, but only do so when the officer took on the "wrong" partisan identity. Not only do co-partisans fail to downgrade their estimation of retired military political activists, they may actually reward such behavior. This normatively weak environment creates the circumstances for political opportunism and further politicization. A subsequent analysis of the social media data for prominent retired officers confirms this finding, showing that these figures can be even more politically polarizing than elected officials. Through the cases provided by retired military involvement in electoral politics, the George Floyd protests, and the January 6 insurrection, the end of the chapter explores how this alternate form of *active* politicization can manifest through either purposeful or unintentional miscalculation of the political environment.

Chapter 7 concludes by packaging these important findings and offering policy recommendations for participants in the civil-military dialogue. These include measures that can be taken to curtail the effects of polarization on civil-military relations and preserve prospects for healthy democratic governance in the future, such as reducing reliance on ex-military figures as political appointees, crafting a positive image in the public space, de-stigmatizing civilian oversight of the institution by civilian leaders, and overhauling military professional education to instill a clearer understanding of the non-partisan norm. These proposals offer options for both sides of the civil-military relationship. For military leaders, they include ways to educate senior officers on the complex landscape of civil-military affairs, socialize the force to the non-partisan norm, and harden ser-vicemembers against political misinformation. For civilian leaders, this chapter includes potential ways to decouple the military from partisan politics, sever the veteran-extremism nexus, and use party platforms to codify a shared need for a non-partisan military.

2

That Fair and Warlike Form

How America Learned to Stop Worrying and Love the Military

Unsurprisingly, the best way to begin any discussion on the future of US civil-military relations is through exploration of its turbulent past and present. The relationship between the American public and its military has endured considerable upheaval over the last several decades, shifting from general skepticism and disdain to seemingly unshakable trust and support. The American public's perception of the military, in that time, has seen armed interventions abroad, significant policy changes regarding conscription and organizational management, and wide variation in military outcomes on the battlefield. The military's regular position at the top of Americans' list of most trusted institution is a relatively recent phenomenon in this regard and not one achieved in isolation. Instead, while the public's esteem for the military has certainly increased, this trend may be more complicated than a cursory look might suggest. During the same period of time in which the American citizens grew attached to their military, they became increasingly detached from each other as partisan tribalism became a defining characteristic of the political landscape.

It is at the intersection of these two important contemporary trends that this book focuses its attention: America's swelling esteem in the armed forces and its surging animus for partisan outsiders. Where the two meet presents the most significant challenge to long-standing normative traditions against the politicization of the military. In order to contextualize the empirical findings that follow, this chapter will outline the emergence of these two concurrent trends, examining how some of the most significant patterns in civil-military affairs are not simply artifacts of a hastily shifting partisan environment, but the culmination of long-unfolding trends in the socio-political ties between the people and their armed forces. It is with a clearer eye toward the current environment that we can classify potential sources and forms of politicizing activity with respect to the military as an institution.

Dangerous Instrument: Political Polarization and US Civil-Military Relations. Michael A. Robinson,
Oxford University Press. © Oxford University Press 2023. DOI: 10.1093/oso/9780197611555.003.0002

First, this chapter will provide some context on the recent history of the US civil-military relationship, charting how an institution that was once one of the least respected in US society arrived at its position today amongst just a few bastions of credibility. It is important to note that while many analysts have focused their attention on the civil-military dialogue as it exists between key civilian leaders and the military, this book will focus more on the military's relationship to the public at large. More recently, civil-military scholars have endeavored to understand how the public may have reached such an improved estimation of the military, from performance in the field to organizational integrity to the "non-partisan" ethic.[1] While these explanations often lack conclusive empirical tests, they provide an important framing device for understanding the trajectory of civil-military relations at the mass public level over the last several decades.

Second, it will explore the concurrent trend of partisan polarization on the fragmentation of the political landscape. Even casual observation of American politics would detect the extent to which partisan identity has more deeply and cleanly divided the public over a variety of subjects. A robust debate has followed over whether the public has polarized on its issue positions across parties, or in fact simply "sorted" into party structures that more cleanly align with their ideological positions. While this is an important feature of the discussion over partisanship today, this analysis also focuses on how civil-military relations is influenced not just by policy disagreement, but rather by the social components of polarization that contribute to tribalism in the public space. Despite existing rationality-driven explanations of military trust, the notion that positive affect for the military might instead be a social function of partisan identity is a potentially dangerous sign for the future of civil-military relations.

The convergence of these two trends results in an environment ripe for politicization of the military by creating political incentives to pull the armed forces into increasingly partisan waters. Though considerable attention has been paid to the high absolute levels of trust the public seems to imbue in the military, this overlooks the underlying partisan gap with regards to impressions of that same institution. Civilian leaders may be tempted to use the military for partisan gain to win points with their constituents, while military actors themselves may be more active in partisan affairs due to weakening norms against such activity. In addition, while "sorting" has certainly contributed to partisan sensibilities about the military, those impressions have also become more extreme— if asymmetrically—across the parties. This type of environment is rife with potential sources of politicization, not only as a result of military behavior, but from the activity of other entities in society. It is here that the chapter will classify a *parallax* model of politicization, based on the notion that politicizing behavior can arise from both actual and perceived ideological movement by any of the civil-military arena's three pivotal actors: the military itself, the major partisan political institutions, and the increasingly partisan public. This vocabulary will be important in the subsequent empirical chapters and will assist in more clearly identifying trends in military politicization.

How Americans Learned to Like the Military

The esteem that the American public holds at present for the military is a noteworthy reversal of fortune. Despite abysmal public perception following the Vietnam War, the contemporary American military consistently registers as one of the public's favored institutions. This pattern for the military with regards to its public image is all the more surprising given the broader context. The public's affect toward the armed forces has not only increased dramatically in absolute terms over this period, but has done so alongside a generalized drop in public confidence for nearly all other public institutions in American society.[2] As we will discover, the result is a puzzling contemporary environment in which the public remains skeptical about its representative political institutions, court systems, and journalists and instead reserves trust for its least democratic apparatus: the military.

Understanding how public esteem for the military is remarkable in today's environment requires some accounting of this relationship over time. It is worth noting that neither changes in American civil-military architecture nor partisan polarization are fully novel concepts in the country's history. Partisan political rancor and even outright politicization of the military predate contemporary events. However, it is only in the last several decades that such behavior can be observed in the United States alongside a standing professional military with high public regard. Following the Vietnam War, the military emerged as one of a host of public institutions that suffered from low public confidence and widespread disillusionment. The unceremonious end of the Nixon administration due to the Watergate scandal heralded a period of not only steadily declining interpersonal trust among the public, but in governmental institutions generally. Haunted not only by the war's outcome, the conscription-era military force was plagued by rampant organizational misconduct, racism, and drug abuse within the ranks.[3] Public discontent over the Vietnam enterprise was compounded by concerns that military officials had misrepresented casualty figures in the worst years of conflict. As both a source of trusted information in the conduct of foreign affairs and an expert community in that same issue area, the military had lost credibility as either.

The dissolution of the conscription military in favor of the All-Volunteer Force (AVF) brought with it what retired Army Colonel Don Snider refers to as

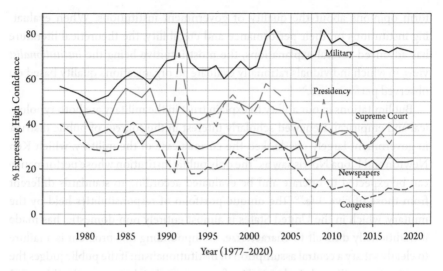

Figure 2.1 Public Confidence in US Institutions (1977–2020)

Note: Figure 2.1 depicts aggregate levels of public confidence in institutions as measured by Gallup "Confidence in Institutions" annual survey (https://news.gallup.com/poll/1597/confidence-institutions.aspx). "High" confidence individuals are those coded as having responded "a greal deal" or "quite a lot" to the standard question: "Please tell me how much confidence you, yourself, have in [institution]". Note: Gallup collection on confidence in the presidency as a public institution did not begin until 1991 survey fieldings.

the "re-professionalization" of the military institution.[4] As shown in Figure 2.1, public confidence in the military steadily rises from 1980 to the present, even amidst a concurrent trend that saw trust in other public institutions decline, such as Congress and the presidency. In addition to critical organizational reforms that reduced misconduct within the military itself, the armed forces were the beneficiary of a rejuvenated budget under the Carter and Reagan administrations and a slowly rehabilitated public image. High-profile military victories in Grenada, Panama, and Operation DESERT STORM provided the American public with a new set of images of the institution and an opportunity to shake off the legacy of Vietnam. But these discrete spikes in public confidence would often return to pre-conflict levels, a trend that would persist until the turn of the century.

The military's status today as one of the most trusted institutions in American society crystallized in earnest following the September 11, 2001, terror attacks and the "Global War on Terror (GWOT)." Since this discrete launching point, aggregate levels of public confidence in the military have never quite returned to pre-9/11 levels, regularly dwarfing public esteem for nearly every other public institution. This is all the more surprising given the major organizational scandals and indecisive campaigns that the military has endured over the same period, a fact which is important to note because of our understanding of how individuals form opinions about the quality of government institutions. When evaluating institutions on their performance and credibility, the theoretical literature has advanced several explanations, the most intuitive being the *institutionalist* view, in which individuals rationally evaluate an organization's quality based on observed performance.[5]

But limitations in our ability to explain trust in the military are both typological and empirical. Renewed scholarly interest in the sources of public distrust in government largely overlooked the curious case of the military, which Ken Newton and Pippa Norris saw as "the only public institution whose performance can be expected to operate and be evaluated according to standards different from those of civic life."[6] The unique portfolio of responsibilities held by the military, which in the United States is almost entirely non-domestic, has made it traditionally difficult to characterize. Compounding this problem is a failure to clearly satisfy a central assumption of institutionalism: if the public judges the quality of the military based on its "performance," what do we mean by this term? Eventually, contrary narratives emerged regarding the source of the military's seemingly unassailable esteem with the American public.

Explaining the Reversal of Fortune

The debate over the sources of public trust in the military is neither a trivial question nor one with an obvious answer. The centrality of many civil-military norms, including civilian control and the professional "ethic," rely considerably on the credibility of the armed forces and the perception of that institution as an expert community. Further still, examining the causes of the public's impressions is necessary to appreciate its weaknesses, as a loss of public confidence may mean a disastrous collapse of one of the last bastions of public trust. But understanding the reason for this curious relationship between the public and its military is not so simple. The reversal of fortune that the American military experienced from its post-Vietnam doldrums of public trust to the prestige it enjoys today requires some understanding of how individuals in society render a judgment about the institution itself. In short, how did the American public develop such a relationship with its military?

Scholars of civil-military relations and institutional confidence have wrestled with the question of public trust in the military through precisely this lens.[7] David Burbach expertly outlines these major patterns of confidence in America's military as a function of different forms of military performance over time, perceptions of the organization's professionalism, and the increasingly predictive nature of partisanship on attitudes about the armed forces.[8] While each of these explanations is unable to completely reconcile the changing political landscape, American foreign policy experiences, and political partisanship with expressed public support for the institution, they are important categories of existing scholarship in this regard. The first discernible pattern of public trust has been traditionally characterized as *performance* theories, in which the outcomes that the military creates on the battlefield are the basis for its support from the public. The second class of explanations have been more loosely termed *professionalism* theories, where the internal processes and ethical standards of the military institution speak more to its capacity as a credible actor in society than war-making. A third includes the perceived objectivity or *non-partisanship* of the institution, namely, its ability to remain outside the partisan political fray and preserve a trustworthy voice in the information space. While other potential explanations have been offered, this book focuses on these three characterizations from Burbach's research as the bulk of the existing civil-military theorizing on sources of the public's recent confidence in its military. Understanding the state of the art in these explanations will reveal not only their empirical shortcomings, but the possibility that public trust is tied to something more emotional and influential in American politics: partisan identity.

Regardless of the typological category of military trust, each requires some objective metric for evaluating the institution itself. This has been historically difficult to achieve with regards to the military. The "performance-trust link," one framework for understanding this judgment by the public, hinges on some evaluation of governmental institutions in the execution of their assigned function.[9] The military's function in society has been notoriously difficult to categorize alongside domestic institutions, but can be broadly construed as fighting and winning the nation's wars. Unlike the armed forces in many other countries, the American military's domestic portfolio of responsibilities outside of disaster relief is traditionally limited. This makes it easier to subscribe to a simple interpretation of public confidence in the military: winning wars wins trust.

This first and "the most obvious" potential explanation for military confidence is a purely transactional assessment of the institution based on its performance in warfare. Using results from a sweeping survey of civilian and military elites in the late 1990s, Paul Gronke and Peter Feaver examined the potential causes of high expressed confidence among the public.[10] As they note, institutionalist explanations for how the public evaluates government performance have often seen this calculation as a product of *process* (perception of the organization's governing principles and ethics) and *policy* (a direct performance-based evaluation).[11] The "battlefield performance" explanation falls cleanly within the latter. As the military's most readily identifiable function within society is to fight and win its nation's wars, it might follow that the institution's performance under these conditions should provide the clearest signal to the public as to its competency and quality.

This explanation for the military's positive image shift in recent decades is not wholly without merit. The case for the performance hypothesis was argued further by David King and Zachary Karabell, offering that the military overcame depressed public support after Vietnam by demonstrating consistent and decisive success in Grenada, Panama, Iraq, and the Balkans.[12] Significant budget overhauls during the Reagan years drove the perception that the military was better trained and better equipped than its Vietnam-era self. These high-profile actions helped to rehabilitate the image of the military in the eyes of Americans, lifting public confidence from 1980 through the initiation of the "Global War on Terror" following the 9/11 attacks. The belief emerged that a new "generation of trust"—Millenials socialized to the military by these victories and not by Vietnam—would solidify this newfound confidence in the military, setting them apart from their predecessors. As Figure 2.2 reveals, despite minor changes in the interim, a similar percentage of Americans believe the United States military is the best in the world (and believes being the best is important) today as did during the late 1990s, when American military dominance arguably reached an apex. If winning wars is important to the public, this line of thought argues that it was precisely performance at this task that explains the military's newfound esteem.

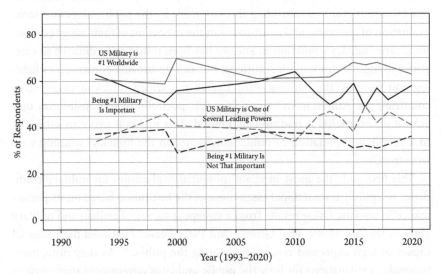

Figure 2.2 Public Belief in Top Status of US Military (1993–2020)

Note: Figure 2.2 depicts responses according to Gallup's Military and National Security survey on questions regarding whether or not the US military was "No. 1 in the world militarily" and whether or not "it is important for the United States to be No. 1 in the world militarily" from 1993–2020 ("Don't know" responses not depicted). Responses show that not only is current public belief in the capacity of the military similar to the period following the collapse of the Soviet Union, but the salience of that capacity has remained unchanged as well (https://news.gallup.com/poll/390356/half-say-military-no-world.aspx).[13]

Despite its intuitive logic and parsimonious claim, the *performance* explanation's empirical support is mixed at best, given the public's likely imperfect understanding of events in wartime.[14] Though Figure 2.1 does reveal a periodic rise in confidence for the military over time, this support increases and stabilizes despite the largely unsuccessful wars in Iraq and Afghanistan that have provided most of the public's recent imagery for military performance. An early and decisive defeat of the Taliban in Operation ENDURING FREEDOM was steadily undone by years of frustration fighting an unfamiliar counter-insurgency, compounded by the competing resource drain of the 2003 invasion of Iraq. Just as in Afghanistan, the lightning-quick conventional defeat of the Iraqi military and "end of major combat operations" was followed by a decent into sectarian internecine conflict. The years leading up to and following the "surge" of American forces were the most damaging in the history of the conflict, both to military personnel and Iraqi citizens. Despite tactical-level success in many areas, these conflicts largely devolved into strategic stalemate; yet, public confidence in the military, at least in the aggregate, failed to reflect these outcomes.

The performance explanation does not—at least on its own—provide a full rationale for the military's change of status among American political institutions. Post-Vietnam battlefield victories certainly track concurrently with much of the improvements to the military's public image that occur between 1980 and 2000. But subsequent frustrations over the military's performance during the Global War on Terror seem to confound a clean explanation for why the public maintains its positive image of the institution. While the *policy* roots of the performance explanation may be insufficient, a competing theory embraces the *process* component. Could the re-organization of the military itself speak more to the public's trust in the institution that its performance abroad?

As the case of the performance explanation attests, settling on a common metric for understanding public trust in the military can be a difficult task. Nonetheless, attempts to classify institutions based on their societal roles or design imperatives have created some useful starting points. Bo Rothstein and Dietlind Stolle argue that publics respond to how well institutions perform their perceived functions within society. For example, "order" institutions like the police or judicial system might be judged based on their ability to provide equity and enforce the laws fairly; by contrast, "political" institutions such as the parliament are evaluated by how well they advance one's ideology as an agent of the public. Using cross-national principal component analysis of the World Values Survey (WVS) in public confidence in institutions, they contend that the military should fall closer to the "order" category of institutions, evaluated based on its impartiality or fairness.[15]

The professionalism class of explanations therefore provide a second theoretical approach that takes into account the importance of organizational *process*, offering that public regard for the military institution is driven by perceived institutional integrity, ethical quality, and embodiment of cherished social norms. Whereas the transactional assessment of the military's battlefield outcomes was the catalyst for trust in the military under performance explanations, in the professionalism realm it is instead the perception of the military as a credible and fair dealing institution.[16] If the military does fall into the general category of "order" institutions, then perhaps it is the internal processes and ethical standards of the profession that drive public confidence in the institution. Minimizing scandals, cultivating a professional ethic, and fair adjudication of ethical failures should provide a suitable metric for understanding if the professionalism explanation holds water.

Again, on first glance this narrative seems to bear at least some merit. If high-profile operational victories were a notable distinction for the military in the post-Vietnam period, so too were fundamental organizational changes in the military itself. The Gates Commission brought with it the end of the conscripted military and the beginning of the "All-Volunteer Force" (AVF), simultaneously curbing the negative association of the military with the draft and ending the need for a deferment system generally perceived as unfair by the public.[17] Major overhauls regarding drug use significantly reduced the rate of substance abuse within the ranks, an endemic problem for the military during the Vietnam era.[18] The re-branding of military service as a self-policing "profession" brought with it the embrace of a military ethic, distinguishing it from other occupations in American society.[19]

Even with these major organizational changes, the professionalism explanation lacks conclusive empirical support. Just as with the performance explanation, the upward trajectory of public trust in the military tracks cleanly with significant organizational reforms over the post-Vietnam period. But this explanation cannot reconcile high (and stable) public confidence with numerous newsworthy scandals, particularly in the post-9/11 period. Revelations of prisoner mistreatment during the 2004 Abu Ghraib prison scandal presented the public with shocking evidence of misconduct at the hands of Army interrogators.[20] Reports of poor conditions and patient neglect at Walter Reed Medical Center in 2007 led to the removal of both the military commander of the hospital and the Secretary of the Army.[21] The military reckoned with widespread sexual assault within the ranks that reached a turning point in 2013, resulting in several calls by Congressional leaders to strip military commanders of the authority to adjudicate such cases on their own.[22] Each of these stories garnered significant coverage in American news media, though as this book will detail later, the exposure to (and influence from) that information is very much a function of one's partisan affiliation rather than objective evaluation.

Military leaders grappled not only with these major organizational scandals during the same period, but with numerous individual cases and acts of misconduct that further complicate the professionalism narrative. The cover-up over the death of Army Ranger and former NFL player Pat Tillman in 2004 made headlines across the country, almost taking the career of General Stanley McChrystal as a result.[23] The Glenn Marine Group scandal resulted in the 2013 conviction of 17 Navy officials for disclosure of classified material to a Malaysian national named "Fat Leonard" in exchange for cash and luxury items given to members of the Seventh Fleet.[24] Though former Army First Lieutenant Clint Lorance was convicted for the 2012 killing of two unarmed Afghan citizens and former Navy SEAL Eddie Gallagher was convicted of misconduct for a 2017 incident in which he posed with a dead detainee for a photo, their subsequent and high-profile pardoning by President Donald Trump conjured uncomfortable comparisons to William Calley and the 1968 My Lai massacre.[25] For a military eager to cultivate an image as a self-policing profession, these cases presented considerable obstacles.

Nonetheless, the professionalism explanation certainly provides part of the answer for the increase in military trust among the public. Polling conducted on political and social institutions by Pew Research in 2019 found that the public believed military officers were the least likely to behave unethically "all" or "most" of the time, and the most likely to face serious consequences when they did.[26] Military officers outstripped nearly every other survey occupation in this regard, an unsurprising finding given consistent polling results on trust in the armed forces.[27] However, if Americans' perception of the fairness of the armed forces as an "order" institution was the sole metric of interest for the public, events such as the sexual assault and Walter Reed scandals should have elicited some change in aggregate public trust. Similarly, the argument that a post-Vietnam wave of professionalization is at the heart of the public's positive affect for the military is confounded by a host of moral failures, both at home and on the battlefield.

A third potential channel for public trust differs from the previous two in that it partially accounts for the political context in which the military exists in the eyes of the citizenry. As discussed earlier, there is a general consensus across civil-military theorists on the virtue and necessity of a non-partisan military and its utility to stable democratic governance.[28] While military elites have become more prevalent in the political discourse domestically, Andrew Hill et al. argue that it is the continued restraint of the institution from engaging in partisan activity and its deeply ingrained deference to civilian leaders that has contributed to high public confidence.[29] Burbach terms this class of theory as the *partisanship* explanation, distinct from *performance* and *professionalism* theories in that the public is responding not to battlefield outcomes or organizational ethics, but on the perception of the military as an objective source of information and a bulwark against political tribalism.[30] In this framework, overt acts of partisanship or political activism on the part of active or retired military elites would be the most damaging behavior the institution could engage in, as it compromises the image of the military as neutral executor of public security. Indeed, the specter of a politicized military has led many to suggest that repeated forays into the political sphere would damage trust in the military institution directly and in government more broadly.[31]

The perception of the military institution as a non-partisan entity is a potentially fruitful explanation, but one that encounters significant difficulty upon inspection of the empirical record. As defined, the partisanship (or more specifically, non-partisan) hypothesis should suffer most from one of the most pervasive trends in US society: politicization. The belief that the armed forces have been "captured" or are more favorably inclined towards a political party or establishment should strike at the center of this base of trust much in the same way organizational scandals or battlefield failures should collapse the previous two explanations we have discussed. On this count, there is considerable doubt that the public is responding to, recognizing, or rebuking politicizing influences when rendering a judgment about military trust. As this book will discuss, the sources of politicization include both external ones (such as civilian leadership placing the military in partisan situations) and internal ones (including actions taking by military actors themselves that can compromise their non-partisan status). Perhaps the most potent source of the latter is an increasingly outspoken retired military community.

Over the same general period in which professional reform and operational success ostensibly rehabilitated the military's public image, its involvement in partisan political affairs also increased. This becomes clearer when one considers the role of retired military officials in shaping this narrative. Major political endorsements have become a ubiquitous feature of the electoral landscape, beginning with presidential campaign endorsements from former Marine commandant P. X. Kelley in 1988 and former Chairman of the Joint Chiefs William Crowe in 1992.[32] Since, bloc endorsements from groups of retired military officers have become commonplace. In 2012, over 500 retired generals and admirals penned an endorsement of Mitt Romney in the *Washington Times*, while candidates Hillary Clinton and Donald Trump boasted lists of dozens of high-profile officers as endorsers for their respective campaigns during the 2016 election.[33] The political conventions of that year featured perhaps the high watermark of retired generals in partisan affairs as retired Army Lieutenant General Mike Flynn and retired Marine General John Allen took the stage at the Republican and Democratic national conventions, respectively.[34]

In addition to partisan endorsements, retired military officials have become a vocal community on matters of policy. The noteworthy 2006 "revolt of the generals" featured recently retired officers issuing a public rebuke of then-Defense Secretary Donald Rumsfeld's management of the Iraq War. In recent years, an even larger community of retired officials have made their voices heard in opposition to administration policies they found objectionable, such as President Obama's policy regarding a proposed intervention in Syria.[35] The landscape of these voices became even more crowded during the Trump administration, where a myriad of policy decisions involving military implementation or organizational regulations were roundly denounced by a host of retired military officials.[36] Contributing to this pattern is the prevalence of retired officers as fixtures on cable news outlets as regular media personalities, especially on networks with established partisan demographics.

Military figures have also been increasingly public figures at the highest positions of government. Though not a new practice, the reliance on ex-military appointees for national security credentials also reached a crescendo during the Trump administration, including the high-profile hirings and firings of retired general officers James Mattis, Mike Flynn, and John Kelly.[37] Amidst a highly charged partisan environment where public trust in the administration was systemically low, the impulse to see such figures as the "adults in the room" frequently placed them in even more precarious political waters.[38] This practice presents potent challenges to the military's preservation of a non-partisan image due to the inability of the public to distinguish retired officers from active representatives of the military institution.[39] In short, considerable data supports the rising concern of internal politicization from the retired community, even if such activities are themselves motivated by a good faith desire to remove the military from partisan politics.

For these reasons, the non-partisan explanation also seems to lack comprehensive explanatory power on the question of public trust in the military. Over the same period in which appointments and endorsements became the most frequent, there is no discernible change in aggregate public confidence for the military institution. This is not for lack of politicizing influences, partisan activism by military figures, or even incidental cases where the active force was pulled into partisan waters. Though the previous discussion briefly listed examples of internally driven politicization efforts, concerns over external ones placing the military in the middle of partisan disputes may be an even more influential pattern of events. Regardless, the fact that public confidence has remained so high in light of these concurrent trends in endorsements, commentary, or political advocacy casts serious doubt on the validity of the non-partisan explanation to singularly provide a complete answer.

Collectively, while each of these explanations do not fully account for all of the military's reversal of fortune, they do provide essential context to the current state of civil-military relations. As later analysis will suggest, the missing piece may be a fuller accounting of the political context in which this relationship between the public and the armed forces occurs. If institutionalist theories of public confidence are to be believed, an institution's performance should result in some correspondingly rational judgment from the public. But this calculation cannot afford to ignore the often subjective cognitive biases that partisanship can inject into this process. Instead, partisans may vary on which type of performance they value. In addition, partisans may have very different levels of exposure to information that challenges their impressions of the institution and their objectivity given social proximity to it.[40] In short, whether you are a Democrat or Republican may not only shape how you feel about the military, but what information you receive that could possibly update that belief. It is because of this potentially significant influence that we must also account for the polarization that has developed in American society alongside shifting trends in civil-military relations.

How Americans Learned to Dislike Each Other

The American public's newfound warmth for the military during this time has been matched only by an increasing chilliness between the major partisan political tribes in American society. While hardly a unique condition in the history of American politics, the "polarization" that emerged between the Democratic and Republican parties in the later portion of the twentieth century represented a clear divergence from the relative consensus of the middle decades. As Lilliana Mason identifies, the 1940s and 1950s were characterized by a demographic parity between the major parties that might seem surprising to observers of American politics today: rural, urban, white, and non-white voters were members of both parties.[41] Today, these groups are neatly defined by their demographics, with the Republican party a narrower community of white, rural, and religious voters and the Democratic party a broader multi-racial coalition of younger, urban ones. Just as with the previous approach to the military's five-decade reversal of fortune, we have to ask: how did we get here?

The collapse of the mid-century comity between the parties followed the Civil Rights era, where passage of major legislation protecting African-American voting rights fractured the tenuous alliance between Northern Democrats and their co-partisans in the states of the former Confederacy. The result was a fundamental re-organization in the demographic alignment of the two parties, with white, Southern conservatives bolting their party for the Republicans and black voters for the Democrats.[42] The parties that emerged from this "sorting" process were ideologically more distinct and internally more coherent; without a meaningfully shared ideological "center," the presence of "cross-cutting" identities among elected officials decreased precipitously.[43] The new political landscape would instead be characterized by parties with far cleaner demographic lines.

Nowhere is this more clearly observable than in the shifting ideological placement of political elites across the major parties. Figure 2.3 depicts the

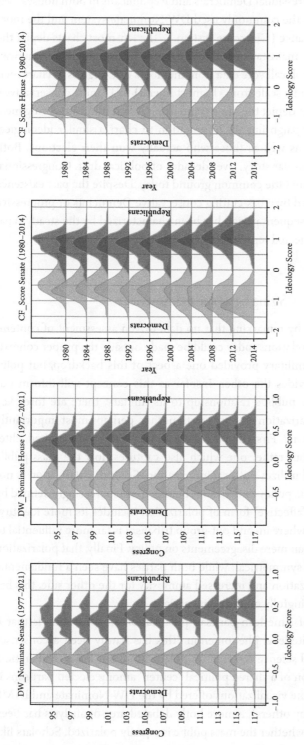

Figure 2.3 US House and Senate Partisan Polarization (1977–2021)

Note: Figure 2.3 depicts the ideological distribution of Democratic and Republican members of Congress and candidates using the DW-NOMINATE measure developed by Poole and Rosenthal and the CF Score measure used by Bonica. The first and second subfigures show the diverging distribution of elected House and Senate members in their ideological proximity between the 95th (1977) and 117th (2021) Congresses; the third and fourth figures show the same measure using Bonica's measure, which incorporates candidates for those same offices as well, from 1980 to 2014.

distributions of Congressional Democrats and Republicans in both houses over several decades using the commonly used DW-Nominate system and the more recent Campaign Finance (CF) score system.[44] The left-most charts depict the former, a quantitative mainstay of political ideology measurement in American politics, that utilizes roll call vote data from members of Congress to chart their ideological location on a scale from -1 (most liberal) to 1 (most conservative). The right-most figures depict the same trend using Adam Bonica's scoring measure, which uses campaign finance information to chart a similar ideological space for candidates as well as those who actually won their elections. Both sets of figures tell a similar story: over decades of political drift, Congressional partisans seem to share little common ground today. Despite the past existence of a "center" populated by cross-cutting conservative Democrats or progressive Republicans, the subsequent period has been characterized by the steady separation of the party's elected representatives.

Sizing Up Polarized America

This chapter opened by remarking that no data-driven assessment of contemporary civil-military relations today could be made outside the proper context: surging trust in the military provided one aspect of this backdrop, but political polarization provides the other. Insofar as this concept will inform our understanding of the public's relationship to its military, there are three key characteristics of polarization that are worth noting, perhaps most importantly by defining what it is *not*. First, that this trend is very likely not a limited, elite-level phenomenon, but rather one which also captures how the mass public seeks, interprets, and utilizes political information. Second, polarization is not simply a function of its policy dimensions, but is a trend increasingly defined by its social ones. This "affective" form of polarization includes its more identity-driven components, where in- and out-group tribalism is far more influential to attitude formation than mere disagreements on policy. Finally, that polarization in this fashion is not symmetrical: while both parties have seen a fundamental ideological re-organization and increased animosity for the other side, this has occurred more meaningfully on the political right.

The first aspect of American partisan polarization worth noting is that it is unlikely a pure elite-level phenomenon. This has hardly been a consensus point within political science research on polarization, but bears deliberation. While the evaporation of a shared political "center" among elected partisans is easily observable in the visualizations offered by the DW-Nominate and DIME datasets (among many others), a more hotly debated area of analysis has been over the question of whether the mass public is equally polarized. Scholars like

Morris Fiorina argue that the public is indeed not polarized in this fashion, instead harboring generally moderate viewpoints despite having more ideologically extreme voting options from which to choose.[45] Consequently, this vision of polarization defines the concept as mass opinion clustering at the ideological poles, particularly when asked on survey instrumentation. But this need not be the case: polarization between partisan subgroups can exist in an influential form even if this extreme clustering is absent.

A competing scholarship in partisan polarization instead argues that it is the relative distance between the two parties at the mass level that matters, not their absolute position on a two-dimensional ideological space. Alan Abramowitz and Gary Jacobsen, among others, offer that the increasing correlation between an individual's espoused partisan identity and their political ideology cannot be simply explained by a small group of the most politically engaged, nor can it be chalked up to the Fiorina's notion of "party sorting."[46] While Americans are more cleanly sorted into the partisan establishments that better summarize their ideological views, it is difficult to ignore the evaporation of traditional understandings of the "median voter," a hypothetical centrist that in theory should guide the parties closer to the ideological middle.[47] Not only do parties rarely cater to such a perceived centrist, but the belief in political "moderates" as volunteered on survey instruments may miss the fact that these individuals are likely to espouse more extreme political opinions than some avowed partisans.[48] Partisan identity not only provides a suitable proxy for understanding individual-level ideological leanings, but over recent decades is likely to overlap considerably with racial, ethnic, and urban-rural divides as well.[49]

Simple policy disagreements can no longer adequately capture the distance between partisans in society when significant portions fail to even see the elected representatives of the other party as legitimate.[50] Polarization can therefore be more helpfully envisioned as Murat Somer and Jennifer McCoy argue: "a process whereby the normal multiplicity of differences in a society increasingly align along a single dimension, cross-cutting differences become reinforcing, and people increasingly perceive and describe politics and society in terms of 'us' versus 'them'."[51] Contemporary reappraisals of polarization have focused on the rise of partisan media as a contributory element. The influence of conservative media outlets like Fox News, for example, remains at the center of ongoing debates as to the sources of and responses to social polarization and the expansion of partisan tribalism across time and issue areas.[52] As we will find in Chapter 4, the significance of media consumption in partisan attitude formation, especially with regards to perception of the military, cannot be understated. In sum, polarization cannot be solely considered the province of the halls of Congress, but rather bears consideration as a societal trend that captures dynamics in the public as well.

This helps to introduce the second dimension of polarization worth noting, that it is best conceived of in terms of its interpersonal aspects rather than just on matters of policy. This idea of "affective" polarization refers more explicitly to the social components of political tribalism, or as Mason remarks, those "political influences that may drive increases in specific types of polarized behavior, judgment, and emotion."[53] Because of its more comprehensive view on the nature of polarization, it fits more cleanly into the definition provided by Somer and McCoy, while empirical research has found it to be a better measure of mass polarization.[54] Existing study in this vein has already revealed that strong affective polarization can distort cognitive processes by affecting perceptual bias, in-group pride, out-group animus, and impressions regarding the expertise of co-partisans over those outside a shared political identity.[55] Individuals are likely to be more favorable to "in-group" members, even going so far as to distort or tailor information consumption to conform with existing information and reduce counter-attitudinal dissonance. Research by Thomas Rudolph and Marc Hetherington suggested that these attitudes are even more acute in political contexts, where social animosity towards "out-group" members outstrips the same sentiment in non-political contexts.[56] With an ever-widening landscape of "political" issue areas, the significance of this social component to polarization is profound.

Affective polarization is not only a more measurable version of this concept, but the more readily identifiable one in contemporary American politics. Out-group animus between political subsets among the public has only surged in recent years. A January 2021 CBS News poll found that a majority (54%) of individuals believed that "other people in America" constituted the biggest threat to America's way of life. This acute form of political tribalism has only increased over time due to a variety of factors, including curated media environments likely to exacerbate stereotypes of partisan out-groups.[57] This ability to mobilize personal distaste for perceived attributes of the "other side" has become even more pronounced in a political environment postured more toward "culture war" issues than substantive policy.[58] This type of polarization also presents more pressing challenges for the state of civil-military relations. As subsequent chapters in this book will discuss, the polarized perception of the military as a political ally (or opponent) is more likely to feed politicization than differing opinions over how to use it.

The final dimension of American polarization that makes it remarkable is that it is not a symmetrical trend: that is, the two parties may exhibit polarizing behavior that is opposite in direction, but far from equal in magnitude. This asymmetry is a pronounced feature in the American political environment, where ideological sorting and a lack of cross-cutting identities is often more observable among the political right and the Republican Party than its counterparts on the political left in the Democratic Party.[59] During the same period in which economic inequality became a bellweather issue in American politics, the parties took decidedly different routes to address their respective electoral fates. As political scientists Jacob Hacker and Paul Pierson note: "the Democratic Party faced cross-pressures that muddied its message and moderated its stances on economic matters. The Republican Party, in stark contrast, radicalized."[60] Enabled by a highly disciplined conservative media apparatus and influential mega-donors, the party's "moderate" wing was considerably weakened.[61] This is not to suggest that partisan establishments of both stripes have not moved along their ideological space; indeed, the same metrics used to spatially track the parties reveal movement by the Democratic party in the opposite direction, though much smaller in magnitude.[62] Concurrently, institutional incentives toward more ideologically extreme candidates have not shaped the parties equally. At the local level, David E. Broockman finds that while Democrats preferred "extreme" county leadership candidates 2-to-1, Republicans favored such candidates on their own side 10-to-1.[63] At the national level, Congressional zoning completed by state legislatures increasingly favors Republicans, growing the number of "safe" districts for Republican candidates headed to Washington.[64] The resulting structural incentives put more emphasis on primary politics—where ideologically extreme candidates are likely to fair better—than on general elections that might encourage moderating one's rhetoric or positioning.

The significance of polarization's asymmetry to civil-military affairs is important when considering how the parties are likely to perceive the armed forces as an institution. The Republican Party's ideological shift is a well-documented phenomenon among political scientists, especially in its extremity relative even to other parties in developed democracies. Pippa Norris's expert-driven Global Party Survey (GPS) classifies the two major American political establishments in very different ways. The parties are heavily divided on matters of social and economic policy, but while panel respondents identified the Democrats as closer to overall median sensibilities as a "liberal progressive" party, Republican political preferences put it in the category of "authoritarian conservative" parties such as Greece's Golden Dawn and India's Bharatiya Janata (BJP).[65] The Manifesto Project's analysis of major party platforms across Western Europe and North America put the modern GOP in company only with the most extreme of Europe's far right nationalist parties, to include the Alternative for Germany (AfD), the Swedish Democrats, and the Finns Party in Finland.[66] Among the many measures used to categorize party ideologies in this measure is public affinity for the military institution, with positive mentions associated with a rightward-leaning political agenda. As will be discussed in Chapter 5, the ideological proximity of the Republican Party to the American military may be closer to seeing the armed forces as part of a shared partisan constituency than mere policy agreement. Though politicians of all affiliations could benefit from politicization of the military for partisan gain, these incentives are likely to impact the two parties differently, just as the larger trend of polarization has so far.

Collectively, political polarization in the United States can be understood more clearly as a function of these three patterns. It is a powerful affective trend with roots in both the elite and mass populations that, while broadly influential to American politics, has exhibited a particular extremity among conservative political institutions. When we juxtapose this pattern of polarization with the previously discussed trend of increased esteem for the military, we arrive at a normatively precarious state of affairs for civil-military relations in the contemporary environment. If Americans are likely to see the military as a credible actor in an environment where the greatest perceived threat to their security is from other Americans, the temptation to use military prestige, leverage military organizational practices, or even deploy military assets for partisan purposes may prove irresistible. This is the environment—one ripe for politicization—that provides the backdrop for this book's empirical findings.

The Problem of Politicization

At the intersection of these two trends amongst the American public—a seemingly untouchable trust in the military and an equally rigid hyper-polarization along partisan lines—is an environment rife with challenges for the preservation of the "non-partisan" military. Not coincidentally, it is also the climate in which politicization is most likely. For a military institution socialized to stay out of partisan politics while hanging its credibility on that image, the prospect of being drawn into the larger partisan fray has manifestly negative implications for civil-military relations as traditionally envisioned. Chapter 7 will outline in greater detail the broader challenges that politicizing the military can present to stable democratic governance and healthy civil-military relations. But the politicization of important government institutions that are non-partisan by design can create significant problems for public trust in government and the ability to address complicated collective action problems.

Partisan political institutions are not without value or legitimate utility to individuals in society, but it is important to note that the military is not designed as one of them. As Rothstein and Stolle note, political parties, legislatures, or executive offices are viewed as conduits for channeling an individual's ideology into policy; however, they argue that this will likely mean confidence in those institutions is more likely to be a function of co-partisanship than objective reason.[67] When institutions that are not designed to perform this ideology-enhancing function are made to do so, the result is likely to be a general collapse in its ability to fairly provide information or execute its assigned functions. The experience of the Supreme Court may provide an important cautionary tale: public confidence in the court has fallen over recent decades, exacerbated by concerns that the "stench of partisanship" has compromised its institutional objectivity.[68] As Kori Schake argues, this comparison and the concerns it raises are apt as "Americans have begun to see our military the way we see the Supreme Court: apolitical when it supports our policy preferences, shamefully partisan when it does not."[69] The circumstances that have resulted from the two parallel trends detailed in this chapter so far have certainly aided in setting these conditions for politicization.

But what do we mean by politicization? This work is not the first to explore the causes and consequences of this concept, nor the first to provide some typological reference guide for the concept of politicization. Ole Holsti conceived of this concept as a function of the extent to which military servicemembers openly identified with a major political party, a trend that has been explored at length by scholars like Jason Dempsey and Heidi Urben.[70] James Golby and Mara Karlin identify thematic criteria for this idea, using the shorthand "PIE" (partisan behavior, institutional endorsement, and electoral influence) to capture the various ways in which politicizing actions might manifest.[71] Golby himself later provides a dichotomy for understanding politicization of military employment as a function of either "civilian activation" or military activism— depending on which side of the civil-military relationship is engaging in certain behaviors.[72] These are useful constructs for understanding specific forms of military politicization, whether in terms of identity structure, political activity, or operational use. From a normative perspective, these are also particularly helpful guides for understanding measures that military officials might take to minimize the effect of politicization or to reduce the exposure of the military establishment to partisan politics. Building on these concepts, this book adopts a modified view of politicization and its various forms by accounting for the notion that politicization is a function of both military *and* civilian behavior, as well as a matter of both perception and observable action.

Parallax Politicization and the Non-Partisan Military

One of the contributions of this book will be to provide a different nomenclature for understanding forms of politicizing behavior around three principal actors in the civil-military relationship: the military, the public, and partisan political establishments. While other agencies or individuals can undoubtedly complicate the non-partisan image of the military, it is this group of entities that are the most important to the model of politicization discussed here. This is because while most categories of politicization examine the importance of action (in particular, actions taken by the military itself), the typology used in this book will incorporate the significance of perception as well. This model of politicization allows for the possibility that while an institution can be politicized by its own actions, a similar effect can be achieved through the movement of other actors around the institution, creating the appearance of partisan bias.

It is important to note that the desire for a non-partisan military institution above faction or interest is not the same as the commonly invoked "apolitical" military that transcends any involvement in politics at all. The use of military force is a fundamentally political act, while their subordination to civilian leadership in the execution of that policy is a cornerstone of contemporary civil-military relations theory.[73] The "apolitical" military is, in this sense, an inappropriate conflation of terms and should instead be construed as the "non-partisan" ethic.[74] An abstention from anything in the realm of the "political," as scholars like Risa Brooks have argued, fails to account for the inescapably political nature of the military profession. In contrast, a commitment to non-partisanship provides much clearer and narrower criteria for the military: to remain outside not politics, but *partisan* politics. Even with this clarity, however, a key argument of this book is that the military may be politicized even if professionals in the institution make good faith efforts to avoid partisan politics.

The two trends identified so far in this chapter demonstrate the importance of several key actors in whether politicization occurs. In discussing the recent history of civil-military affairs, the relationship between the mass public and the military was of particular importance; similarly, the evolution of partisan polarization was a study on the interaction between that same public and the major partisan institutions in society. As a result, capturing the dynamics of politicization demands some accounting of these three entities: the military institution itself, the observing mass public, and the partisan establishments. Each is significant in determining how politicization occurs or is interpreted. The *public* observes partisan political activity of the other actors, calibrated by the scale offered by signposts among trusted elites and political parties. Against this backdrop, the public renders a judgment about the objectivity of the *military* based on its perceived position (or movement) between these heuristic guides. But the belief that the military has "moved" toward a certain *partisan political establishment* does not need to be rooted in actions taken by the institution; instead, the movement of these actors relative to each other can create a perception of that effect without the military needing to do anything at all. To make matters more complicated, the observing individual may exist (or move) along that same ideological spectrum while trying to render such judgements, even if they do not consciously acknowledge it. The result is a dynamic environment in which both civilian and military actors can engage in behavior that has a politicizing effect.

This is an important distinction to what in this book is termed the Parallax Model of politicization, borrowing from the concept in observational mechanics where the movement of an observer relative to distant objects can change based on new perspectives, creating the illusion of movement between them.[75] In the most common example, a person on Earth will observe a nearby star's position relative to far-distant stars differently depending on their position in orbit around the Sun. If we envision the public as the observer, the military as the nearby object, and major partisan institutions as the ideological backdrop, it is not difficult to imagine how the movement of one these bodies relative to the observer—or the movement of the observer themselves—may in fact create the parallactic appearance of movement between the other two. This model provides a way of spatially understanding politicization as not only an act of choice by military actors, but of civilian ones as well.

This is the political environment modeled in Figure 2.4, where the observing mass public calibrates its understanding of the military's placement on an ideological spectrum relative to the major partisan institutions in the background. Below the main figure is a depiction of how the public might observe an ostensibly "non-partisan" military, that is, one that is not perceptibly closer to one party or another. This is not meant to capture the empirical reality of the American case; rather, cultural closeness between the military and political conservatives is well-documented and would oblige a different placement. However, this is done for the purpose of the model, to provide an ideal-type place to begin from which politicizing activity can be observed as a deviation from the status quo. In this model, military politicization can manifest in one of four different forms, which differ in either (1) the relevant agent of action or (2) the purposefulness of their activity.

In the first two cases, the military itself is the agent of action: what differs is the animating force behind that activity. *Active* politicization refers to instances in which the military, under its own motivation, takes actions that move its position closer to one of the partisan institutions. In the other form, *passive* politicization, the military is still the agent of action, but it is instead responding to directives from superior agencies or civilian leaders that are instead moving the military toward their own partisan establishments. In the example of our Earth-bound observer, active and passive behaviors indicate when our nearby military star drifts (or is pulled) toward one of the distant guideposts, without any real movement from those markers or the observer. Both therefore capture instances in which the public would see a military institution's own activities inching it closer to one political party's preferences. While the former categorizes cases in which this is voluntary, the latter accommodates the asymmetrical relationship between civilian leaders and the military and the possibility that such actions are instead compulsory.

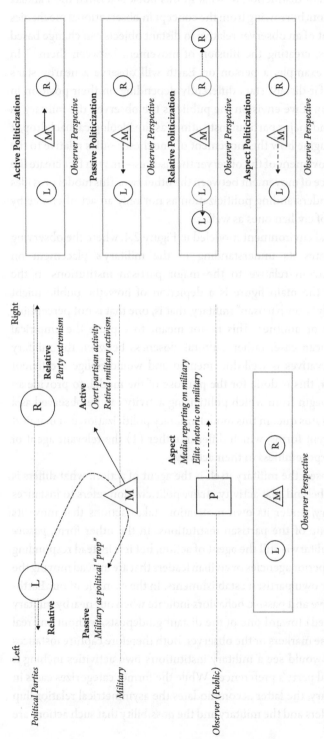

Figure 2.4 Parallax Model of Politicization

Note: Figure 2.4 depicts the parallax model's four forms of politicization. The observing public (P) calibrates their judgment of the military (M) against the ideological spectrum populated by the major political parties (L, R). In the active form, the military moves of its own accord toward a certain political party, creating the shift observed by the public; in the passive form, this same shift is observed by the public, but it is designed by civilian leaders, not the military. The relative form shows how when the parties move apart, particularly in an asymmetric fashion, the new distance between them can leave a fixed military appearing closer to one than the other. The aspect form shows when the observer moves towards an ideological extreme, the belief that the military has not kept pace with their new calibration of the ideological spectrum can create the impression it has moved in the opposite direction.

The other two classes of politicization include those instances in which the military is not the agent of action, but rather appears to move closer to one political party's sensibilities because of the movement of other actors in the environment. In *relative* politicization, the movement of political parties along the ideological spectrum can create the impression that the military is now closer to one or the other. This is particularly likely if the movement by the parties is asymmetrical, a feature of American partisan polarization already described above. If the parties that provide some left-right ideological calibration for the public themselves shift, institutions in the erstwhile "center" may appear to be in a new position in relative terms, despite their fixed position in absolute ones. By contrast, *aspect* politicization occurs when the opposite is true: the military and political parties remained generally fixed, but the ideological movement of the observer forces a new perspective in which the military may appear to have moved closer to one party than the other. Returning again to the original stylized example, these classes of behavior capture when bodies *other* than the nearby military star are in motion: either the distant guideposts (relative) or the Earth-bound observer themselves (aspect). While the first two classes of behavior categorized politicization as a more tangible effect, these classifications of behavior are significant because they account for politicization as a function of perception.

Active politicization emanates from actions taken within the military institution itself, directly creating the impression that the military is more closely aligned with one political party in particular. This most closely approximates Golby's "military activism" in type, with the most obvious form of active politicization occurring when the military engages in overtly partisan activity. Active-duty military leaders can politicize their institution through end-arounds or the "slowing" of civilian policy choices and create the impression that the armed forces are at odds with specific partisans.[76] This can also occur with retired officers, who still carry the imprimatur of the institution in the eyes of the public.[77] Such actors becoming ubiquitous figures in politics as appointed officials, media commentators, and political activists can result in this type of active politicization. This concept captures measures taken by representatives of the military that create the appearance of "movement" toward one partisan establishment over another. Civil-military scholars have warned that the credibility of the armed forces may very well be conditional on its appearance as non-partisan. Compromising this image would, among other things, erode the veracity of military counsel and the reliability of information it provides.[78] It is important to note that active politicization encompasses any activity by military actors that creates the appearance of implicit alignment—whether or not this is intentional or not is less relevant. For example, even if "politicking" or "alliance-building" measures taken by the military to advance its own organizational preferences do not have a partisan agenda in mind, such measures can still politicize the institution as they inevitably come at the expense of one political party over another.[79]

This type of behavior can manifest in a variety of ways. As detailed previously, partisan political endorsements and advocacy by retired general or flag officers (GOFOs) have grown steadily over time, reaching a fever pitch during the turbulent Trump administration as fears over its normalization became a topic of debate among civil-military scholars.[80] Now, candidates regularly publicize lists of dozens or hundreds of retired officers as standard fare during campaign season.[81] Many drew attention to the dangerous precedent set by this active variety of politicization, when retired Marine General John Allen and retired Army Lieutenant General Mike Flynn appeared as keynote speakers for both major party nominating conventions in the 2016 election season. At the most extreme end, actual politicians or candidates for office with military experience often make that affiliation a centerpiece of political messaging, implicitly leveraging the credibility of the larger military.[82] But military figures need not dive directly into partisan political machinery to risk politicizing the institution. Policy advocacy, political commentary, or editorial publications can achieve this effect due to the public's inability to tell the difference between active and retired military figures.

Nonetheless, actively politicizing events are the easiest to detect in contemporary civil-military affairs, if for no other reason than they are more visible. Concerns over the "poor" state of civil-military relations in the 1990s emanated from the perception that military leaders expressed their personal distaste for President Bill Clinton by lobbying Congress for specific foreign policy outcomes or highlighting cultural tensions over issues like service for open homosexuals.[83] To historians like Richard Kohn, this was not merely an artifact of a singular dislike for Clinton, but a general rightward shift among the military, creating the appearance that it "began thinking, voting, and even espousing Republicanism with a capital R."[84] In short, active politicization requires some purposeful behavior by military actors that more closely align the institution with the specific preferences of a particular political party. Chapters 3 and 6 will use examples of this behavior from the Bush, Obama, Trump, and Biden administrations to contextualize empirical findings on military policy advocacy and retired military activism.

By contrast, passive politicization comes from outside the institution, when civilian leaders or the public place the military in partisan political situations. Whereas active politicization occurs when implicit institutional allegiance to a political party is *given*, passive politicization occurs when it is *taken*. The motivation for such behavior is certainly not a new feature of American politics. As an institution with high public trust, the armed forces are a tempting target for use as a political implement, whether to provide legitimacy to policy recommendations or credibility through appointments to governmental posts.

Passive politicization includes placing the military in positions where political spotlights become difficult to avoid, or setting conditions wherein the routine execution of military functions can be viewed as politically partisan. Put simply, active politicization creates the impression that the military has moved toward a certain political party; the passive variety instead appears as though the military has *been moved* toward one.

Politicization of this type has also proven a reliable fixture of the political environment. For example, civilian leaders have often used ex-military appointments to high-ranking political posts as a strategy to garner credibility or public support. Public engagement with the military can also achieve this effect, such as speeches in front of military audiences or highly visible trips abroad to visit servicemembers. It is again important to note that the intent to politicize the military is not a requisite for such to be the outcome; instead, the distinguishing characteristic is the locus and direction of agency. Nonetheless, the most potent manifestations of passive politicization occur when blurring the lines of implicit endorsement are by design. Norm-breaking behavior identified by many civil-military scholars fits this mold, such as military scenery being used to legitimate controversial policies like the "Muslim ban," or in advocating that active-duty servicemembers engage in partisan activism with Congress.[85] Direct appeals to the military as part of a voting constituency loyal to the commander-in-chief or their party are perhaps the most easily visible and normatively problematic versions of passive politicization.[86]

Relative politicization is neither the result of active military behavior nor external actors targeting the military for political value, but instead is a feature of the public's ideological anchoring in a shifting political environment. The active and passive categories detail how politicization can occur when the military pushes or when it is pulled: this third form captures one instance of how it can occur even when the military is standing still. Relative politicization therefore arises when the military "appears" to move closer to one party than another, but only due to the shifting partisan political ground beneath their feet. As previously discussed, largely objective means of ascertaining the parties' position on a left-right ideological spectrum have found that polarization has widened the gap between them, even if this gap is deeply asymmetric. The public, recalibrating their understanding of the political "center," may conceive of institutions that once resided at that imagined place as drifting toward one side or another.

For example, imagine the public viewing a simple political spectrum as depicted in the third chart; it would observe a politically progressive party (L) on one end and a politically conservative one (R) on the other. The military, along with other institutions attempting to stay out of the partisan fray, would emerge around the center. Now imagine that one partisan establishment moves to the extreme end of its own ideological space. This could occur through actual polarizing forces we have already observed in American politics, as well as evidence of more subjective forces that lead partisans to over-estimate the ideological extremity of their opponents.[87] In an attempt to find the new political "center," the public shifts perspective to keep it in frame. However, institutions that were formerly clustered around the previous center now appear to have drifted closer to the other end of the political spectrum. Though no actions were taken by these groups, the shift of partisan establishments from each other creates the illusion of movement for those in between.

This type of politicizing force is rarer, but captures instances in which civil-military norms, organizational ethics, or professional standards among the military remain locally fixed, but shifting political sensibilities *relative* to the military's policy change in such a way that their new location in the eyes of the public appears more partisan. For example, various news sources reported on statements made by the active duty service chiefs following the 2017 Charlottesville rally in which white supremacist groups publicly clashed with counter-protesters. Statements from the military service leaders amounted to largely standard denunciations of racial violence in the military and elsewhere, with Army Chief of Staff General James McConville reaffirming that extremism of this sort was "against our values."[88] On their face, the statements reflected no tangible change in military policy; however, these sentiments were reported as a "rare rebuke by the top brass of their commander-in-chief" due to their apparent distance from those of the White House, statements from which surprised many observers by expressing a reluctance to convincingly denounce the same extremist groups.[89] In 2022, the Air Force publicly announced that "assignment, medical, legal and other resources" were available to LGBTQ servicemembers and dependents likely to be affected by a string of state laws targeting gender-affirming care and education.[90] Though the statement was characterized as an "unusual move" by the news media, the press release merely reminded Air Force families of existing services and did not constitute any meaningful change in policy from the military; instead, the major change was the spate of legislative moves initiated by the state legislatures in question.[91] In these cases, no military behavior outside the status quo had actually taken place; rather, reporting of "subversive" intent reflected how the partisan political guideposts had instead shifted relative to the military. In the spatial terms of this model, by adopting more ideologically extreme positions, the military's inertia appeared to many observers as a movement *away* from one party, rather than the party itself moving. The concluding section of Chapter 5 will use examples from the Trump administration to illustrate both relative and passive forms of politicization and provide a context for data patterns on partisan cognitive biases about the military.

Finally, aspect politicization occurs when the public observer experiences a significant ideological shift that re-positions the perceived placement of the military with respect to the parties. This is another example of military politicization that can occur without any overt actions taken by the military, but instead is the result of the observer's relative position to the political parties and the armed forces. While mass partisan polarization, particularly the affective variety, has been shown to be an important fixture of contemporary American politics, this brings with it a preference for specific media outlets and sources of information. As a result, partisans are likely to receive starkly different pictures of the military when it comes to both war- and peace-time reporting, depending on their partisan ideology and preferred media source. Accuracy aside, if these preferred media sources provide specific types of information on military activities to their partisan audiences, the result may be a reappraisal of the military's position relative to the major partisan institutions in society. While this may appear to the observer as gaining information about the military's movement, it is in fact a socialization of the observer themselves; an inability to distinguish the difference can be accredited to an inflated sense of "moderation" among voters even when they in actuality quite partisan.[92] As a result, repeated exposure to information or narrative construction regarding the military can create the impression (even if misleading) that the military represents partisan interests.

This form of politicization can therefore occur when specific narratives about military culture and organizational practices emerge for decidedly partisan purposes. Media personality and Fox News commentator Tucker Carlson elicited strong rebukes from the Pentagon for repeated segments on the "feminization" of the military by disparaging pictures of female servicemembers in maternity flightsuits. The remarks elicited sharp criticisms from senior military leaders decrying Carlson using his platform as one of the highest-rated cable news hosts to denigrate American servicemembers.[93] As with the case of relative politicization, the military had not meaningfully changed policy or took overt politicizing action: the policies addressed in the broadcast were in fact developed under co-partisans in the previous administration. Nonetheless, the remarks were clearly intended for a partisan audience to re-evaluate their estimation of the military as an objective political body. This form of politicization is likely to become more common as tailored forms of media consumption, whether through conventional or digital means, become available to partisan audiences seeking to reduce dissonant information. Chapter 4 will use data on partisan media consumption and recent examples of media narrative-shaping around the military by partisan interest groups or news outlets to show how aspect politicization can manifest in practice.

This chapter has outlined the convergence of two important and concurrent trends in the American political environment: an increasing affinity among the public for its military and a decreasing regard for partisan outsiders as a function of polarization. Where these two trends meet has created an environment where politicization is not only possible, but likely to be incentivized as partisan skirmishes take on more existential stakes. As the last chapter in this book the challenge of politicization has clear implication for the maintenance of the military's non-partisan ethic in a liberal democracy. The Parallax Model of politicization provides some vocabulary for understanding the different forms that this pattern can adopt, to include instances where movement toward a specific political party is either compelled or illusory. The complex media environment and polarizing political landscape only compound this challenge for the military to maintain credibility as an objective guarantor of national security.

The chapters that follow discuss empirical findings gathered through original survey experiments and observational data collection in order to understand how partisan polarization has affected the state of civil-military relations and, by extension, the extent to which politicization is likely to persist as a challenge for the United States. Each chapter will discuss how perceptions of the military's voice in politics, the depiction of the military in media, the tolerance of the public for non-partisan military activity, and the role of the retired military community has been shaped by recent developments in American politics. In each case, several of the model cases detailed here will be relevant for understanding the sources of politicization and the key actors involved.

‖ 3 ‖

Deafening Whisper

The Utility of the Military Voice

Before we can understand the possible ways that the military voice can be a source of politicization, it is first necessary to explore the influence that military actors can have on public opinion, particularly on issue areas in which the armed forces have an outsized role. The importance of public support for foreign military intervention is a prominent feature of international relations and security theory. Political elites and key decision-makers, particularly in costly arenas such as military intervention or foreign affairs, must consider not only the material costs of military action, but the public and political costs as well. Public approval for these types of policies can often shape the realm of feasible options for political leaders and underpins much of our understanding about how democratic systems of government decide to launch, sustain, and conclude conflicts abroad.[1] As the modern information environment allows broad access to elite opinions and preferences, the shaping influences of public opinion on complex issues such as foreign policy are of considerable interest to both policy-makers and academics. For our purposes, understanding how and why military voices influence the public is a necessary place to begin any study of politicization.

A sizable literature in political science has been devoted to understanding how elites in society can shape public support for foreign policy or war initiation. These efforts have studied the ability of the media, partisan political leaders, policy experts, and international institutions to influence public opinion on these complex issue domains.[2] Political communications scholars have argued that the potency of these "cues" are understood to vary considerably depending on the credibility of the source, the political awareness of the recipient, or the substance of the message.[3] However, the relative influence of traditional social and political elite groups such as partisan leaders and the media has become less certain, particularly as public distrust in these organizations increases in democracies like the United States. Over the past two decades, this trend has been coupled with

Dangerous Instrument: Political Polarization and US Civil-Military Relations. Michael A. Robinson,
Oxford University Press. © Oxford University Press 2023. DOI: 10.1093/oso/9780197611555.003.0003

a increasingly public focus on the opinions and policy-making relevance of one of the few institutions with high levels of public trust: the military. Given the central role that elite members of the military play in both the development and execution of these policies, the impact of military speech on such subjects may be substantial. If the military institution is likely to experience more politicizing behavior from both within and without, one important concern is how valuable the military voice is likely to be as a political tool.

This analysis focuses on the influence of the military institution in shaping public attitudes on intervention abroad, contributing not only to recent work on elite cue effects and the study of public support for war, but to the state of civil-military relations. First, the chapter will propose several testable hypotheses regarding military elite cue effects on public opinion formation. Given the high degree of source credibility that military elites have enjoyed over the past several decades, otherwise professionally taboo public appeals issued by these figures will have a substantive effect on public approval, even when issued in contradiction to the public preferences of the president. The second section introduces survey experimentation to measure the effect of military elite cues on public support for military intervention, building on existing study by using a competitive information design.[4] Third, the design of the survey incorporates trust in the military alongside the level of public trust in a variety of governmental and social institutions in order to better understand the moderating influence of this individual-level characteristic on the potency of elite cues.[5] Finally, this chapter will conclude with examples of military advocacy in practice and the possible sources of politicization implied by the experimental findings. If military actors—whether through retired speech, media leaks, or direct commentary— are able to move public opinion on policy, their capacity for influence is likely to be a source of active politicization more broadly. Using the examples of the 2006 "revolt of the generals" over Iraq policy and the 2010 episode between the Obama administration and leaders in the Afghanistan theater, this chapter illustrates the active politicization that can emerge as a result of military speech.

Elite Cues and the Military

Active engagement by military figures in political discourse, particularly in matters of foreign policy, is a normatively fraught subject in civil-military affairs. As discussed previously, different civil-military philosophies prescribe different roles for the military in political decision-making.[6] However, many of these works find common ground in the assertion that the military owes not just subject matter expertise to political leaders, but institutionalized subordination. Senior military officers are both formally and normatively discouraged from actions or statements that could be construed as subversive of sitting civilian leaders, especially the president as commander-in-chief. Despite being professionally discouraged, military cues on policy may still be issued for a variety of reasons.

One explanation comes from understanding the formulation of policy as a bargaining process between civilian decision-makers and the elite advisors they enlist for counsel on complicated issues. Elizabeth Saunders argues that intra-elite bargaining is essential in foreign-policy formulation, both as a means for developing robust and successful strategies and for co-opting key elites in order to prevent them from publicly signaling against the policy later.[7] Sufficiently co-opting these elites gives them a vested interest in the policy's success and less ability to publicly appeal on flaws in the policy. Applied to the military context, these concessions may involve civilian commitments to specific strategies desired by the military elite, bureaucratic advancement or promotion, or providing increasing resources to the military commensurate with the task.[8] However, a failure to bring these key leaders into the decision-making process in a way that sufficiently mollifies their misgivings or incorporates their preferences can create incentives to seek end-around strategies in order to shape the decision space of the civilian leadership through the public.

Another potential reason for military cuing could be fundamentally divergent preferences between military and civilian leaders that is exacerbated by bureaucratic factors. Jim Golby argues that military elites appointed under a different administration or not appointed by the president are likely to have different foreign policy attitudes than the executive across a range of possible issue domains.[9] Similarly, executives who have inherited the military appointees of a previous administration may be less likely to lend weight to their advice. As a result, civilian leaders may more forcefully push foreign policy or security agendas in spite of contrary military advice in the private sphere, incentivizing military defection in the public sphere in an effort to shape the process. However, recent survey research by Ronald Krebs, Robert Ralston, and Aaron Rapoport seems to suggest that the audience is likely a willing one, with the public increasingly accepting of open military advocacy (or opposition) to policy and more likely to insist that civilian leaders defer to their counsel on matters of conflict.[10] Interestingly, civilian leaders may be skeptical of military advice that a growing share of Americans want to hear publicly; not only does this indicate a complex information environment, but a weakened norm against military speech.

This focus on divergent preferences, unrestrained by a sense of accountability to a political patron, is particularly important given another source of military elite cues: an increasingly vocal retired military community. These elite figures have generated intense debate on the normative implications of military dissent and the political consequences of former military leaders offering conflicting opinions to sitting political elites.[11] Regardless of the normative propriety of retired military speech in traditional civil-military relations, they present an understudied and potentially significant empirical puzzle. What's more, this community is worthy of consideration as part of the larger military elite community, as they draw on the same shared pool of institutional credibility as their active duty counterparts.

Bureaucratic patronage or intra-elite bargaining failure present some explanatory insight into why the military elite may issue these public signals at all, despite the proscriptions against them. Many civil-military scholars have argued that such political interventions by military elites could degrade the credibility of the larger institution.[12] However, this does not remove incentives for individual cue-givers to exploit a common pool of clout with the public for short-term gain. Despite strong reason to believe that these types of signals will be influential, the elite cue literature exhibits only a limited empirical accounting of their impact. This is particularly curious given the increasingly public and political role being played by active and retired military elites in government and warrants a more tailored analysis.

Public Opinion and Elite Cues

A considerable effort in political science has sought to understand the dynamic by which the public develops opinions about complex issues. The formative models of public opinion-shaping subscribe to the notion that individuals are unable to efficiently form expert opinions on every issue in the political sphere, resorting instead to the heuristic offered by cues from trusted elites.[13] Empirical efforts testing the potency of these cues have explored the influence of partisan leaders, policy experts, academics, and international institutions.[14] This body of work ascribes a great deal of influence to elite figures in their ability to shape public attitudes on policies or candidate choice through cuing.

An important consideration in measuring these effects has been the relative importance of the cue's substance ("the message") against characteristics of the source ("the messenger"). Richard Petty and Tom Cacioppo identify these two channels as central (where the message's substance is analyzed) and peripheral (where the cue source's credibility is assessed) modes of thinking. This Elaboration Likelihood Model (ELM) argues that peripheral processing is more likely when the information environment is distracting, the issue under debate complex, and the stakes of the decision impersonal.[15] Given the distant and complex nature of foreign policy to the individual, we should expect increased reliance on source characteristics when measuring signal persuasiveness. The military's privileged position as executor of foreign policy and high regard in the public's esteem should posture military elites for considerable influence on such issues.

Empirical exploration of military advocacy or opposition to foreign intervention suggest that these voices may be influential. Important experimental survey research by Jim Golby, Kyle Dropp, and Peter Feaver has found that key military actors may be able to sway public attitudes on military operations, while survey work by Ronald Krebs and Robert Ralston suggests that their impact may be conditional on the partisan identity of the audience.[16] The experimental design in this chapter includes a number of design features that account for influence patterns among partisans, incorporate a competitive-cue environment more representative of the respondent's information space, factor in the partisan identity of the president, use a broader array of military cue-givers (including retired elites), and measure individual-level confidence in the military institution as a potential moderator. The state of the art in this area of civil-military relations scholarship therefore helps to structure some guiding hypotheses.

The rest of this chapter categorizes these hypotheses into three groups. The first addresses the influence of military elite cues as they relate to characteristics of the source itself, namely, its credibility. These peripheral mechanisms include the existence of influence effects in the aggregate, the role played by perceived trustworthiness and reliability, and the robustness of cue effects across different types of military sources. These are intended to gauge both the latent political influence of military elites and the importance of source credibility in that process. The second proposes a hypothesis relating the substance of the message to the effectiveness of the elite cue. This test serves to measure the significance of signal direction relative to other voices in the respondent's information space, in this case the president. Finally, the third set of hypotheses is designed to analyze the effect of multiple signals on the strength of the military cue. These leverage the competitive cue framework of the design to assess the influence of military elites in a partisan context and demonstrate how military signals might be ripe for appropriation in a polarized environment.

Source Credibility

The first hypothesis regards the ability of the military source to move public opinion in absolute terms. As previously discussed, cues that originate from credible elites may influence public opinion formation across a range of issues. Given highly specific subject matter expertise, perceived objectivity, and broad confidence from the public, military elites should be a potentially influential voice in the information space. One should therefore expect military cuing to be persuasive on matters specific to that base of knowledge, such as military intervention. Additionally, military cues may be normatively costly to transmit given professional imperatives against political activity by representatives of the military institution. For these reasons, policy cues from military elites should be influential to individual-level attitude formation.

- **H1A (Military Influence)**: All else equal, public approval for a proposed military intervention will be higher [lower] with supportive [opposing] military cues than without them.

The second hypothesis accounts for understanding the role of source credibility by directly considering the perceived reliability of the military elite. Credible sources may serve as a useful gauge for finding one's ideal point policy on issues with which the respondent is unfamiliar, particularly as the issue becomes more complex or distant.[17] This credibility is largely understood to be the product of the source's perceived trustworthiness, expertise, and ideological or political like-mindedness.[18] Ideological alignment with partisan elites is more easily measured through individual-level partisan identity or political ideology. Though it is harder to measure like-mindedness between the individual and the military than it is with political leaders, one can proxy for this connection by measuring the level of institutional trust the respondent expresses in the military establishment.

- **H1B (Confidence in the Military)**: The effect of military elite cuing will increase positively with the level of institutional trust the respondent expresses for the military establishment.

Third, in order to further establish the role of source credibility in this process, the next hypothesis accounts for the variety of ways in which military signaling might be transmitted. Military elites operating in this framework have a variety of options to influence the possible decision space of civilian leaders and the mass public.[19] In recent decades, one strategy of particular import to civil-military tradition has been attempts by these figures to utilize a high level of public trust to "end-around" political decision-makers. Appeals of this sort provide a potentially potent tactic for military elites to influence policy through the public. However, due to the normative proscriptions against military leaders engaging in such behavior, they are also emblematic of politicizing behavior that is likely to alter public perception of the objectivity and non-partisanship of the military institution. Accounting for the different ways this might occur couches concerns over politicization in a modern context; as a result, this chapter accounts for three possible methods of signaling.

First, serving military elites can influence the public discourse by speaking or writing through conventional media outlets. Risa Brooks captures this option in her typology of domestic political strategies for the military elite, distinguishing public appeals from the normal disclosure of military counsel by (1) its public nature and (2) its outright endorsement or admonishment of a proposed policy alternative.[20] This tactic is not purely an artifact of the contemporary civil-military environment. General Colin Powell's letter to the editor of the *New York Times* and article in *Foreign Policy* in 1992 opposing the contemplated intervention in Bosnia placed the enterprise in serious doubt in the final month of a contentious presidential campaign.[21] Though this typology does not specifically consider Congressional testimony a true example of a public appeal, General Eric Shinseki's testimony in the lead-up to the 2003 Iraq War that scrutinized the White House's war plans for the invasion was both a public signal and one seemingly in opposition to administration policy preferences.[22]

Public appeals are simplest to employ, as senior military officers interact with conventional media outlets on a regular basis. However, the visibility of these cues can present trade-offs to their effectiveness. The first is that concurrence may be indistinguishable from independent judgment when public cues are in accord with civilian-led policy, such as General David Petraeus's 2004 *Washington Post* editorial supporting the ongoing strategy in Iraq or Lieutenant General H. R. McMaster's 2017 *Wall Street Journal* editorial advocating the Trump administration's "America First" foreign policy.[23] When civilian and military cues are in alignment, individuals may simply surmise that this is the public reflection of some private sphere bargaining process or coordination. Political leaders are likely to have co-opted the military into the decision-making process outside the public eye and little "surprising information" is disclosed by both elite groups espousing the same position. More simply, because of the professional expectation of military support to the civilian leadership, concurrent military cues may simply reflect a fulfillment of this supportive role. However, they could also present an implicit statement about cost, likelihood of success, and feasibility, as research on international organizational cues has shown.[24] Here, supportive comments by senior military officials could provide comfort to those with interventionist preferences but uncertain opinions about a specific case.

Prepared statements, interviews, or articles also have a high probability of being received by the public and enjoying wide media circulation. As a result, there is a higher probability that the signal will be received by a broader audience among the public. However, the second potential effect of this openness is that the signal's influence may be limited, particularly among active duty officers, if the public perceives that any statements made by such figures are screened beforehand. Powell's public remarks on the 1992 Bosnia debate were highly publicized and ignited considerable debate about the limits of appropriate military influence, although he has since remarked that these comments were permitted by the Department of Defense before their release.[25] This is not always the case, however, and public statements can also trigger a wider dialogue over the merits of civilian-led policy. During the air campaign in Kosovo in 1999, outspoken ground invasion proponent General Wesley Clark was asked by the press to gauge the success of the air war on Serbian forces. Clark, who had been marginalized by other senior defense officials for his views on the necessity of a ground operation, offered that "without being there on the ground, it's very difficult to give reliable information," remarks seen by some as a subtle attempt to "box in" the Clinton administration's policy space.[26]

Second, communicating cues to the public need not utilize traditional transmission channels and can instead by conducted through less overt means, such as targeted information "leaks." As noted previously, prepared statements and conventional media use may theoretically limit the effectiveness of the cue in certain circumstances. A potentially potent tactic also available to military elites, specifically active-duty officers, is to allow private information to be acquired by or leaked to the press in an effort to circumvent normal decision-making channels. There are several reasons to believe media leaking or private information "spillage" can be effective. Public opposition to such tactics on normative grounds has weakened over time. Schake and Mattis's survey of civil-military attitudes found that while leaking information in response to "unwise orders" is considered the least legitimate response by the public, approval of this tactic has increased four-fold since 1998 across both veteran and civilian elements of the mass public.[27] More recent survey work by Golby and Feaver suggest that this attitude has only grown in the interim, with the public more likely to accept military resistance to "unwise" civilian orders.[28] For the audience, the release of classified or private information could be an inherently useful elite signal in their attitude formation regarding policy. Given the newsworthiness of unauthorized information seizures and staff-level leaking of private information, it is reasonable to argue that this type of signal can be highly influential because it lacks the impression of pre-approval that deliberate statements might carry. The private origin of the message instead heightens the "surprising" nature of the information and increases its perceived credibility. Through this mechanism, the public can be exposed to information about misgivings held by military elites over the feasibility, cost, and likely duration of a conflict.

Targeted leaks of private information can be a potent tool for military leaders seeking to shape policy. An example of this tactic in practice was the release of internal documentation detailing General Stanley McChrystal's troop level recommendations to the Obama administration in 2009. The headquarters staff in Afghanistan, concerned with a potentially unfunded mandate to achieve rapid success there, was accused of acting to shape the decision space of the newly elected Obama administration by pushing for a "surge" influx of additional forces. Finding themselves "boxed in" by the leak, the White House approved the Afghan "surge" in accordance with a proposed military course of action.[29] Signals of this type similarly carry the imprimatur of military source credibility while providing "surprising" or private information that the public would not see otherwise.[30]

Third, one of the most potent cue-givers representative of the larger military establishment is that of the retired community. Though traditionally understudied, contemporary research has begun to evaluate the effect of this community on public receptiveness to endorsements of major partisan candidates and levels of support for high-profile political issues.[31] In keeping with the previous discussion on actor trustworthiness and expertise, retired officers have become increasingly visible actors on matters treading well into the realm of partisan politics. For this reason, there are several explanations for why this community warrants consideration in both the study of elite cues and as a potential source of politicization.

Retired officers are increasingly present in the public sphere as cue givers, whether as security analysts for major media outlets or as independent subject matter experts. Over several administrations, retired military officers have engaged in public criticism, advocacy, or activism on issues such as security strategy in Iraq, Syria, and North Korea, the allocation of the federal budget, and policies governing the open service of homosexual or transgender individuals, torture, and relations with the media.[32] The increased popularity of such figures as media commentators or analysts has made retired military influence a ubiquitous feature of the information landscape, especially given the additional platforms afforded to military elites by social media.[33] Furthermore, retired officers draw on the same shared pool of institutional credibility as the active officer corps and issue cues from the same position, but without the rigid legal proscription against speaking publicly. Recent study into the impact of retired officials drawing on this credibility pool has concerned scholars and policymakers alike, for fear that such repeated interference may actually degrade the integrity of the wider military institution.[34] The importance of high source credibility among retired officers even after they have left the military became more salient following numerous high-profile appointments of retired military officers to key bureaucratic positions in government during the Trump administration.[35] In short, retired officers warrant consideration as a distinct signaling mechanism from the military community.

These different signal mechanisms—deliberate statements, undisclosed leaks, and retired elites—reflect the wide variation in military elite sources to which the individual may be exposed when acquiring information and forming policy attitudes. Whereas the previous hypotheses explore the magnitude of military elite influence and the role of institutional confidence on that same influence, it is reasonable to suspect that this effect is largely consistent across different types of military sources. Given that a military identity is the constant feature across these different sources, this third hypothesis provides an opportunity for further evidence of source credibility's central role in military elite influence.

- **H1C (Consistency of Military Influence):** The effect of the military cue will be robust across different types of military sources, including active duty, undisclosed, or retired elites.

Collectively, this first set of hypotheses speaks directly to the importance of source credibility on individual-level receptiveness to military elite cues. It first tests whether such elites can have an effect on support levels for a given policy (H1A); this effort reflects past empirical designs measuring military elite influence in the context of the elite-cue literature. However, they also explore the role of peripheral processing and the importance of source-specific characteristics in this process by measuring the moderating effect of institutional confidence (H1B), and the robustness of the military cue across different strategies (H1C).

Signal Direction

The second thematic hypothesis regards how the cue's substantive direction might influence the public on its own. Much of elite cue theory includes the assertion that individuals in society may lend special weight to cues that are deemed surprising information or counter to the perceived preferences of the cue source. Elite communities with stated preferences on particular issues provide little new information by supporting those positions. However, when partisan leaders or other elites issue cues that are counter-to-type or costly, these cues can be particularly informative to individuals, even if the individual does not share ideological alignment with the source.[36] This dynamic is identified by Matthew Baum and Tim Groeling, who find that costly and "credible communication"—such as criticism of the president from a co-partisan—is far more influential to the public than unsurprising, expected, or "cheap talk."[37]

Applied to the case of military elites, such surprising information may be the military advocating or opposing specific policy options in violation of traditionally accepted professional norms against such activity. More specifically, that an aspect of the military's "type" includes restraint against oppositional cues that contradict the commander-in-chief's preferences. As a result, statements or actions that violate this long-held norm should be considered costly or "counter-to-type" informative signals:

• **H1D (Costly Signaling)**: Military cues that are professionally costly—issued in contradiction to public executive preferences—will be more effective than those issued in concurrence with the executive.

The notion that military elite signaling might be more effective due to their costliness is generally dependent on an image of the public where traditional civil-military norms are shared and salient. Chapter 6 will show that when military elites can be more cleanly identified with a "side" in the partisan landscape, this assumption for the public experiences significant problems. However, this chapter's initial empirical foray into the effects of military speech provides a military actor with no overt partisan identity; as such, the basic logic that an objective military voice might be more credible when risking professional sanction remains a viable hypothesis.

Effect of Multiple Signals

The third set of hypotheses addresses the effect of multiple signals on the influence of the military elite cue. As designed, another advantage of this empirical strategy is the competitive structure, allowing for the incorporation of individual-level characteristics like partisanship in understanding the influence of military elites. While both partisan and military cues have been shown to have an independent effect on attitude formation, the strength of that influence in a partisan environment with competing voices has yet to be explored. Such a dimension is of particular importance in light of empirical research suggesting the salience of partisanship on both perceived source credibility and sensitivity to information about foreign policy ventures.[38] This dynamic is of considerable interest in situations where the information is expected to have the least effect: does military opposition degrade support among co-partisans? Does military concurrence increase support among contra-partisans?

Analysis of these competitive cues again speaks to the importance of source-specific characteristics of the military elite. With exposure to multiple cues, the individual is forced to weigh the relative credibility of the sources when rendering an expressed opinion. Polling on the prospect of military intervention reveals the potentially wide disparity in public confidence between different voices in the debate, most notably the president and the military.[39] Whether partisan political cues or military elite cues maintain a residual effect after considering the other is unclear, though there are theoretical reasons to support either case. Across the elite-driven politics literature, the effect of partisan resistance or "motivated reasoning" plays a significant role. Individuals may attend to co-partisan preferences while downplaying contradictory information.[40] However, military elites may present an objectively credible source of information, potentially tempering partisan biases or providing substantive policy cues. Accordingly, this approach considers the following hypotheses testing the effect of military cues in this partisan context:

- **H1E (Oppositional Effect Among Co-Partisans)**: Military elite cues that are oppositional will decrease support for a policy advocated by a co-partisan president.

- **H1F (Supportive Effect Among Contra-Partisans)**: Military elite cues that are supportive will increase support for a policy advocated by a contra-partisan president.

There are several testable implications of these hypotheses. If military actors can offer signals that bring individuals closer to agreement with a contra-partisan president, this would indeed present evidence for the strength of the military signal. Rather than ignore the information, this would indicate that individuals instead expended more cognitive resources in addressing the dissonance it presents and updated their impressions of the policy. Similarly, the impact of oppositional cue effects on drawing support away from a president's co-partisans would suggest that not only do military elites have an independent political influence, but one that remains relevant even after considering strong co-partisan voices. Individuals presented with oppositional military signals can also choose to either ignore the information or allow it to update their support for the policy. While the former suggests that partisan bias or resistance takes precedence, the latter is evidence for the robustness of military influence amidst competing voices from a trusted political source.

Collectively, these three groups of hypotheses approach the latent political influence of military elites from several different perspectives. The first analyzes the role of source credibility on the effectiveness of military cues: whether this influence exists at all or is conditional on the mechanism of transmission. The second assesses whether aspects of the message's substance compound this effect; namely, its direction relative to the preferences of civilian leaders. The last set of hypotheses tests the durability of these cues in a partisan context, specifically evaluating whether such signals can influence individual attitudes against the expected direction.

Research Design

Testing these various sets of hypotheses involves the employment of a survey experiment with specialized design features. The survey was fielded to a nationally representative opt-in panel in December 2016 and was designed to measure the effect of military elite cuing on proposed armed intervention policies.[41] The design incorporates competitive cue environments and explicit assignment of presidential partisan identity, including variation in the transmission mechanism of military elite cues. After the standard demographic battery of questions collecting information on various individual-level characteristics, respondents were asked to read and offer an opinion on a short news story detailing a proposed military intervention being considered by the United States, the substance of which varied along two dimensions.[42]

The first dimension varied the president's partisan identity as either a Democrat or Republican. One idiosyncrasy of this experiment worth noting was the period of time in which it was fielded. The timing of the survey occurred during the post-election period in 2016, in the waning months of the Obama administration where the public was aware that the incoming president would be Donald Trump. This timing provided both a challenge and an unexpected opportunity in the context of the survey's aim. Survey experimentation randomizing the partisan identity of the president can often be limited by the fact that only one party can be tangibly imagined in the moment. At any given time, one party will have representation in the White House, while the survey is essentially asking the respondent to imagine an amorphous figure for the other party for comparison. The timing of this survey provided a rare window where both partisan identities could be realistically projected onto the presidency, though deeply informed by the individual personalities in question. To be sure, the personality traits of Obama and Trump carried their own pre-dispositions in the public eye, which likely includes some immeasurable effect of pre-treatment. Nonetheless, respondents would not be asked to "invent" figures when assigned to either condition of president partisan identity. In all conditions, the president advocates support for a proposed military intervention; the timing of the survey would make this cue more tangible, if susceptible to individual perceptions of the incoming and outgoing commanders-in-chief.

The second dimension varied the nature of military influence as either silence (*control*), a supportive signal (*support*), or an oppositional signal. Supportive signals came in the form of a statement to the press by an active-duty senior military commander in the region. Oppositional signals came in one of three possible forms: a contrary statement by an active-duty officer similar to the *support* condition (*oppositional statement*), a leaked internal memorandum from the regional military headquarters (*oppositional leak*), or cable news commentary from a retired senior military commander (*oppositional retired*). Military signals differed only in transmission mechanisms and direction, offering no governing logic for support or opposition.

The resulting structure yields a 2 × 5 factorial design with 10 possible experimental conditions. Respondents were assigned to one of these conditions, asked to read the corresponding vignette, and subsequently provided their level of agreement with pursuing the proposed policy, which was randomly presented as either a humanitarian or conventional military intervention. Respondents offered support on a five-point scale ("strongly disagree," "disagree," "neither agree nor disagree," "agree," "strongly agree"). In the conventional scenario, the news story depicts a small former Soviet state as the victim of increased aggression from Russia as border skirmishes and mobilization threaten the country. In the humanitarian condition, the news story reflects an authoritarian regime clashing with protesters as domestic resistance to the regime breaks into violence. Additionally, respondents were asked as part of the demographic battery to rate their level of confidence in a random-ordered display of social and political institutions, including the military.[43] After measurement of their support for this policy, respondents receiving either vignette were re-randomized into a new treatment condition and asked to read and provide their level of support for the other scenario. Each respondent therefore went through random assignment, news story exposure, and approval measurement twice, with the order of the scenario's presentation randomized.

The design was structured to provide information in a competitive environment. In all conditions, the president was on record as being in support of a potential intervention, with the partisan identity of the president randomized between the two major parties. A completely symmetrical design would include a dimension in which the president publicly opposed the intervention; however, in order to preserve both statistical power and ecological realism, this dimension is not included. The format of the vignette and the randomization of partisan identity were chosen for several reasons. First, the information was formatted in order to best replicate the manner in which many Americans actually consume news media, in short news summaries rather than in long substantive articles. Second, the president was assigned a randomized party identity in order to allow for analysis of partisan alignment between individuals and the president on cue effectiveness. The resulting design provides numerous avenues to measure the utility of the military voice in a complicated political landscape.

Data Analysis and Findings

The initial results of the experiment suggest that, in the simplest sense, military signals do influence public opinion in the aggregate. Figure 3.1 displays the change in aggregate levels of public approval compared to the control condition, labeling respondent treatment conditions and pooling over both scenarios. Notable immediately is the suppressive effects of military opposition to public support for intervention: mean support level among the public drops considerably between the support (+2%) and opposition (−8%) conditions. Conditional on the military weighing in on the debate, the direction of military influence creates a 10 percentage-point swing in support among the public. These initial findings bear out the central claim of H1A, with effects recovered while pooling across both partisan assignments of the president, the different treatment conditions of military cues, and any respondent characteristics.[44]

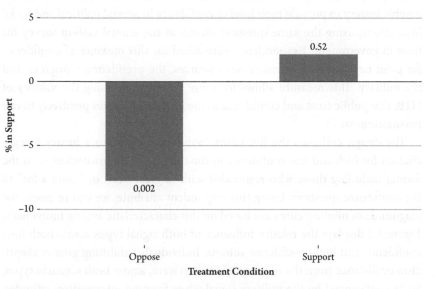

Figure 3.1 Public Support for Interventions by Treatment Condition

Note: This figure reports the change in support for proposed military intervention, pooling across both intervention scenarios. Individual responses were recoded as a binary variable for support for the intervention if they answered "strongly agree" or "agree" to the policy, and 0 if otherwise. The "Support" treatment condition reflects those respondents assigned to military cues in support of the policy, where "Oppose" reflects those respondents assigned to any of the conditions where military cues were issued in opposition. Reported figures display p-values for two-tailed t-test for difference in means between treatment and control conditions. $N_{SUPPORT} + N_{OPPOSE} = 1579$.

While this does not yet allow for specific inference about the role of source credibility, it is noteworthy that such effects were achieved through mere endorsement/opposition to the policy. The structure of the experiment and the design of the news vignettes and military cues isolate the effect to characteristics of the source. Because the wording of the cue is held constant, we have reason to believe that any variation in effect size is either the result of the specific source's perceived credibility or the manner in which the signal is sent. While this suggests that source credibility is a potentially important function in determining the effect of military cues, analysis of the following two hypotheses will more directly measure this argument.

Confidence in Military Institution

How is this effect moderated by expressed trust in the source? In order to allow for further investigation of the effect of source credibility on how these military cues are being internalized, respondents were asked a part of the demographic battery to provide their level of confidence in several political and social institutions, using the same question format as the annual Gallup survey for trust in government. Respondents were asked for this measure of confidence for print newspapers, television news sources, the presidency, Congress, and the military. This measure allows for more precisely assessing the validity of H1B, that public trust and confidence in the institution relates positively to cue persuasiveness.

The design collapses the five-point confidence scale into a binary categorization for *high* and *low* confidence in the military as an institution, with the former including those who responded with "a great deal" or "quite a lot" to the confidence question. Using this respondent attribute, we can re-assess the magnitude of military elite cues based on this characteristic among individuals. Figure 3.2 displays the relative influence of both signal types across both low-confidence and high-confidence subsets. Individuals exhibiting greater skepticism or distance from the military institution were, across both scenario types, far less influenced by the military signal when forming intervention attitudes. However, high-confidence individuals in the sample were more susceptible to military cuing on average; this is particularly true for oppositional cues for which the magnitude of the effect is statistically significant and nearly three times the magnitude of that in the low-confidence group.

This finding seems to lend increased support for the argument that source credibility matters when considering military elite cues (H1B). Trust in the institution visibly moderates the effect size of the signal, though the substantive information provided by the oppositional cue remains more powerful. Indeed, past research on military elite cues by Golby et al. suggested that Republicans

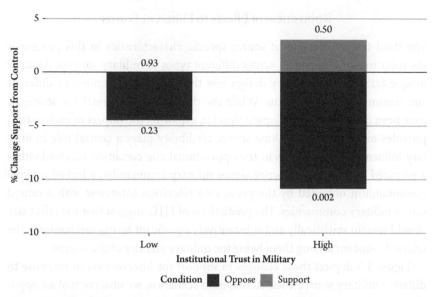

Figure 3.2 Effect of Oppositional Cues by Institutional Confidence

Note: This figure reports the effects of military cues based on respondent-level confidence in the military institution across both scenarios. Respondents were characterized as "high" trust if they responded "quite a lot" or "a great deal" to the confidence measurement question and "low" trust if otherwise. Reported p-values denote significance in two-sided t-test for difference in means between treatment condition and control condition. $N = 1564$. Among high confidence individuals, N_{Dem}=414, N_{Rep}=498; among low confidence individuals, N_{Dem}=468, N_{Rep}=184.

might be more susceptible to such signals on average.[45] These results suggest that, more specifically, these cues are most persuasive among those with pronounced confidence in the institution. However, the basic assertion that Republicans are more likely to be in the high-trust condition is also valid. Republicans in the survey largely expressed high confidence in the institution (73%), compared to a comparably lower rate among Democrats (46%). Across the entire sample, 55% of respondents expressed high confidence in the military; within this group, 46% identified as Republicans and 37% as Democrats. Compared to the actual Gallup polls conducted in the previous year (2016), this 55% figure is low compared to the nationally recorded level at the time of 73%.[46] Given the role of expressed confidence in cue persuasion established here, this has the effect of biasing my treatment effect downwards. As such, it is reasonable to believe that a more representative sample with higher levels of expressed confidence in the military would have exhibited even larger treatment effects in response to military cuing. While confidence in this regard is more tightly correlated with Republican identification, the broader inclusion of the trust metric reveals that even Democrats can be moved by such cues if they trust the source.

Robustness of Effects to Different Forms

The third test of the role of source-specific characteristics in this process is the robustness of this effect across different types of military sources. Another unique feature of the survey design was the random assignment of different cue transmission mechanisms. While the different oppositional cue strategies have been quantitatively collapsed thus far, exploring the impact of each in turn provides more insight into how source credibility plays a central role in military influence. Respondents in the oppositional cue condition received either a prepared op-ed from an active senior military commander, a leaked internal memorandum obtained by the press, or a television interview with a retired senior military commander. The predictions of H1C suggest that the effect size should remain statistically and substantively significant across mechanisms, the relevant constant among them being the military identity of the source.

Figure 3.3 depicts these changes in support for intervention in response to different military source cues. Across both scenarios, we observe that all oppositional cues are substantively able to suppress public approval for the policy on their own. Active-duty op-ed statements seem to be the least dramatic in terms of negative influence, depressing public support by roughly 5 percentage points from the control condition. The reduced effect is potentially the product of the

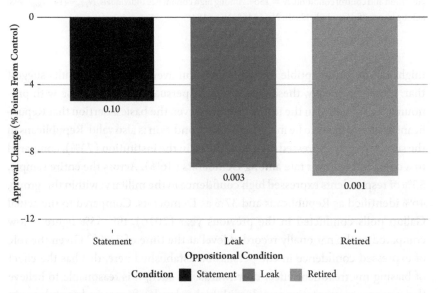

Figure 3.3 Public Support by Opposition Strategy

Note: This figure reports the effects of oppositional military cue conditions across both conventional and humanitarian scenarios. "Statement", "Retired", and "Leak" labels indicate approval levels for those respondents assigned to the deliberate statement, retired commentary, or media leak experimental conditions, respectively. Reported figures display p-values for two-tailed t-test for difference in means between treatment and control conditions. Total oppositional cue sample $N = 1191$.

more deliberate cue transmission process discussed earlier, in which the assumption of pre-approval by government officials may render them less "surprising." The media leak strategy was more effective, suppressing public approval by nearly 10 percentage points across both scenarios. These results seem to support the notion that military source credibility combined with private information makes for a potent signal.

Finally, the retired military community displays similar influence among the public in shaping attitudes. The receipt of an oppositional cue from a retired senior military commander suppressed public approval by nearly 11 percentage points across both scenarios. Consistently, retired military elites were able to shape public support for the policy as much or more substantively than their active duty counterparts in both scenarios, indicating that this community is likely drawing on a shared credibility pool, while less constrained by norms of public silence on policy. Though they have not been incorporated into past empirical design strategies, these results not only validate the importance of military credibility, but also the increasingly ubiquitous role of retired elites in public attitude formation.

The results indicate support for H1C, insofar as military oppositional signals are influential across different modalities. While the different military source results are statistically indistinguishable from each other, they individually maintain statistical significance from the control condition, indicating the strength of military oppositional cues to different types of sources. Allowing for variation in the specific military cue-giver's status and transmission mechanism more broadly demonstrates the robustness of military elite cues; the most crucial characteristic held constant across all conditions is the military identification of the messenger. More specific to our purposes, the positive support for H1A-C demonstrates the critical function that source credibility provides in the effectiveness of military elite cues on public opinion.

Signal Direction and Influence

The importance of source credibility does not necessarily negate the substance of the message itself and the information such signals provide. While the cue in my experimental design contains no substantive argumentation, its direction relative to presidential preferences (H1D) may be inherently influential given its informative value or potential costs. Military elites offering contrary signals to the commander-in-chief may provide updated information about the intervention's requirements or probability of success to the public, degrading confidence in the policy's potential outcome. These signals may indicate to the public that the elite community charged with policy formulation and policy execution—the president and military, respectively—have divergent attitudes about the same scenario. This uncertainty could influence individual-level calculations about whether to support the policy.[47] The substantive value of the oppositional cue may also be a function of the costliness of conveying it. As stated previously, perceived professional or institutional costs to the military in issuing such a contrary signal could imbue the signal with greater informational value if the public believes it is offered in spite of likely professional sanction.

Though the precise pathway is not identified in this design, one observation worth noting is that oppositional cues are likely given influence because of the unique position of the military institution in society. Whether as a statement about elite discord and the potential prospects of the intervention, or as the result of normative costliness for issuing the statement at all, both mechanisms include attributes of the military elite as critical considerations. Military elites, particularly active-duty figures, are therefore powerfully positioned to influence public support through dissent with policy due to their position in the national security structure and in the public's esteem. These findings suggest that civilian decision-makers risk potential damage to a public base of support for intervention by not suitably co-opting military preferences. However, the results so far have not yet incorporated the inescapable force of partisanship in understanding the effect of military speech.

Military Cues in a Partisan Context

Generally, it appears that cues offered by the military prove influential in shaping public approval for armed intervention. Additionally, there is strong evidence to suggest that it is the credibility of the military source that facilitates this level of influence with the public. A final contribution of this original empirical design is analysis of how this influence is affected by competing voices in the information space, most importantly those of partisan elites. There has been considerable attention paid to partisan leaders in the elite-driven politics literature and on the effects that partisanship have on perceived credibility or on resistance to new information.[48] However, such analysis has not been conducted when elite signals are in opposition with others, particularly over the subject of armed intervention and when the military elite voice is heard. As a result, measuring military cues in a competitive environment increases our understanding of their effect in a realistic, partisan environment.

In order to test the third set of hypotheses, one can examine the shift in public approval for an intervention advocated by presidents of either party with respondents of different partisan identities. Figure 3.4 depicts this change in support by partisan identity of the individual and the president, across both treatment conditions and pooling across both intervention scenarios. Again, these hypotheses analyze the most interesting potential cases, in which military

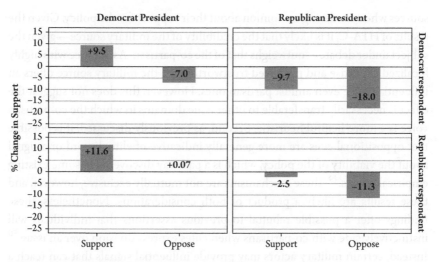

Figure 3.4 Interaction of Partisan Identity and Military Cuing Effects
Note: This figure reports the effects of military cue conditions in each of the four combinations between respondent and presidential partisan identity. The horizontal axis varies the president's partisan identity while the vertical axis varies the partisan identity of the respondent. Results are pooled across both conventional and humanitarian intervention scenarios. Baseline is control condition for the relevant cell. Respondents identified as Democrats and Republicans includes "leaners" on seven-point scale of partisan identity. Blue and red-bordered cells indicate partisan alignment, gray-bordered cells indicate contra-partisan alignment. $N = 1564$.

cues may actually be able to erode that support among co-partisans (H1E) or create support among contra-partisan dyads (H1F). Faced with information contrary to their individual partisan pre-dispositions, partisan respondents might be expected to marginalize or ignore the military cue in favor of reducing the dissonance that such opposing information presents.

Among co-partisan dyads, however, this expected rejection of the oppositional military signal is not clearly reflected in the results of the experiment. Democratic respondents exposed to an oppositional signal reduced their support for the proposed intervention by roughly 7 percentage-points compared to Democrats in the control condition, even when the operation was proposed by a Democratic president in both cases. Similarly, Republican respondents exhibited a nearly 11 percentage-point reduction in support for the intervention when exposed to an oppositional signal despite its proposal by a co-partisan Republican president. Collectively, these results offer evidence in favor of H1E: despite a contradictory position from a co-partisan political elite, the military elite cue retains a residual effect when the two are placed in competition.

There are several potential explanations for such a pattern. First, the competitive framework of the design forces individuals to weigh the credibility of the two sources when rendering an opinion about their support for the policy. Given the results of H1A-C, it is likely that the credibility of the military source—given the subject under debate—outweighs that of the co-partisan. As a source with highly localized expertise and perceived trustworthiness, the military source offers an influential voice even amidst partisan ones. However, this does not suggest the effect is necessarily transferable to other issue domains in which the co-partisan voice is a more helpful heuristic. Second, as previously discussed, it is possible that oppositional cues are more generally indicative of elite discord or a signal about the viability of the policy, which is a pathway discovered in some existing empirical efforts.[49] These mechanisms are not mutually exclusive, however, and these results are likely a product of both considerations. Nonetheless, these findings offer a possible rebuttal to previous assertions that individuals will instinctively side with co-partisans when elites express division over an issue.[50] Instead, certain military actors may provide influential signals that can reach a variety of individuals.

The pattern of response in contra-partisan dyads is more mixed for the hypothesis that military cues can elicit support from outside the president's party (H1F). On one side, Republican respondents offered a supportive cue by the military elite increase their approval for a Democrat-proposed military intervention by nearly 11 percentage-points. This constitutes a substantive and surprising challenge to partisan expectations for the Republican audience. However, not only did Democratic respondents exposed to a supportive signal not increase their support for a Republican-proposed intervention, their support actually decreased by roughly 9 percentage-points compared to the control condition. These results offer partial support for H1E in that supportive cues, at least for Republicans, can positively influence support for a contra-partisan policy.

Again, there are several explanations for either pattern among partisans. Given the null effects of the oppositional cue among Republicans for a Democratic president's proposal, it is clear that these indicate "floor effects." Military opposition may present no new or surprising information for Republicans that influence their opinion regarding the policy. However, military support is highly informative given the change in approval patterns. As contra-partisans are likely skeptical of the president's proposal, military elite support may offer a useful "second-opinion" that can calm these uncertainties and offer a useful policy cue.[51] It is also possible that military support for a Democratic president offers a substantively surprising endorsement given the conservative image of the military and party stereotypes regarding national security.[52] Democratic respondents, however, seem more rigidly skeptical of Republican proposals, using the military cue not as a "second-opinion" but rather as further reason to doubt the policy's soundness. This may also reflect partisan perceptions of both the outgoing and incoming president; in the aftermath of an electoral defeat, Democratic respondents skeptical of the incoming Trump administration may have been generally resistant to any proposed intervention despite military endorsement. This pattern predates information the public would have gained during the course of the Trump administration, which Krebs et al. find drove Democrats toward an uncharacteristic deference toward the military as a check against the Republican president.[53] While we find mixed support for H1F, the potential influence of military cues to elicit support among some contra-partisans is nonetheless suggestive.

Taken together in Table 3.1, these findings offer additional support to the argument that military elites possess considerable latent political influence with regards to shaping public opinion on military action, perhaps even in a partisan context. The competitive framework used here forces respondents to sift through multiple voices when rendering an opinion. While the mechanisms may be different, the source credibility of the military cue drives effects on both sides of the partisan aisle. This argument is further supported by the fact that the experiment does not provide respondents with any substantive information about policy preferences by the military cue-giver. Instead, individuals in all treatment conditions are reacting to a simple endorsement or opposition to the policy. This "peripheral" attention to the message makes the source's unique attributes more significant in its persuasiveness.

Collectively, the results of this experiment provide a suitable starting point for exploring our central line of inquiry: the impact of the partisan landscape on civil-military relations and the likelihood of politicization. The public's affect for the military institution proves an important moderating variable for under-standing when military speech is likely to influence the public's thinking. These findings are particularly interesting given more recent survey research by Jim Golby and Peter Feaver; with regards to Afghanistan policy, a plurality of civilians rendered no opinion at all about the future of the intervention, while blame for failures was largely laid at the feet of contra-partisan civilian leaders.[54] With divided elites, low foreign policy knowledge, and high confidence in the military, the utility of the military voice is seemingly substantial. Across different transmission mechanisms, military actors were able to erode support for the president's stated preferences, in some cases even among the commander-in-chief's co-partisans. These effects are certainly modest given the constraints of the experiment. While the competitive design provides greater ecological realism, the hypothetical military speaker had no observable partisan alignment and spoke only on an issue within their general expertise: military intervention. Nonetheless, the military voice has important utility in shaping public opin-ion on complex issues across different modalities and in different conditions;

Table 3.1 Summary of Principal Findings and Support for Testable Hypotheses

Hypothesis	Support	Findings
Source Credibility		
A Military elite cues influence public support.	✓	Military cues create 10 %-pt swing across all conditions compared to control.
B Influence increases with expressed confidence.	✓	Oppositional cues three times more effective with high-confidence individuals.
C Effect robust to different military sources.	✓	Effect statistically and substantively significant across military sources.
Signal Direction		
D Direction of policy cue matters.	✓	Oppositional cues nearly four times more influential than supportive cues.
Effect of Multiple Signals		
E Oppositional cues can dissuade co-partisans.	✓(D) ✓(R)	Democrats and Republicans reduce support by 7 and 11 %-pts, respectively.
F Supportive cues can attract contra-partisans.	✗(D) ✓(R)	Republicans increase support by nearly 11 %-pts; Democrats actually decrease support.

Notes: Table 3.1 depicts the level of support for each testable hypothesis and a brief description of the empirical findings for each; hypotheses are grouped by point of analysis (source credibility, signal direction, and the effect of multiple signals). Results for H1E and H1F allow for mixed support based on partisan identity of the respondent; (D) indicates the hypothesis' validity for Democrats, (R) for Republicans.

however, the use of this voice runs afoul of traditional civil-military norms reviewed earlier, making it a possible source of *active* politicization.

Sources of Politicization

Given the significance of these results, it is worth noting how their findings relate to the potential for politicization in a polarized partisan environment. In all cases explored by the experiment, the actor with agency in speaking publicly was military in nature: whether active-duty or retired, in each condition they were representative of the military institution and acting largely of their own accord. As a result, such behavior more cleanly fits within the *active* category of politicization. What might this look like in practice? In order to illustrate the nature of military elite signaling and its capacity for active politicization, this chapter's final section examines two cases of military dissent: the 2006 "revolt of the generals" under the Bush administration and the 2009–10 Afghanistan review process under the Obama administration. In both cases, representatives of the military institution engaged in public oppositional dialogue with the commander-in-chief or senior civilian leaders that frayed existing civil-military normative traditions and adequately embodied this form of military politicization.

In the first case, retired military officials waded into the political information space, issuing high-profile opposition at a critical phase of the Iraq War. The US military effort in Iraq following the defeat of conventional Iraqi armed forces in 2003 had stalled considerably by the second term of the Bush administration. Increasing sectarian violence across the country cast doubt in public and elite circles that the administration could effectively resource and manage both the Afghanistan and Iraq theaters, leading to a partisan split in support for the war unprecedented since Vietnam.[55] Initial misgivings about the need for a much larger force in the run-up to the Iraq invasion, most publicly voiced by former Army Chief of Staff General Eric Shinseki, re-emerged in a new debate about the prospects for the mission's success and the embattled leadership of Secretary Donald Rumsfeld, whose Pentagon had marginalized Shinseki in subsequent policy-shaping following the general's remarks to Congress.[56]

Even before the considerable strategic shift that followed the 9/11 attacks and the "global war on terror," senior military officials in the Pentagon and abroad experienced a major bureaucratic shake-up with the appointment of Donald Rumsfeld as Secretary of Defense. Rumsfeld's interpersonal style and managerial philosophy struck many senior military leaders as abrasive and uncompromising, coupled with a desire to streamline the organization and assert more direct control over military leaders. The negative reversal of fortune in the Iraq War seemed to vindicate Shinseki's original warnings and increased criticism of Rumsfeld's management of the Pentagon, which many military leaders felt perpetuated poor strategic choices by stifling debate.[57]

Concerns over Rumsfeld's bureaucratic management of the Defense Department evolved into a broader referendum by the retired military community on the wisdom of the Iraq War and its governing strategy. Retired Marine Lieutenant General Greg Newbold, who served under Rumsfeld in a key staff position during the initial phases of the Iraq War planning, was the first of several recently retired senior military officers to voice public disapproval for Rumsfeld's management of the military and the larger Iraq War's strategic direction.[58] In an article written for *Time* in mid-2006, Newbold openly rebuked the secretary's handling of Shinseki's warning in 2003 and characterized the administration's commitment to the Iraq fight as having been "done with a casualness and swagger that are the special province of those who have never had to execute these missions—or bury the results."[59]

Newbold was not alone in this open criticism of the war and its civilian leadership. Retired Army general officers Paul Eaton, Charles Swannack, John Riggs, and John Batiste, along with retired Marine Lieutenant General Paul van Riper, all issued public statements or articles calling for Rumsfeld's removal from leadership of the Defense Department.[60] Most of the officers involved had, like Newbold, observed first hand the flaws in the Pentagon's management of the Iraq War and argued that it had suffered directly from Rumsfeld's leadership style. Eaton, who had been saddled with the task of rebuilding the Iraqi army in 2004, retired earlier than planned following his statements that such an effort would take several years to be completed effectively. Like the rest of the officers involved, Eaton wrestled with professional norms of restraint in his disapproval of the Iraq strategy. However, after viewing the 2006 Quadrennial Defense Review, a Defense Department articulation of strategic priorities and budgetary forecasts, Eaton found its "appalling" focus on conventional threats during a counter-insurgency war unacceptable, voicing his discontent in a *New York Times* op-ed.[61]

The collective furor caused by these elite military figures reinvigorated a debate over the strategic direction of the Iraq War, Rumsfeld's future in the Pentagon, and the political will to see the mission through to completion. The "revolt of the generals" was all the more difficult to ignore with figures like Swannack and Batiste—recent division commanders in the Iraq War— immediately following their retirement with a foray into the political discourse of the war's conduct. The generals' discontent contributed to a sharp turn in public opinion against the embattled Secretary of Defense, despite President George W. Bush's statements of support to stand by Rumsfeld through the length of his second term.[62] By the time Rumsfeld offered his resignation in November, the

2006 midterm elections had swung against the Republican party. Congressional Republicans were "infuriated" that Bush had not facilitated the secretary's ouster earlier, convinced that Republican candidates suffered at the polls from carrying the weight of Rumsfeld's public image, irreparably damaged by the generals' "revolt."[63]

If this public appeal by the retired military elite was in any way influential, it was also costly for the military institution's preservation of a non-partisan image. The renewed conversation over Iraq strategy was met with heated debate over the appropriateness of the "revolt" in the context of civil-military professional norms. Critics denounced the generals as subversive to the principle of civilian control and setting a dangerous precedent for active-duty officers to more forcefully resist policies with which they did not agree.[64] While many applauded the "revolt" as a display of patriotism and professional integrity, others saw the action as potentially damaging to the credibility of the active-duty officer corps. Richard Kohn contends that the opinions and misgivings of retired military elites may very well be indistinguishable from those of active officers in the eyes of the public; this community is therefore legitimized by the same credibility of the larger military institution, but less constrained by norms of the civil-military relationship.[65] Many have since used the incident as a cautionary tale of the dangers of the "paradox of prestige," where repeated attempts to leverage the public's positive affect for the military by individual actors can cumulatively damage that same level of trust.[66]

This case captures some of the key aspects of active politicization, where representatives of the military institution engage in behavior which alters its position as objective and non-partisan actor in the eyes of a public observer. The "revolt" created significant political disruption: pressure from the retired military community, many of whom had only recently departed the battlefields of Iraq before offering their criticisms publicly, may actually have worked against the very outcomes for which they aimed. In his own memoirs, George W. Bush states this much directly: "there was no way I was going to let a group of retired officers bully me into pushing out the civilian secretary of defense."[67] The desire to deny the retired officers in question tangible and immediate results for their actions was likely behind the delay in Rumsfeld's departure, even if this eventual end was fulfilled.

The episode also displayed the professional price of having defied the long-held norms of civil-military relations through active politicization. Norms of restraint have governed the relationship between military and civilian leaders for decades, making public appeals like the "revolt" infrequent. As a result, the historical rarity of military dissent makes cuing costly for the same reason they may be credible. Events such as the "revolt" display the institutional cost of cue-giving from military elites. Regardless of various judgments about its success in achieving policy change, the actions of the generals complicated the long-term independent credibility of the military as "fair dealer" in policy advice to civilian leaders. Peter Feaver argues that the event complicated Iraq policy decision-making regarding the subsequent "surge" strategy due to concerns over protest resignations by senior military leaders that would have been politicized by Bush's partisan opponents.[68] The collective impact of active politicization events on the public's impressions of the military institution cannot be undervalued, even in cases where the actors in question are, as Martin Cook argues, "apparently devoid of any partisan political motive."[69] The fact that the individual cue-giver does not directly internalize sanctions on the behavior creates a potentially damaging "tragedy of the commons" as retired officers try to leverage the institution's credibility for personal gain.

Just as a the 2006 "revolt" had created political problems for the Bush White House on the direction of the Iraq War, a series of military public statements and information leaks regarding the future of the Afghan War had a similar effect on the Obama administration years later. In an effort to re-assess the broader strategy for American military efforts in the country, key advisors in the newly elected Obama White House advocated for the replacement of serving theater commander General David McKiernan with General Stanley McChrystal. Largely reliant on recommendations from Defense Secretary Robert Gates and Chairman of the Joint Chiefs of Staff Admiral Mike Mullen, Obama approved the change, with the added responsibility of conducting a review on the state of US efforts in Afghanistan and a recommendation for future strategic decision-making.[70] The recommendation would inform potential troop levels required to support the fledgling Afghan security forces and protect the population from insurgent groups that had gained momentum with the diversion of key resources to support the Iraq conflict.

By early 2009, the new president had already expressed trepidation to increasing US presence in Afghanistan; during the preceding campaign, Obama had stressed a re-prioritization away from the "war of choice" in Iraq and affecting a responsible stabilization and withdrawal from Afghanistan.[71] A troop increase that further entangled the United States with the Afghanistan War was generally undesirable among key administration officials, many of whom harbored distrust for the military establishment. Vice President Joe Biden would concurrently push for a competing strategy dubbed "counter-terrorism plus," a smaller-footprint military approach that focused on developing human intelligence networks and decapitating insurgent group leaders.[72] The political stage into which McChrystal's evaluations would enter was politically fraught before the assessment even began.

McChrystal's classified report, passed to the Pentagon by August, seemed to clash directly with any political aspirations of a timely withdrawal. The assessment highlighted a lack of reliable intelligence, unwilling coalition allies, and a restrictive focus on the force protection of US servicemembers as the drivers behind a security environment where the Taliban held considerable advantage. The report offered three force structure alternatives: a increase of 10,000 troops to focus on training Afghan soldiers, of 40,000 troops for a concerted counter-insurgency campaign against the Taliban and al-Qaeda affiliates, and of 85,000 troops for a more dedicated counter-insurgency campaign. The assessment contended that without a resource commitment commensurate with the objectives the president had articulated, the larger operation could result in "mission failure."[73]

The assessment's gloomy forecast for US success and its advocacy for such a potentially large influx of troops into the theater created political problems for administration officials, who wished to keep the finer details of troop requests out of the public discussion. In mid-September, the assessment was leaked to the *Washington Post*, which promptly published McChrystal's misgivings to the American public.[74] Though the assessment was partially sanitized, the general theme of impending mission failure should the administration not comply with military recommendations created the impression among Obama staffers that the president's options had been effectively circumscribed. The environment destabilized further shortly after, when in a speech to the International Institute for Strategic Studies (IISS) in London, McChrystal directly rebuked the feasibility of a small-footprint strategy like the one being advocated by Biden.[75]

Obama conveyed his frustration over the leak and these remarks to Gates and other key advisors, viewing the incident as a clear attempt by the military to "box in" the president's options over the Afghanistan conflict and force a troop increase that would involve the United States in that war for much longer. With the 40,000-troop request public knowledge and projected to cost in upwards of $1 trillion over ten years, the leak constrained Obama's ability to explore smaller options in the face of the McChrystal report. While it did not result in the middle-ground option of 40,000 soldiers requested by McChrystal directly, it had pressured for a more aggressive choice from the Obama administration despite both publicly and privately announced preferences to the contrary. Obama had intended for the McChrystal review to serve as the basis for a private discussion with the military about future strategy; the leak and London speech had effectively broadcast military preferences to the American public. Key advisors also made clear that with their advice public knowledge, Obama would likely have to relieve Mullen and McChrystal should he make a decision that contradicted their advice.[76]

However, the incident was exceedingly costly for both the key figures involved and for the larger military institution. The leak of a classified mission assessment and McChrystal's subsequent remarks were interpreted by civilian officials as a clear attempt to circumscribe the president's decision-making autonomy. Peter Feaver characterized the incident as "the defining moment in civil-military relations under Obama's watch" while a new debate on the stability of the political-military relationship emerged again.[77] McChrystal personally found himself on the outside of much of the subsequent strategic decision-making and his now-public clash with the Obama administration had set the conditions for his removal months later when a *Rolling Stone* article published disparaging remarks about administration officials made by senior military staffers in McChrystal's headquarters.[78]

The event had also politicized the nature of military advice to sitting civilian leaders. McChrystal's removal did not assuage the fundamentally divergent preferences expressed by the military and political elite over the issue of wartime strategy. While civilian officials felt manipulated by an indirect military appeal to the public, military elites felt the entire ordeal was representative of a fundamental breakdown in understanding between the two parties on the resourcing of political objectives in war. The feasibility of those objectives for a speedy withdrawal and a stable Afghan government were never questioned by the military elite, only the resources needed to achieve them; the divergence seemed to suggest that "if the president wanted a different answer, he needed to ask a different question."[79]

The incident more importantly illustrates the cost of *active* politicizing behavior despite the utility of the military voice. The individual-level costs to the cuegiver were observable by the tarnished relationship between the Obama team and McChrystal's headquarters after the incident. The military lost a potent voice in Washington as part of the strategic discussion and the general's removal in 2010 was easier to facilitate in the environment the leak incident had created. The institutional costs of the ordeal are perhaps far more apparent. A reinvigorated debate on the health of American civil-military relations again called into question the non-partisan and independent nature of military advice. An already distrustful relationship between the new administration and the military was made worse, putting subsequent military advice under added scrutiny; indeed, it is likely that the episode informed how future president Joe Biden would incorporate military forecasts into his own calculations to withdrawal from Afghanistan in 2021. During this critical phase of the conflict, however, the event provided the grounds for further partisan politicization. Congressional Republicans conditioned their support for any Afghan strategy on approval by senior military leaders like McChrystal; Senator Lindsay Graham offered continued Republican support "as long as the generals are O.K. and there is a meaningful number" of at least 30,000 troops.[80] The civil-military climate engendered by the leak resulted not only in fraying the relationship between the

White House and senior military leaders, but providing a basis for politicization of the military as an institution.

In both cases, there is little reason to believe that the desires of the relevant military actors were anything other than to shape policy in a particular direction, rather than to align the military institution toward or against a political party. However, politicization as conceived in this book need not spring from a conscious intention. Instead, the institution can be politicized merely through the perception that its activities or behaviors are driven by allegiance to a particular partisan tribe, or at least in opposition to another. In an environment where an increasing number of issues are "partisan" in nature due to polarization's dwindling consensus, the number of areas in which military and civilian actors— even those acting without intent to politicize—can achieve these effects grows. This is particularly true for active politicization, as any direct actions by the military or its representatives are likely to redound to the benefit or detriment of a political party. The McChrystal troop estimate leak provided Congressional Republicans grounds to further tribalize the troop package debate over Afghanistan to Obama's chagrin, just as the "revolt" provided a device for anti-war Democrats to pressure the Bush administration for reforms.

The findings of this chapter provide an empirical launching point for the remainder of this book. The combined effect of partisan polarization and high public confidence in the military has been an environment where politicization is more likely, even detached from partisan motivations. As primary figures in the formation and execution of policy with a durably high level of trust with the American public, these figures continue to play a key role in political debates on policy both in uniform and after departure from the service. The foundations of modern American civil-military relations are rooted in normative prohibitions against policy activism by military actors. Yet, this dynamic is difficult to sustain in an era where the line between the two areas is increasingly blurred. The norms of Huntington's idealized philosophy oblige an institutionally separate military whose elites trade autonomy for the expectation that they do not engage in public debate with their civilian superiors. As we will discover, this conflict between the latent influence of military voices and the prohibition against their use is one of the most challenging aspects of the modern civil-military landscape.

This is because the military has become an increasingly vocal entity in the development of foreign policy. Through targeted survey experimentation, this chapter has demonstrated how individuals substantively attend to elite cues on military intervention, even when they are issued in contradiction to the president, whether a co-partisan or political opponent. When offered information about military attitudes on a proposed policy, some respondents used oppositional cues as a useful "second opinion" or used substantively surprising information on policies with which they have little information, even if the policy was recommended by a contra-partisan president. This experimentation provides a modest contribution to our understanding of elite cues and the military. While the design more accurately represents the competitive information space of the outside world, it is important to note that the military actors here espoused no information on their partisan sensibilities and spoke only on an issue close to their professional expertise, foreign policy. As we incorporate the significance of partisan polarization into this analysis in subsequent chapters, the employment of military voices in politics provides not only a clear example of active politicization, but a tempting target for co-optation or distortion in other forms of politicizing behavior.

Using the Iraq War's "revolt of the generals" and the Afghanistan troop estimate leak as contextual examples of active politicization, such military signals can be effective, if potentially costly to the source's credibility. While this chapter reveals how military speech can drive elite civilian perceptions of military politicization, Chapter 6 will further unpack the implications of the retired community as a potential source of active politicization in the eyes of the mass public. For our purposes here, the results of this chapter demonstrate that not only do military figures possess considerable latent political influence, but that this influence is largely tied to the perception of the military elite as a credible figure and reliable source. This naturally begs a question pursued by the remainder of this book: if the military voice can be an effective political tool, how does this voice function in the highly polarized environment of American politics? For an understanding about how partisans of different stripes are likely to attend to a credible military voice, we require some accounting for how the public gathers information necessary to render a judgment about the military's credibility.

4

Return to Sender

Media Reporting and the Partisan "Credibility Gap"

If military voices are influential ones because of their perceived credibility, what are the sources—and limits—of that credibility with the American public? So far we have explored how military actors might be able to influence mass opinion through active means, exploiting the public's positive esteem for the military as an institution. However, we have yet to incorporate how political polarization influences who finds the military "credible" in the first place. While patterns of confidence in the military are unique for several reasons, one of their more puzzling characteristics is a pronounced divergence in partisan attitudes despite the military's non-partisan professional norms. Seemingly out-sized support among conservatives has been explained in the past as the result of partisan realignment, defense policy preferences, and shifting post-conscription military demography.[1] Yet, while these help to explain the static existence of a baseline partisan "confidence gap," they fail to account for the dynamic aspects of partisan separation over trust in the military.[2] Because of the necessity of new information in evaluative processing when judging the credibility of an institution like the military, this chapter argues that the confidence gap between partisans is not simply the result of different preferences, but of divergent pathologies in how partisans receive and employ updating information. Understanding the nature of this gap will contextualize how different forms of politicization can emerge as a result, particularly those that hinge on how the public forms attitudes about the military.

The next two chapters will probe the underlying demography of public attitudes on the military, providing a basis for how partisan polarization has divided perception of this ostensibly trusted institution. Partisan identity, as we will see, drives two significant and formative behaviors with regards to forming an impression on the credibility of the military: how one acquires information on the institution itself and how one employs that information to form opinions. This chapter will explore the former as the first step in the process. As a

Dangerous Instrument: Political Polarization and US Civil-Military Relations. Michael A. Robinson,
Oxford University Press. © Oxford University Press 2023. DOI: 10.1093/oso/9780197611555.003.0004

smaller percentage of Americans have first-hand exposure to the military through
service or interactions with those who have served, their exposure to military
performance, organizational integrity, and professional behavior is in large part
shaped by third-party sources. How does partisan identity shape the types of
information to which individuals are exposed? What categories of politicization
is this information environment likely to engender?

This chapter will explore precisely these questions. First, it briefly discusses
the nature of this growing trend of polarization in assessment of the military
institution. The principal aim of this section is to demonstrate the partisan
separation on evaluation of the military institution and to review existing explanations for this divide. Second, it proposes a dynamic theory for explaining
the partisan confidence gap by, first, considering the impact of selective information exposure and, second, incorporating the influence of partisan attitude
polarization on impressions about military credibility (explored in Chapter 5).
As a result, consideration of both *selective exposure* to information and *biased
updating* can help to better explain polarization in military trust. Third, this
chapter will assess the validity of these two explanations by examining original
text data and observational data on reporting habits to map media consumption
patterns across partisans. During critical and high-volume phases of military
reporting, conservative Republicans were less likely to be exposed to negative
updating information about military performance than their Independent or
Democratic counterparts. This asymmetry in exposure to information between
partisan subgroups may drive a subsequent divide in how those groups employ
new information in forming an opinion on the military's credibility. The final
section of the chapter will discuss how this information environment sets the
conditions for politicization of the armed forces. Because of the ability of media
or other interest groups to shape how the public perceives the military relative to
other political fixtures—such as the major political parties—partisan influences
on military reporting can set the conditions for *aspect* politicization in particular.

The Partisan Gap in Military Credibility

The ability of an individual or organization to shape public attitudes can most
simply be described as a product of their credibility with the audience. As
detailed in Chapter 3, considerable theoretical effort has been made in articulat-
ing the ways in which attributes of information sources such as knowledge, trustworthiness, and like-mindedness can scale the persuasiveness of their messages.[3]
Public trust in political and social institutions is an essential part of a functioning
democracy, not only as a reflection of popular approval of institutional performance, but as an expression of the trustworthiness of information and policy

signals that come from these institutions. In an environment where the value and veracity of political information from traditional sources are contentious and increasingly characterized by "echo-chamber" media exposure, the process by which individuals seek credible elite voices and form policy preferences is significant.[4] This is especially true given the tendency for individuals to rely on these voices the more confusing or distracting the information space becomes.[5]

The broad trend of declining confidence in a variety of political and social institutions previously discussed has renewed debate over the process by which individuals decide to express trust in them and the implications this trend has for the long-term viability of democratic values.[6] Given the increasingly central role that active and retired military elites play in policy formation, governance, media commentary, and business, scholars have devoted more attention to the potential influence of this elite bloc. The capacity of military officials to shape public opinion on policy, influence public support for military intervention, inform the public perception of success probability during war, or grant credibility through endorsement relies on the military institution's considerable clout with the public.[7] High levels of support for the military come during a time where decisive military victories are elusive and a sizable portion of society admits mixed understanding of the military.[8] However, they also come during a period of increased dissatisfaction with representative institutions, political polarization, and growing acceptance of authoritarian measures in government.[9]

But if confidence in the military is so high, why would it be a problem to have an institution broadly trusted by the American people? The answer is not so simple. Despite the comparably high public confidence the institution enjoys relative to others in society, pooled data of expressed public trust in the military can be misleading. First, it is often unclear exactly what individuals are conveying when they respond that they trust the military. The institutional trust literature is largely devoid of dedicated study on public attitudes toward the military, while those that approach the subject focus on high aggregate levels of confidence captured in most polls.[10] Second, only recent studies have incorporated the importance of increasing polarization within the civilian public itself, which draws attention to the fact that while aggregate trust in the military is high, partisan subsets of the American public clearly disagree on the same question.[11] This leaves the puzzling pattern of partisan separation in evaluation of the institution's credibility. While traditional civil-military relations norms prescribe a non-partisan military outside the realm of day-to-day politics, individuals in US society exhibit widely divergent attitudes in assessing the credibility of the institution.

This is evident in the extent to which partisans are themselves polarized over their impressions of the military, despite the appearance of broad consensus that aggregate poll numbers sometimes suggest. Table 4.1 reveals some evidence of this partisan split in confidence for the military across several instruments in

Table 4.1 **Confidence among Partisans for Select US Institutions (2018–2020)**

	NPR/PBS (2018)*			Gallup (2019)			Gallup (2020)		
	Dem.	Rep.	**Gap**	Dem.	Rep.	**Gap**	Dem.	Rep.	**Gap**
Institution									
Presidency	7	37	30	9	77	68	16	83	67
Democratic Party	26	3	23	-	-	-	-	-	-
Republican Party	2	23	21	-	-	-	-	-	-
Military	44	65	21	58	90	32	61	91	30
Media/TV News	23	4	19	32	9	27	33	7	26
Supreme Court	22	27	5	21	51	30	33	53	20
Small Business	-	-	-	58	83	25	74	87	13
Banking System	16	17	1	27	37	10	39	43	4
Congress	7	9	2	14	7	7	14	14	0

Notes: Reported figures depict levels of partisan confidence in select US institutions across both the Gallup Institutional Confidence survey (2019, 2020) and the NPR/PBS/Marist Poll (2018). Figures are percentage of the sample that responded with high levels of confidence in the institution listed; Asterisk (*) indicates institutions where figures were computed using highest ("a great deal") confidence response; Megan Brenan, "Amid Pandemic, Confidence In Key U.S. Instituions Surges", Gallup, August 12, 2020; Domenico Montanaro, "Here's Just How Little Confidence Ameircans Have in Political Institutions", NPR, January 17, 2018.

recent years, reporting Democratic and Republican levels of confidence for a variety of institutions in US society. Adopting Rothstein and Stolle's nomenclature, these include representative, power-checking, and order institutions.[12] This figure captures not only the divide amongst partisans over the credibility of the military institution, but contextualizes this gap across other institutions in society. Partisan separation regarding the military rivals the same gap in magnitude among other institutions that are highly susceptible to partisan calculations, such as the presidency and the media. As detailed in Chapter 2, we can conceive of partisans in the public as "polarized" based on their relative distance from each other, even if they are both generally approving of the institution. Surprisingly, while we might expect evaluations of the military to resemble low-polarization institutions such as the courts or the banking system, this is not the case. Rather, partisans seem to harbor meaningfully different levels of confidence in the institutional quality of the military.

This polarization in partisan attitudes toward the military presents several challenges, not the least of which to stable civil-military relations. First, an inability to objectively evaluate the credibility of select institutions in society contributes to a broader devaluation of fact-driven political discourse. A military institution that can maintain high levels of public confidence among certain partisans despite organizational scandals or frustrations on the battlefield could negatively influence the ability of individuals to properly learn the lessons of foreign policy failures.[13] Second, as partisan sorting deepens political and social polarization, the capture of military confidence into a partisan identity has potentially damaging implications for the preservation of civil-military norms. While democracy and civil-military scholars argue that a military institution removed from partisan political fights is necessary for the preservation of democratic values, the perception of partisan "capture" of the military institution could be damaging to the integrity of the armed forces and of the very credibility it carries with the public.[14] In addition to weakening principles of civilian control and eroding public support for an "all-volunteer" force, these effects set the conditions for several forms of politicization outlined in the Parallax Model.

But what explains this partisan gap? The notion that partisan calculations should inform impressions about the performance or institutional quality of the military is particularly curious given its non-partisan mandate. The military institution has a specific role in society, to fight and win the nation's wars; however, despite the organization having no explicit partisan role, partisans arrive at different evaluations of the institution's credibility over time and in response to major events. What explains this divergence? As we will see, existing scholarship suggests that elite-level alignment on policy preferences or military demographic changes could explain such an arrangement, with political conservatives more culturally aligned with the military. However, these explanations cannot account for the expansion of the partisan gap across different administrations and states of military performance. This chapter proposes a corollary theory, that separation in perceived institutional credibility—particularly during wartime—between partisans is the product of the different processes by which these groups receive new information about the institution. Specifically, how partisan polarization in media consumption and depictions of the military may shape this process. In such an environment where partisan institutions (and their associated media arms) can shape public perception of the military, the probability of politicizing behavior increases.

Extant Explanations

Many security scholars have studied the importance of partisan identity as a salient consideration in civil-military relations, whether in the context of how civilians and the military divide on the use of force, the public's knowledge and perception of the military in society, or the political demography of the military itself.[15] These analyses satisfyingly chronicle the evolution of elite-level dynamics or the political identification of the military, even if they speak less to the polarization that exists between subsets of that public in evaluating the credibility of an institution they commonly observe. Indeed, a conservative Republican preference for the military institution has been a persistent trend for several decades and one addressed laterally in broader discussions of civil-military relations in the United States. But what explanations have been advanced that could explain, at least statically, the partisan "confidence gap" toward the military?

First, some have pointed to closer proximity between the military and the Republican party at the elite level as one source of this slant. The party's post-Vietnam role in loosening many of the bureaucratic restrictions that the Kennedy and Johnson administrations had placed on the military led to a period of autonomy and expansive authorities in the Pentagon, developed further under the patronage of the Reagan-era buildup and the Goldwater-Nichols bureaucratic re-organization.[16] The party leadership also seized on a critical opportunity to capture national security and patriotism as key aspects of the its post-war identity, filling the political void left by a Democratic party that retreated from interventionist rhetoric and favored domestic programs over expanded military funding. Even the military's image was better rehabilitated under Republican presidents, as William Odom states, that though "the Democrats have treated the military as the source of bad national strategy in Vietnam [...] the Republicans defended the military against the charge."[17] In this line of argument, this connection was deepened by increasingly aligned preferences for the use of force abroad, a shared "militant internationalism," or increasing skepticism of more ideologically distant Democratic leaders.[18] This accord between political conservatism at the elite level, therefore, provides one lens for understanding why certain partisans may feel differently about the military.

Second, the rightward-changing demography of the military itself has also been a subject of study among civil-military scholars. Huntington early identified the emerging identity of the post-conscription force aligned with the specific regions of the country, while the post-Vietnam all-volunteer military took on a far less representative profile than society at large. With the adoption of the "southern strategy" by Republicans in the 1960s and 1970s, Republicans leveraged their position as the "national security party" and its geographical inheritance of the American South to increase its electoral connections to servicemembers. Between 1976 and 1996, military officers had become far more outspoken in their identification with the Republican party, increasing from 33% to 70%, even though the larger society only increased identification with the party from

25% to 33% over the same period.[19] Political attitudes among military officers have swung in favor of the Republican party, with those identifying as Democrats joining at lower rates and leaving at earlier times than Republican counterparts.[20] In addition, evidence suggests that the relationship may run both ways: recent survey work points to the idea that conservatives in the broader public find more common political ground with the institutional values of the military.[21] This attachment is a persistent feature of the contemporary environment: surveys by Ronald Krebs and Robert Ralston have further revealed that this same community of conservatives is more likely to see military service as a function of patriotism or sacrifice and the military itself as emblematic of core conservative values.[22] Similarly, Heidi Urben finds that Republican servicemembers are more likely to feel comfortable expressing their political selves than Democrats and more likely to see their values shared by other servicemembers on social media.[23] Perhaps alarmingly, a preference among military servicemembers for Republican candidates was seen as so reliable that military absentee ballots for the opposing party were flimsily used as justification for alleged fraud in the 2020 presidential election.[24] Collectively, in addition to some shared worldview at the elite level, there is strong reason to believe that cultural affinity at the mass level may also contribute to the gap.

These efforts make a collectively compelling argument for explaining the existence of (1) a preference alignment on foreign policy between Republicans and the military at the elite level and (2) an increasing cultivation of military servicemembers as an extension of the party's constituency at the mass public level. However, this does not directly address why the conservative public would continue to imbue the military with high levels of seemingly unconditional trust over time, especially in response to decades of war, organizational scandals, periods of out-party rule, or individual misconduct cases. The remainder of this chapter will argue that the missing component is an understanding of how institutional confidence should be seen less as an objective valuation of an organization's performance than it is an extension of partisan polarization and cognitive bias. With limited first-hand understanding of an institution, individuals are largely dependent on other elites in society for information by which to form an opinion, such as the organized media.[25] However, media environments trafficked by different partisans may exhibit widely different sensibilities in their reporting patterns, resulting in uneven frames and volumes of information about the military.

Such thinking is at the core of this theory: an increasingly polarized and ideologically sorted public, subjected to different information flows and exhibiting different levels of cognitive bias, contributes to widening polarization in what should be an objective evaluation of institutional performance. As such, this theory envisions two complementary elements of the same evaluative process with regards to assessment of the military institution. First, the *selective exposure* hypothesis argues that partisans are predisposed to receive widely different types of information pertaining to military performance, shaping the usable store of data with which partisans issue judgments of credibility. Second, the *partisan bias* hypothesis argues that how partisans use new or newly salient information in forming opinions differs greatly between subgroups, with affective polarization biases driving uneven levels of perceived military credibility. This chapter will explore the first step in this process, examining how individuals acquire information about the military through media consumption and how these dynamics contribute to potentially politicizing activity.

In the following section, we explore a more dynamic understanding of the partisan credibility gap by including consideration of this highly fragmented and polarized media landscape. Individuals with limited exposure to the military institution require third-party information in order to form attitudes about its performance. Just as research has shown that strong partisans are more likely to be politically active, exhibit polarized attitudes, and downweight disconfirming information, they are also more likely to display increased in-group bias and fail to objectively evaluate the quality of certain public institutions.[26] In seeking to understanding the nature of the credibility gap, this chapter investigates how individuals of different stripes may be predisposed to perceive military activity, performance, and institutional quality differently based on partisan selective media exposure.

Partisan Media and the "Credibility Gap"

Just as no accounting of contemporary civil-military relations is complete without consideration of the role of partisan polarization, no discussion of that same polarization is complete without some understanding of the changing media landscape. The diffusion of cable television in the 1980s heralded a shift away from the traditional three-network American newscasts of the preceding period. The end of the Federal Communication Commission's (FCC) so-called "Fairness Doctrine" during the Reagan administration formally recognized media firms as businesses, rather than public institutions responsible for the "public interest."[27] Instead of the traditional "point-counterpoint" balance enshrined in the Fairness Doctrine's mandate for media, the environment set the conditions for the evolution of "niche news" outlets tailored to audience preferences, to include partisan sensibilities.[28] The expansion of the media environment beyond cable television in recent decades has compounded this Balkanization of media, with the internet, social media, and talk radio providing a wide array of options for partisans to select based on the valence of their content.

The nature of this fragmented media environment as a contributing force to (and symptom from) the polarization of American politics is a well-documented phenomenon among political science and communications scholars, particularly in their diagnosis of the highly coherent and effective messaging of conservative media. This is not to suggest the fragmentation of media is an entirely one-sided affair: for example, Matthew Baum and Tim Groeling's analysis of news media content from across several sources early in the Iraq War revealed detectable reporting biases across networks favored by both progressives and conservatives compared to the largely non-partisan wire services.[29] The existence of partisan-friendly media outlets has led to (and responded from) a tendency among the audience to seek these sources out over others, reducing dissonant information regarding political issues or the characterization of political opponents.[30] While supply and demand effects are both operating in the growth of the partisan media marketplace, the same asymmetric polarization evident among the public at large is observable in the media environments trafficked by those same individuals. But just as polarization patterns overall affect both partisan tribes, though unevenly, a similar pattern in partisan media makes the dynamics of conservative channels particularly interesting. In particular, the lack of "cross-cutting" identities that polarization scholars have found among the political right is analogous to the narrow, but ideologically coherent, media environment most heavily trafficked by conservatives.[31]

For example, the rise of Fox News as the favored news source for partisan Republicans on cable television is perhaps one of the most important artifacts of this decades-long process of media fragmentation. Developed in 1996, the "fair and balanced" network was conceived as a counter-punch to the conservative perception of a media environment hostile to Republican political interests. Its primordial roots reach back to Fox president Roger Ailes's Nixon-era memo "A Plan for Putting the GOP on TV News" arguing for the creation of a conservative media bastion on television and ushering in a sea change in the political information space.[32] Since, the network's reach to conservative audiences and influential role in American political discourse has become undeniable. In 2020, Republicans rated the network as the most trustworthy source for political information in the run-up to that year's presidential election, with nearly 60% responding that they had gotten their news from Fox in the previous week.[33] This is not only a reflection of demand-side preferences from the audience, but the ability of the network to influence political belief structures on the supply-side.[34] Again, this is not to suggest that progressives do not enjoy their own preferred cable networks: a substantial proportion of them cite CNN, ABC, CBS, and MSNBC as regular television information sources.[35] But individual sources in the comparably polyglot progressive media environment are far less influential than their more monolithic conservative analog. Scholarly research of Fox's coverage of major political events has uncovered a substantial level of influence to shape belief structures among its audience on the Iraq War, the "birther" conspiracy theory claiming President Barack Obama was not born in the United States, the COVID-19 pandemic, and the legitimacy of the 2020 presidential election.[36] Polarization is undoubtedly a state of politics with many causes, but given the simultaneity with which polarized belief structures and out-group animus have moved alongside the fractionalization of media, it is difficult to disentangle the influence such outlets may have likely had on the emergence of these concurrent trends.[37]

While platforms like Fox remains a key data point for communications research into polarization, the environment in which individuals acquire political information exhibits a vast array of "echo chambers" all along the ideological spectrum. The end of the "Fairness Doctrine" and the rise of cable television certainly set the conditions for news outlets to develop around a business model that provides tailored information to a specific audience. The addition of online news and social media—as we will find later in this book—also provides partisans of various allegiances the opportunity to seek out information in a way that conforms with existing belief structures. However, just as political polarization writ large has taken on a decidedly asymmetric pattern, so too has the corresponding media environment. While Democrats and Republicans certainly have preferred media sources from which to acquire political information, the conservative landscape is far more coherent. Republicans overwhelmingly acquire their news from a small number of preferred sources, such as Fox and actively distrust the rest; by contrast, Democrats and Independents tend to receive news from a variety of sources and have greater trust in the media institutions overall.[38] Expression of factually inaccurate information and conspiracy theories has also been shown to be widely asymmetrical between the parties, with higher levels of belief among political conservatives.[39] The significance of this pattern of media consumption is important for our purposes in this chapter: if partisans are in fact gathering different information about the institutional quality of government institutions like the military when rendering judgements about "trust" or "confidence," there is reason to suspect that the partisan fragmentation of the media environment itself is likely part of the story.

Selective Information Exposure

If media exposure informs how partisans might be drawing conclusions about the military's credibility (or proximity to partisan establishments), there are two ways in which this might be the case. The first is that partisans are sub-jected to different *volumes* of information regarding military performance or organizational conduct. Demand-based reporting biases and voluntary selective exposure to certain outlets can result in the individuals of various partisan identities having different probabilities of hearing updating information. For example, if the military suffers an operational defeat or experiences an organizational scandal, partisan media outlets may simply choose to report on military issues at higher or lower volumes during the relevant period. If an individual with high affect for the military does not hear the negative story about the military from their preferred source, it may be cognitively easier to dismiss it as aberrant or untrustworthy if they incidentally encounter it from others. Larry Bartels argues specifically that while skepticism of new information that challenges one's priors may be Bayesian, it is not rational. Indeed, this off-hand rejection of new data "in extreme cases [...] may approach delusion" in its censoring of potentially important information.[40] We can form the first testable implication of this pattern in order to account for the possibility that media outlets with partisan audiences may exhibit this type of reporting bias with respect to military-related stories:

- **H2A (Asymmetric Reporting)**: News outlets with established partisans audiences will report negative stories about the military at different rates.

The second form of information exposure bias may be that partisans are subjected to different *frames* when military information is reported. With respect to issues regarding military competence and professionalism, these stories may be presented in a way that insulates the institution from public criticism or highlights organizational failures. Even if H2A predicts certain outlets may under-report these stories, particularly high-profile events involving the military would still likely oblige even biased partisan sources to report on them. However, the nature of that reporting may be heavily subject to "lead story" effects and issue framing by focusing on some aspects of the military's performance while ignoring or downplaying others.[41] We can capture this potential avenue of information selectivity in H2B:

- **H2B (Asymmetric Framing)**: When negative military stories are reported, media outlets with established partisan audiences will exhibit different frames with respect to criticism/insulation of the military institution.

In both cases, the events of reality fail to effectively update factual beliefs due to filtering by partisan-favored media sources. Given the direction of the partisan credibility gap, in which Republicans exhibit consistently higher levels of trust in the military, H2A might further propose that conservative media outlets reporting on political issues will significantly under-report issues regarding military failures, strategic missteps, professional misconduct, and other stories critical of the military institution compared to non-conservative outlets. This would logically result in a Republican audience with less access to updating information by which to form new evaluations of the military. Whether this is the result of supply-side news biases, demand-side audience preferences, or a combination of both, is not the purview of this analysis, as all of them contribute to the logic of H2A. In addition, H2B might further predict that when these stories are reported, they will be framed by conservative-friendly outlets in such a way as to minimize direct damage to the prestige and credibility of the armed forces. This chapter examines both of these hypotheses in the following section by analyzing reporting habits and patterns among news outlets with defined partisan audiences during the Iraq War. This period is particularly useful in testing the information exposure hypothesis because (1) new information about military conduct and performance was readily available and (2) this event temporally aligns with the beginning of the partisan "gap" on military trust more broadly.

However, even if individuals have a variety of options in how they evaluate the military institution given new information, they are still largely reliant on third parties to provide that information. Barring personal experience or direct exposure to the institution's actions, many individuals instead rely on information from other elite communities in society, such as political leaders and the news media when forming attitudes on such institutions.[42] This assumption is particularly important when considering the military institution, given its day-to-day distance from the mass public and the decreasing probability of the average citizen having first-hand information on military performance.[43]

Partisan political identity serves as the principal lens through which individuals likely gain information about institutional performance. For a structurally and normatively non-partisan institution as the military, partisan alignment should theoretically provide no additional information that is predictive of performance evaluation. Instead, it is possible that polarization in expressed trust for the military is partially the result of such expressions being subsumed into partisan identities and maintained by controlled information exposure. If support or opposition to specific government institutions becomes a mark of partisan identity or a signpost for ideological conformity with the larger group, it is likely to become more closely aligned with individual partisan identity. As Christopher Achen and Larry Bartels observe (emphasis added):

> A party constructs a conceptual viewpoint by which its voters can make sense of the political world. Sympathetic newspapers, magazines, websites, and television channels convey the framework to partisans. *This framework identifies friends and enemies*, it supplies talking points, and it tells people how to think and what to believe.[44]

Partisan media consumption habits are therefore the centerpiece of understanding the volume and type of information that the public acquires about the military. Recent study has concluded that conservative Republicans are far more likely to consume news media from a single source rather than a multitude of news outlets.[45] This has not meaningfully changed over recent years, where conservative skepticism of mainstream print and news media sources has become commonplace.[46] As such, we should expect that the reliance on third-party information about the military institution is more potent among these individuals, who are more likely to receive thematically coherent information. Similarly, as previously discussed, the existence of media "echo-chambers," particularly among established partisans, serves to minimize exposure to contrary ideas, bolster existing beliefs, and increase alignment with pro-attitudinal information.[47] Furthermore, the active distrust among political conservatives for a much wider swath of media sources compounds this effect: in addition to trafficking a limited plurality of information sources, this partisan subgroup is also more likely to reject contrary information as non-credible depending on its source. A 2017 report from Gallup found that while 62% of Democrats believed that the news media "gets the facts straight," only 14% of Republicans felt the same way. This distrust of the press permeates every medium, from television to print media to internet news.[48]

The role of partisanship in interpreting wartime events is not a new phenomenon. Adam Berinsky found that respondents identifying as Republican during the Bush administration were more likely to underestimate the number of casualties the United States had sustained in the Iraq conflict and more likely to have a higher perceived probability of success for the war's outcome.[49] However, what remains is some accounting for how this partisanship interacts with the amount and type of information those same partisans are likely to receive in producing impressions about the military. If stories that otherwise might update their opinion of the military's performance or professionalism are not widely reported by their preferred media outlets, strong partisans may be more likely to dismiss individual disconfirming stories as either untrustworthy, biased, or unrepresentative of the institution writ large. Concurrently, stories or themes that are reported at higher rates may be more likely to lodge with their audiences, establishing a sense of salience and recency. If partisan networks or publications exhibit widely different reporting patterns, this may be contributing to the "credibility gap" among their audiences.

Selective Exposure and Military Performance

In order to assess the impact of divergent information availability across news outlets with established partisan audiences, this section analyzes reporting trends on the Iraq War in 2007 across major media sources in different forms. This military reporting period provides a useful case for several reasons. First, this period represents a high watermark of information on military activity, making detection of disparities between partisan media outlets more readily detectable. In terms of American military casualties, 2007 was the deadliest year of the conflict and the second deadliest for Iraqi civilian deaths. Second, the debate over the Bush administration's decision to "surge" additional combat forces into Iraq made this period one of the most politically contentious as well. The major political parties at home sparred over the rising death toll, material cost, and uncertainty surrounding the strategic direction that the "surge" embodied. Finally, this period makes a useful case for analysis in that it aligns closely with the beginnings of the partisan divergence on expressed confidence in the military as an institution. While the personnel and material cost of the war reached its peak during this period, the "surge" was also responsible for achieving significant gains in the military's objective to achieve security for the nascent Iraqi government and minimize insurgent violence, even if these gains were not visible until the end of the year. In addition, extant research on this period reveals it to be one illustrative of deeper trends in partisan media reporting rather than a unique idiosyncrasy of the Bush years.[50] As such, the notion that partisans of different stripes may have emerged from this critical period with very different understandings of the military's performance may be traceable to their respective information environments.

The first dimension we examine is the frequency with which stories that might otherwise update partisan attitudes on the military are reported across different sources. For example, as coalition forces engaged more frequently with insurgent forces during the war's most casualty-producing year, partisan outlets that reported more on Iraq stories generally were likely to make knowledge of friction and potential stalemate more accessible to audiences. By contrast, outlets that reported on Iraq stories less often may have cut off a line of information supply to their audiences, leaving viewers or readers unable to form new opinions or more reliant on pre-existing priors. Due to the fact that the partisan "credibility gap" has manifested with conservative Republicans espousing much greater affect for the military than Independents or progressive Democrats, examining the difference between outlets with established partisan audiences can help us to understand the information environment. In order to test the theory that certain sources may underreport stories of war performance (H2A), this empirical efforts uses the Pew Research Center News Coverage Index (NCI) dataset, which records and codes the duration, substance, and frequency of online, radio, television, and print media news segments based on a series of rotating sampling processes.[51]

This analysis specifically examines the prominence and frequency of stories coded in the NCI dataset as pertaining to Iraq combat events, casualties, reconstruction efforts, evaluations of the Iraq troop surge, and other events relevant to the conduct of the war's execution. These stories are coded distinctly from "homefront" stories involving memorialization and Iraq veteran issues and "policy debate" stories concerned less with the war's conduct. As a result, this category exclusively captures news stories that best reflect the performance of the military during the critical "surge" period to a national audience. These include cable news outlets with the highest ratings exposure at the time (CNN, MSNBC, FOX) and print media outlets classified as "Tier 1" by Pew based on national distribution and circulation (*New York Times, Washington Post,* and *Wall Street Journal*). This dataset also includes radio programs with headline feeds (ABC News Headlines), national audiences (NPR), and the highest cumulative audience programs that year (Sean Hannity, Rush Limbaugh).[52] Broadly examining such a variety of news sources captures a fairly adequate picture of the media environment partisans would have experienced regarding information on the military's performance in Iraq.

Figure 4.1 displays the results of this analysis for the major cable news channels. As previously stated, a preponderance of self-identified Republicans consume most of their news from Fox, while Democrats and Independents are likely to sample from a variety of sources including CNN, MSNBC, and PBS. Of particular import for this analysis, therefore, is the contrast between these groups of media outlets when reporting on the Combat Events category. Evident from these results is that Fox devoted lower levels of average air time to such stories in 2007, with segments of far shorter collective duration compared to the other news channels. This lower reporting frequency indicates a sharp departure from the opening (and more visibly successful) phase of the war, in which Fox quickly outpaced its competitors in coverage.[53] The change in reporting patterns also contrasts with the run-up to the invasion in which prowar narratives dominated.[54] During the "surge," the most notable gaps in relative coverage between outlets are concurrent with increased concern over the refugee crisis (March), the deadliest months of the year (April-July), and the period following General David Petraeus's report to Congress (September). During these periods, conservative media is out-reported by as much as two to three times by other networks on these stories. As reported in Table 4.2, over the entire measured period, the average percentage of daily coverage time spent on ICE stories on Fox amounted to roughly half of that spent by CNN and MSNBC, and close to a third of that spent by PBS. Coverage of Iraq stories more generally, including homefront and policy stories, exhibit an even starker contrast between outlets.

Cable news was not the only way partisans were likely to acquire information about the military's performance in Iraq. Incorporation of print newspapers with national distribution yields a similar pattern of reporting asymmetry. Figure 4.2(a) captures the prominence given to ICE stories over time by each of the

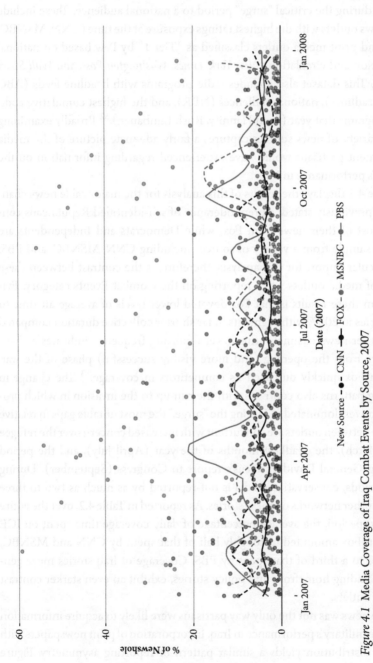

Figure 4.1 Media Coverage of Iraq Combat Events by Source, 2007

Note: This figure depicts media coverage of Iraq Combat Events (ICE) and related news stories as coded by Pew Research News Coverage Index (NCI) Dataset. Points represent day totals for percent of newshole for cable news sources with largest audience reach. LOESS smoothers are added to depict broader trend of moving averages over time (span = 0.10).

Table 4.2 **Descriptive Statistics, Iraq War Reporting: Cable News (2007)**

| | Mean Percentage of Sampled Newshole | | | |
News Source	PBS (1)	CNN (2)	MSNBC (3)	FOX News (4)
Combat Events (ICE)	9.18 (< 0.001)	6.12 (< 0.001)	6.85 (< 0.001)	3.62
Domestic/Homefront	27.12 (< 0.001)	6.57 (0.07)	10.75 (0.01)	4.62
Policy Debate	26.38 (< 0.001)	13.03 (0.01)	25.28 (< 0.001)	9.97
Observations	431	468	243	394

Notes: Reported figures depict average percent of daily newshole dedicated to segments on Iraq War stories across the entire 2007 news year. Values in parentheses ( ) indicate p-values for two-tailed t-test for difference in means between reported news source and Fox News as reference category.

three Tier 1 print sources sampled. While the *Wall Street Journal* does not rank as high on likely information sources for conservatives as Fox, Pew Research continued to reveal as recently as 2020 that it is the only newspaper that self-identified conservatives trust more than they distrust.[55] Even at minimum span, the LOESS smoother cannot capture a yearly trend of reporting for *WSJ* because there are too few data points of reporting on these stories. This should not be surprising; compared to the *New York Times* and the *Washington Post*, the *Journal* is far more business-focused and devotes fewer column inches to foreign affairs on the whole. However, it remains that among preferred print media sources, an even wider partisan disparity in access to updating information about the military's war performance exists in this medium than in cable news.

We can also include consideration of radio sources as an additional medium: of the top five media sources utilized by "consistent conservatives," Fox News (88%) and local news (50%) are followed closely by radio programs from Sean Hannity (45%) and Rush Limbaugh (43%).[56] However, Figure 4.2(b) reveals that these do not constitute a side channel by which information about war events might have been communicated. Again, the LOESS smoother has too few reporting points to calculate a yearly trend from the conservative outlets. This is in comparison to National Public Radio and ABC News Headlines which regularly spent in excess of 10% of their sampled air-time on ground events and combat actions coming from the Iraq War. As a well-trafficked news medium by self-identified political conservatives, these findings contribute to the pattern developed in Figures 4.1 and 4.2(a). Across cable news, print media, and talk

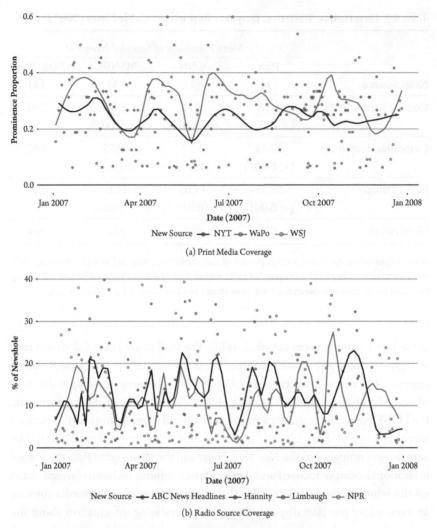

Figure 4.2 Media Coverage of Iraq Combat Events by Source, 2007
Note: This figure depicts media coverage of Iraq Combat Events (ICE) and related news stories as
coded by Pew Research News Coverage Index (NCI) Dataset. Points represent day totals for percent
of newshole or prominence proportion. LOESS smoothers are added to depict broader trend of moving
averages over time (span = 0.15). Smoother lines for WSJ (4.2a), Limbaugh (4.2b) and Hannity (4.2b)
not visible because of insufficient data points over observed time.

radio, outlets with established partisan audiences exhibited wide disparity in the
volume of reporting for a critical phase of the war.

Was this purely an artifact of the environment as of the "surge" period in Iraq?
It is unlikely that this pattern of reporting across media types and outlets was an
idiosyncrasy of that specific year or the possible negative reflections on military
institutional quality that it may have incurred. This is more clearly visible through

an extended analysis of the same cable news sources to reporting on specific "sub-story lines" coded by the NCI dataset outside the Iraq Combat Events category.[57] Noticeably less airtime was committed on average by Fox News to stories such as the troop increase, the Pat Tillman friendly-fire cover-up scandal, and stories comparing the conflict in Iraq to the Vietnam War. These patterns appear to persist even outside one specific phase of the Iraq War. Examining print media reporting over a longer period of time revealed that *Wall Street Journal* readers were far less likely to be exposed to any stories regarding the Abu Ghraib prison scandal (2004), the Haditha massacre (2006), the Walter Reed Medical Facility scandal (2007), or stories regarding sexual assault in the military (2013) than readers of the *New York Times* or the *Washington Post* over the same periods.[58]

In another alternative accounting of these reporting trends, one could argue that conservative-friendly media outlets like Fox News were not reporting more favorably on the military as much as for a co-partisan president in George W. Bush, to whom the Iraq War was indelibly attached. The best point of comparison for this period in 2007 Iraq during the Bush administration is the similarly described "surge" of forces into Afghanistan in 2010 under the Obama administration. Both years involved a politically controversial increase to troops deployed in these areas and were both the deadliest years of their respective conflicts. Figure 4.3 displays the results of using the 2010 version of the NCI dataset and conducting the same analysis of network-specific reporting patterns on the Afghanistan Combat Events (ACE) substory category. Notably, we still observe that Fox News reporting on the military's activities in Afghanistan came in under its competitors at MSNBC, PBS, and CNN for most of the calendar year. While not the final word on the issue, this pattern outside of a Republican administration does draw into question the notion that conservative media under-reported war events in 2007 simply to protect a co-partisan president's favored foreign policy initiative.

The media environment depicted in this analysis reveals a reasonably consistent asymmetry in reporting across different partisan news sources on the subject of Iraq War events, more specifically the stories about casualties, reconstruction frustrations, and regular assessments of the "surge" strategy that might otherwise have informed a new assessment of the military's execution of the campaign. As a critical story topic for informing the public on military performance, the difference in information between partisan subgroups comes into closer focus. Media outlets such as Fox News, more heavily trafficked by conservative Republicans, were less likely to report on military scandals or poor wartime outcomes. As a result, we can find some support for H2A, in that partisans on both sides of the political spectrum would have had different levels of availability to updating information on military performance and institutional quality. The next

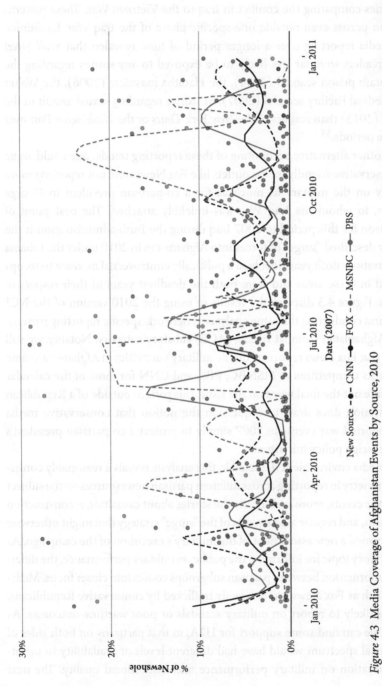

Figure 4.3 Media Coverage of Afghanistan Events by Source, 2010

Note: This figure depicts media coverage of Afghanistan events and related news stories as coded by Pew Research News Coverage Index (NCI) 2010 Dataset. Points represent day totals for percent of newshole or prominence proportion. LOESS smoothers are added to depict broader trend over time (span = 0.15).

section examines how this asymmetry in reporting is potentially compounded by uneven framing of military information across news sources.

Evaluating Asymmetric Framing Hypothesis

Examining high-volume news periods like the "surge" phase of the Iraq War provides a useful picture of the reporting patterns of the various news sources frequented by partisans during an important opportunity of evaluation for the military. One potential critique of these patterns is that they speak to descriptive patterns of story frequency, rather than the substance of certain stories—such as Iraq War events—when they are reported. It is reasonable to assert that certain sub-storylines, such as the "Comparisons to Vietnam" or "Pat Tillman Scandal" stories, are damaging enough to military prestige in themselves that a gap in reporting frequency likely results in a commensurate gap in substantive portrayal of the institution. The difficulty US forces encountered during this critical period, with mounting casualties, the "surge" of several brigades into the Baghdad area, and high-level leadership turnover, made even objective reporting on battlefield events potentially damaging news about military performance. Collectively, we observe some evidence for H2A in the reporting patterns depicted during this period for individuals to update their judgments on military performance. In particular, across different media and sources, conservative outlets consistently reported less on Iraq War events than centrist or left-leaning media outlets.

In order to assess the second hypothesis governing selective media exposure, simply observing reporting volumes can only help so much. Even if partisan outlets were likely to report on military activity with various degrees of frequency during the relevant reporting period, what remains to be seen is how those stories were likely to be framed once they were reported. Given the salience of the Iraq War, it would have been impossible for news outlets of any type to ignore the story entirely; as such, it is just as important to the idea of partisan selective exposure that one understand the substantive valence of military reporting. Closer inspection of cross-outlet trends in cable news reporting during this same period allows for this level of fidelity. Selecting on the same three primary television news outlets from earlier (CNN, MSNBC, and Fox), the LexisNexis Academic database allowed for collection of all broadcast transcripts for calendar year 2007 which contained the term or root *iraq/iraqi* and were sub-coded by the database as pertaining to the Iraq War. After removing missing data and detectable duplicates, the final dataset of 1,951 broadcast transcripts captured the substantive discussion of news segments dealing primarily with the Iraq War during the same timeframe analyzed previously. This dataset served as the textual corpus for content analysis on the topic distribution across news sources within the Iraq War subject.

Unsupervised machine learning and text-as-data analysis have become an increasingly effective tool for allowing a textual corpus to inform the researcher about the variety of substantive topics being addressed in a body of text. The method used here is an extension of the Latent Dirichlet Allocation (LDA) multilevel architecture, the Structural Topic Model (STM), in order to allow the text of the transcripts themselves to inform what subjects are being discussed across news sources. The STM pre-supposes a set of k potential topics being discussed in the text, across which a probabilistic distribution of words exists, and that documents are similarly a mixed distribution across topics.[59] This allows the text to characterize its own topic distribution based on those words that occur most frequently.

After collection, the transcripts were pre-processed to produce a functional version of the dataset as a textual corpus (stemmed, lemmatized, and stripped of punctuation, numbers, and capitalization), running several topic models on the constituent broadcast segments. Several iterations allowed for me to remove proper nouns with high frequency, such as the names of reporters and commentators referenced directly. Once a sufficient number of these "stop words" had been removed, the resulting structural model allowed me to infer some of the most identifiable thematic threads of the transcripts. Using these words and the substantive material in the top ten articles best captured by each topic, the topics were assigned a descriptive label according to the content of reporting and the tone of the discussion.

Using the news source as a covariate, we can visualize the predicted topic proportion over the entire text corpus for each news source with uncertainty bands at the 95% level. Figure 4.4 depicts some of the more coherent and clearly identifiable topics based on word probability and the substance of the broadcasts themselves. Each graphical depiction shows how different topics composed various levels of the content share across the media outlets over 100 simulations— expressed as the predicted mean topic proportion—given the substance of the transcripts. Topics depicted in Figure 4.4(a) indicate those with notably higher frequency in the Fox subset of the corpus, while those topics in Figure 4.4(b) were more prevalent in the MSNBC and CNN transcripts.

In order to provide some thematic consistency to the topics identified by the model, the topics themselves were assigned titles that captured some of the major ideas consistent within each of the most internally coherent topic areas. Indeed, many of the patterns identified during analysis of the Pew dataset seem to re-emerge. The MSNBC and CNN-favored topics in Figure 4.4(b) included direct commentary of material losses, strategic frustration, and mounting coalition military casualties. The "New Course in Iraq" and "Iraq Withdrawal"

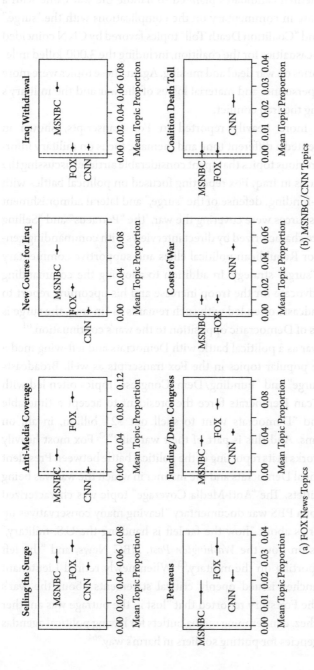

(a) FOX News Topics

(b) MSNBC/CNN Topics

Figure 4.4 Expected Topic Proportion by Source (STM), Cable Broadcast Transcripts, 2007

Note: This figure depicts the expected topic proportion for each of these eight topics estimated by the topic model by source. Model programmed and visually depicted using STM package in R.[60] Topics are grouped by the media outlet that led reporting on those topics. Labels indicate substantive impact of frequently occurring words and the content of top ten broadcast transcripts captured by topic prevalence. Uncertainty bands represent 95% confidence intervals following 100 simulations. With K=35, the average expected mean topic proportion ≈ .028.

topics, most heavily reported by MSNBC, were temporally frequent around the announcement of the "surge" strategy in early 2007 and later in the year when the "surge" strategy was coming under increasing scrutiny. The stories drew increased attention to the debate over the viability of the new strategy and discussion of a timetable for removing US forces. Media focus shifting to how the 2008 presidential candidates planned to handle the war came with a commensurate increase in commentary on the complications with the "surge." The "Costs of War" and "Coalition Death Toll" topics favored by CNN coincided with periods of high-casualties for the coalition, including the 3,000-killed milestone and specific stories on war dead and missing. Again, these topics were more concerned with the personnel and material losses of the war and the military's difficulty in navigating the Iraq conflict.

However, topics more heavily reported in Fox transcripts, shown in Figure 4.4(a), represented a different tone and thematic focus on military information. Unlike the previous topics that spent considerable airtime discussing the military's complications in Iraq, Fox reporting focused on political battles with Democrats over war-funding, defense of the "surge," and lateral admonishment of how other media sources were covering the war. The "Petraeus" and "Selling the Surge" topics were characterized by direct interviews with commanding general David Petraeus or Republican political elites and supportive commentary of President Bush's "surge" strategy. In addition to allowing the commanding general to directly advocate for the troop increase and his upcoming report to Congress, these broadcasts often led with such remarks as "in Iraq, the surge is working" or critiques of Democratic opposition to the war's continuation.[61]

Framings of the war as a political battle with Democrats and left-wing media were generally more popular topics in the Fox transcripts as well. Broadcasts in the "Selling the Surge" and "Funding/Dem. Congress" topics often led with comments such as "can Democrats force the president to accept a timetable for pulling out?" and "Democrats want to shell out $21 billion, in all, on non-military programs. And this is part of their war bill?"[62] Fox most heavily outpaced other networks in its reporting of the political battle between President Bush and Congressional Democrats and the manner in which the war was being reported in other outlets. The "Anti-Media Coverage" topic was characterized by admonishments of a PBS war documentary "leaving many conservatives up in arms," critical stories about "how the far left is handling the U.S. military," and negative reports on how the *Washington Post*, NBC News, and "the left wing press" were reporting on the military.[63] When newly retired Lieutenant General Ricardo Sanchez issued openly critical statements about the war's governing strategy, the Fox story reported that "lost in the outrage was another statement from Sanchez, condemning media outlets for having political agendas and blasting news agencies for putting soldiers in harm's way."[64]

Across these topics, we observe some support for an asymmetric framing pattern (H2B) during this critical reporting period. As individuals sought out and received various types of information regarding the conduct of the war, they were subject to different distributions of framing or "lead story" effects based on which outlet they were likely to traffic. Whereas centrist and liberal media sources were more likely to frame discussion of the Iraq War as a dialogue on military frustrations, personnel and material loss, rising sectarian violence, or discussion of a rapid withdrawal, conservative outlets were more likely to discuss the conflict in terms of homefront political fights over funding and the "surge," the Democratic opposition in Congress, or criticism of how other media outlets were reporting on the military. A detectable disparity in the substance of Iraq stories across outlets conforms with previous research on partisan media report-ing and audience belief structures. In a 2003 University of Maryland survey probing belief in false statements over the Iraq War, researchers found that only 23% of public broadcasting listeners believed at least one of the claims (which including the discovery of WMD in Iraq and links between Saddam Hussein and Al-Qaeda) while 80% of FOX News watchers believed at least one.[65] In addition to spending less time discussing the military's performance on the ground, topics more prevalent on conservative media often seemingly came to the defense of the military institution by insisting that other media outlets were subverting the armed forces or that political opponents were harming the war effort.

Given the patterns of reporting measured in the preceding section, these results indicate a perceptibly skewed information environment between par-tisans with regards to the volume and content of information they received about the military. The result is a seemingly "one-sided information flow" whose substance was far more conditional on the partisan identity of the viewer than objective realities on the ground.[66] These findings conform with other explo-rations into motivated partisan reasoning that have found such individuals are likely to seek out confirmatory information and rigidly adopt the corresponding belief structures.[67] Media consumers who identified as Democrats or Indepen-dents were likely to traffic in environments that reported on the Iraq War more frequently, focusing largely on costs and concerns over strategic quagmire when they did. Republicans were less likely to receive negative information on the war's progress during one of the most important years of its conduct; furthermore, conservative-friendly outlets were likely to look favorably on the yet-untested "surge" and avoid discussions over the costs of the conflict. Given the increased reliance of this partisan subset for fewer news sources, these individuals are less likely to encounter contrary information outside a unified narrative. While not the authoritative word on the subject, this analysis certainly lends credence to the notion that partisan divergence over trust in the military is, at least in part, compounded by very different stores of information. As the next chapter will discuss, strong partisans who are reliant on a select few media outlets may also be particularly susceptible to biased updating when presented with new and contradictory information.

Sources of Politicization

If at least some of the partisan gap on trust in the military can be explained by access to different stores of information, what influence might this environment have on the likelihood of military politicization? What we have observed in this chapter has been an understanding of how partisanship and media consumption may influence how individuals arrive at different conclusions about the military's capacity or organizational integrity. But those same judgements are also likely to be a function of that observer's affinity for the institution in a partisan sense. Reaching back to our Parallax typology of politicization, it is important to remember that institutions can be politicized even if the only activity or public speech occurring is from actors external to that institution. If political party leaders or trusted media elites frame a particular image of the quality, performance, and trustworthiness of a government agency or organization, it is not unreasonable to suggest it will shape how the observing public re-calibrates their placement of that body relative to a partisan political spectrum. The analysis of this chapter suggests that when it comes to public perception of the military, this may very well be a possibility: given some type of military behavior on the battlefield or at home, the likelihood of different outlets to report on them may likely shape how their respective audiences draw conclusions about the institution's quality.

Since the target of such reporting is the audience, this artifact of the environment leaves open the possibility of *aspect* politicization. As detailed in Chapter 2, this form of politicization captures when the public receives information that alters its perception of the military in relation to the fixed ideological backdrop provided by partisan elites or organizations. In this category, the political parties may not meaningfully move their own positions, nor does the military engage in any behavior that qualifies as active politicization. Instead, media- or elite-driven narratives surrounding military events may move the viewer's own ideological position and recast the armed forces' proximity to partisan institutions from the audience's new vantage point. Through repeated exposure, these individuals may arrive at the conclusion that the military exhibits the sensibilities of a specific partisan political establishment or specifically opposes those of another.

How might this type of politicization manifest? Third parties can often contribute to aspect politicization by drawing attention to some military institutional behavior that directly supports or opposes the partisan agenda of one of the major parties, even if this is not the principal intent of the military decision-making bodies. Some of the most potent examples of this concept in practice occur over organizational reforms or policies that touch on deeply held partisan social issues, but these are not an exhaustive list of instances in which this form of politicizing behavior can happen. Aspect politicization captures when third-parties signal to the audience that the military policy, behavior, or performance is indicative of hostility or embrace of a specific partisan political establishment, even if this is not empirically the case. Instances in which the military engages in behaviors or policy changes that seemingly redound to the benefit of one party's agenda (or the detriment of the other) therefore provide fertile ground for aspect politicization if third-party sources of partisan information seize on them. As we have seen in this chapter, one of the conduits for this type of third-party messaging can be trusted media outlets trafficked by partisan audiences.

For partisans, media reporting can provide an important lens for them to form attitudes on the level to which institutions like the military are to be trusted or considered amenable to their interests. One of the most consistent findings in this chapter—that conservatives are less likely to see critical information about the military—will find additional validation in Chapter 5 when we explore how those same individuals process critical information that they *do* receive. This might suggest that partisan Republicans are immovably attached to the military as an extension of their own constituency. However, it is important to remember that this type of media influence can work both ways: the same apparatus that can positively depict the military institution to its audience can also provide more critical portrayals. To this end, Chapter 6 will reveal the pressure point by which partisans are likely to lose confidence in the military: the perception that it supports institutional preferences from the other side of the ideological spectrum. In these instances, trusted media sources can provide partisans new information about the credibility of the armed forces with respect to their favored partisan establishment.

One example of this dynamic in practice is observable in conservative media coverage of military leadership in the first year of the Biden administration. The change in party control of the White House followed a turbulent year that included the extremist violence of January 6, 2021, and attack on the Capitol building as well as the protests following the murder of George Floyd, both instances in which domestic military deployments featured prominently. Months into office, conservative media shifted its coverage of the military institution with attention toward organizational policies and practices deemed out of step with the preferences of its partisan audience members. New Defense Secretary Lloyd Austin's initiative to "stand down" military forces for a day in order to facilitate a concerted discussion about political extremism in the ranks followed high-profile reporting over the number of veterans (and active servicemembers in some cases) who participated in the attack on the Capitol in January. The Pentagon was criticized in some corners of conservative media, who characterized the decision as a "purge," even calling for cuts to the military budget if such policies were not abandoned. In a direct appeal to the audience, Fox's Laura Ingraham remarked "Why should we fund a organization that the Democrats plan to use, not to protect us, but to restrain us in order to protect themselves and their grip on power?"[68] Though uncharacteristic of a longer tradition of conservative reporting on the military, the coverage can be seen as an attempt to influence a partisan audience's perception of the military from like-minded institution to partisan implement.

The following months included similar reporting on military activity with a particular eye toward the institution's ostensible hostility to Republican interests. Former Trump advisor Sebastian Gorka took to the conservative NewsMax outlet to denounce military leaders for their statements about addressing racism in the ranks and admonished an Army soldier as a "disgrace" after she appeared in a recruiting ad that showed her upbringing rallying for equality with her two mothers.[69] Outrage over "culture war" issues like combat flightsuits for pregnant women, the "feminization" of the military compared to competitor states, and the prioritization of climate as a security challenge became popular talking points depicting the military as hostile to conservative political values.[70] When Chairman Mark Milley was questioned by House Republicans over the concept of "critical race theory," Fox host Tucker Carlson argued that Milley's response had aimed a "race attack" at Americans and that the general was "not just a pig, he's stupid."[71] This surprising change in tone regarding the military is a reminder of the fragile foundations of public confidence in the armed forces and the influence of third-party media influences in aspect politicization.

The changing information environment for the likely-Republican audience of conservative media during this period would depict a much different military than previous exposure to the same sources was apt to provide. This offers an important illustration of how media outlets can affect the practice of aspect politicization by shifting public perception about the military itself. The change in both frequency and substance of stories regarding the military's organizational activities seems to suggest a desire to signal to audience members that not only were the armed forces hostile to Republican political preferences, but were props in support of an opposing partisan agenda. At the time of this book's publication, this pattern of reporting amongst traditionally military-friendly media sources has continued, with elected officials often expanding these criticisms through public statements and even proposing legislation aimed at curtailing specific policy initiatives.[72] Whether or not this manner of reporting will shift attitudes about the military among Republicans remains to be seen, but results from Gallup's 2021 institutional confidence survey found a remarkable 10-percentage point drop in Republican confidence in the military, down to 81% espousing "a great deal" or "quite a lot" from 91% just a year earlier.[73] While still remarkably high, it is possible that the shift in media reporting has updated the perceived utility of the military as a partisan ally for some conservative audience members.

Interest groups or party-aligned activists may also be able to provide the third-party voices necessary for aspect politicization, particularly if their signals are carried through the same media channels analyzed here. The same window of analysis in which this chapter's analysis drew its focus, the "surge" period of the Iraq War, provides an example of how other third-party influences can shape partisan perceptions of the military. In September 2007, General David Petraeus's anticipated report to Congress, alongside Ambassador Ryan Crocker, provided an opportunity for the senior military and civilian representatives in Iraq to update the American people on the conduct of the "surge" after the most damaging six months of the entire war. On September 10, the morning of their testimony, the *New York Times* published a full-page advertisement sponsored by liberal anti-war group MoveOn.org, with Petraeus's photo emblazoned with the title "GENERAL BETRAY US." The advertisement accused the Pentagon of inaccurate methodologies for tracking casualties coming from the war, as well as directly denigrating Petraeus for allegedly engaging in a public misrepresentation of the state of the conflict to the American people.[74]

The advertisement and the resulting media coverage energized the larger partisan debate over the state of the conflict, with Congressional Republicans immediately denouncing the ad and the *Times* for running it. Bush swept in to Petraeus's defense, remarking that "... most Democrats are afraid of irritating a left-wing group like MoveOn.org—or more afraid of irritating them than they are of irritating the United States military."[75] While several prominent Democrats also decried the ad, the result involved dueling Senate resolutions from both parties. John Cornyn (R-TX) authored the Republican response calling for a formal denunciation of the ad, while Democrats authored a competing measure that would denounce MoveOn's ad as well as those from the 2004 campaign that had attacked the military service of presidential candidate John Kerry. The publication of an advertisement directly targeting the credibility of the senior commander in the Iraq War closely reflected the existing partisan divides over the issue of the war itself.

The incident's illustration of aspect politicization from media sources lies in its effect on the audience, most notably progressive Democrats likely skeptical of the war and culturally less aligned with the military as an institution. A Pew Research survey taken just a week after Petraeus's testimony revealed that nearly half of Democrats (49%) believed the general "made things seem better than they are," compared to only 13% of Republicans who agreed with the same characterization of his testimony. Compared to a July survey from the same firm, Democrats were seven percentage points more likely to agree that Congressional Democrats were "not going far enough" to challenge Bush's Iraq policy, 61% up from 54%. The partisan gap on the state of war reached a new high compared to the summer as well, with Republicans more likely to see the military as making progress against the insurgents and reducing civilian casualties, to the tune of 51 and 31 percentage points higher than Democrats, respectively.[76]

The MoveOn advertisement episode provides a useful example of aspect politicization in that military activity that was conducted within its institutional bounds—namely, fighting and reporting on the state of wars—was portrayed in specific media outlets with the intention of painting the military as hostile to the interests of one partisan establishment, in this case war-skeptical Democrats. Despite the fact that the advertisement's accusations were loosely attached to the facts itself, its intent and possible effects are illustrative of an attempt to change the observing public's understanding of the military institution.[77] As this chapter has found, third-party voices in media can be powerful shapers of public perception, particularly toward institutions with which the public has little firsthand knowledge. In this case, partisans among the political left were likely to consume information about the military with a particular bent: namely, that it was covering up information about a damaging war, which would redound to the benefit of partisan opponents in the Bush administration in the run-up to an election year.

Third-party voices, particularly those conveyed through trusted partisan media sources, provide some of the most significant sources of aspect politicization. However, as articulated earlier in this book, these forms of politicization do not stand alone and in fact often set the conditions for other forms to manifest and compound the challenge of maintaining a "non-partisan" image for the military. Active politicization—when military actors engage in some behavior that might signal advocacy or opposition to partisan political institutions—can provide the most potent raw data for aspect politicization. Media sources may then report on that same military behavior with a partisan slant, further altering the perception of the institution in the eyes of the public. Aspect politicization can then also lead to the passive variety: partisan media reporting on military activity can cue partisan elites or elected officials to expand the narrative to a larger audience, putting the military into the position of partisan political prop. As we will explore in subsequent chapters, the interconnectivity between different forms of politicizing behavior is one of the most complicating factors for normatively preserving a "non-partisan" military force.

In this chapter, we have found some evidence that partisan voices in the media space can meaningfully influence how individuals consume information about the military. Examining several high-reporting periods on military activity across various forms of communication and outlets has shown that partisans in American society were likely to experience very different perceptions of their military as an institution during a critical phase of war reporting. These analyses provide another modest contribution to the study of political communication with respect to public institutions, particularly relevant amidst a wide-scale decline in public trust for nearly every government body except for the military. Perhaps more importantly, analysis of the information environment during these periods reveals a notable asymmetry in how partisans were likely to see the military's performance during complicated wars and controversial organizational scandals. In keeping with the "credibility gap" we observe between partisans, Republican-friendly outlets were generally more favorable in their portrayal of the armed forces. Using brief examples from the early Biden administration and late Bush administration, we observe how media outlets and interest groups can instead move the perspective of the observing public themselves in aspect politicizing behavior (even counter to type in the former example). But this chapter explored only the selective exposure portion of a larger theory on information processing: the next step involves understanding how these partisans employ that information in rendering judgments about the credibility of the military itself.

5

No Time to Explain

Cognitive Biases and Partisan Perceptions of the Military

If partisans are likely to gather different types of information about the military, how might this influence their resulting impressions about the credibility of the military as an institution? In deconstructing the seemingly unshakeable trust of the American public in its military, we observe a widening gap between partisans that underlies ostensibly high aggregate numbers. Partisan Republicans consistently register greater confidence in the military compared to Independent and Democratic counterparts in American society; while traditional explanations based on policy preferences and military demography certainly help to account for some of this trend, the expansion of the gap requires a more dynamic story. In the previous chapter, we explored one potential source of the divide: deepening variation in the types and amounts of information that partisans were likely to receive about the military from trusted or preferred media sources. Just as Republicans were more likely to register higher amounts of trust with the military over time, there is also evidence that their preferred media outlets were more likely to report on the military favorably than those trafficked by other individuals.

The second part of this dynamic accounting of the "credibility gap" requires analysis of how those same partisans employ on-hand information, stereotypes, or pre-conceptions about the military when judging the institutional quality of the military. As described earlier, understanding what is meant by "trust," "confidence," or high "performance" when it comes to the armed forces is notoriously difficult. For representative political institutions like Congress or the presidency, this concept of trust may proxy for approval of job performance that is more readily observable by the domestic public, or the propensity to believe information that comes from the institutions themselves.[1] By contrast, the military's portfolio of responsibilities is unique among public institutions in society; namely, to fight and win wars abroad. Therefore, we gain some insight into the partisan "credibility gap" by analyzing this question of

Dangerous Instrument: Political Polarization and US Civil-Military Relations. Michael A. Robinson,
Oxford University Press. © Oxford University Press 2023. DOI: 10.1093/oso/9780197611555.003.0005

performance—what do individuals look for when evaluating the military, given the information they are likely to have?

Even if partisans are likely to acquire very different information about the military itself, the "credibility gap" between them could be a perfectly rational pattern if partisans simply grade the armed forces on different metrics. However, if this fails to be the case, the answer may lie in something more closely tied to the concept of affective polarization we have thoroughly discussed so far. Specifically, the failure of individuals to rationally evaluate an institution's "performance" may not only reflect a failure to acquire useful, updating information, but a pathological attraction or aversion to the institution based on partisan tribalism. Applied to the "gap" between partisans over the military, this could indicate a political environment more susceptible to politicization. The belief that the military is either an extension of or threat to a valued partisan political "in-group" would present significant challenges to the preservation of the "non-partisan" ethic and a weakening of key civil-military norms among the public.

This chapter explores precisely this question. First, it will briefly discuss how existing scholarship has yielded competing theories of rational behavior and diverging partisan preferences. Given an observable set of behaviors or store of political information, what might account for partisans coming to different conclusions about a commonly visible outcome? Second, it will detail the results of original survey experimentation designed to provide some insight into this very area of inquiry. How do partisans respond to information about military "performance"? Whether in terms of battlefield success, organizational integrity, or avowed "non-partisanship," the theories reviewed in Chapter 2 provide a variety of rubrics by which individuals may judge the military's institutional quality. If partisans simply disagree on which matters most, the credibility gap may simply reflect rational choices. However, analysis of the survey's findings casts doubt on this interpretation. Whereas some respondents express clearer preferences for military behavior and update negatively in response to poor outcomes, others prove generally resistant to new information about military failures. The implications for civil-military relations are clearest in the environment this creates for politicization, particularly the *passive* and *relative* varieties.

Cognitive Biases and the Credibility Gap

As detailed previously, the credibility gap between partisans is more completely accounted for by considering the methods by which individuals acquire and process new information about the military institution. This updating process theoretically includes two important (though not necessarily sequential) steps: one in which individuals acquire information regarding the military and another regarding how individuals allow that information to update their judgements about the credibility of the military institution. Whereas the previous chapter focused on the former, this chapter will examine how the latter may also help to explain the polarization of attitudes over the military. The store of information individuals acquire from partisan media sources not only provides the basis for making these judgements, but can also clue audiences into the partisan utility of an institution's behavior, the impact that the institution may have on issues of particular partisan import, or even which institutions can be seen as ideologically proximate extensions of their political "in-group." If partisan calculations provide the basis for assessing the performance of institutions like the military, rather than objective evaluation, this biased form of processing may further deepen the challenge of politicization.

Given the magnitude of the military's credibility gap, how might cognitive biases help us understand why partisans in society arrive at different expressed opinions about a non-partisan entity? We have already seen how part of this story is one of media consumption and its different valences. But an incredibly rich literature in political science has focused on the varying processes by which individuals update their impressions of policies or institutions in response to new information. One approach contends that even partisan individuals are capable of responsibly using information to update their own prior beliefs in a credibly Bayesian fashion. This conceptualization of fundamentally unbiased learning "holds that new information moves people with different partisan affinities (but similar levels of prior information) in the same direction and to approximately the same extent."[2] When approval for a policy or leader across different partisan subgroups seems to track in a parallel fashion, they argue, this is clear evidence of unbiased learning: partisans are responding to common information shocks in a similar way.

However, another approach argues against this interpretation: if a truly unbiased process were at work, partisan subgroups should not be moving in parallel, but converge on some common understanding as new information outweighs individual-level priors in the Bayesian framework.[3] Instead, the "Bayesian" parallel trends assumption used as validation of unbiased learning is actually the most potent evidence against it. In this contrary accounting, often termed "selective perception," there is instead some irreducible partisan bias that separates political subgroups despite observation of some common picture of factual information.[4] Additionally, scholarship in political messaging has found that strong partisans, particularly those with the political sophistication to mount a more informed defense, will seek out confirmatory information, downweight disconfirming arguments, and lend more credibility to information that confirms their prior understanding.[5] Applied to the case of institutional affinity for the military, the

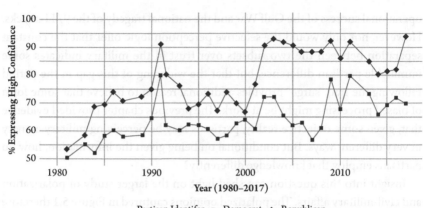

Partisan Identifer -■- Democrat -◆- Republican

Confidence in Military by Major Party Identification

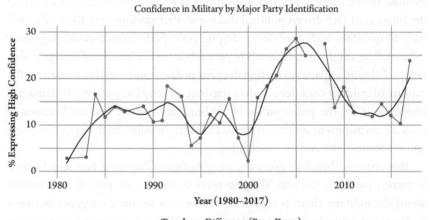

Trend -•- Difference (Reps-Dems)

Partisan Gap in Expressed Confidence

Figure 5.1 Public Confidence in Military Institution by Partisan ID (1980–2017)

Note: Figure 5.1 depicts high expressed confidence in the military institution conditional on stated partisan identity as captured by Gallup June Wave "Confidence in Institutions" survey instrument. "High" confidence categorized as answer of "a great deal" or "quite a lot" to the five-point Gallup question for institutional confidence. LOESS smoother (span = 0.3) depicts increasing polarization gap between partisan subgroups for clarity.

failure of partisans to reach a common understanding should lead us to believe that a potentially partisan-motivated bias is at work.

Figure 5.1 depicts how this gap between partisans has shifted over time. Using responses to Gallup's annual battery on confidence in American political and social institutions, the case for a truly "Bayesian" or unbiased process seems unlikely according to the logic offered by "selective perception." Indeed, partisans do trend in parallel over certain periods of time and even experience shocks similarly, such as the spike in confidence across both groups following the operational success of the Gulf War and the national tragedy of the 9/11 attacks. However, not only would the selective perception logic offer that the constant separation between the two subsets over trust in the military indicates some immutable partisan difference, but that the widening of this gap in the period following the Iraq "surge" provides additional reason to believe that some form of biased processing might be at work. The previous chapter provided evidence that, given some objective reality, partisans may be perceiving military activity in very different ways. But conditional on being given the information, how do partisans employ that knowledge differently?

Insight into this question can shed light on the larger study of polarization and civil-military affairs. The polarized opinions captured in Figure 5.1 therefore requires study for several reasons. As previously discussed, failing to objectively evaluate the credibility of select institutions in society contributes to a broader devaluation of fact-driven political discourse. Partisanship that allows the military to maintain high confidence despite poor performance could negatively influence the ability of individuals to properly learn the lessons of foreign policy failures.[6] Again, as partisan sorting deepens political and social polarization, the capture of military confidence into a partisan identity has potentially damaging implications for the preservation of civil-military norms. The implications of such an environment on the potential for military politicization are numerous and the focus of the end of this chapter.

This analysis therefore takes the insights from Chapter 4 one step further. If certain partisans are less likely to receive negative or critical information about the military, there is reason to believe in a similar divergence between partisans on attitude formation downstream. What happens when partisans *are* subjected to the information? Using original survey experimentation, this chapter explores the reaction of partisan individuals to negative information about the military institution. This sidesteps the supply issue of media "echo-chambers" and puts partisans to a choice: given this information, does one update their understanding of institutional credibility for the military? As we will find, conditional on exposure to knowledge of battlefield failures, professional misconduct, or partisan activity, Republicans fail to change their impressions of the military, compared to Democrats and Independents who feel worse about it. The implications of these findings are that a sizable portion of the public may not receive critical information, and conditional on them doing so, may be resistant to its influence.

Partisan Biases and Military Credibility

While much has been made of the high *aggregate* level of public trust in the military, the gap between Democrats and Republicans—the latter a traditional mainstay of military support—is an inescapable underlying condition. As detailed in the previous chapter, positive support for the military along partisan lines has been in part ascribed to elite-level similarities on the use of force or the demography of the military itself.[7] However, there is comparably less accounting for the dynamic effects of partisanship in solidifying these attitudes. In reality, partisans may be coming to very different perceptions of the quality of entities like the military not only because of different information sources, but because of the same cognitive biases that have characterized the politicization of other institutions.

As a companion to the "selective exposure" hypothesis proposed in Chapter 4, the "partisan bias" hypothesis asserts that partisans are using different evaluative processes to transfer information into judgments about the credibility of the military institution. Conditional on new updating information reaching the audience, it still may be the case that partisans differ in how they evaluate the performance or institutional quality of the armed forces. However, differences in expressed opinion need not indicate the existence of pronounced partisan bias. This chapter therefore considers two potential explanations for how partisans might arrive at different conclusions about the military institution in response to new or newly salient information.

The first potential explanation for the partisan credibility gap considers the possibility that individuals simply have different understandings of what is preferable. If this is the case, disparate attitudes need not be indicative of biased processing. As described in Chapter 2, in a "top-down" institutionalist accounting of public trust, government bodies engage in their assigned roles and receive evaluations from the public based on their performance. In this tradition, expressed trust in institutions is endogenous, a rational valuation of those institutions based on their perceived performance.[8] This process of creating confidence in institutions requires that government produce positive outcomes that are, in turn, rewarded by the public with expressions of trust in the institutions that are responsible for them. William Mishler and Richard Rose seize on one of the main limitations of this field in that, "although institutional theories agree that political trust is endogenous, they disagree about which aspects of performance are important or how performance is assessed."[9]

Most of the limited study dedicated to understanding institutional evaluations of the military has relied on similar thinking, arguing that public trust is a rational valuation of perceived performance. As detailed in Chapter 2, numerous scholarly efforts have sought to characterize what types of behavior or performance individuals value most with regards to the military, ranging from purely transactional evaluations of battlefield performance to organizational professionalism.[10] But as some have noted, the specific challenge in explaining patterns of trust in the military institution comes from the difficulty in capturing a meaningful metric of performance.[11] Fewer studies have considered that these criteria might differ based on the political or ideological leanings of the individual.

In short, partisans may simply use different yardsticks to measure military "performance." Previously, we encountered how existing civil-military relations theorists have traditionally captured these classes of activity. The first potential driver of public esteem for the military is, as Gronke and Feaver remark, "the most obvious" one, a purely transactional assessment of the institution based on its *performance* in warfare. As the military's singular function within society is to fight and win its nation's wars, it follows that the institution's performance under these conditions should provide the clearest signal to the public as to its competency and quality. A second theoretical approach takes into account the importance of organizational practices and "process," that public regard for the military institution is driven by perceived institutional *professionalism*, ethical quality, and embodiment of cherished social norms. Here, individuals in society expect the military to embody certain virtues or maintain organizational standards of integrity while preserving warfighting capacity. Finally, public trust figures may instead capture responses to the military's development as an impartial and *non-partisan* elite community in society. While military elites have become more prevalent in the political discourse domestically, many scholars argue that it is the continued restraint of the institution from engaging in partisan activity and its deeply ingrained deference to civilian leaders that has contributed to high public confidence.[12] This category of preferences differs from the first two in that the public is responding not to battlefield outcomes or organizational ethics, but to the perception of the military as a fair broker and credible source of information. From these three preference sets the following hypothesis is drawn:

- **H3A (Divergent Standards):** Certain partisans will value different classes of military behavior (performance, professionalism, non-partisanship) more in rendering their opinions about institutional credibility. These differing preferences allow for partisans to evaluate the institutions rationally, but on different evaluative criteria.

These different classes of evaluative criteria allow for the possibility that partisans across society merely have divergent preferences with regards to the optimal behavior of their military. As a result, H3A argues that partisan divergence in expressed confidence is the result of different political subsets expecting certain types of behavior from the military and rewarding or punishing the institution in accordance with their perceived accomplishments or failures in that class. This would be observable if partisans displayed clear and distinct prioritization in which types of military behavior affected their perceptions of trust. The main empirical effort of this chapter tests this hypothesis using experimental methods designed to measure partisan preferences for military performance.

However, if partisan individuals express no clear preference for military behavior relative to each other, we can no longer assume that a truly unbiased learning is taking place. In this case, a difference in expressed opinion at the conclusion of the updating process between partisan groups is attributable to cognitive biases that prevent a similarly updated evaluation of the institution. Conditional on access to useful information on military failures, one would expect a commensurate re-evaluation of the institution that took this information into account; if they did not, some biased process is affecting the nature of that evaluation:

- **H3B (Partisan Bias)**: Certain partisans employ a biased process in evaluating the credibility of the military institution in response to new information. Conditional on receiving negative information on military institutional quality, some will reject, downweight, or "backfire" their estimations of military credibility.

In theory, H3A allows for an unbiased process of evaluation to take place and contends that partisans simply disagree on the most important criteria by which to evaluate the military's credibility. However, H3B captures the possibility that, even without more *a priori* information on the military and with the ability to express preferences differently, a subset of individuals will actively reject updating information or interpret the meaning of that information in a way that insulates the military institution from damage.

Why might this be the case? As we have seen, the effect of partisan sorting on the extremity of issue positions and out-group animus has expanded dramatically in recent decades.[13] The nature of "affective polarization" argues that partisan identity carries with it a social dimension that can distort objective thought processes regarding policy or governmental quality. Joseph Bafumi and Robert Shapiro argue more pointedly that the influence of solidified partisan attitudes may have potentially damaging implications for rational opinion formation more broadly (emphasis added):

> Strong partisan attitudes may lead to *rigidity of attitudes and opinions in the face of new and credible discrepant information.* Not only might such new information be avoided through selective exposure, but its accuracy and validity might be denied as a result of "motivated bias" or flawed reasoning or no reasoning at all.[14]

Expressions of confidence in the military could, therefore, be not purely rational evaluations of institutional credibility, but rather ones tinged by emotional statements of partisan and social identity. Strong partisans have been found to be particularly more likely to counter-argue contrary information, to express anger or bias in response to threats to party status or prestige, or in the case of political conservatives, to express far more dogmatic thought processes or ideological intensity.[15] For example, Krebs and Ralston argue that Moral Foundations Theory (MFT) provides some conceptual framing for this civil-military attachment: not only do political conservatives look favorably at the military for its values, but are themselves more likely to value "binding" traits like in-group loyalty as a social good.[16] While many of these in-group defensive patterns are detectable in attitudes about co-partisans, it would be particularly curious to find such a dynamic at work in attitudes about an institution with a decidedly non-partisan structure and code of ethics. Nonetheless, H3B accounts for the possibility that this process is at work, particularly among strong conservative partisans, influencing how new information about the military is received and processed.

This manner of processing would indicate a different cognitive mechanism among partisans with respect to the military's institutional performance. The broader trends identified in Figure 5.1 and in Chapter 4's analysis of media consumption would suggest that Republicans are more likely to look favorably on the military institution and might therefore be resistant to critical information of that same entity. We have other reasons to suggest why this might be the case through analyzing existing survey data. Figure 5.2 depicts the results of principal component analysis (PCA) of responses to the American National Election Studies (ANES) and Gallup annual institutional confidence surveys. PCA provides a method of dimensionality reduction, expressing variation across multiple responses in a few number of dimensions; we can visually observe how respondent answers to ANES "feeling thermometer" (0-100) and Gallup's confidence questions load on each of the first two principal components (PCs). By examining how specific institutions correlate in their factor loadings, we can draw surface-level inferences about how different partisans view these institutions.

The graphical depiction in Figure 5.2 using the 2012 ANES data (the last year that the military was listed for feeling thermometer measures) and the 2016 Gallup institutional confidence measures rendered in a numerical fashion. In the ANES data, we observe that the military's loading looks very different across partisan subgroups: for Democrats, it correlates strongly with other branches of government, whereas the military appears alongside partisan allies like the "Tea Party" for Republicans. A similar trend emerges in the Gallup data: both partisans express trust in the military in a similar fashion to the police, but this cluster among Democrats corresponds with institutions like the presidency, whereas the same military-police loading is closer to religious institutions among

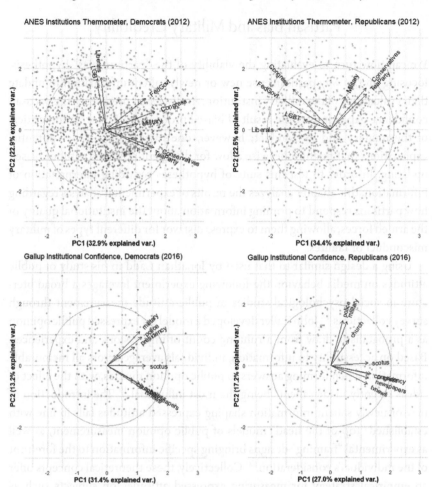

Figure 5.2 Principal Component Analysis of Institutional Affect/Confidence, ANES (2012) and Gallup (2016)

Note: Figure 5.2 depicts the results of principal component analysis (PCA) on the feeling thermometer scores for several institutions in US society according to the 2012 ANES (the last year ANES measured thermometer data on the military) and 2016 Gallup institutional confidence survey, broken down by partisan subgroups. First two principal components depicted for clarity. Unit circle denotes maximum value of factor loading for each institution's rating among these subgroups. American National Election Studies, 2012 (www.electionstudies.org).

Republicans. While not conclusive on their own, these points of analysis provide a strong intuition that conforms with larger trends in Republican partisan affinity for the military and its competency and trustworthiness.[17] If Republicans are more likely to see the military as an extension of the party "in-group," they may be more likely to engage in cognitive defense of the institution when exposed to negative information.

Partisan Bias and Military Credibility

We can now turn to evaluating the viability of the "partisan bias" hypothesis, focusing on the way partisans use new or newly salient information to update their evaluations of the military institution. As discussed previously, the partisan confidence gap is in part the result of biased processing of information critical of the military and its conduct; however, one must also consider potential explanations that might otherwise allow for divergent opinions without biased updating. In order to test this suite of hypotheses regarding interpretation of information, this chapter analyzes the results of experimental analysis regarding how partisans respond to priming information about the institutional quality of the armed forces, allowing them to express disfavor for different types of military misconduct or failures.

Using a design similar to that used by Jonathan Ladd in his study of public attitudes on media behavior, the following experiment leverages a broad literature in social psychological studies of public attitude measurement through survey collections.[18] John Zaller developed a model for expressed public opinion as a probabilistic draw from a running count of impressions and experiences. Based on accessibility to information, individuals average across all memorable information when forming answers to public opinion queries, with the effect of "ideas recently made salient" being the most influential.[19] The introduction of new or newly salient information shaping expressed attitudes falls in line with established "top of the head" models of public opinion measurement, as well as experimental "framing" designs bringing specific information to the forefront of the individual's consideration.[20] Collectively, these theoretical concepts offer an empirical strategy for measuring expressed attitudes on subjects such as institutional confidence. Experimental framing can raise the short-term salience of specific information in line with the "top-down" accounting of public trust, providing an opportunity to measure the effect of specific actions by the military on public confidence in that institution.

In this experimental design, individuals were subjected to updating information that increased the salience of institutional quality in the military. Respondents were drawn from a nationally representative opt-in panel conducted by YouGov in March 2017, resulting in a final sample of 1,000 individuals randomly assigned to one of four experimental conditions. Following a standard demographic battery, the *control* condition was asked two questions regarding their level of interest in news stories regarding US foreign policy and military operations, but unlike the treatment groups read no news stories or priming vignettes. This group served as the statistical baseline for confidence levels in three measured institutions—the military, the presidency, and the Congress—which were measured on an 11-point scale (with semantic Likert anchors) following the two news interest questions.

All respondents were prompted that the study was measuring the extent to which stories about security issues and the military were reaching the public. In the control condition, respondents were asked (1) if they actively followed news stories about US foreign policy and (2) about US military operations. Each of the other three treatment groups was respectively prompted with two news snippets describing stories related to the military that had occurred in the last several years and asked if they had heard these stories. All groups were then asked at the end to measure their level of confidence in the military, the presidency, and Congress, in order to prevent the respondent from clearly detecting the dependent variable of interest. The news stories given to each group were structured to vary the content of new information according to three classes of divergent preference criteria discussed previously. The first treatment group (*non-partisan*) was prompted with news stories that detailed partisan activity by retired military officers during the 2012 and 2016 presidential campaigns. The stories discussed large blocs of retired generals and admirals who had openly endorsed candidates Barack Obama, Mitt Romney, Donald Trump, and Hillary Clinton. This was designed to allow respondents to express preferences of military behavior in terms of non-partisanship and objectivity.

The second treatment group (*performance*) was exposed to two stories that detailed battlefield ineffectiveness or incompetence in the Iraq and Afghanistan wars, including a botched hostage rescue attempt by the Navy's SEAL Team Six in 2010 and the accidental bombing of a Medecins Sans Frontieres clinic in Kunduz, Afghanistan, in 2015.[21] These were designed to allow respondents to express preferences in terms of battlefield outcomes and strict performance criteria. Finally, the third treatment group (*professionalism*) was prompted by news stories that described ethical failures by the military institution, including a 2012 Defense Department report describing the firing of nearly 30 generals and admirals due to offenses ranging from sexual assault to misuse of government funds, and a story discussing the 2009 conviction of several US soldiers accused of the rape and murder of an Iraqi family in 2006.[22] This thread was designed to allow respondents to express preferences in terms of professional or ethical standards of conduct.

Evaluating the Preferences Hypothesis

The nature of this design allows for more specific testing of potential biased updating or the influence of divergent preferences. By varying the nature of newly salient updating information, we allow partisans to express their preferences in different ways, a flexibility that builds on past empirical efforts and offers an avenue for the possibility that a rational process may be at work if partisans simply have different conceptions of what type of military behavior is positive or negative.[23] If H3A accurately captures the operant process between partisans, Democrats and Republicans should meaningfully respond in a negative way to specific classes of military misconduct. For example, if one partisan group values battlefield effectiveness as a criteria for evaluation, but another places more stock in the professional integrity and organizational practices of the institution, then divergent opinions at the end of the updating process need not come from systematic partisan bias.

Despite this accommodation made by the design, the results indicate a profoundly asymmetric use of the new or newly salient information among partisans. Figure 5.3 reveals the change in expressed confidence in the military institution from the control condition by partisan subgroup, assessed using the respondent's identification on the three-point partisan identity scale. While Democratic respondents express marginal concern for partisan military activity, they indicate a more defined preference against military performance failures in the tactical setting and professional misconduct, where expressed confidence was reduced by 8% and 13%, respectively. These results seem to provide empirical replication

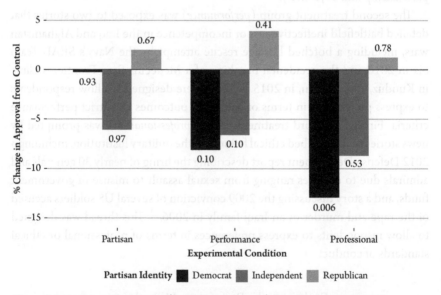

Figure 5.3 Experimental Results (Partisan Breakdown), YouGov—March 2017

Note: This figure depicts deviation in expressed confidence in the military institution as measured by the 11-pt scale in all experimental conditions. Respondent patterns broken down by identification into Democrat, Republican, and Independent subsamples based on self-identification on three-point partisan identity scale. Reported p-values reflect significance at 95% level for two-tailed t-test for difference in means between experimental and control subgroups. $N_{Total} = 957$

of the broader fluctuations we observe among Democrats in Figure 5.1, where confidence in the military institution dips in tandem with the most violent years of the Iraq War and the various strategic stalemates of the subsequent decade. If we expect negative information about battlefield outcomes or organizational failures to rationally result in reduced esteem for the military, Democrats and Independents seem to display this internal logic to varying degrees.

Republican response patterns, however, indicate no change in expressed opinion regardless of treatment condition. In all experimental states, Republican changes in confidence for the military institution were positive and statistically insignificant. This also seems to replicate the broader trend observed in Figure 5.1, where Republican confidence patterns seem unmoved by indecisive foreign wars and internal scandals that substantively affected Independent and Democratic levels of trust. Even though the design allows for Republicans to express different preferences from Independents and Democrats, no negative information about the military results in an updated expressed opinion. We might expect that a single treatment might be unable to substantively move public opinion about the military's institutional quality; however, the same treatment moved Democrats and Independents in a negative direction to a statistically significant degree, while Republicans remained unaffected. As a result, the unbiased learning process captured in the "Bayesian hypothesis" and tested in H3A finds little support with these findings.[24]

The results indicate that Republican respondents proved resistant to new negative information in their evaluations of the military, despite Democrats and Independents doing so. If there exists little evidence for H3A, what might explain the wide variation in updating across partisan subsets regarding common observation of the military institution? What remains is analysis of H3B: if certain partisans (in this case Republicans) are resistant to information critical of the military and express no clear yardstick for evaluating that institutional rationally, we have reason to suspect partisan biases may be at work. Whether by blaming military failures on political leaders rather than the armed forces, attributing misconduct to individual failures rather than organizational ones, or downweighting the value of the information because of its contrary narrative, we have strong reason to believe that even with available information, Republican respondents are interpreting information in a far more favorable fashion or polarizing against its message.

Evidence for Partisan Bias

The importance of potential partisan bias becomes clearer when analyzing the experimental results among strong partisans. Figure 5.4 depicts the percentage change in expressed trust and confidence in the military institution from the

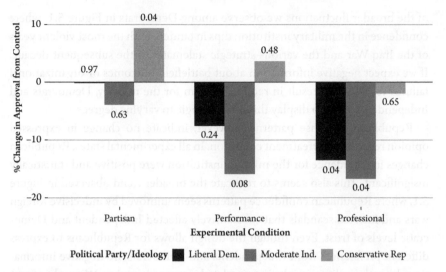

Figure 5.4 Experimental Results (Strong Partisan Breakdown), YouGov—March 2017

Note: This figure depicts deviation in expressed confidence in the military institution as measured by the 11-pt scale in all experimental conditions. Respondent patterns broken down by combined identification into Democrat, Republican, and Independent subsamples based on self-identification on three-point partisan identity scale and sorted political ideology as conservative, moderate, and liberal on a five-point scale. Reported p-values reflect significance at 95% level for two-tailed t-test for difference in means between experimental and control subgroups. $N_{Total} = 500$

control condition by sorted partisan groups. Moderate Independents are also included and remain a useful quantitative baseline for the expressed attitudes of individuals with less incentive for partisan biasing or an obvious desire to minimize dissonance with partisan narratives. At first inspection, we observe that sorted Democrats again trend much closer to the attitudes of Independents across the different treatment conditions. While unaffected by news of partisan military activity, they express less confidence in the military in response to news of professional misconduct (−13.4%). By comparison, moderate Independents expressed a similar distaste for battlefield failures (−15.8%) and ethical or professional scandals (−16.7%) when rendering updated impressions of the military's institutional credibility.

However, closer analysis of strong Republicans reveals a broader polarization than is observable in Figure 5.3 when pooling across the entire partisan subgroup. In addition to strong Republicans expressing no degradation in their evaluation of the military across treatment conditions, this group responded with a substantively and statistically significant *increase* in expressed confidence in the institution of nearly 10% in the *non-partisan* condition. This is particularly surprising given the ostensibly limiting "ceiling effects" one should expect from the conservative Republican control group's mean confidence level of 9.55 on an 11-point scale. This response indicates a defensive polarization away from the expected direction of the treatment and a dramatic departure from the processing that dictated the response of both moderate Independents and liberal Democrats. While these latter groups expressed a clear distaste for certain categories of military behavior, the sorted Republican subgroup actively increased its support for the same institution being evaluated by political out-groups.

These results present evidence for the assertions of the partisan bias hypothesis (H3B), that polarized motivated reasoning is affecting what should be a rational valuation of institutional performance. In addition to Republican respondents remaining largely unmoved by new information, the response pattern displayed by strong conservative partisans is indicative of a motivated counter-arguing of disconfirming information. This "backfire effect" is a well-documented trend in response to weak issue framing and among strong ideological partisans, particularly when introduced to negative information about political in-group members.[25] Past study on this phenomenon by David Redlawsk has found that in a "direct challenge to the notion of voters as rational Bayesian updaters," motivated reasoning led individuals to increase support for a favored candidate after receiving negative information about the candidate.[26] The response patterns exhibited in these experimental results indicate a similar biasing of new information, in an effort to counter-argue information that confounds pre-existing beliefs in favor of interpretations that support those beliefs.[27] It is telling that such a seemingly unexpected increase in strong Republican trust comes in response to information about military support to co-partisan political candidates, further highlighting the central role played by partisan identity in rendering their evaluation. In comparison, such knowledge did not affect strong Democrats or moderate Independents in their evaluation of the military institution.

This response pattern among Republicans is surprising in its reflexive defense of an outside institution, but makes more sense within the existing study of affective polarization and its associated biases. Not only has partisan identity been demonstrated to have strong social components that increase animosity regarding political out-groups, but these same mechanisms strengthen the defense of in-group members against disconfirming information, making rational evaluation of institutional quality unlikely.[28] The results of this experimental design indicate that Republicans have to a certain extent incorporated support for the military institution into the social fabric of their partisan identity, defending it as one would a co-partisan. Their defense of the institution in the face of negative information supports recent study that Republicans are more ideologically coherent as a group and that such "identity politics" are indeed much stronger among Republicans due to a lack of cross-cutting identities.[29] As discussed later this level of partisan bias risks compromising the ability of these partisans to objectively evaluate an institution's performance or to closely scrutinize the outcomes of militarized foreign policy ventures.

Additional support for the partisan bias hypothesis can be found by examining observational survey data as well, in cases where partisans observed a common set of updating information in dramatically different fashions. This process has manifested in a variety of ways, with different effects on expressed confidence in the military institution across partisan subgroups. In 2007, the deadliest year for coalition forces in Iraq, public confidence in the military hit its temporary nadir, with 69% of Americans expressing high confidence in the institution.[30] Mounting casualties, uncertainty over the success of the "surge" strategy, shifting leadership, and political divisiveness were compounded by decreasing public confidence in the accuracy of battlefield reporting. Between 2003 and 2007, Democratic confidence in the accuracy of battlefield reports from the military dropped from 78% expressing "a great deal" or "fair amount" to 32%. Republican confidence dropped as well, but three in four still had high confidence in reporting by the military. Instead, Republicans passed their distrust to the press, in whom only 29% of Republicans expressed high confidence, down from 81% in 2003. Half of Democrats, by contrast, maintained high confidence in the press reporting from Iraq.[31] In the midst of growing distrust about the military's wartime performance, Democrats attributed blame to the institution itself, whereas skeptical Republicans instead passed blame for inaccuracy to the news media. In addition to highlighting Republican distrust of competing media reports detailed in the previous chapter, this also sheds light on how updating information was rationalized to support a prior rather than influence an updated evaluation.

When military misconduct and accusations of large-scale sexual assault problems within the institution peaked in 2013, partisans again split over the nature of the problem and its proposed solutions. While half of Democrats directly attributed the reports of sexual assault to "underlying problems with military culture," nearly 70% of Republicans ascribed the incidents to individual acts of misconduct detached from the institution as a whole. When considering the best way of handling the problem, 58% of Democrats stated that Congress needed to directly intervene to change military law or strip military commanders of their legal authority. In contrast, a similar percentage of Republicans believed that the military should be left to handle the problem internally without outside interference.[32] Again, with partisans given similar information about negative military activity, these groups interpreted and employed that information in widely different ways. Conditional on both subgroups believing the factual nature of the information (a potentially weak assumption given the findings of the previous chapter), Democrats negatively updated their evaluation against the military institution, whereas Republicans drew fundamentally different interpretations that insulated the institution from more direct criticism.

These cases lend additional credence to the validity of the partisan bias claim, that skewed interpretations driven by partisan sentiment lead some to draw systemically more friendly or adversarial interpretations from the same information about the military. Though short of decisive inference, examination of the cognitive resources expended by partisans on either side can inform our understanding of the mental process at work. Taber and Lodge argue that the sort of disconfirmation bias predicted by H3B could manifest in those respondents taking "more time and cognitive resources denigrating and counterarguing attitudinally incongruent than congruent arguments."[33] Across treatment groups, we observe these patterns in a similar fashion. *Non-partisan* group Democrats and Republicans spent almost the same amount of time completing the survey. This is unsurprising as this experimental condition was where partisans actually expressed similar attitudes. However, Republican respondents in the *professionalism* and *performance* conditions spent on average nearly 20–25% more time completing the survey than their Democratic counterparts.[34] Again, though not conclusive in its own right, further study should examine this causal pathway more closely.

The fact that strong Republicans in this analysis exhibit a seemingly partisan bias in defense of a non-partisan institution is particularly curious and potentially damaging to preserving the non-partisanship of the military. Both the experimental results and observational survey data on military failures have shown Republicans are more likely to consider military misconduct a product of individual actors rather than large organizational flaws. These defensive patterns reflect a political tribalism among Republicans with respect to the military, conforming to patterns of in-group favoritism and partisan biases.[35] When confronted with the prospect of inaccurate information coming from the battlefield, Republicans were far more likely to blame the news media, while Democrats and Independents more directly charged the military itself. It is telling that just as military confidence has been consistently high among Republicans, an equivalent pattern is found among Democrats for the mass media.[36] Though it may be overly simplistic to ascribe partisan affiliations to either institution writ large, Republican distrust in a liberal-favored institution like the mass media has the dual effect of discrediting new information and striking at a perceived partisan opponent. As such, Republican trust in the military would not be a purely rational valuation, but rather an expression of partisan attitudes. Collectively, these patterns provide strong reasons to suspect that the partisan "gap" in confidence is likely to continue.

Collectively, the results of the experiment and the validation it finds in macro-trends of public trust in the military promote strong support for a cognitive bias born of partisan affiliation when interpreting information regarding the military institution. While political Democrats and Independents seem to utilize new or newly salient information in the expected fashion, updating their opinions of the organization based on knowledge of negative actions or behavior, Republicans seem to defend the institution as they would an extension of their own political party. Given the non-partisan nature of the military, this is particularly puzzling and normatively precarious. If partisan confidence in military elites is seen by politicians to be highly durable, the latter may increase appeals to the military as a political device for electoral gains or policy support, bringing the military institution closer into the political fold and risking a dangerous erosion of civil-military balance.

The implications of these results are significant for our understanding of politicizing behaviors and the circumstances which can lead to them. If the military is seen as a reliably favorable partisan ally (or unfavorable opponent) by a portion of the population, this can create incentives for civilian politicians to engage in forms of *passive* politicization or using the armed forces as a polit-ical "prop" for partisan gain. What's more, the belief that the military is more proximate to one political party may create the misperception among partisan leaders that the armed forces will be favorable to its activities. When partisan establishments take on increasingly extreme positions or policies, the resulting *relative* politicization can reveal to individuals the "daylight" between the military and the major parties, knowledge of which can change how the public views both institutions.

Sources of Politicization

If partisans diverge on how they perceive the military, what kinds of behav-ior they expect from it, and even the news they receive about it, what does this environment mean for potential sources of politicization? In the previous chapter, we observed how media reporting and third-party rhetoric about the military might shift the public observer along some ideological space, leaving the impression that the institution, failing to keep pace, has drifted away from them. This *aspect* politicization focused on the public's relationship to the military as influenced by actors generally outside the major parties; however, evidence that those same individuals are likely to respond very differently to information about the military once they receive it sets the conditions for other types of politicizing activity. If partisan political elites recognize that the military institution can be a conduit to credibility with their constituencies, knowledge of the patterns observed in this chapter's analysis may create incentives for *passive* politicization: namely, the use of military actors, iconography, and implicit support for partisan political gain.

As identified by many prominent civil-military analysts, the Trump administration period provides a fruitful source of illustration for this class of politicizing
behavior. Both political upheaval and norm violations during this period, according to Peter Feaver and Richard Kohn, saw civil-military policy-making "strained
close to the breaking point."[37] The administration's attitude toward existing civil-
military norms and processes, as well as the outsized role that military figures
played in some of the it's most dramatic moments repeatedly set the conditions
for various forms of politicization.[38] Pauline Shanks Kaurin argues that such
a period obliges consideration of "unprincipled principals" in the relationship
between civilian leaders and the military, and how the administration's turbulent
civil-military record prompts a re-examination of subjective control in US civil-
military relations.[39] This is not to suggest that other presidential administrations
have always refrained from using the military for partisan political gain. On the
contrary, the temptation to use military actors or icons as political "props" has
been a persistent feature of electoral politics. However, this period provides a
wealth of valuable examples of *passive* politicization in particular, which can take
on a variety of forms.

First, perhaps the most readily observable form of passive politicization that
occurred during this period included direct appeals to the military as a partisan
political constituency. In a speech to servicemembers stationed at MacDill Air
Force Base in February 2017, Trump remarked on the outcome of the recent
presidential election stating: "We had a wonderful election, didn't we? ... And I
saw those numbers, and you liked me and I liked you. That's the way it worked."[40]
These types of direct invocations regarding the military's support as a partisan
voting constituency were not rare. Trump publicly incorporated the military as
part of a supportive base of "the tough people," including "Bikers for Trump"
and the police.[41] The normative problems this variety of politicizing behavior
presents for the preservation of a non-partisan military ethic are manifest: this
form of rhetoric can engender in the public the belief in a military captured
by partisan institutions or beholden to specific partisan "in-groups." In its most
extreme form, this type of passive politicization can influence how civilian
leaders are likely to envision the employment of the military itself, a prospect
Golby reviews thoroughly in his discussion of the Trump administration's legacy
of politicization.[42] Following the initial protests in the wake of George Floyd's
murder, Trump encouraged Minnesota Governor Tim Walz on social media to
confront the "thugs," stating explicitly that "the Military (sic) is with him all the
way."[43] Taken broadly, political rhetoric depicting the military as partisan ally is
perhaps the most readily observable form of passive politicization.

Second, additional patterns of passively politicizing behavior include the
use of military iconography or imagery for partisan political gain. The Trump
administration period again offers several useful examples of this behavior in

practice. The president quickly realized a key campaign promise to effectively bar immigration from seven Muslim-majority countries in January 2017. However, the president would sign the controversial "Muslim ban" in the Pentagon's "Hall of Heroes," a memorial to military servicemembers presented with the Medal of Honor.[44] The incorporation of the location's symbolism, as Kori Schake notes, "to associate the military with his policies," represents a more implicit form of passive politicization.[45] Similar concerns voiced by civil-military scholars emerged over the president's decision to involve high-profile military hardware in the country's 2019 Independence Day festivities. The move again raised concern over the passive politicization of the military through the use of military iconography. Retired Army Lieutenant General Dave Barno remarked, "This looks like it's becoming much more of a Republican Party event . . . and it's unfortunate to have the military smack dab in the middle of that."[46] Given the limited direct exposure between the public and the armed services, the military's ability to maintain a non-partisan image to the public becomes a considerably harder task if public-facing icons or symbols are appropriated for partisan advantage. As Chapter 7 will discuss, the use of military iconography, gear, and symbols by right-wing extremist groups compounds this problem, one drawn into sharpest relief after the deeply partisan causes of the January 6 attack. By incorporating such symbolism into partisan political strategies, the prospect of passive politicization increases even without conscious agency by military actors.

Third, while the most normatively problematic forms of politicization depicted in the parallax model are likely to occur when actors engage outside their institutionally sanctioned roles, politicization can still happen even when those same individuals act within the bounds of their authority. The Trump administration's tenure included numerous instances where the military institution found itself in partisan political waters as a result of legal, if controversial, executive decisions. These policies frequently involved the military in controversial issue areas due to their strong partisan utility amongst Republicans, such as immigration, LGBTQ rights, and foreign policy. Civil-military scholars pointed to the administration's pre-midterm election deployment of nearly 5,000 active-duty servicemembers to the country's southern border as a clear case of politicizing both the active force and the military budget, which had to be repurposed to circumvent Congressional blockage of the border wall.[47] Representing a traditionally evangelical voting constituency, the president abruptly ended the Obama administration policy allowing for the open service of transgender servicemembers, citing the "tremendous medical costs and disruption" such individuals posed to the military.[48] Overruling several ongoing and adjudicated military justice cases, Trump issued executive clemencies and pardons for several servicemembers tried or convicted for various acts of misconduct, to include war crimes while deployed.[49] After extensive lobbying by Republican members of Congress like Duncan Hunter and Fox News personalities like Pete Hegseth, themselves both former military officers, Trump effectively reversed the military's own judicial findings, remarking on social media that, "We train our boys to be killing machines, then prosecute them when they kill!"[50] While these decisions reside within the institutional powers and responsibilities of the presidency, they can still achieve politicizing effects by blurring the lines between the partisan political agenda of the president's party and the implicit sanction of the military institution.

As detailed in previous chapters, none of these forms of politicization can be considered in isolation; instead, they are likely to contribute to or emanate from other forms involving other key actors. The knowledge among partisan political leaders that the military institution exists within the social identity construct of their "in-group" constituency may not only set the conditions for *passive* politicization, but contribute to *relative* politicization as well. This form of politicizing activity occurs when elite-level polarization increases dramatically and party positions or rhetoric take on relatively extreme values compared to historical positions. When this occurs, even a military institution that has remained generally fixed (or modified its policy only slightly) may seem to have shifted dramatically. In reality, the partisan political ground has moved underneath its feet. If partisan leaders believe the military to be a ready-made constituency, it may adopt more extreme positions believing the institution will likely go along with it or fail to admonish it. When this expectation isn't met, the extremity of the party may expose the "daylight" between the two institutions, creating an impression to the partisan observer of a military hostile to their "in-group" interests.

One example of this concept in practice occurred following the events of January 6, 2021, when violent rioters attacked the Capitol in Washington, DC, during the validation of the 2020 election results. The following week, Army General and Chairman Mark Milley authored a letter to military servicemembers with the Joint Chiefs of Staff decrying the violence as illegal and assuring the joint force that president-elect Joe Biden would be sworn in as the next commander-in-chief, despite the propagation of factually inaccurate beliefs that the election was invalid.[51] While the circumstances of the 1/6 attacks (and the letter itself) were nearly unprecedented and accompanied the deployment of thousands of National Guard soldiers in response, the military's support of peaceful transitions of power in the American political system is hardly a controversial position, nor one that had ever been imperiled enough to oblige military speech on the issue.[52] However, the result was a considerable gap between the political position of a partisan institution and the stated position of the military's senior leaders. An

Ohio National Guard officer garnered media attention for openly decrying the letter as "seditious," remarking on social media that the military service chiefs were "either scared or in bed with the left."[53] Such reporting on this "relative" gap increased the possibility that to a co-partisan observer, the military was likely to appear as hostile to an important "in-group" belief in a fraudulent election, which even months later a majority of Republican partisans maintained.[54]

A similarly relative-politicizing event occurred during the fallout from the "Unite the Right" white supremacist event in Charlottesville, VA, during the summer of 2017, when military organizational values again appeared in sharp contrast to vastly different positions set among the incumbent party over denunciation of extremist groups. Counter-protesters at the event clashed with attendees, including many visibly displaying white supremacist and neo-Nazi flags and icons, seeking to prevent the removal of statues depicting leaders of the former Confederacy. The resulting violence resulted in the death of one of the counter-protesters when Alex Fields rammed a crowd with his car, further elevating the event to national visibility. In the following week, numerous military leaders, to include the service chiefs and various military units, publicly denounced the violence and the extremist ideologies of the white supremacists involved, mainly through comments issued on social media. However, the comments contrasted sharply with those of the president; instead, many interpreted them as surprisingly mild admonishments over the incident, offering that both "blame" and "very fine people" were present on "both sides."[55] The contrast between these two sentiments is an illustrative example of relative politicization. The military's position on organizational values with regards to extremism had not meaningfully changed. Instead, the remarks were newsworthy because of their notable contrast to the position adopted by the White House, of which a majority of the public disapproved and a plurality believed put white supremacists on "equal footing" with their opponents.[56] Nonetheless, the chiefs' statements were instead reported as a "rare rebuke" of and "apart" from Trump's, as well as a "near historic development for U.S. civil-military relations."[57] In reality, a relatively extreme position revealed the distance between a partisan guidepost and the military; as a result, an observer may have drawn similar conclusions about a military "rebuking" its commander-in-chief.

Passively politicizing behavior can also set the conditions for its active counterpart, by placing military actors in precarious partisan situations. One example of this behavior in practice was the noteworthy extent to which military actors were appointed as high-ranking officials in the administration.[58] As a general trend, military appointments to posts typically occupied by civilian experts have increased across both parties. However, though high-profile ex-military appointments are not new, the administration placed such figures closer to the political functions of the executive branch, while the president regularly referred to them as "my generals" and serving officers as "my military."[59] The installment of recently retired Marine General James Mattis as Secretary of Defense was met with consternation from political opponents concerned about the preservation of civilian control of the military, concerns that continued with Joe Biden's nomination of former Army General Lloyd Austin to the same post.[60] Civil-military scholars similarly admonished the appointment of retired Marine General John Kelly to the post of White House Chief of Staff. David Barno and Nora Bensahel argued that "having a retired general serve in such an unabashedly partisan role" risked conflating the military and civilian spheres altogether, eroding the trust between the two.[61] Even this early in the administration, Daniel Drezner specifically questioned if American confidence in the military had reached a "tipping point," speculating as to whether "Trump's elevation of the military to such a high-profile role" imperiled the public's trust in the institution.[62]

While the passively politicizing effects of these appointments alone may have run afoul of existing civil-military norms, further active politicization can follow when these military figures are forced to engage in the partisan political space as a result. A risk for partisan politicians relying on military figures for credibility or the implicit support of the institution comes due when those same figures no longer serve the interests of the administration. A partisan constituency's attachment to military figures—the very reason for installing them—may make it difficult to untangle without incorporating the same type of affectively polarizing language to discredit them. Before Mattis's exit as Defense Secretary, Trump remarked to the *Wall Street Journal* that he feared the retired general was "sort of a Democrat," a partisan jab which would manifest fully two months later when Mattis departed citing irreconcilable differences with the administration's policies toward US allies.[63] Kelly's departure followed a turbulent series of clashes with the president; nearly a year later, Kelly would openly admonish Trump's conditioning of security aid to Ukraine for partisan political purposes, over which Trump was impeached in early 2020.[64] Army Lieutenant General H. R. McMaster, the administration's pick for National Security Advisor following the inauspicious departure of retired Army Lieutenant General Mike Flynn, decried the failure of the administration to properly address the threat of Russian aggression shortly before his departure at Trump's insistence.[65] If reliance on military appointments can increase the likelihood of passive politicization, this practice can also make active politicization more common by placing those same military actors into increasingly partisan political environments.

Certainly the Trump administration has no monopoly of passively politicizing activity. On the contrary, political speeches with partisan overtones are not a new feature of the civil-military landscape, nor is the use of military symbolism for partisan political utility the sole province of a single faction. The unexpected appearance of two soldiers from American Samoa during the 2020 Democratic National Convention elicited consternation from many observers concerned over the use of the military during such a partisan event, leading to an internal military investigation.[66] Following Republican Congresswoman Majorie Taylor Greene's 2021 speech at the Conservative Political Action Conference in which she mistakenly referred to the American territory of Guam as a foreign country, the territory's Congressional representative sent uniformed Guamanian servicemembers to Greene's office to "say hi."[67] Such episodes reflect *passively* politicizing activity of this nature is observable across time and different political institutions. The impact and frequency of such events are therefore likely to vary along these two dimensions as a result. One of the main contentions of this book is that politicization of the military is likely to be perceived in very different ways depending on one's partisan identity and the valence of the military's behavior.[68] But as continuing research into civil-military friction has shown, the Trump period provides an illustrative wealth of politicization cases, particularly the passive and relative varieties enabled by the high partisan affect for the military examined in this chapter.

As previously discussed, the intent to politicize does not need to be present for politicization to occur. Virtually any directive from the commander-in-chief is likely to reflect the worldviews and preferences of the executive, which are themselves likely to favor their own partisan institution over another. When it comes to external actors politicizing the military, the magnitude of politicization can be just as much a product of the public's perception as the actor's intent. As the last chapter of this book will outline, increased passive politicization is not just attributable to intentional use of the military as "political prop," but a lower threshold of issues wherein the public is polarized. However, partisan political calculations, informed by a knowledge of social attachment or rigidly positive affect for the military among the partisans in society, are likely to continue creating incentives for politicization.

The results of both Chapters 4 and 5 jointly communicate important features of the civil-military landscape. First, that partisans are likely to acquire very different information about the military, a reality that is compounded by the affinity among partisans for curated media environments that limit disconfirming information. Second, partisans are likely to use new information—particularly critical information—about the military in very different ways depending on their social affect for the institution and cognitive biases incumbent to individual-level partisanship. Finally, these two patterns collectively set the conditions for additional forms of politicizing behavior. If partisan leaders are aware of these biases among the public, it can lead to using the military as a "prop" for political gain (passive politicization), exposing large ideological differences between the military and extreme party positions (relative politicization), or even putting military actors in partisan environments where their behavior is likely to compromise the military's non-partisan ethic (active politicization). In short, civil-military sensibilities about non-partisan activity by the military may be weaker than previously theorized.

In the next chapter, we explore this idea directly: are individuals likely to sanction military actors caught in this web of politicization? In order to analyze the strength—or weakness—of civil-military norms amongst the public, we look at one representative arm of the military institution that has garnered increased attention from scholars and policy-makers alike: retired military officers.

6

Delusions and Grandeur

Weakening Civil-Military Norms and Politicization

Many of the results reviewed so far may convey seemingly contradictory ideas: the military voice can be a particularly effective one in some contexts, but the credibility of that voice to the public is likely to be filtered through a complicated web of pre-conceptions and cognitive biases incumbent to affective partisan polarization. Paradoxically, the elite community most trusted by the public is the one (at least theoretically) most normatively proscribed from using that influence in political activity. However, the ubiquity of military elite voices in the political sphere has nonetheless increased, in part due to retired military officials whose post-service careers include media commentary, political activism, or legislative lobbying. Recent scholarship in military politicization has suggested that continuous interventions by these figures into politics could be met with a broad public devaluation of the institution's credibility.[1] The central assumption of these arguments is that military credibility is conditional on its image as a non-partisan entity. However, while the necessity of this "non-partisan norm" is nearly a consensus among civil-military scholars, the proposition that the public considers this norm important has been subjected to surprisingly little empirical scrutiny. Despite increasing political activity and partisan activism by both active and retired officers, public confidence in the armed forces remains (in the aggregate) the highest among institutions in US society, even as democratic "backsliding" remains a noteworthy concern for political observers.[2]

In the previous chapter, we found that exposure to negative institutional behavior by the military was unevenly received by partisans of different allegiances. Democrats and Independents were influenced by knowledge of battlefield failures or ethical scandals, while Republicans were generally resistant to negative informational updates. Interestingly, few were influenced by the knowledge of partisan activity by members representative of the institution. What does this mean for the strength and salience of traditional civil-military norms governing the involvement of the military in partisan affairs? In this

Dangerous Instrument: Political Polarization and US Civil-Military Relations. Michael A. Robinson,
Oxford University Press. © Oxford University Press 2023. DOI: 10.1093/oso/9780197611555.003.0006

chapter, we explore this puzzle in particular: how does political activity by military elites influence public perceptions of their credibility and that of the military institution? Review of the extant literature would suggest that the public can respond to such information in one of several ways. First, they can respond as a *principled* public that uniformly sanctions elite sources that are perceived as violating the professional norm against such activity. This pattern, reflective of the civil-military normative consensus, would indicate that individuals lend less credibility to partisan sources and do so objectively, with no bias towards their own political ideology. Second, they can respond as an *indifferent* public that does not allow political activity to update their impressions of military elite credibility in a significant way. Such a response would indicate that repeated exposure to military figures in partisan politics has already eroded the salience of this norm to the point where additional information about violations is unlikely to matter much.

However, this chapter argues that while the *indifferent public* underestimates the influence of military political activity, the *principled public* overestimates the objectivity of the audience. As a result, there is strong evidence for a third hypothesis: the *partisan public*. This image of the public departs from the previous two in that it is neither principled nor objective; individuals selectively view military partisans as less credible not for violating a professional norm, but for adopting a politically contrary position. In this framework, military credibility is not conditional on adopting non-partisan attitudes, but rather on adopting the "correct" partisan attitudes. Focusing on retired military elites in original survey experimentation, this research effort finds greater evidence for this version of the public, indicating a weakening of a non-partisan norm considered to be an important structural component of democratic societies. The final section of this chapter will discuss how such an environment of partisan polarization both incentivizes further active politicization and limits the reach of military elites in broadcasting information.

This chapter will proceed as follows: first, it outlines the fundamental conflict between the normative demands of civil-military scholarship and the predictions of the body of work in public opinion formation. The purpose of this section is to demonstrate that while military elites satisfy many of the theoretical criteria to be credible sources in providing political information, that civil-military theory broadly considers such activity to be normatively and functionally problematic. Second, it argues that an objective norm against political activity by the military may be weaker than previously contemplated and offers a typology for the different attitudes the public may adopt in response to knowledge of military politicization. This section will outline the potential response patterns empirically measured by my survey instrument, in whether such norms against a partisan political military are objectively strong (*principled public*), objectively weak (*indifferent public*), or selectively weak (*partisan public*). Third, it will incorporate the results of original survey experimentation designed to measure how military politicization (1) influences the public's estimation of the endorser's credibility and (2) influences the perceived credibility of the larger institution. Whether the public adopts indifferent, principled, or partisan attitudes in each domain has decidedly different and significant implications for civil-military relations. Finally, this chapter will provide illustrative context for this state of civil-military norms amongst the public, one which sets the conditions for *active* politicization and providing incentives for retired officers to wade into partisan political waters, despite the potential implications for the institution.

Political Activity and Military Credibility

In a complex information environment, a lack of expertise among the public on certain issues should inform how credible expert sources are chosen. As discussed in Chapter 3, communications scholars have found that when issues are personally important, individuals "centrally" attend to the substance of the argument; however, when the information environment is distracting or the issue is exceedingly complex, these same individuals "peripherally" attend to the attributes of the source itself.[3] Political issues like military intervention, foreign policy, or international agreements fit into this mold of complexity, where individuals may rely more on attributes of the source of information than on its substantive content.[4] Among the characteristics most closely tied to source credibility are *trustworthiness* and *knowledgeability*, which collectively speak to the source's credibility in the eyes of the individual; elite communities with high public esteem and subject matter expertise should be the most influential, particularly in technical or complex political issue domains.[5]

However, it is worth considering that for public entities like the military, this credibility is likely to be a product of two different levels of concern: the individual source and the broader institution. The relationship between both levels of credibility has been studied at length in marketing research governing the effectiveness of corporate sponsors and their public brand. The extent of elite *endorser credibility* from an individual source operates in conjunction with the *corporate credibility* of the larger institution that the individual represents.[6] Both the perceived expertise and trustworthiness of the individual source and its parent organization act as reinforcing or supportive forces in persuading the public about the reliability of their claims.[7] As such, this analogous literature in business research envisions both trustworthiness and expertise as significant insofar as they influence attitudes towards the endorser, the corporate firm, and "purchaser intent," linking perceived credibility to a higher likelihood that the "product" will be accepted by the public.[8]

We can extend this logic to public opinion formation on political issues, in which an individual source and its institution operate in the roles of endorser and corporate entity, respectively. Just as corporate endorsers and firms seek to develop public credibility in order to increase purchaser intent, so too do political elites look to maintain the same public credibility in an effort to persuade individuals in society to adopt specific policy preferences. As discussed later, this more comprehensive framework for understanding public perceptions of elite credibility allows for a better method of examining changes in trustworthiness and expertise among specific elite communities like the military. The notion that an institutional brand may inform the influence of individual military actors is all the more important given empirical research by Jim Golby and Peter Feaver that suggests the public is unlikely to be able to identify specific military figures or ascribe to them a personal brand of credibility.[9] As an institution with high levels of public confidence, the military and its elites should serve as powerful voices of influence, combining broad public appeal, subject matter expertise, and a professional reputation as trustworthy dispensers of information.

Military Credibility and the Non-Partisan Norm

As reviewed earlier in this book, the "normal" theory of civil-military relations in the United States reflects a general aversion to a "political" military of any type.[10] However, while an important line of inquiry in this chapter is how partisan activism might harm this normative framework, this is not to suggest that a politically knowledgeable military is fundamentally undesirable. It is therefore important to distinguish between the types of political competency that satisfy the two "imperatives" and those that violate them. The complexities of modern warfare have made striking the delicate balance between the functional and societal imperatives increasingly difficult. While a politically "neutral" military may be desirable from the societal perspective, a military that does not understand the political dimensions of warfare quite clearly violates the functional imperative. This philosophy springs from one of Clausewitz's most significant observations, that political concerns are inseparable from war: "its grammar, indeed, may be its own, but not its logic."[11] A politically "neutral" military, therefore, is quite different from a politically illiterate one. More recent scholarship has observed the tension between these two imperatives and the involvement of the military in "politics." For example, Risa Brooks argues that a lifetime of professional socialization to being "apolitical" can leave military officers unaware of the political nature of their work, which paradoxically "alleviates the impulse for self-scrutiny about what it means to be apolitical and what the behavioral and intellectual bases are for such a stance."[12] A politically competent military may well satisfy a functional imperative for effectiveness in wartime; however, an ostensibly partisan one violates the societal imperative for civilian control and the corresponding norm against partisan activity. As a result, it is important to distinguish political awareness and understanding among military elites from active participation or agenda-setting in that process.

This is not to suggest the line between good faith military behavior and politicizing partisanship has become any easier to detect, particularly among those no longer bound by regulatory constraints on speech. Though this "non-partisan" norm has been broadly codified in the legal proscription against serving military servicemembers publicly advocating for a political cause or candidate in person, technological advancement in communications has rendered many of them dated.[13] The availability of social media platforms has made the open proliferation of partisan political attitudes from military servicemembers less costly and more threatening to traditional civil-military norms.[14] According to Richard Kohn, this gap between normative standards and the law is particularly pronounced among retired military elites, who, unencumbered by such regula-tions and acting as political appointees, media commentators, policy activists, or business lobbyists, nonetheless "represent the culture and the profession just as authoritatively as their counterparts on active duty."[15]

This pattern is the predictable convergence of the two trends identified at the beginning of this book. The reality that one of the most trusted institutions in US society is the same one normatively discouraged from engaging in partisan politics is prone to create paradoxes or negative incentives for political actors, some of which we have already observed. Numerous scholars have expressed concern that the very credibility the military enjoys among the public is inex-tricably tied to its ability to remain a non-partisan institution. Jason Dempsey argues that a failure by military elites—both active and retired—to refrain from political activity will result in a loss of trust from the public and an increas-ingly politicized force.[16] In addition to compromising the veracity of military advice provided to civilian leaders while in uniform, Dempsey argues that the very credibility that provides military advice its value will be degraded by a broader society that only imbues trust in the military because "it is seen as being above the political fray."[17] Mackubin Owens similarly argues that while the military must be politically literate for its functional role in warfare, a politicized military "will lose legitimacy in the eyes of the American people" and hamper its ability to functionally contribute to the maintenance of national security.[18] However, this conditional relationship between military credibility and non-partisanship requires a principled audience for whom the non-partisan norm is salient and strongly held. While there appears to be considerable theoretical consensus on this point, there is little empirical validation for the argument that the non-partisan norm is salient among the public; as the next section will discuss, there is instead strong reason to believe that this norm has weakened considerably.

Challenging the Normative Consensus

Given the theoretical focus on its existence, the notion that the non-partisan norm is strong among the American public is one that demands some empirical exploration. As it stands, this theoretical consensus hinges on a key assumption about the public: that it objectively views civil-military norms as salient and that these norms are strong enough to override partisan calculations on how they perceive the military. Several patterns in the contemporary environment call this assumption into question. First, there is strong reason to believe that the public is not as principled or normatively grounded as scholars believe. Figure 6.1 depicts levels of public approval for select surveys items in the World Values Survey (WVS), the 1999 Triangle Institute for Security Studies (TISS) survey fielded by Peter Feaver and Richard Kohn, the 2013 YouGov Civil-Military Attitudes survey conducted by Schake and Mattis, and a 2015 YouGov survey on military interventions in politics.[19] Between WVS waves in 1995 and 2020, US respondents believing that "having the army rule" was a good or fairly good "way of governing the country" went from 6% to 21%, with even larger support among "millennials."[20] Though still a minority opinion, this constitutes a significant increase in support for illiberal governance in clear violation of not only the military's non-partisan norm, but broader democratic norms of civilian governance.[21]

The YouGov survey conducted by Schake and Mattis similarly uncovers a weakening of traditional civil-military norms against political or activist behavior. Compared to respondents asked the same question in the TISS survey, the percentage of respondents believing that leaking material to the press was an acceptable action by military officers in response to "unwise orders" increased from 5% to 19%.[22] Golby, Cohn, and Feaver draw attention to this trend, noting that one of the most "disturbing" findings was the high levels of individuals who seemed accepting of "improper civil-military norms."[23] The 2015 YouGov survey audience also revealed weak resistance to the notion of domestic political intervention: nearly 30% of respondents would support the military taking control of the federal government, a figure which increases to 43% in the event of a perceived constitutional violation. More than half (53%) agreed that "active duty military personnel should be active in politics if they want to be." These shifts in public attitudes regarding the proper role of the military in politics and society provide strong reason to believe that traditionally held norms of the "non-partisan" military may be less salient than previously believed.

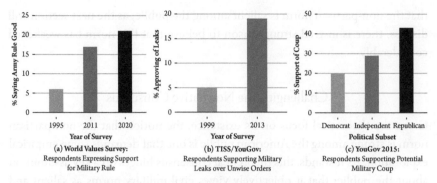

Figure 6.1 Degradation of Civil-Military Norms among the Public

Note: This figure depicts changes in select civil-military norms across several historical surveys, the World Values Survey (1995, 2011, 2020), the Triangle Institute for Security Studies Survey (1998–1999), the Schake/Mattis YouGov Survey (2013), and a YouGov survey exploring attitudes on domestic political military intervention (2015).[24] Figure 6.1(a) depicts the percentage of WVS respondents who answered "fairly good" or "very good" to the question: "I'm going to describe various types of political systems and ask what you think about each as a way of governing this country. For each one, would you say it is a very good, fairly good, fairly bad or very bad way of governing this country?" Figure 6.1(b) depicts a comparison of the percentage of respondents who approved of military officers responding to unwise orders by deciding to "leak the material to the press to alert others to this problem." Figure 6.1(c) depicts the percentage of respondents in the 2015 YouGov surveying answering "yes" to the question "Is there any situation in which you could imagine yourself supporting the US military taking over the powers of the federal government," displayed by partisan identity on a three-point scale.

Second, there is also evidence to suggest that the public may not exactly be less principled than previously theorized, but instead more systematically indifferent. It is worth noting that the American public's growing esteem for the armed forces has unfolded alongside a similarly decades-long escalation in the frequency of military activism, particularly from the retired community. One of the most visible ways this activity has manifested is in the incorporation of retired military personalities to partisan election campaigns. Jim Golby, Kyle Dropp, and Peter Feaver, examining the 2012 election season, found that while public knowledge of this political activity—in violation of theoretical norms—had little influence on public trust in the military, it did make individuals more likely to feel that this activity was appropriate, potentially indicating that "such norms are obsolete."[25] In this view, repeated exposure to military involvement in partisan politics may have already influenced perceptions of the institution; as a result, new information about politicization might be less meaningful in updating attitudes. A weakening of the non-partisan norm not only questions the theory of a principled public, but suggests the public may be indifferent enough that political activity has no effect on expressed confidence in the military source.

But partisan activity exceeds simple endorsements for political candidates. Media commentary and political activism by military elites have also become more popular in political debates over a wide range of issues. Across several administrations, retired general officers have engaged in collective activism over defense policy, security strategy, organizational practices, or budgetary priorities.[26] Retired military officers commonly serve as analysts and commentators on cable news, pen independent editorials on foreign policy and security strategy, and have been appointed to increasingly central and partisan roles in government.[27] A more targeted analysis of the effects of political activity on military credibility requires including knowledge of these types of behaviors among the public as well.

In short, the civil-military relations literature offers two potential theories of public response to political activity by military elites: a principled and norms-based public in which credibility hinges on the perception of non-partisanship, and an indifferent public toward which political activity has little effect on public trust. While recent trends in public opinion and normative sentiment call the first into question, testing the second requires more precise measurement that explores not only institutional-level effects, but the micro-foundational influence of partisan behavior on the credibility of individual elites. As the following section will outline, there is reason to believe that both of these characterizations of the public are insufficient. As such, this chapter argues a third potential image of the public, neither normatively grounded nor indifferent, but rather decidedly partisan.

Theorizing Public Response to Military Politicization

This chapter builds on the findings we have uncovered so far by examining how partisan political activity by military elites effects public perceptions of politicization and credibility. In order to address this question, we can draw from existing research a series of testable hypotheses that envision different pathologies for the public in responding to knowledge of partisan military activity. Each of these images serves either to validate existing assumptions about the public's preferences or to challenge these same assumptions. In addition, this effort examines how each of these depictions of the public would manifest along two measurable levels: (1) how knowledge of political activity by a military elite source affects impressions of that source's credibility and (2) how this knowledge influences the perceived credibility of the broader military institution. Both patterns have independent and interactive implications for the quality of civil-military relations and the future of potential military politicization.

The Principled Public

The first theoretical image of the public is that most commonly embraced by the existing civil-military scholarship, which is termed here the *principled public*. In this framework, military credibility indeed depends upon the preservation of a non-partisan image; the public embraces the norm of a non-partisan military and the necessity of such an institution to the proper functioning of democratic society. In line with the basic assumptions of the formative civil-military theorists, the military is viewed as a fundamentally martial and conservative organization whose institutional subordination to civilian leadership—regardless of partisan identity—is essential to the preservation of both democratic norms and effective government.[28] As discussed previously, considerable theorization in this regard has more recently predicted that partisan activity will directly damage military credibility due to public backlash.[29] Knowledge of political activity by representatives of this institution should therefore be greeted by broad disapproval from the public, regardless of the position espoused by these representatives.

This notion is rooted in a generalized image of the public as an objective audience with fixed collective preferences in favor of non-partisan military behavior. Partisan behavior or the perception of being a tertiary partisan battlefield may therefore degrade public trust and make the professional advice of uniformed officers less credible to civilian leaders and the public.[30] This sentiment has been more recently voiced by former Chairman of the Joint Chiefs of Staff Martin Dempsey in reference to remaining non-partisan: "That's how we maintain our trust with the American people. The American people don't want us to become another special interest group. In fact, I think that confuses them."[31] The distinguishing feature of the *principled public* is that it responds with generalized distrust for the military speaker—and potentially the institution—to perceived partisan activity. This erosion in credibility, however, is not sensitive to the ideological substance of such activity; instead, this image assumes an audience that shares a common preference for the military to remain out of politics, even if such figures were to engage in behavior favorable to one's partisan "in-group."

The testable implications of the principled public form the theoretical baseline of this analysis and test of the consensus opinion in the civil-military relations literature. An idealized example of this pattern is depicted in Figure 6.2(a); the perceived credibility of partisan military elites is objectively diminished, while partisan identity plays no significant role in their evaluation. In this framework, civil-military norms against such behavior are both highly salient and broadly accepted. As such, the principled public would respond according to the predictions of the following hypothesis:

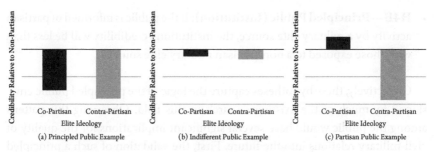

Figure 6.2 Idealized Representations of Credibility Effects

Note: This figure depicts idealized examples for each of the proposed hypothetical images of public response to knowledge of military partisan activity. The conditions "Co-Partisan" and "Contra-Partisan" refer to the ideological direction of activism by the hypothetical military elite in reference to that of the individual. The y-axis depicts the change in perceived public credibility in either condition relative to a non-partisan military elite with no known partisan activity. Figure 6.2(a) depicts the principled public, with uniform sanctioning of the source across conditions. Figure 6.2(b) represents the indifferent public, with little response to information across conditions. Figure 6.2(c) shows the partisan public, combining both a significant sanctioning of contra-partisan elites with a negligible or marginal increase in co-partisan credibility.

- **H4A—Principled Public (Elite Source)**: If the public is informed of partisan activity by a military elite source, that source's credibility will be less than that of a non-partisan military elite source.

The principled public hypothesis incorporates the same assumptions regarding the normative value of a non-partisan military that much of the civil-military scholarship has advanced. Compared to a non-partisan source with the same expertise and qualifications, the public would objectively devalue the credibility of a partisan source due to his or her participation in partisan behavior that contradicts established norms. More specifically, we should expect to see a reduction in the perceived trustworthiness of the source relative to a non-partisan source. However, if the effects of partisan behavior are particularly strong, the principled public may even reduce its estimation of the source's expertise, even if held constant across elite profiles.

At the second level of analysis, we can apply a similar logic by which exposure to such partisan sources aggregates to attitudes about the larger military institution. While it is reasonable to expect the influence of partisan activity by a single elite source to have more modest effects on the individual's judgment of the broader military establishment, the principled public hypothesis predicts that the public will generally reject this behavior as normatively inappropriate. This assertion is strongly represented in civil-military studies exploring the partisan identity of the military itself and the implications of a perceived partisan shift by the institution.[32] Once again, the public is envisioned as a principled whole that broadly embraces a shared preference for a non-partisan military:

- **H4B—Principled Public (Institution)**: If the public is informed of partisan activity by a military elite source, the institution's credibility will be less than with those exposed to a non-partisan military elite source.

Collectively, these hypotheses capture the logic of the principled public envisioned by much of the existing research in this field. Observing this pattern among the public would have several significant implications for the quality of civil-military relations into the future. First, the validation of such a principled audience would confirm a long-held belief that not only is the non-partisan norm salient among the public, but that partisan or ideological variation among the public itself is not a significant factor in updating perceptions of military elite credibility. This would also confirm the existence of a mutually valued political norm that has escaped polarization or self-serving partisan attitudes. Second, the appearance of such a sentiment among the public would indicate that the incentive structure for military politicization is, as Golby et al. argues, "a self-negating tool."[33] Military elites seeking to leverage the high public esteem of the institution for their own purposes would instead find an audience unreceptive to their messaging.

The Indifferent Public

A second possible image of the public is starkly different in terms of its observable implications. While the *principled public* broadly embraces the non-partisan norm, the *indifferent public* is generally unmoved by violations, either because the norm is not salient or the audience believes it is already invalid. As previously discussed, there is strong reason to believe that, across several areas of interest, civil-military norms in society have weakened with regards to the proper role of the military institution in politics. Extant research suggesting that political endorsements can have localized effects in swaying public opinion, but not significantly negative effects on estimations of public trust in the institution are indicative of this vision of the public.[34]

The basic intuition of the *indifferent public* is that military elite participation in partisan activity only marginally effects military credibility and that weakened or non-existent norms regarding such activity contribute to indifferent attitudes. There are several reasons why such patterns might be observed. First, the broader trend of low confidence in traditional elite or expert communities may be drawing individuals to attend to sources they perceive as credible, regardless of the propriety of their engaging in public opinion-shaping. Second, it is possible that the public already views the military and its elites as influenced by partisan attitudes, making additional information about such activity relatively unpersuasive.[35] In either case, the indifferent public's estimation of military elite credibility is neither significantly strengthened nor weakened due to partisan activity, but rather so commonplace that knowledge of norm violation is not new information.

Accordingly, the observable implications of this image at the individual (endorser) level are quite clear. Figure 6.2(b) reflects an idealized example of the indifferent public, with partisan behavior resulting in insignificant effects on perceived credibility relative to a non-partisan source. If civil-military norms are generally weaker than previously theorized, then being informed of political activity by a specific military elite source should elicit a minimal response in accordance with the following hypothesis:

- **H4C—Indifferent Public (Elite Source):** If the public is informed of partisan activity by a military elite source, that source's credibility will not be significantly different than that of a non-partisan military elite source.

This hypothesis predicts that individual sources who engage in partisan political behavior will not suffer noticeable damage to their perceived credibility with the public. It is possible that such a pattern, even if it appears in the aggregate, could be localized to separate political subgroups in society. For instance, evidence of an indifferent public may be present among partisans of one identification, but not another. Alternatively, it may be the case that an embrace of such indifference is indicative of a more generalizable degradation of the non-partisan norm across the public. In either scenario, the incentive structure for continued military elite influence would be very different than that predicted by the *principled public*: elites would not need to worry about losing credibility with the public when engaging in political debates.

Such an incentive structure for partisan activity would be even more durable if the public rendered indifferent attitudes regarding the larger military institution. An indifferent public at the endorser level (H4C) would make political activity a low-cost enterprise for individual elites; however, a similar attitude at the organizational level would make such activity even less costly. The common-pool credibility problem predicted by many civil-military scholars does not exist in this framework, as neither the institution nor the individual suffers in terms of credibility with the public for the partisan activity of representative elites:

- **H4D—Indifferent Public (Institution):** If the public is informed of partisan activity by a military elite source, the institution's credibility will not be significantly different than with those exposed to a non-partisan military elite source.

These hypotheses capture the broader logic of the indifferent public. While the principled public indicates that the non-partisan norms of civil-military theory are salient and viewed objectively, patterns reflective of the indifferent public are representative of substantially weakened norms regarding the same behavior. In this framework, public perception of trustworthiness and expertise will remain largely unchanged in response to information about partisan activity, showing that such behavior is not informative to the public nor offensive to its normative sensibilities. Such weakened norms pose little obstacle to increased future military politicization.

The Partisan Public

The third image of public response to military political activity proposed here is the *partisan public*. In this framework, individuals sanction military elites for partisan behavior not because it is normatively prohibited, but because it is politically incongruent to their partisan identity or ideology. This hypothesis departs from the previous two images in several significant ways. First, while the *principled public* takes as given a strong normative consensus among the public against partisan military behavior, the *partisan public* hypothesis assumes that these norms are weak or non-existent. Second, the *partisan public* engages in selective sanctioning of elite credibility based on partisan leaning, rather than the objective patterns of credibility loss predicted by the *indifferent* and *principled* public images. In short, this vision of the public accounts for the likely impact of partisan tribalism on evaluations of military credibility in response to partisan activity: individuals only sanction military partisan activity if it benefits the other "side."

Additionally, this image allows for the prospect that the partisan public may not only selectively lower their estimation of elites on the other side of a political debate, but may actually increase their perceptions of credibility among military elites who endorse an opinion closer to their own. This assertion draws on existing study on social polarization and the biasing effects of shared partisan identity on objective thought processes.[36] It is reasonable to expect that erosion of contra-partisan elite credibility will outweigh any potential increase in co-partisan credibility in magnitude. This is largely in line with past study that has found that out-group animosity is both strongest when phrased in partisan terms and substantively more powerful than in-group favoritism.[37] In its simplest form, the *partisan public* weighs military elite credibility as it would any other source of information, not according to principled adherence to civil-military norms, but according to partisan like-mindedness:

- **H4E—Partisan Public (Elite Source)**: If the public is informed of partisan activity by a military elite source, that source's credibility will be less among those of the opposite partisan identity, compared to the non-partisan source. Source credibility among like-minded partisans, however, will be unaffected or will increase.

The observable implications of this hypothesis can take on several forms. Figure 6.2(c) depicts the most likely manifestation of the *partisan public*, wherein elite credibility is asymmetrically sanctioned by the public based on the individual's partisan or ideological leaning. The *partisan public* assumes a subjective audience; sanctioning of credibility is limited to contra-partisan elites, rather than the objective sanctioning observed among the principled public. The prediction of H4E is therefore that individuals will devalue the credibility of contra-partisan elites, with marginal effect on their assessment of co-partisan credibility. Particularly strong indicators of this hypothesis include co-partisans evaluating the military source as *more* credible for having engaged in such behavior, relative to the non-partisan source.

Extended to the institutional level, the *partisan public* should similarly weigh the military's credibility in the context of the source's direction of partisanship, not the normative implications of that partisanship. As before, it is reasonable to expect these effects to be more modest than at the endorser level; however, the same general pattern should emerge. Military partisan activity is likely to result in lower levels of confidence in the military, so long as that activity does not redound to the benefit of one's partisan institution:

- **H4F—Partisan Public (Institution)**: If the public is informed of partisan activity by a military elite source, the institution's credibility will be less among those of the opposite partisan identity, compared to those exposed to the non-partisan source. Institutional credibility among like-minded partisans, however, will be unaffected or will increase.

In both hypotheses, total expressed credibility should be much lower when the military actor in question and the individual are in partisan conflict. Both testable implications expect this to manifest mostly as a shift in perceived *trustworthiness* of the source or institution. However, particularly strong partisan effects may even influence the perceived *expertise* of these sources relative to the non-partisan source, even if the qualifications of both profiles were held constant. This extreme version of the partisan public not only changes their impression about the more subjective reliability of the source, but also the seemingly more objective experience or knowledgeability of that same source based on partisan thought processes. This image of the public not only depicts a weak state of civil-military norms across individuals, but suggests that the environment may be incredibly ripe for *active* politicization.

Testing Elite Credibility and Partisan Activity

In order to test the validity of these hypothesized images of the public—and by extension, the strength and salience of the non-partisan norm—the remainder of this chapter uses the results of original survey experimentation designed to measure how partisan political activity by military elites affects public perceptions of credibility. The survey was fielded in November 2017 to an opt-in panel of 1,038 respondents acquired through the survey firm Qualtrics; respondents were prompted that the survey's intent was to ascertain public attitudes on several policy issues under debate. Before answering these questions, however, respondents were randomly assigned to one of three conditions and asked to view a profile of a prominent elite who had offered public opinions on these issues. In all three categories, respondents were exposed to a profile of a retired military officer that contained information on six broad attributes. The first three included *overseas experience, academic qualification,* and *command responsibility,* attributes that speak directly to the expertise of the profiled elite and that were fixed across all treatment conditions. The profile also included information about post-retirement activity, such as *media presence, partisan alignment and endorsements,* and *policy advocacy or criticism,* which were intended to provide an image to the public of the elite's affiliation and level of partisan involvement.

These latter three attributes varied according to the assigned treatment condition of the respondent. In the baseline and functional control group, *non-partisan,* respondents were exposed to the profile of a retired senior military commander with multiple combat tours, command experience at the highest levels, and several academic degrees, whose post-retirement activity included historical research, non-partisan academic council membership, and a lack of political endorsements for major party candidates. In the second and third groups, respectively categorized as *activist left* and *activist right,* the elite's military experience and qualifications were the same as the non-partisan; however, their post-retirement activity included prominent media presence on cable news networks, joining major party campaigns as national security advisors, and public advocacy or opposition to administration policy. These profiles were developed using attributes from several prominent military commentators and political activists, with the post-retirement attributes designed to draw maximum contrast to the non-partisan category and ensuring the respondent has a clear picture of the elite's partisan alignment and behavior.[38]

After being exposed to the elite's profile, respondents were asked two four-question batteries measuring the perceived credibility of (1) the individual source and (2) the source's organization, in this case the military. Both of these measurement scales are adapted from an analogous literature in business research. As previously discussed, the concepts of "endorser" and "corporate" credibility in this field can be effectively applied to the realm of political information. The credibility of individual elite voices or "endorsers" and their organization's "corporate" reputation are just are important to the sale of a political message as they are to a business's sale of a product. The connection between these two measures has been well-established as reinforcing and influential, with impressions about endorser credibility affecting larger "attitudes-toward-the-brand" that shape corporate or organizational reputation.[39] This design adapts the same general logic to assess not how perceptions of credibility affect attitudes towards an endorsement (termed "attitude-toward-the-ad"), but rather how negative information measurably affects these perceptions of credibility.

In order to capture these attitudes of endorser credibility, the design of this chapter adopts a strategy similar to Ronald Goldsmith et al. which uses a modified version of the Likert scale measures of individual *expertise* and *trustworthiness* developed by Roobina Ohanian in measuring credibility.[40] The measure of individual source expertise asked respondents to offer a seven-point score on the degree to which the source is "experienced" and "knowledgeable"; similarly, respondents were asked for the same measurement on the source's perceived level of being "trustworthy" and "reliable" as an analogous measure for the source's trustworthiness. These attributes were selected from a longer list provided by Ohanian's study and based on their high internal construct validity and in order to reduce survey fatigue and unnecessary redundancy. This four-question battery provides three dependent variables: (1) a 14-point additive scale for expertise, (2) a 14-point additive scale for trustworthiness, and (3) a collective 28-pt scale for total source credibility of the individual military elite.

We can build a similar measure for corporate entities through an additive construct for measuring institutional credibility, building on past research regarding corporate reputation.[41] Similar to the measurement for individual credibility, this scale is built from two four-question batteries that gauge attitudes on institutional expertise and trustworthiness, respectively. After registering individual elite credibility attitudes, respondents were then asked for a seven-point, semantically anchored Likert measurement on the degree to which they agreed or disagreed that the military "has a great amount of expertise" and "is skilled at what they do" (expertise) and that the respondent trusts the military and believed it "makes truthful claims" (trustworthiness). This again provides three measures for subsequent analysis: (1) a 14-point additive scale for institutional expertise, (2) a 14-point additive scale for institutional trustworthiness, and (3) a collective 28-point scale for total institutional credibility. Finally, respondents were asked for their opinions on two issues under debate, after exposure to the position of the military elite being reviewed. These included the level of support for a pre-emptive strike on the North Korean nuclear program, in which the military elite is on record as an advocate, and a federal budget proposal for reducing funding to the State Department and foreign aid, for which the military elite was a vocal opponent. These measures were not important to the analysis, but rather provided a motivating logic for the individual to assess the credibility of the military actor offering an opinion.

Data Analysis

So how does partisan activity by retired military officers affect the public's estimation of their credibility? As previously discussed, this is a level of analysis that has escaped close empirical scrutiny and speaks more directly to the individual incentives for military elites to engage in partisan activism. The images of the public described by H4A–H4E have distinctly different features and significant implications for the strength and salience of civil-military norms among the public; furthermore, the validity of these hypotheses depends not only on the broad trends among the public, but how these patterns emerge among established partisans. Figure 6.3 depicts the aggregate effects of partisan activism on perceptions of individual elite credibility compared to the non-partisan retired officer. Immediately clear is the statistically and substantively significant decrease in the credibility of activist military elites across each metric. Partisan military elites with left- and right-alignment suffered a 3.4% and 9.1% loss to their total assessed credibility, respectively.

This initial visualization can also help to draw out some important observations about the effect of partisan activity on judgments of credibility. First, the right-activist military partisans are subject to a significantly higher loss in

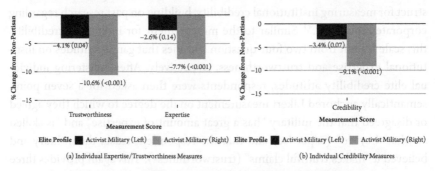

(a) Individual Expertise/Trustworthiness Measures   (b) Individual Credibility Measures

Figure 6.3 Loss of Credibility for Military Activists, Aggregate Results

Note: This figure depicts the change in perceptions of expertise, trustworthiness, and credibility for military partisans in reference to the non-partisan elite profile. This measure pools across all respondent attributes including partisan identity and education. Posted figures reflect magnitude of effect and p-values for two-tailed test for difference in means between activist categories and the non-partisan reference category. Respondents assembled from opt-in panel from Qualtrics during November 2017, N = 1038.

credibility from the general public than activist-left partisans. This trend was apparent across both the expertise measure (-7.7%) and the trustworthiness measure (-10.6%) and is partially attributable to the negative way in which political independents responded to knowledge of partisan military elite activity. Second, there is a surprising decrease in the perceived *expertise* of the elite source $(-2.6\%$ and -7.7%, respectively) despite the source's qualifications remaining fixed across conditions. Interestingly, partisan military retirees are generally viewed as less knowledgeable or qualified than non-partisans. A cursory look at the results might suggest that the public is generally principled in its rejection of such behavior; however, closer inspection shows that this is not the case.

Analysis of these effects across partisan subgroups in fact provides little support for the notion of a principled public. Figure 6.4 depicts the same change in measured expertise, trustworthiness, and total credibility for military activists relative to the non-partisan profile, but organized according to the partisan identity of the respondent. These results, which show consistently selective and asymmetric sanctioning of contra-partisans, provide strong evidence for the predictions of the partisan public hypothesis (H4E). Across both partisan groups, these results are strikingly similar and substantively significant. Among Republicans, activist-left military elites experienced significant reductions in both perceived trustworthiness (-22.6%) and expertise (-17.2%), losing substantial overall credibility (-19.9%). However, these same measures for activist-right elites were marginally positive and statistically insignificant among those same Republicans. A similar pattern is observable among Democrats: activist-right military elites suffered lower perceived trustworthiness (-18.4%) and expertise (-15.5%), resulting in a sizable erosion in total credibility (-17.0%). Perhaps even more indicative of the partisan public than their Republican counterparts, Democrats not only sanctioned contra-partisan retirees, but expressed a statistically significant *increase* in the perceived trustworthiness $(+8.0\%)$, expertise $(+5.6\%)$, and overall credibility $(+6.8\%)$ for co-partisan activist-left military elites.

This strong asymmetry in response reflects the expected patterns of the partisan public (H4E). Individuals strongly sanction the credibility of contra-partisan military elites, while the reliability of co-partisans is either unaffected (Republicans) or increased (Democrats). The difference in magnitude reflects the predictions of previous study in partisan affective biases, in which out-group animosity is a more potent force on political perception than in-group favoritism.[42] In short, once the aggregate treatment effects are analyzed conditional on individual partisan identity, there is comparably little support for either the principled (H4A) or indifferent (H4C) publics. Instead, we find more evidence for a partisan public: it is difficult to claim that the audience normatively rejects partisan involvement by retired military actors if they only

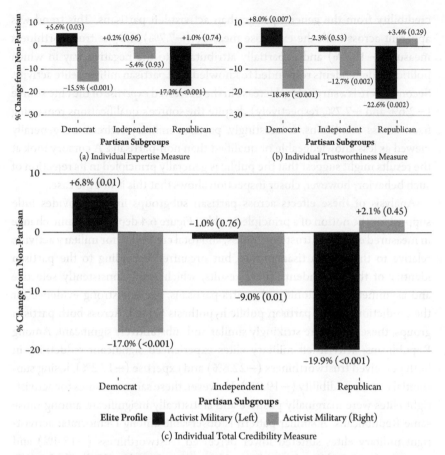

Figure 6.4 Loss of Credibility for Military Activists, by Partisan Identity

Note: This figure depicts the change in perceptions of expertise, trustworthiness, and credibility for military partisans in reference to the non-partisan elite profile, according to self-identification on three-point partisan identity scale. Posted figures reflect magnitude of effect and p-values for two-tailed test for difference in means between activist categories and the non-partisan reference category. N_{Dem} = 402, N_{Ind} = 367, and N_{Rep} = 269.

respond negatively to behavior that runs afoul of their own partisan sensibilities. At the individual "endorser" level, these results suggest that retired military activists should expect to lose credibility for engaging in partisan politics—but only with those who disagree with them anyway.

The second dimension of this analysis is the impact of exposure to such partisan sources on *institutional* credibility. As previously discussed, the significance of "corporate credibility" on the influence of individual representative elites may be significant; Barbara Lafferty and Ronald Goldsmith argue that "the impact of the endorser, even if highly credible, will not be as important as the credibility of the company" when rendering opinions about that organization's trustworthiness and expertise.[43] Of particular interest in this analysis is the reverse effect: how attributes of individual representative elites might influence attitudes about the organization. Civil-military scholars that warn against the politicization of the military elite frequently focus on the institutional ramifications of such activity, including the prospect of a significant common-pool problem if partisan activism results in a loss of institutional credibility rather than individual sanctioning.[44]

The sequence of the survey makes the partisan activity and behavior of the individual elite "newly salient information," providing a useful opportunity to allow such calculations to influence attitudes about the broader institution by bringing this information to the "top of the head."[45] In order to evaluate the image of public attitudes about the institution, this instrument includes a similar analysis using the previously described corporate credibility measures. As in the individual-level analysis, the aggregate results are more balanced, with exposure to left- and right-aligned activists resulting in a modest but statistically significant reduction in the overall credibility (-1.6%, -2.8%) of the military institution. However, closer inspection of the general results that accounts for the individual-level partisanship of the respondent reveals less principled indicators of the public's normative sensibilities.

Figure 6.5 depicts this change in measurable expertise, trustworthiness, and overall credibility of the military institution among the same political subgroups. Though more modest in size, exposure to contra-partisan military elite activism translated into similar effects as we observed at the individual level. Democrats exposed to activist-left elite profiles found the military marginally more credible ($+1.4\%$); however, those exposed to activist-right profiles found the same institution less trustworthy (-6.4%), less qualified (-4.1%), and less credible (-5.2%). A reciprocal trend emerges among Republicans, who found the military less trustworthy (-7.7%) and credible (-5.5%) when exposed to activist-left profiles relative to the non-partisan condition. These trends are comparable in magnitude and inverse in direction, largely in line with the predictions of H4F. Similar to the results at the endorser level, there is little support for the other hypotheses as the effect on co-partisan credibility is marginal (in opposition to H4B) and substantively significant (against the predictions of H4D).

Collectively, the results present strong support for the partisan public hypothesis. Individual elites lose substantial credibility among the public when engaging in partisan behavior, but only among those on the opposite side of the political debate. These findings also challenge the notion of a principled audience with an objective consideration of the non-partisan norm. Instead, military elites with established partisan records are viewed as less trustworthy—making political messaging more difficult to a substantial portion of the public—and less qualified, even when these objective facts about the source were held constant.

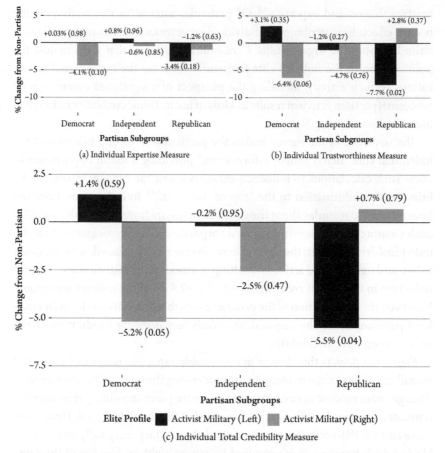

Figure 6.5 Loss of Credibility for Military Institution, by Partisan Identity

Note: This figure depicts the change in perceptions of expertise, trustworthiness, and credibility for military partisans in reference to the non-partisan elite profile, according to self-identification on three-point partisan identity scale. Posted figures reflect magnitude of effect and p-values for two-tailed test for difference in means between activist categories and the non-partisan reference category. $N_{Dem} = 402$, $N_{Ind} = 367$, and $N_{Rep} = 269$.

However, this effect is compartmentalized to individuals on the other side of the military actor's partisan identity. This provides a strong basis to believe that partisan identity is a critical determinant in public attitude formation about the acceptability of military involvement in political affairs. Recent survey research by Ronald Krebs, Robert Ralston, and Aaron Rapoport has found that this is an important individual-level discriminator; the findings of my experiment not only conform to this idea, but also to their assertion that civil-military norms are much weaker among the public than previously believed.[46] What's more, these results conform with recent work by Golby and Feaver suggesting that military figures openly weighing in on divisive issues could redound to the detriment of the wider institution in terms of the public's trust.[47] If the public is indeed this partisan, the conditions are present for the normalization of politicizing activities.

Creating an Environment for Politicization

Collectively, evidence for the partisan public from these results presents a significant challenge for civil-military theorists. The weakening of political norms among the public has seemingly reached into attitudes regarding the proper place for military elites in the political discourse. As a result, the weakened state of the non-partisan norm revealed here offers a rebuttal to the argument that military credibility is conditional on the appearance of non-partisanship. While this design focused on retired military elites rather than serving officers, it is exactly these ex-military figures who have the ability to leverage public esteem for the armed forces in public messaging, doing so with growing visibility.[48] The increasing frequency and acceptability of this behavior creates a different environment of incentives: while the individual elite risks losing credibility with contra-partisans, they also have the ability to gain credibility with a like-minded, if narrower audience. However, the results of this analysis suggest that while a common-pool problem may exist, the incentive structure for military elites to avoid politics is not as self-defeating as previously theorized.[49] Instead, there is strong reason to believe that military elites can garner increased credibility and influence—or at least not lose them—among a select and politically like-minded audience, losing influence only among those on the opposite side of the ideological spectrum. While this environment may deter those seeking a broad audience among the public, it would have no such effect on those trying to cultivate a political "afterlife" to their career, seeking favor with an major partisan establishment, or searching for a suitable base for policy activism.

Military elites can replicate these favorable demographies by tailoring political audiences through digital media. In order to illustrate this point, this chapter also incorporates data collected on the social media follower networks of several military elites. As thoroughly studied by Heidi Urben, social media platforms have become an increasingly popular mechanism for military servicemembers to communicate political information; as such, this section examines the ideological identity of the followers that military elites draw based on their level of activism.[50] This process leverages the principal assumptions used by Pablo Barbera in modeling political ideal points through Twitter data. Individuals incur a cost by deciding to receive information from specific sources through "following," both in terms of minimizing cognitive dissonance and in the opportunity cost of forgoing access to competing information; in short, "these decisions provide information about how social media users decide to allocate a scarce resource—their attention."[51] While Barbera uses follower network information for Bayesian analysis of elite ideal points, the distributions themselves are of specific interest here in understanding the audience attracted by certain military elites. In a similar fashion, this section uses the political ideal points estimated through the CFScore measurements based on campaign finance contributions developed by Adam Bonica, a metric for ideological measurement that has demonstrated strong internal validity and adaptive use over traditional roll call measures.[52] Using this ideal point measurement for political elites, we can construct ideological distributions for the follower networks of different military elites.

Figure 6.6 depicts the distributions of these military elite follower networks on a single ideological dimension provided through the CFScore measure, from −1.5 (most liberal) to 1.5 (most conservative), with collection occurring in late 2017 and early 2018.[53] Perhaps unsurprisingly, active duty officers (italicized) had decidedly balanced distributions, indicating access to a broad political audience. As partisan activity by uniformed officers is the most closely scrutinized and easily detectable, such centrist follower networks conform to expectations. Similarly balanced military elite accounts include those of the Joint Chiefs of Staff and retired Chairman Martin Dempsey, who has cultivated a noteworthy individual brand of non-involvement in partisan political matters.

However, these distributions become increasingly skewed towards a more narrow audience as elites become more involved in political opinion-shaping. Just as the previously discussed experimental conditions took care to draw a strong contrast between different types of post-retirement media exposure, policy activism, and political endorsements, so too do we observe that activity along these dimensions draws an increasingly partisan follower network. For substantive comparison, data collection included the distributions of elected officials (in bold) serving during the time of collection whose principal pre-election careers were military service, in order to demonstrate a theoretical "upper bound" for perceived partisanship by military elites. For balance, members of both parties in both houses of Congress (Senators Tammy Duckworth (D) and Tom Cotton (R), and Congressmen Seth Moulton (D) and Ryan Zinke (R)) are included. Retired officers who have since taken posts in academia, such as Yale senior fellow Stanley McChrystal and former Fletcher School of Law and Diplomacy dean James Stavridis, possessed slightly less centrist distributions, though they maintained access to a generally broad audience.

Military elites serving as media commentators or security analysts on major cable news networks, such as Mark Hertling (CNN), Jack Jacobs (MSNBC), Barry McCaffrey (MSNBC), Morris Davis (MSNBC), and Jack Keane (FOX), instead possessed some of the more partisan follower audiences in the sample.

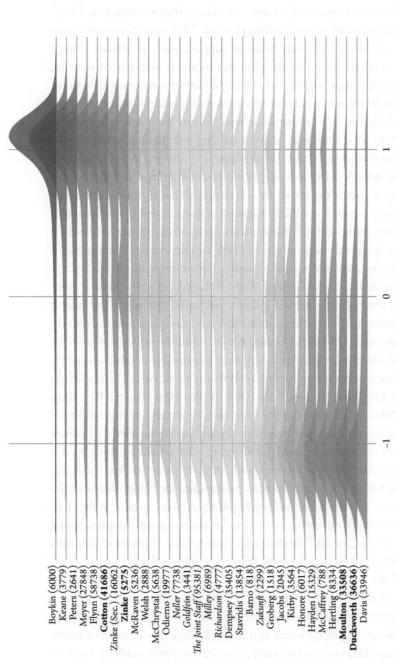

Figure 6.6 Military Elite Follower Network Distributions (CF Score Ideology)

Note: This figure depicts the ideological distributions of military elite Twitter follower networks, measuring political ideal points based on Bonica's CF Score measurement of other elected officials followed by the same users. Height of distribution re-scaled based on distribution maximum values. Darker coloration indicates more extreme mean values for the distribution. Bold-faced military elites indicate elected officials whose principal pre-political careers were as military officers. Italicized elite profiles indicate active-duty serving figures at time of collection. Figures depicted in parentheses are counts of ideologically assessed users who followed at least two political officials, not a count of the entire follower base. Profile information gathered between October 2017 and March 2018.

Retired military officials vocal on specific issue domains drew similar follower networks. These include Russel Honore, the former commander of Hurricane Katrina relief efforts who criticized Trump administration efforts in Puerto Rico following Hurricane Maria, and Jerry Boykin, the former leader of the Army's Special Forces Command, whose "incendiary rhetoric regarding Islam" generated significant controversy in military circles.[54] Advocacy for specific issue domains with established partisan bases of support, such as climate change policy, religious evangelism, or immigration may be just as influential in drawing a partisan audience as more traditional political endorsements or contributions.

Military elites who have found post-retirement service as political appointees can attract similarly one-sided audiences as well. Former National Security Advisor Michael Flynn drew a follower network strikingly similar to elected Republican officials on the same side of the ideological spectrum. In the time since his firing as National Security Advisor, Flynn became an increasingly partisan figure, speaking at events organized by adherents of the "QAnon" conspiracy theory and advocating for the military's seizure of government in the fashion of the 2021 Myanmar coup d'etat.[55] Normatively egregious actions of this sort far outstripped nearly any other retired officer in the sample, even if others garnered similar quantitative distributions of followers. For example, former NSA and CIA chief and retired Air Force General Michael Hayden, as well as several other retired officers, drew slightly skewed follower networks toward the left side of the political spectrum, though through far more commonplace political speech. Hayden was a frequent critic of the Trump administration's relationship with the US intelligence community and management of Russian cyber intrusion, going so far as to caution serving intelligence analysts to "think twice" before taking assignments in the White House.[56] Finally, it is also clear that military elites with high visibility—even without the high rank of general or flag officers— are capable of garnering partisan audiences through activism. Medal of Honor recipients Dakota Meyer and Florent Groberg, though relatively junior in rank and responsibility, demonstrate this potential. Meyer appeared on Fox News segments in support of Trump administration policies and its relationship with the media. Groberg, a "self-described lifelong Republican," was a speaker at the 2016 Democratic National Convention and a public supporter of the presidential candidacy of Hillary Clinton.[57] Both figures attracted distributions of followers more representative of elected partisans than active-duty officers.

Analysis of the social media environment helps to provide some understanding of how some retired military elites are responding to the incentive structure suggested by this chapter's experimental results: namely, that these figures can cultivate highly coherent and tailored audiences of support rather than mixed groups likely to sanction their entrance into partisan affairs. Furthermore, examining platforms like Twitter provides insight into a form of media "echo-chamber" development that was not investigated in Chapter 4's look at portrayals of the military institution through traditional media. While, as Pablo Barbera concedes, the "self-selected minority" of Twitter users constitutes a small sample relative to the American electorate, it is cross-sectionally diverse and allows for measuring the partisan appeal of non-political figures, such as military officers.[58] Across the spectrum of measurable military elites, increased political activity results in ideologically narrower audiences. At the highest levels of media presence and partisan activism, these military elites are indistinguishable from elected politicians in terms of the public audience they attract. As the experimental results demonstrate, it is possible that co-partisans who attend to these types of military elites may even view them as more credible than non-partisan or contra-partisan elites. However, this comes at the cost of access to a broad audience in shaping policy preferences, with potentially negative consequences for the ability of this expert community to influence public attitudes on policy.

The uneven and selective nature of the partisan public's response to political activity represents a departure from the previously theorized assumptions of a principled public. The latter assumes an objective audience, in which individual elites engage in political behavior to the detriment of the very institution that provides their credibility; taken in repeated interventions, partisan activity that "trade[s] on the reputation of the active force" results in decreasingly credible military elite voices across the whole of society.[59] However, the partisan public presents a different incentive structure. A similar common-pool problem of credibility exists, but rather than individuals negatively leveraging the institution's credibility, politically active military elites can potentially increase their favor among like-minded partisans, damaging institutional credibility only among those on the other side of the political debate. The existence of narrow and ideologically coherent social media follower networks and tailored media environments, in addition to the experimental results of this analysis, demonstrate that the partisan public reflects an environment susceptible to *increasing* military politicization, rather than the self-defeating logic of the principled public.

Sources of Politicization

These results regarding public attitudes on military engagement in partisan politics indicate a landscape potentially ripe for increasing forms of *active* politicization. In Chapter 3, we observed examples of this concept in the form of targeted military speech on specific issue areas or even media leaks from active-duty officials over foreign policy. This chapter has expanded our understanding of the sources and consequences of active politicization, particularly by retired military officials, in an environment where public distaste for partisan political activity by such figures is not so readily rejected out of hand. As a result, there are two likely sources of active politicization this climate might engender from retired military officers weighing an entrance into the political arena.

First, the environment is likely to create politicizing pressures by incentivizing retired military actors to purposefully leverage their former institution's credibility with select partisan audiences. This category of behavior involves when retired military figures intentionally "choose a side" in partisan skirmishes and repurpose public esteem for the institution in an effort to advance one party's political prospects over another. If a traditional understanding of the public presumed that such activity was likely to be sanctioned by a broad audience, the knowledge that it is instead likely to be rewarded by a narrower audience could influence how military retirees assess risk and reward for engaging in partisan political activity. This type of opportunistic behavior can take on several forms, ranging from the mild to the more normatively egregious.

In its more recognizable form, this type of active politicization is most likely to manifest in endorsements for partisan political candidates or even military figures using institutional regard for the military to run as candidates themselves. Since their inception during presidential elections, retired military endorsements for candidates have only grown in frequency and volume in the intervening years, exploiting a new "political gray area" where the line between normative propriety and individual freedoms are harder to disentangle.[60] However, political campaigns now make use of bloc retired military endorsements as regular currency during election cycles and tout the support of recognizable retirees as evidence of implicit backing from the country's favored institution. The 2016 and 2020 election cycles featured retired military officers as nominating convention speakers, individual high-profile endorsers, or members of bloc-letters supporting or opposing specific candidates for office. Research on military endorsements has found that they are both unlikely to move partisan attitudes on voter intent and likely to be an attempt at group solidarity with other retirees than ideology advancement.[61] Nonetheless, this invocation of military experience reflects a more intentional form of active politicization, attempting to positively impact the prospects of one partisan institution over another.

These forms of endorsement or opposition need not occur within the context of electoral cycles to involve retired military officers in partisan skirmishes. Individual or bloc messages can communicate opposition or support to existing policy while incorporating the military's institutional prestige as an implicit source of credibility. The Trump administration faced regular admonishment from retired military officers concerned with a shift toward illiberal governance, while the early months of the Biden administration met with bloc opposition from retirees calling the results of the 2020 election into question and declaring Biden a "Marxist."[62] It is important to note that these actions reflect, in many cases, the positions of small numbers of retired military officials compared to the population of general and flag officers. Nonetheless, they are often the subject of intense news coverage, providing outsized influence to political discourse relative to the number of retired military elites involved. As Peter Feaver argues, the 2021 letter against Biden was "newsworthy mainly because it was signed by retired military officers who, in so doing, violated the norms of their profession and contributed to the erosion of healthy civil-military relations in the United States."[63] Even if such activity does not explicitly endorse one partisan establishment, rhetoric that redounds to the detriment of one side over another may still have a greater politicizing effect if it is perceived as such from an increasingly partisan public.

The most normatively egregious form of retired military activity within this first category are those actions supporting political extremism or even violence. This is perhaps the most recent expansion of the spectrum of retired military engagement in partisan affairs and need not involve high-ranking retired officials at all. Instead, former military servicemembers can achieve the same politicizing effect regardless of rank by using the visual trappings of the military institution to support inherently violent political agendas. The presence of military veterans at the January 6, 2021, attack on the Capitol building became a focal point of subsequent reporting on the attack, including indelible photos from the scene depicting former servicemembers in tactical gear engaging in physical damage to the Capitol with intent to violently disrupt the political process of validating the 2020 election results.[64] Subsequent research of those arrested for the attack revealed retired or former military individuals featured prominently as members of organizations like the Proud Boys and Oathkeepers, groups that intentionally recruit from ex-military and law enforcement populations in an effort to provide mainstream palatability for their cause.[65] The decidedly partisan animating causes of the insurrection and the involvement of military servicemembers among the attackers compounded the politicizing effect of the attack through the use of military icons, tactical gear, and Revolution-era flags to blur the line between the active force and violent extremist groups.[66] This form of activity represents the most deleterious form of active politicization by former military servicemembers, not only enforcing the belief that the armed forces have experienced partisan "capture," but through exploitation of a partisan environment that may not wholly sanction such behavior.

Second, active politicization can result not only from purposeful opportunism, but simply if retired military officials assess the likely impact of their speech according to outdated appraisals of credibility and partisanship. As discussed previously, politicization can occur just as much out of perception and unintentional effect as it can from purposeful action taken by any of the key actors involved: the public, the major political parties, or the military itself. While the opportunistic source of active politicization reflects an intentional desire to leverage military esteem with the public for partisan utility, retired officials with no intention of politicizing the military this way can still do so if they believe that they can break through increasingly rigid partisan divides. Retired military officers that privately adhere to norms of non-partisanship or have publicly cultivated a brand of non-intervention may believe that their own credibility is sufficient to provide reasoned and non-partisan thought in contentious spaces. However, the nature of the partisan public may in fact confound these expectations, leaving such retired officers in the same position as intentionally politicizing figures. In this sense, military speech may be actively politicizing not because it is influential, but because it is unable to alter sensibilities among partisan audiences.

A more recent high watermark in retired military speech provides some illustration of this form of activity; namely, the nearly unprecedented rebuke of administration policy in response to the 2020 protests following the murder of George Floyd.[67] Nationwide protests that resulted in the activation of National Guard forces in multiple states and the District of Columbia were met with high-level discussion in the Trump administration to invoke the Insurrection Act, which would have allowed for the deployment of active-duty forces to states where protests were ongoing. Concerns over such an invocation, compounded by private remarks by Defense Secretary Mark Esper for governors in affected states to "dominate the battlespace," resulted in numerous admonishments from retired military officers worried about the implications of using active-duty forces in American cities.[68] The debate took on uniquely partisan dimensions as the president's Congressional allies became the strongest advocates for domestic deployment of the military in response to the protests.[69] Normative civil-military concerns over the issue flared again when Chairman of the Joint Chiefs of Staff Mark Milley appeared in a photo taken shortly after protesters were forcibly dispersed to allow senior administration officials to walk to a nearby church, for which Milley publicly and quickly apologized.[70] Retired military officers offered a variety of statements against the proposed Insurrection Act measure and the prospect of continued military presence in response to the protests. The nature of these statements, captured by Dan Maurer, spanned concern over Constitutional inviolability and the protection of free speech and assembly, worries about "battlespace" rhetoric regarding law enforcement, and fears over the application of military force domestically.[71]

The retired military officers who offered these statements included a broad community of individuals, many of whom had no prior record of politicizing speech at all but rather expressed concern at the prospect of military politicization in invoking the Insurrection Act against the protesters. Retired Army General Joseph Votel warned against the potential damage that such measures might inflict on public trust in the military, calling on senior leaders to advise against such a decision: "the purpose of such counsel is to ensure that the U.S. military does not become politicized."[72] In an article for Harvard's Belfer Center, retired Army General Vincent Brooks similarly cautioned against the use of the military for episodes like the church photo-op, which "politicized them by their presence."[73] The prospect of military deployments domestically even earned the admonishment of retired officers who had made concerted efforts to avoid partisan political spaces and encourage other retirees to do the same, such as retired Army General Martin Dempsey and retired Navy Admiral Mike Mullen, who characterized the administration's actions as "sickening" and "very troubling."[74] In addition to several retired officers offering like-minded commentary, the two former Chairmen of the Joint Chiefs of Staff explicitly mentioned the uniqueness of their speaking out given the exigencies of the moment and their historical restraint from such activity.[75]

This form of active politicization is distinct from the previously characterized opportunistic variety because it does not emanate from a position of purposeful intention; indeed, it is noteworthy that many of the statements involved in the Floyd protest case invoke *concerns* over military politicization as their animating cause. How does the partisan public environment set the conditions for such activity? Partisan attitudes envisioning military officers as institutional guardrails to civilian leadership can engender such a climate: in the case of the Floyd protests, this manifested in commentary that retired officers were "finally speaking out against Trump."[76] But retired military officers who have refrained from partisan political activity may also operate under the impression that their latent credibility as a non-partisan may allow them to break through partisan gridlock as an objective "fair dealer." However, the results of this chapter's analysis seem to suggest that this reflects a fundamental misreading of the depth of partisanship in American politics. Instead, seemingly credible actors— exposed to the relatively novel forces of the partisan public—are likely to be marginalized at best, or politicized at worst. For an example of this dynamic at work, one need look no further than the involvement of retired Marine General and former Trump Defense Secretary Jim Mattis during the same episode. Mattis, who had previously declared an intention to refrain from public criticism of administration policy until "the time's right to speak out," broke his silence over the Insurrection Act debate, denouncing Trump as an inherently divisive figure proposing the use of the military to violate the Constitutional rights of fellow citizens.[77] In a YouGov poll taken shortly after the protests, Mattis's approval among Republicans had dipped to 21% (compared to 51% following his resignation), following weak or indifferent support of Mattis's comments from Congressional Republicans.[78] Active politicization can still occur even if the speakers involved are well-intentioned or non-partisan actors, because the partisan public (and the corresponding information environment) is unlikely to process and interpret their comments as such.

These cases provide an important distinction between the ways the partisan public can lead to different forms of active politicization. In the first type, opportunistic retired military elites intentionally utilize the public's esteem for the military institution for targeted partisan gain. Even if the behavior is likely to be sanctioned by partisans across the aisle, these individuals are likely outside the retiree's concern, as co-partisans are unlikely to sanction the behavior. However, the second type reflects a different response to this new incentive structure. Due to outdated appraisals of the depth of partisan polarization among the public, retired military officials with non-partisan credibility may believe themselves capable of bridging divides in moments of crisis. However, these efforts are likely to be either marginally influential or spun as partisan activism, even if this was not the organic intent of the speaker. In both cases, either a working knowledge or misunderstanding of the partisan public can lead to actively politicizing behavior by retired military officials.

The study of civil-military relations has consistently embraced the imperative of maintaining a non-partisan military, as both a normative defense of liberal standards of civilian control and a functional requirement for coherent and successful security policy. While the military has emerged as one of the most trusted organizations in society, civil-military scholars often contend that this is because of the careful maintenance of an objective image to the public. The very credibility of the institution is, in this framework, conditional on the institution's appearance as non-partisan. However, amidst broader trends in selective information exposure, partisan polarization, and the discrediting of expert communities, the perceived trustworthiness and expertise of the military institution makes it a source of considerable latent influence regardless of the norms against political activity. Instead, the level of military elite activism—whether in commentary, advocacy, or partisan endorsements—has steadily increased despite these traditional norms.

This chapter outlined several theoretical images of the public's preferences with regards to the "non-partisan norm." These included the *principled* image theorized by much of the existing civil-military literature and the *indifferent* image suggested by the limited empirical work towards this question. This chapter adds to these constructs the *partisan* image of the public, in which the non-partisan norm is weakened to the extent that military elites only risk suffering a loss of credibility among a specific political subset of the public and may even be able to gain credibility among another. Using original survey experimentation designed to measure how exposure to partisan military elites effects both individual- and institutional-level perceptions of credibility, we observe that there is little evidence for an objectively enforced and mutually embraced non-partisan norm across the public. Instead, military elites with a record of partisan behavior are only sanctioned among political opponents; as such, these elites more closely resemble partisan figures or elected officials, but with the imprimatur of the military institution. The institution itself similarly suffers a loss of credibility among those exposed to contra-partisan elites, drawing a firmer connection between the actions of representatives and the preservation of the military's corporate credibility.

This environment creates several challenges for the stability of civil-military relations and the durability of traditional norms of liberal governance. First, this analysis reveals a weakened state of civil-military norms amidst broader shifts in public sentiment away from other traditionally taboo concepts, such as military, technocratic, or authoritarian rule. Increasing military politicization is therefore a potentially damaging prospect for the maintenance of traditional democratic processes, even if the regime is not existentially threatened. Second, the partisan public creates a unique incentive structure for military elites seeking to cultivate a political "afterlife" to their careers, by allowing access to an ideologically coherent—if narrower—audience. Finally, through illustrative cases of its effects, the partisan public environment can lead to active politicization by either opportunistic military retirees seeking partisan political gain, or by decidedly non-partisan figures operating under a mistaken belief that they can bridge the partisan divide. In both cases, the tribalism of the surrounding political environment and the weakness of civil-military norms against military partisanship contribute to increasing politicization into the future.

Collectively, the principal findings of this analysis present several significant challenges to the future quality of civil-military relations, democratic norms of civilian control, and the value of military advice on policy matters. Empirical evidence for a *partisan public* is indicative of a deeper weakening of the non-partisan norm, long-held to be both salient and broadly accepted among the public by civil-military scholars. Such a lack of aversion to military intervention into partisan political affairs provides little reason to doubt that military politicization into the future will continue, particularly among those elites seeking to cultivate favor with a partisan establishment. The prospect of garnering an ideologically coherent and attentive audience is evident in the types of audiences different military elites draw conditional on their level of partisan behavior. The weakening of the non-partisan norm is more problematic for the preservation of democratic regime quality when viewed alongside the concurrent rise in public acceptance of authoritarian processes, illiberal rule, and unprofessional military elite behavior. Finally, there is strong reason to believe that with repeated forays into the political arena, retired military elites complicate the integrity of the larger institution with civilian leaders who rely on their objective counsel.

Missing in Faction

The Future of Civil-Military Relations

The preceding chapters have probed emerging trends in American civil-military affairs, revealing important patterns as to how the public perceives the armed forces as an institution through the deeply influential lens of partisanship. While certainly not the final word on the subject, these collective insights give us a new level of understanding into the state of civil-military relations, using data-driven observational and experimental techniques during a particularly illustrative period of normative change and upheaval. As American political affairs continue to reflect the shape of partisan polarization, the effects of this environment on the public's relationship with the military are worthy of consideration by national security leaders, civil-military relations analysts, and democracy scholars. The Parallax Model of politicization provides us one approach for understanding how polarization can complicate this relationship by re-contextualizing what it means to be "politicized." In a time when information exposure, cognitive biases, and even our appraisal of objective fact are likely to be filtered through partisan tribalism, military politicization need not be intentional or even the result of actual behaviors. Instead, merely the perception that the military represents a possible partisan adversary is all that is required to compromise this relationship between the people and the armed forces.

The introduction of this book outlined the many challenges that this environment of hyper-polarization and civil-military normative decay can pose to American political stability and decision-making. By creating a political climate where politicization of the military institution is more likely, polarization risks compromising the trust of the public in its armed forces and distorting its role from non-partisan guarantor of national security to yet another partisan battlefield. The evolution of targeted media environments and weakening of civil-military norms amongst the public can also hamper the very effectiveness

Dangerous Instrument: Political Polarization and US Civil-Military Relations. Michael A. Robinson, Oxford University Press. © Oxford University Press 2023. DOI: 10.1093/oso/9780197611555.003.0007

of the military in its core function: fighting and winning wars. Increasingly ubiquitous political activism by the retired military community risks the presumption that serving officers are mulling a political afterlife, compromising the quality of advice given to civilian leaders while in uniform. In addition, the weakening of a civil-military "firewall" between the armed forces and partisan politics erodes a critical ingredient to liberal democratic governance during a period of widespread "backsliding" among developed democracies. Throughout the course of this book, empirical analysis of the contemporary civil-military climate has uncovered several findings that validate these concerns, as well as a model for understanding how politicization of the military can manifest in a variety of forms.

In Chapter 3, we observed that military actors can be potentially influential voices in the political information space, particularly with those who have high estimations of the military's institutional credibility. Survey experimentation probing this idea found that whether in the form of direct statements, media leaks, or even speech by retired officers, military input could meaningfully affect how the public forms attitudes on complicated political matters like foreign policy. While this finding suggested that military voices can shape public attitudes, it did not yet incorporate how partisanship interacts with the process, determining the manner in which those voices can be co-opted or re-purposed for partisan gain. Using examples from the Bush and Obama administrations, this chapter classified such speech as emblematic of *active* politicization, cases in which representatives of the military willfully take actions that create the impression the institution is more amenable (or hostile) to one party's interests than another.

The significance of partisanship to this story came into sharper relief in Chapter 4, revealing that how the public determines military credibility in the first place may be a product of their partisan identity and its associated media consumption habits. Examining both observational data over time and text data from a high point in military war reporting, this chapter uncovered significant patterns of how partisanship and media exposure intersect with perceptions of the military. It revealed that partisans are likely exposed to very different depictions of the military depending on their preferred news sources, which are themselves an extension of partisan identity. Conservative Republicans were less likely to be exposed to critical information about the military than other segments of society, while Democrats and Independents were more likely to read or hear stories about organizational mismanagement, ethical scandals, or strategic quagmires abroad. Using examples from both the Iraq War period and more recent media developments, this chapter provided examples of how partisan media stories on the military can result in *aspect* politicization. Using targeted reporting to "push" the observer along the ideological spectrum can create the impression that the military has in fact drifted in the opposite direction by failing to keep pace with the individual's partisan preferences.

This influence of partisanship on public perception of the military and the "gap" between the parties was a centerpiece of Chapter 5's analysis, showing that trust in the military institution may be partially tied to partisan identity as well. Analyzing the results of survey experimentation regarding negative military performance, the same partisan trends emerged. Conservative Republicans were less likely to incorporate new information about poor performance in updating their impressions of the military than their Democratic or Independent counterparts, being more likely to see the military as a social extension of a shared partisan constituency. The incentive structure this creates for using the military as a partisan "prop" can result in *passive* politicization, illustrated through numerous examples from the Trump administration period. While the use of the military for partisan gain has been a near-constant feature of American politics, the knowledge that a segment of the population rigidly adheres to trusting the military above other institutions provides more incentive for passively politicizing activity. Such measures include high-profile appointments in government or the use of military iconography to create impressions of implicit support for a partisan agenda. This also risks the growth of *relative* politicization: if party establishments believe the military (or its supporters) to be a ready-made constituency, it may create incentives for extremity in political position-taking. Using examples from the same period, there is evidence to suggest this may instead reveal the "daylight" between the two institutions if the military does not follow suit, creating the impression of institutional hostility toward a particular party in the eyes of the public.

Finally, Chapter 6 extended this line of inquiry to its logical conclusion by testing the strength of civil-military norms among the public, particularly in the context of retired military political activism. Rather than "principally" rejecting such behavior as inappropriate regardless of partisan valence or even "indifferently" brushing such information away as uninformative, the public interpreted knowledge of such behavior as unacceptable only if it was not in support of their own partisan institution. Not only does this suggest that the "non-partisan" norm assumed by many to be salient among the public is in fact quite insignificant, but that the resulting political environment is ripe for *active* politicization in the form of retired military speech. Using examples from recent election cycles and political flashpoints, this environment proves susceptible to either purposeful or unintentional forms of politicizing behavior. While the more deliberate form can come from retired figures exploiting an accurate assessment of the public's partisanship, even well-intentioned actors can contribute to politicization through a misreading of the public's desire for non-partisan voices to break through the gridlock.

This concluding chapter takes stock of these findings and reconsiders the state of civil-military relations by offering what existing patterns are likely to exacerbate the ongoing prospect of politicization and what measures can be taken to curtail its most deleterious effects into the future. As areas of political consensus shrink and affectively polarizing "culture wars" between the two partisan tribes expand, the limits of public confidence in the military institution may soon be exposed as more fragile than previously theorized. What's more, increasing political animosity or even violence in pursuit of partisan aims threatens to further pull the military into troubled waters, whether as order enforcers or active participants. However, this book's contribution to our empirical understanding of the civil-military relationship may suggest steps that policy-makers, civilian leaders, and military professionals could adopt to forestall continual politicization of one of the country's most important institutions.

Exacerbating the Politicized Landscape

Before providing possible measures for ameliorating military politicization in the future, it is important to identify active considerations that risk inflaming this trend. With so many concurrent patterns in both American politics and civil-military relations to evaluate, it is often difficult to parse the causality or direction in which they occur. One of the many purposes for this book's analysis was to untangle some of these threads by directing attention to how increasing partisan polarization and increasing affect for the military were not only related, but resulted in a new political climate where civil-military norms were likely to emerge much weaker. The insights gathered from the preceding chapters offer a host of important data points for understanding this future environment: the power and coherence of media ecosystems, the selective influence of military voices based on partisanship, and the erosion of normative prohibitions against partisan activity by military actors. From these we can derive several influences that are likely to contribute to continued military politicization into the future.

The first source emerges from an observation made throughout this book: namely, that many of the archetypes articulated by the Parallax Model can contribute to (and emanate from) other forms, resulting in a potentially escalatory feedback loop of politicization. Each of these categories of politicizing activity is potentially troubling in their own right to advocates of the "nonpartisan" military. Each either shifts the institution's preferences in line with (or against) select partisan sensibilities or creates the impression of the same as the three actors (public, military, and parties) move relative to one another in some ideological space. In his analysis of politicization activity during the Trump years, Jim Golby offers that such activity, including the frequency, gravity, messaging, and political context components are linked rather than exist in isolation. Indeed, this understanding of politicization provides a useful measure for diagnosing the causes of such behavior and a method for assessing severity across cases.[1] Often left unaccounted is some understanding of the ways various politicizing actions interact and the resulting magnification of effects they can produce.

One advantage of the Parallax Model's classification scheme is that these ideas are not mutually exclusive, nor do they exist truly independent from one another over time. For example, individual acts of politicization can lead to a cascade of other forms across multiple actors or reciprocal behaviors between institutions that continue cycles of politicizing activity. For example, when the military or its representatives purposefully engage in partisan political affairs, this form of *active* politicization may provide a basis for partisan media sources to report on such activity as evidence of military institutional hostility or amenability to a favored partisan institution, a form of *aspect* politicization. This media strategy, in turn, may provide essential cues to partisan political leaders as to the sensibilities of their constituencies, leading to actions by party elites to either exploit favorable shifts by intensifying party positions (*relative* politicization) or counter-balance the inciting event by reversing policy (*passive* politicization). The connectivity of these forms of politicization provides one of the most significant challenges for maintaining the military's non-partisan image.

Actively politicizing behavior, for example, may provide the raw data for other forms of politicizing activity. For example, the 2021 publication of a bloc letter signed by over 120 retired general and flag officers denouncing the Biden administration for launching a "full-blown assault on our Constitutional rights in a dictatorial manner" provides a simple example of active politicization.[2] Using the military's institutional credibility with the public and their own rank within that institution, the letter sought to depict the military as "pawns" of partisan opponents in the Democratic party. However, despite the fact that the letter was signed by a small fraction of the community of retired officers, it drew disproportionately higher media attention and exposure to a much larger audience. The resultant reporting included rebukes of the letter from former Chairman Mike Mullen as reflecting "right-wing Republican talking points" and comparisons by the press to a similar letter issued by serving generals in France warning of civil war if the government failed to protect its "civilisational values."[3] In this case, actively politicizing behavior by one group of retired officers increased the probability of resultant aspect politicization when the story was reported to wider audiences, especially in partisan ecosystems where both the initial statement and its detractors could be used to depict the military in different ways.

Second, the probability of military politicization into the future may increase as a result of a lowering threshold of party consensus and a much larger frontier of partisan skirmishes. As discussed, this book's definition of politicization includes a wide variety of behaviors. The perception of the military as a partisan ally or opponent can result from both purposeful design and unintentional consequences. Central to this understanding of politicization is that perception of the military in a partisan light is just as important as whether it is factually accurate. Politicization, therefore, need not be the result of an intentional deviation of any actors from their Constitutionally envisioned role, illegal activity, or partisan designs for the military. Instead, it may result from any decisions made with respect to the military in which the political parties do not agree. As polarization escalates and the consensus threshold drops, friction along a greater breadth of issues can be perceived as politicizing due to the nature of the environment. For example, long-standing differences in party preferences over LGBTQ rights provided the basis for accusations by conservative Republicans that the Obama administration was politicizing the military in enacting the 2011 repeal of the "Don't Ask, Don't Tell" prohibition against open service by gay, lesbian, or bisexual individuals and the 2016 lifting of similar policies regarding transgender servicemembers.[4] Reciprocally, the reversal of the latter in 2017 under the Trump administration was heralded by right-wing media as an end to "social experiments" in the military and decried by the *New York Times* editorial board as an "about-face on a basic human rights issue."[5] The case provides an illustration of how decision-making made completely within the regulatory authority of all actors involved can result in *passive* politicization, the perception that the military is being moved to suit the partisan preferences of civilian leaders.

However, the probability of such politicization increases as more areas of political discourse become ones in which partisans cannot find consensus. If there has been a shift in this dynamic in recent years, it has been in the expansion of partisan warfare to areas where consensus may have been a reasonable expectation in the past. In short, the more areas in which partisan leaders are fighting, the more likely any actions they take with respect to the military can be perceived as politicizing. Though this expands the universe of cases that can be considered forms of politicization, these cases can still vary wildly in terms of their normative implications to civil-military relations. Polarization over state- and federal-level policies governing the vaccination of the public against the COVID-19 virus in the first year of the Biden administration demonstrated the depth to which partisan accord even over areas of public safety and health had evaporated.[6] As a result, mandated vaccination of military servicemembers became a deeply partisan issue, "politicizing" what otherwise should have been the uncontroversial position of insulating the force from a dangerous illness.[7] Demands from members of the special operations community for exemptions from the order were taken up by Congressional Republicans as a cause celebre, an episode that went all the way to the Supreme Court before returning a firm ruling upholding the policy.[8] In another series of partisan flare-ups, efforts to push back on the order's implementation among National Guard soldiers by the governors of Oklahoma and Texas led to high-profile friction with the Pentagon, including Texas Governor Greg Abbott's warning that Biden "is not your commander-in-chief" (referring to the Title 32 authority of the governor over National Guard soldiers).[9] Such incidents are emblematic of the increased speed with which areas of partisan disagreement can spread to military domains. As the landscape of political areas where partisans disagree continues to expand, the resulting environment provides additional opportunities for military (or military-adjacent) activities to be perceived in a politicizing fashion.

These exacerbating factors, derived from many of the empirical findings in this book and contemporary events in civil-military affairs, suggest that challenges to the preservation of a perceptibly "non-partisan" military will be persistent and sizable. Widening partisan disagreement, increasingly powerful media "echo-chambers," and eroding bi-partisan consensus are well-studied areas among scholars investigating the causes and consequences of polarization on American society and governance more broadly. But the insights of the preceding chapters allow for us to add to this landscape a sensitivity of trust in the military based on partisan identity, stark divides in the types of information partisans consume about the military's performance, and generally weak resistance to partisan activity by military actors, especially retired military officers. This environment and its likely extrapolation into the future provide a scene ripe for the politicization of the military, casting it as partisan entity, voting constituency, defender of democracy (to in-groups), or slow-rolling "adults in the room" (for out-groups). Nonetheless, this book's major findings suggest that military leaders, civilian policy-makers, professional journalists, and the public can adopt a variety of measures that would assist in curtailing a general loss of confidence in the military and preserving a stronger democracy as a result.

Improving Civil Military Relations into the Future

Before discussing some of the measures that such communities can take to curtail damage to the civil-military relationship, it should be noted that these efforts are circumscribed by the larger political environment. One of the most important distinctions in this book's depiction of politicization is that such activity can occur in both effect and intention: whether the military is being "politicized" is as much about perception as reality. As noted, this widens the range of possible actions taken by civilian and military leaders that can have politicizing effects; however, it also sets the boundaries of what many actors, particularly military figures, can meaningfully do to combat the root causes of the environment. In short, though the most effective way to reduce the probability of any particular action being seen as politicization is to de-polarize the outside environment, this book assumes that such a sea-change is unlikely in the near future. Instead, these recommendations both acknowledge the limited agency that military figures have in shaping the partisan political environment and assume that polarization will persist (or even deepen) in the near term.

Nonetheless, military and civilian institutional leaders possess the ability to shape a future civil-military relationship characterized by trust and executed in line with Constitutionally envisioned roles for the parties involved. Attending to the most challenging components of military politicization requires changing an incentive structure that currently allows for varied forms of incorporating the military into partisan political enterprises. To this end, both military and civilian leaders may be able to reform not only how their institutions address the subject of civil-military affairs, but ensure that both servicemembers and civilians properly understand the role of the armed forces in democratic governance. This includes an appreciation of the many ways military politicization can manifest—through the actions of the military itself, political leaders, or the public—and the implications of a wholesale loss of confidence in the armed forces. While some measures may be the sole province of a specific institution, some may in fact be joint ventures between both sides of the "dash" in civil-military relations.

Military Professional Education

One area that military leaders can directly manage to improve prospects for its institutional credibility is to improve how it educates officers on the subject of civil-military relations. As previously outlined, a likely source of continued strain against the non-partisan military ethic is the notion that military officers at the highest ranks cannot avoid partisan political waters as areas of consensus between the two parties evaporate. This does not mean that these individuals need be unprepared for how to navigate such terrain, nor does it require that they violate the non-partisan norm in doing so. As Risa Brooks notes in her definitive "Paradoxes of professionalism," an unnuanced adherence to the Huntingtonian "apolitical" ethic may in fact develop officers who are unable to discern "blind spots" in their understanding of the inherently political nature of the military profession.[10] A lack of education regarding the difference between political and *partisan* political activities can lead to critical missteps at best, or a pathological avoidance of essential job responsibilities at worst. The intent of military professional education in this regard should not be to develop "political" officers, but rather politically *literate* ones who are able to navigate a complicated civil-military landscape while preserving the institution's credibility. Changes to professional military education regarding civil-military affairs should therefore seek to achieve several important aims.

First, military officers should be socialized to the complexity of this landscape from early in their careers, providing a clearer picture of not only the national security decision-making apparatus, but the legal authorities and responsibilities incurred by each actor in that structure. Updates to formal civil-military education are made difficult by the complexity of the political environment, where senior military leaders are likely exposed to a variety of competing institutional pressures and mandates. As Lindsay Cohn, Max Margulies, and the author outline, military officers are simultaneously socialized to horizontal responsibilities within their organization and vertical allegiances to the chain of command and subordinates.[11] The obligations of command, mission accomplishment, professional norms, and democratic governance, to name a few, may not always be in accord; instead, the probability of politicization increases as these nodes come into conflict, putting senior officers in a position where the "right" answer may not be immediately evident. To be clear, military officers are well-socialized to the supremacy of the civilian chain of command, as well as the concept of "manifestly" illegal orders, which do not require acquiescence by servicemembers in execution.[12] However, this standard may be insufficient in the face of an environment where legality is difficult to ascertain and different loyalty structures may issue contradictory mandates.

Recent patterns in national security affairs illustrate how gray areas unaddressed by the "normal" theory of civil-military relations can create ethical and professional quandaries for military officers with national visibility. The experiences of Army Lieutenant Colonel Alexander Vindman and Navy Captain Brett Crozier offer examples of this complexity in practice, as well as how politicization of the armed forces more broadly can result from its often contradictory mandates.[13] While Crozier found himself caught between *authoritative* orders of the chain of command and the *supervisory* obligations to those under his command during the COVID-19 pandemic, Vindman was similarly caught between two *authoritative* arms of government when Congress and the White House issued contradictory orders to produce testimony during the first Trump impeachment trial.[14] These are not unique cases of civil-military friction, nor do they represent singular circumstances unlikely to be repeated; instead, they illustrate a clear need for officers to be made aware of the complicated ethical and legal landscape that can impede preservation of a non-partisan military. Desirable educational reforms include a thorough understanding of both Constitutional frameworks for military oversight and the professional norms of the military itself, to include its "non-partisan"—not "apolitical"—ethic. Officers in the military's educational pipeline should have regular opportunities to engage with civilians from across the national security enterprise, gain cross-cultural understanding of different organizations, and update their own knowledge regarding the civil-military dialogue. Concerted discussion among the profession on how to reconcile competing principles (and principals) will help to advance a clearer understanding of normatively sound behavior amidst polarized politics. This requires that leaders of the profession set aside concerns that such an important dialogue is prohibitively "political" and instead embrace the necessity of clarifying these roles into the future.

Second, future discussion of the American civil-military architecture should attempt to familiarize rising military officers to the end user of military service: the American public. Of the many authorities and institutions to which professional officers owe allegiance, an inescapable byproduct of military service is the provision of security to the public that transcends partisan identity. This obliges military educational institutions to ensure that officers—particularly future senior leaders—embrace the professional ethic that puts the public good and the preservation of civilian control ahead of personal partisan sensibilities. Making this point of instruction a priority is all the more important given recent patterns that indicate a weakening of this principle across society. Recent survey experimentation and analysis of cadets at the United States Military Academy at West Point suggest that junior officers are less likely to possess this normative grounding than previously theorized, at a time when partisan rhetoric can often depict the military as a factional body.[15] In short, the services cannot afford to rely on relatively intermittent formal schooling opportunities to proliferate these ideas of the military profession. Instead, senior officers should exploit chances to educate junior members of their commands on the values of the organization and its place within a larger system of democratic governance.[16] Nonetheless, there is also a sizable role for educational institutions to provide a forum for discussion and development throughout a servicemember's career by contextualizing these lessons within the broader enterprise of American national security and democracy.

While hardly exhaustive, these measures provide some method of socializing military officers to both the complicated landscape of civil-military affairs and the best principles for navigating it. As Heidi Urben notes, calls for reform of the professional military educational space have become a mainstay of policy recommendations in recent years. To this end, equipping military officers with a better understanding of the sources of potentially politicizing activity they are likely to observe provides considerable added value.[17] To be sure, such an effort requires that senior military leaders achieve professional consensus on how servicemembers can adroitly navigate this environment while satisfying their constitutional roles in society. Comparably simpler is a normative grounding in the professional ethics of non-partisanship that can stymie attempts at certain forms of politicization by arming officers with an understanding of their likely causes. Though it will be more difficult, it is also important to have a concerted discussion among professional leaders as to how military officers can reconcile democratic principles, civilian control, and organizational norms amidst increasingly fractious politics.

Crafting a Public Image

Preventing deeper military politicization, as several observations in this book have shown, requires a strategy of responsible engagement with and through media. If the military is to benefit from its acculturation of a non-partisan image, it also requires better control over the ability to build that image in the eyes of the public. The power of partisan media and its shaping influences over how the public derives its impressions about the armed forces suggest that the military needs to take an active role in telling its own story, or risk having it told for them. As detailed in Chapter 4, the public's lack of firsthand knowledge about the military makes information gleaned from third parties—including partisan media outlets—that much more influential in shaping attitudes among the people. This requires defense leaders to build a culture where productive engagement with journalists is a priority, rather than reflexively keeping the press at a distance. As retired Admiral James Stavridis notes, this is essential in conveying both accountability and trustworthiness to the public.[18] By taking active steps to craft a responsible public image as non-partisan national security guarantor (rather than partisan constituency), the military can responsibly separate itself from political tribalism while remaining engaged with the public directly.

First, military institutional leaders can take steps to solidify a positive, non-partisan brand with the American public. While there exists a variety of ways in which military leaders can address the causes and consequences of politicization on the margins, it is important to note that there is also an institutional limit to what they are able to change while rightly respecting civilian control. Outside of *active* politicization from inside the establishment itself, the military may be subjected to politicizing behaviors over which it has little agency. While the military is limited in its ability to prevent these activities, especially if they emanate from civilian leaders in the chain of command, they can maintain consistent messaging as to military organizational values and the professional ethic without violating essential frameworks of civilian control. For example, the 2019 pardons issued by the Trump administration to various servicemembers accused or convicted of war crimes sparked controversy in part for reversing the military's own internal judicial process.[19] As military ethics scholars Pauline Shanks Kaurin and Bradley Strawser note, the episode reflected a "dreadful breakdown of the American civil-military trust" and risked misrepresenting the military as an institution that endorsed extra-judicial violence.[20] While the armed forces are correctly limited in their ability to counter-message procedurally legal actions by civilian leaders, a well-established narrative among the public that the military effectively polices misconduct within its ranks could have cushioned the impact of such politicization. Making clearer where the military's principles lie can increase the chance that violations of those values from externally politicizing activity can be better contextualized, rather than creating a misperception of military malpractice. That narrative is best developed through public messaging about the military's organizational values and its institutional marketing, professional branding, and engagements in the public space.

Second, this type of messaging can serve to combat more extreme forms of partisan activity within the ranks by educating the public about its armed forces. As this chapter will discuss later, while the January 6 attackers included military servicemembers, the majority of those with military affiliations were veterans and not active-duty personnel.[21] While the distinction is well appreciated in national security circles, the military should not take for granted the public's ability to discern the difference. The purposeful use of military iconography, symbols, and tactical equipment—as well as recruitment of military veterans— by partisan-aligned extremist groups is intended to blur the line between violent organizations and an institution with high public esteem, the military.[22] In addition to policing such ideologies within its ranks, the military can take active steps to ensure the public knows the difference between veteran and active-duty communities, between those wearing military-style equipment and actual military servicemembers, and between the symbolic trappings of military credibility and true members of the profession. David Burbach, Danielle Lupton, and Lindsay Cohn outline how ambiguity in this space can be damaging to democratic norms and civil-military relations when it conflates police organizations and military forces; it stands to reason that further uncertainty in discerning the military from private citizens would be even more problematic.[23] Efforts made by the military to clarify these distinctions would be the natural extension of broader messaging designed to demonstrate what the military does (and does not) stand for, such as the ongoing push to rechristen military bases bearing the names of former Confederate officers.[24] Such measures are an example of broadcasting organizational values to the public while drawing brighter lines between the military and partisan-inspired or extremist doppelgangers.

Finally, part of this campaign to positively shape the military's image should include curbing deleterious activity by servicemembers in the same public space. While countering partisan-inspired political violence within its ranks is part of this effort, the military should also consider revising its policy regarding social media use by military servicemembers. Heidi Urben's research of social media activity and political sentiments in the military services has uncovered a troubling volume of divisive political rhetoric espoused by servicemembers online and demands a fundamental re-assessment of the outdated prohibitions of DoDI 1344.10, to include consideration of social media activity as avenues for "disparaging" remarks.[25] Existing loopholes, as Urben notes, allow for known military speakers to engage in damaging partisan speech (in many cases directed at serving civilian leaders) in a fashion that risks damaging the larger institution's credibility and *actively* politicizing the armed forces as a whole. This book's findings confirm that social media may continue to provide ready-made partisan constituencies for retired military officials engaging in (possibly extreme) political rhetoric. To continue to ignore the same utility this space provides to active-duty personnel may only compound a greater erosion of the military's non-partisan credentials. Including considerations of social media use by servicemembers into the professional education of senior officers may assist in both concurrent efforts at digital literacy and limit potentially damaging violations of the organization's non-partisan norm.

Adopting New Perspectives

As many of the preceding empirical findings suggest, emerging challenges to traditional non-partisan norms are not only a function of long-unfolding political trends, but of more recent changes to historically reliable patterns in civil-military relations. In addition to professional education and shaping public perception, leaders in this space should be willing to embrace different mindsets with regards to possible sources of (and solutions to) politicizing activity toward the military. Part of this new perspective includes understanding the shifting sources of public support for the military as an institution and the agency of military leaders in managing it. Not only has this book shown that a misreading of this landscape (even by well-intentioned actors) can lead to politicization, but that even historically reliable sources of public confidence are increasingly unstable. Similarly, another way in which civil-military leaders can stay ahead of potential normative problems is to incorporate wisdom from non-US cases. Comparative political scholars in the civil-military relations space have uncovered valuable and potentially instructive lessons regarding the dangers of politicization that American leaders can no longer afford to ignore. Both measures provide new angles by which to properly assess the political landscape in which military officers and civilian leaders operate and to defuse potential sources of politicization.

First, leaders in the military should recognize that while the armed forces continue to enjoy high levels of trust from the American public, not every threat to this esteem is within the hands of military leaders to control. If military leaders subscribe to outdated notions of the civil-military relationship, the resulting miscalculations could deepen the erosion of important norms. The experimental results of this book suggest a partial answer to former Chairman Martin

Dempsey's inquest on public trust in the military and "what it would take to screw it up": in short, a failure among military leaders to properly appraise the fragility of that same public trust. Broadly speaking, some of this miscalculation may be attributable to flawed measurement techniques and the limits of survey batteries to accurately assess public confidence. Jim Golby and Peter Feaver's more advanced application of item-count experimentation to the subject finds that public attitudes about the military may in part reflect some social desirability bias by survey respondents seeking to project a supportive image to the military, while privately harboring more skeptical attitudes.[26] Such nuanced probes into the nature of public trust in the military may illuminate the soft foundations at the heart of publicly expressed confidence in the armed forces. Until such thinking is adopted more broadly, military leaders may fail to properly assess the potential sources of politicization in the future by relying on obsolete information.

Improving the accuracy with which military leaders assess their surrounding environment requires some appreciation of the shifting sources of public trust in the armed forces as an institution. Even here, traditional assumptions regarding the ways that the military can lose confidence among the public are up for debate. For example, partisan-driven support towards the military may be less reliably stable than in past decades, even among traditionally military-friendly conservatives. Ronald Krebs and Robert Ralston identify this potential sea-change in partisan esteem for the military highlighting recent shifts in how conservative political leaders and media outlets speak about the military itself.[27] Uncharacteristically hostile coverage of military leadership from conservative media during the early months of the Biden administration provides some illustration of this sensitivity in practice, with highly rated media personalities admonishing military leaders for specific political sensibilities or even calling for a reduction in military funding as a result.[28] A decline in confidence in the military reflected in more recent survey data seems to capture this trend at work, reflecting the shifting perceptions of partisans toward the armed forces.[29] As Daniel Drezner remarks, this is likely indicative of a change in their evaluative calculus, choosing to "distrust any institution not entirely in sync with their ideological priors" and assessing the military's reliability solely through that lens.[30] This is not to suggest that Republicans will no longer exercise greater support for the institution than Democrats, nor does it mean that these seemingly contrary patterns in conservative reporting on the military (during a Democratic administration) would persist should party control of the White House change. However, it does suggest that the partisan sources of confidence in the military may be more movable than in years past: if historically reliable bastions of pro-military affect are no longer so reliable, advocates for preserving the non-partisan norm should take stock. For uniformed leaders, this means accurately assessing external sources of politicization; similarly, retired military figures weighing the possibility of public remarks in this space should properly assess their potential influence against the possible damage they might do to the institution.

Second, national security decision-makers, academic scholars, and military leaders alike can benefit from internalizing the lessons of non-US cases in civil-military breakdown in order to avoid the most deleterious effects of politicization. Study of US civil-military affairs has often kept comparative case studies at arms length. With low coup-propensity, few instances of protest resignations, and traditionally strong democratic institutions, the conversation regarding the United States has often overlooked the informative value of other states in the international system. The political turmoil of the 2020 presidential election and the involvement of military figures in largely unprecedented partisan political territory should, alongside declining confidence in government, provide a justification for embracing new paradigms. Critical institutions and leaders in national security can no longer afford to construe civil-military relations outside a broader context of comparative political scholarship.[31] Whether as instructive guide or cautionary tale, these cases may prove important to military officers and civilian leaders amidst the challenges of polarization in the American context.

The experiences of other countries can be informative to contextualizing ongoing patterns in US civil-military affairs, especially given the cross-regionally sweeping trends of authoritarian drift, institutional decay, and societal militarization. Risa Brooks thoroughly outlines the value of such lessons, couching recent developments in American civil-military relations in a broader comparative context. Through this lens, watershed developments at the intersection of partisan polarization and civil-military affairs are not American idiosyncrasies so much as data points in a larger pattern of behavior. The dangers posed by "societal-military coalitions" and declining confidence in democratic institutions are more readily apparent in the context of comparative cases in Europe and Latin America where such patterns have resulted in a militarization of policy.[32] Recent comparative political scholarship by Vincenzo Bove, Mauricio Rivera, and Chiara Ruffa uses the experiences of Algeria and France to explore how deference to the military—an increasingly regular feature in the American context—can result in both "push" or "pull" factors bringing the armed forces into unprecedented policy-making roles.[33] These cases not only provide knowledge of the potential dangers of politicization, but a vocabulary to express these concerns that has historically remained absent from discussion of US civil-military affairs. Such examples are illustrations of potential outcomes from unchecked politicization of the military and a warning to US leaders as to its dangers. Following recent political flashpoints and concerns over peaceful power transitions in the future, American observers of civil-military relations can no longer afford to ignore comparative lessons where partisan politics drew the military into domestic skirmishes or even political violence.

Similarly, just as American military education should ensure adherence to the norm of non-partisanship among the officer corps, it should incorporate lessons from comparative cases in which this norm was placed in competition with the preservation of democratic institutions. To be clear, this does not run counter to the prevailing policy suggestions of this book: instead, it encourages a professional dialogue amongst and between civilians and the military over the possible tension between obedience to orders and support to the larger enterprise of democracy. This dilemma is more readily observed in non-US cases in which political leaders attempt to include the military in autocratic measures within ostensibly democratic systems of government. Such a scenario in an American setting would undoubtedly complicate the civil-military "problematique" by creating more direct tension between the military's organizational mandates. Prioritizing defense of democratic institutions in the face of autocratic decision-making may run afoul of civilian control, while prioritizing objectivity could permit the military to passively—if obediently—become party to eroding that same democracy. Manaswini Ramkumar's discussion of the Indian military's precarious situation during the 1972 emergency declaration issued by Indira Ghandi provides some insight into this dilemma. Facing the twin challenges of incorporation into anti-democratic measures by one political movement and open co-optation by an opposition movement, military commanders were able to suitably distance themselves from both efforts.[34] While hardly exhaustive, such cases provide grist for meaningful conversations within the profession regarding the proper role of the military in democratic governance. Valuable lessons from comparative political scenarios can therefore help to contextualize challenges that US military leaders have observed or may encounter in the future.

Rebuilding the Non-Partisan Norm

One inescapable observation from this book's findings is the role of non-military actors in eroding traditional norms against politicization. While Huntington's notion of subjective control has certainly escaped dedicated analysis for years, its precepts seem especially important to the contemporary landscape: the institutional and legal barriers to maintaining a non-partisan force seem inadequate in the face of politicizing activity. While the recommendations so far have focused largely on measures that military leaders can take to reform their own institution and culture toward de-politicization, many areas of this problem are in the hands of external bodies to control. Of the various typological forms of politicizing behavior outlined in the Parallax Model, three of the four result from activity guided by extra-military actors or institutions. Whether in the use of military policy as a partisan tool (passive), the role of media or activists in shaping public perception of the military itself (aspect), or the extremity of the political parties in influencing how the public calibrates partisanship (relative), politicization can occur even without unprofessional activity by uniformed officers. As a result, the reconstruction of these norms requires not only that military leaders engage in an unbiased view of their surrounding environment, but for civilian leaders to actively take measures that reduce politicizing forces on the military.

The military community of course has a large role to play in reconstructing non-partisan norms through institutional and collective activity. As previously discussed, the active force can incorporate formal education regarding civil-military relations and democratic norms into its professional advancement process. But the retired community can also shape this outcome by engaging in interpersonal or collective efforts to curtail forays by other retired officers into overtly partisan political spaces. While individuals or small blocs of officers often make headlines for such activity, they represent a small minority of the thousands of retired officers of general and flag rank. The community would benefit immensely in heeding calls to make both this numerical disparity and the non-partisan professional ethic known to the public and reduce the potential reward for such activity.[35] This is not to suggest that all retired military actors intentionally act to degrade these norms; as this book has shown, such figures may in fact only speak because of concerns over politicization itself. Nonetheless, reducing unintended politicizing effects requires that active-duty and retired servicemembers cultivate a professional culture where adherence to valued norms of objectivity persist even after the end of one's service. These internal considerations aside, it cannot be understated that non-military actors also have the ability to shape the durability of the non-partisan norm.

First, strengthening this normative foundation requires not only an effort from military leaders, but a change from the American public in what it reasonably expects from the armed forces as an institution. The political environment depicted in the preceding chapters is one where partisanship may not only incentivize military actors to politicize the profession, but may create similarly negative incentives for external actors to pull the military into partisan political skirmishes. The concurrent trends of surging confidence in the military and plummeting trust in other areas of government make the military a tempting source of credibility in a political climate where this quality may be in low supply. This does not, however, make such expectations reasonable within the context of American democracy. The public instead needs to adopt a clear-eyed appraisal of its military, decoupled from both party and interest, that appreciates the value of a non-partisan force to national security and democratic governance. This also obliges the public to objectively evaluate the performance of the military in its organizational competency: as Kenneth Schultz argues, polarization over major foreign policy enterprises may result in reflexive attitudes based on partisan identity rather than thoughtful interpretation of their key lessons.[36] A public that cannot rationally evaluate the military's institutional quality nor the inherent value of its non-partisanship is likely to repeat past foreign policy mistakes and continue deputizing military voices into partisan debates.

As a result, civilian leaders can play an important role in cultivating an objective attitude among the public about the military's performance as an institution. As we have observed, individual-level impressions about the armed services are likely a patchwork of pre-conceptions, partisan identity structures, media consumption, and even social desirability biases stemming from the "patriotic ritual" of expressing trust in the military.[37] Failing to adopt an unvarnished assessment of the military's value not only leads to poor policy outcomes, but eschews the responsibility of the public to conduct proper oversight of its military. Encouragingly, the prospect of bipartisan measures designed to more closely oversee military organizational practices provides one potential area of future political consensus.[38] Partisan leaders have an opportunity to signal to their respective audiences that the military is an agent of government, one that should be evaluated based on its performance, rather than societal affect or patriotic obligations. Engagement in this type of objective, consensus-driven oversight might also serve to reshape our understanding of the "civil" side of the civil-military relationship. While the term has traditionally conjured images only of the executive, these measures may return much needed agency to the Congressional component of civilian control.

To be sure, the scope of this type of attitudinal shift among the public is ambitious: operating without additional legal or institutional restraints on politicizing activity, bolstering the non-partisan norm amongst the public also requires top-down leadership from political elites. Party leaders have agency in shaping the extent to which military actors play (or do not play) a role in partisan politics. For example, building strong positions on the enforcement of civil-military norms within party platforms can assist in formalizing opposition to politicizing the services in pursuit of partisan political gain. This may not only signal to the public where the normative sensibilities of their leadership reside, but also temper the exacerbating force of extreme party polarization on the probability of politicization into the future. For example, the Democratic party's 2020 platform specifically included provisions to prevent "politicization of the armed forces and distortion of civilian and military roles in decision-making," reflecting at least some acknowledgment of the challenge.[39] Such declarations are best met with tangible action, however, as scholars expressed concern over the Biden team's subsequent appointment of retired military officers to high-ranking positions in the administration and transition, seemingly working at cross purposes to the platform pledge.[40] Nonetheless, declaring and codifying a commitment to civil-military norms within party platforms can provide clarity and institutional support that signal important political values to the public.

Second, political elites can take direct measures to ensure the military stays out of partisan politics. One way to achieve this is to reduce the extent to which politicization provides partisan utility by actively limiting military appearances in electoral contexts. Indeed, the prescriptions of this section are perhaps the most ambitious in that they require self-restraining actions by the interested parties: no amount of insistence on enforcing civil-military norms will completely remove the incentive for political parties to play up cultural proximity to the military or highlight the past service of candidates for office. But political elites should also take note of civil-military relations scholarship suggesting that these strategies are far less lucrative than they may appear at first glance. Jeremy Teigen's research into veteran Congressional candidates finds that any edge they may enjoy at the ballot box is greatly dependent on geographic context rather than an inherent veteran advantage. Elevating candidates who make their past service a centerpiece of the campaign will likely serve to conflate the partisan and military realms for comparably little gain.[41]

Recent analysis of voting patterns by veteran members of Congress also questions the notion that they are more likely to engage in bipartisan behavior. Research by G. Lee Robinson et al. finds that "the potential benefits of increasing bipartisanship in Congress should therefore be weighed against the possible politicization," given that the link between veteran status and "across the aisle" sensibilities is uncertain at best.[42] Military leaders may have a part to play in forestalling politicization from veteran candidates by re-approaching existing policy governing the participation of inactive servicemembers in political campaigns. As Jessica Blankshain and Lindsay Cohn argue, National Guard and reserve component personnel serving in this capacity as partisan actors further blurs the line between the military and electoral politics.[43] Broadcasting the limited utility that repeated appeals to military service have in the partisan political realm may not address this problem at the purely normative level, but in reshaping the cost-benefit calculus of this practice in electoral politics.

More pressingly, recent flashpoints in which the military has been thrust into unprecedented partisan political environments suggest that civilian politicians' role in rebuilding the non-partisan norm extends beyond the context of just campaigns. As discussed throughout this book's empirical chapters, politicization is also the result of an increasing society-wide tendency to see the military as a panacea for social or political problems outside its formal responsibilities. Frustration with legislative or bureaucratic process has contributed not only to a growing embrace of illiberal governance in the United States, but has extended partisan fights to secondary battlefields where favorable outcomes are deemed more likely. Civilian leaders can bolster the non-partisan norm by ensuring that specific areas of political process and communication remain off-limits for the military.

This requires that civilian politicians use their influence as political elites to prevent creating a permission structure for anti-democratic activity or political violence. For example, uncertain political circumstances during the turbulent 2020 election period obliged Chairman Milley to remind the public that the military has "no role" in the adjudication of free and fair elections in American governance.[44] As Lindsay Cohn and Steve Vladeck point out, this is not even a matter of executive branch authorities, but rather a prohibition that is "expressly forbidden by law."[45] While remarks like this from senior military leaders were normatively encouraging amidst the uncertainty about a peaceful transition of power, partisan leaders should take steps to ensure that such clarifications are never necessary. While this chapter's recommendations include educating future military leaders on the complicated landscape of national security and creating politically "literate" officers, this effort should also make clear where the irrevocable boundaries of military authority reside. Anti-democratic activities can put uniformed servicemembers in a precarious situation, increasing the tension between professional military deference to civilian orders and legal obligations to constitutional democracy. All actors in the civil-military relationship should ensure that no circumstances emerge in which the military is seen as a referee for elections or put military officers in a position for which they are neither professionally trained nor constitutionally empowered.[46] Placing the focus back on proper democratic institutions of government to perform these functions is essential to the process.

Civilian leaders can also support the non-partisan norm by ensuring that political rhetoric refrains from sanctioning violence of any type. As previously mentioned, the aftermath of the Floyd protests and January 6 reveal how the presence of the active services, veterans, and military iconography amidst highly charged partisan skirmishes is both indicator of and contributor to a weakened non-partisan norm. Taking clear steps to openly condemn violence, civilian politicians can not only prevent conditions where the military may need to respond to civil unrest, but also denounce extremist organizations that target veterans for membership. Political elites should endeavor to marginalize the role of violent groups in partisan political discourse and cut off any access to mainstream legitimacy that may empower their incorporation of military servicemembers or veterans. This not only defuses a key source of military politicization, but serves a larger objective of ensuring that non-violent conflict resolution remains a hallmark of American governance.

Making the Military a Hard Target

While these recommendations have focused on how organizational policy or professional education can address the most common sources of politicization, both military and civilian leaders would do well to consider the means to combat more egregious forms of politicizing activity. Regrettably, the events of January 6, 2021, and its aftermath represent a watershed moment not only in American politics, but for US civil-military relations. First, the incident captures the volatility of the political environment and the increased likelihood of military actors being involved in partisan skirmishes into the future, despite the lack of any formal procedural role.[47] Subsequent analysis of the event intensified concerns about the prospect of political violence into the future. Senior retired military officers would later pen editorial warnings to the public regarding such a possibility during future elections or implicitly citing the event as grounds for "unprecedented concern."[48] Second, the episode is illustrative of how partisan-inspired political violence can lead to military politicization. The deployment of National Guard soldiers to secure the Capitol following the attack was not only the second such deployment in less than a year, but became a point of political contention for months after.[49] Finally, detailed investigation into the event's origins and conduct revealed the extent to which former (and in some cases, active) servicemembers were among the rioters, both as lone actors and as part of organized paramilitary organizations.[50] The episode reflects a troubling low point in partisan politics, but also an example of how the military can be easily pulled into such flashpoints moving forward.

The findings of this book inform additional measures that military leaders can take to address the challenge of politicization and protect the institution against the most pernicious aspects of partisan politics. As concerns over the normalization of political violence increase, one dimension of increasing concern is denying access by extremist groups for whom military recruitment has become normalized.[51] It is important to note that this does not call for political activism, nor does it advocate for walling off the military institution from all things "political." Instead, military leaders cannot afford to mislearn the lessons of past politicization events by engaging in a wholesale retreat from politics. Rather, given that military servicemembers are themselves drawn from the same mass public so riven by partisan polarization as their civilian counterparts, institutional leaders in the armed forces should take steps to guard these individuals from polarization's most extreme byproducts while remaining responsibly engaged in the civil-military relationship. The potentially disastrous effects of political extremism within the armed forces—or as a source of politicization—are ones that should be taken seriously by both civilian and military leaders.

First, military leaders can take steps to make servicemembers "harder targets" when it comes to political misinformation, both as recipients and proliferators. Concerningly, one significant finding of this book's empirical effort is that actively politicizing speech from military servicemembers—whether in service or retired—can erode public trust in the institution and portray the military as yet another partisan battlefield. This problem is compounded by a vulnerability among servicemembers to the same misinformation and disinformation that characterize the larger media ecosystem. Peter W. Singer and Eric Johnson argue that senior military leaders should take steps to increase digital media literacy training within the ranks as a means of protecting the force.[52] This type of education serves not only to harden servicemembers against pernicious information operations efforts from abroad, but to arm individuals with a capacity to detect similarly deleterious sources of misinformation in an American media environment often characterized by partisan bias. A failure to discern factually accurate from misleading or partisan information has resulted in a variety of challenges for the Defense Department, from vaccine refusal among the military during the COVID-19 pandemic to growing military social media "echo-chambers" that often advance incorrect information or normalize political violence.[53] Equipping servicemembers with a greater awareness of the information environment and the ability to apply critical thinking to open source political discourse can aid in bolstering the non-partisan norm.

Second, mitigating partisan-inspired political extremism in the ranks is another area where military leaders can take steps to harden their organizations. Distressingly, following the events of January 6, the notable presence of both active military servicemembers and veterans among the insurrection's many participants directly highlighted the vulnerability of that population to disinformation and the potential dangers of such activity in the form of political violence.[54] Screening procedures designed to prevent extremists from entering military service are indeed important, but unlikely to meaningfully reduce extremist sentiment in both the active force and the veteran community without broader attempts to combat this ideology. As Carrie Lee and Celestino Perez, Jr., argue, professional military educational institutions and senior military leaders can better seize on the opportunity provided by "stand-down" events to facilitate meaningful discussion about the dangers of extremism, rather than permit dismissive attitudes that could further damage civil-military relations. Perhaps most importantly, they argue that military leaders cannot afford to refrain from discussion over issues regarding extremism just because those same issues have become a topic of consternation in partisan political circles.[55] Instead, the military services can better insulate their organizations from partisan politicization by enabling leaders to enforce a truly "non-partisan" normative ethic and counter-message against extremist content without parting company with professional standards of conduct.

Finally, defense leaders should not only bolster the armed forces against the ideological challenge of extremism, but work to more tangibly sever any nexus between servicemembers—past and present—and extremist organizations themselves. The growing scope and scale of partisan polarization has contributed to a similar rise in not only ideological extremity, but in the ubiquity of organizations designed to advance extreme political agendas or even violence. Scholarly research into the expansion of organized groups like the Oathkeepers, Proud Boys, or Three (III) Percenters has shed light on the extent to which these groups often rely on active recruitment of military servicemembers and veterans.[56] As a result, military leaders should take steps to ensure that the public does not visually conflate these groups—often attired and branded as military-adjacent—with the actual military. More pointedly, military leaders should engage in meaningful dialogue with servicemembers that discourages alignment with such groups, even if membership is not explicitly prohibited by regulation. Both hardening the military against misinformation and combating extremism on an ideological level contribute to this effort; but military professionals cannot afford to underestimate the challenge posed by such groups and any recruitment efforts targeted at active-duty personnel and veterans. While the defense establishment has far less control over the actions of the latter category once they have left the service, it can still adequately inform individuals before their departure.

This book's purpose has been to provide some additional insight into the state of American civil-military relations by examining the relationship between the public and the armed forces in a time of extreme partisan polarization. The singular status that the military has enjoyed in the public's good graces alone presents a puzzle worth understanding; its decidedly partisan undercurrents and impact on the durability of American political institutions provide yet more. It is not the first word on the subject, nor will it be the last. Future scholarship will no doubt examine these patterns and many others in the essential context of political tribalism, democratic "backsliding," and curated media environments. But the key insights gained from the preceding chapters should provide some measure of understanding with respect to how the interplay between the public, political parties, and the military itself can shape public perception of their armed forces.

The contribution offered by this book's analysis of survey and observational data will no doubt augment richer datasets in the future. To be sure, survey data can often reflect transient attitudes, may be sensitive to question wording and timing, or even fail to account for desirability bias over issues like civil-military norms. Nonetheless, this book offers important perspectives into the state of civil-military relations by adding to a growing dialogue on how this relationship has changed and will likely change into the future. The period of time where data collection principally occurred for this book is one of significance for the study of civil-military relations, providing a wealth of illustrative cases for military politicization, its likely causes, and its potential consequences. For military leaders, scholars, and civilian national security decision-makers, its observations provide a new vantage from which to observe important trends in this area of study.

APPENDIX

Chapter 3

Sample Statistics and Supplementary Results

Table A3.1 **Covariate Balance across Treatment and Control Conditions**

Respondent Demographic	*Control*	*Support*	*Opposition*
Party Identification			
Democrat	44.7%	40.9%	44.9%
Republican	38.4%	36.3%	31.8%
Gender			
Male	48.0%	46.9%	44.9%
Female	51.9%	53.0%	55.0%
Age			
25th Percentile	35	31	33
50th Percentile	51.5	49	45
75th Percentile	63	62	61
Race			
White	71.1%	76.2%	71.3%
Non-white	28.8%	23.7%	28.6%

Notes: Percentages reflect segment of survey population assigned to each experimental condition or class of conditions (*Opposition* collapses all oppositional cue conditions into a single population) broken down by key demographic values.

Table A3.2 **Randomization Check: Logit Regression with Treatment Assignment as DV**

	Dependent Variable: Treatment Assignment			
	Opposition (1)	Support (2)	Opposition (3)	Support (4)
Democrat	0.063	−0.137	−0.086	0.020
	(0.132)	(0.163)	(0.132)	(0.164)
Male	−0.100	0.037	−0.167	0.098
	(0.129)	(0.159)	(0.130)	(0.162)
Age	−0.003	−0.003	−0.001	−0.001
	(0.004)	(0.005)	(0.004)	(0.005)
White	−0.077	0.255	0.086	−0.103
	(0.149)	(0.189)	(0.148)	(0.182)
Constant	0.613***	−1.388***	0.472**	−1.398***
Observations	1,000	1,000	1,000	1,000
Log Likelihood	−674.263	−496.029	−672.993	−485.841
Akaike Inf. Crit.	1,358.526	1,002.058	1,355.986	981.681

Notes: $\dagger p < 0.10,$ $^* p < 0.05,$ $^{**} p < 0.01,$ $^{***} p < 0.001.$

Table A3.3 **Logistic Regression on Binary Support Variable**

	Dependent Variable: Binary Support Indicator			
	Conv. (1)	Hum. (2)	Conv. (3)	Hum. (4)
Control1	−0.117		−0.192	
	(0.218)		(0.226)	
OpposeCue1	−0.534***		−0.644***	
	(0.184)		(0.191)	
Control2		−0.086		−0.119
		(0.210)		(0.215)
OpposeCue2		−0.467***		−0.494***
		(0.179)		(0.183)
Congress			0.248***	0.332***
			(0.086)	(0.082)

Table A3.3 **Continued**

	Conv. (1)	Hum. (2)	Conv. (3)	Hum. (4)
		Dependent Variable: Binary Support Indicator		
Military			0.339***	−0.010
			(0.082)	(0.073)
Presidency			0.160**	0.144**
			(0.075)	(0.071)
Constant	−0.809***	−0.607***	−3.049***	−1.743***
	(0.154)	(0.152)	(0.366)	(0.325)
Observations	1,000	1,000	997	997
Log Likelihood	−549.291	−597.601	−517.958	−577.920
Akaike Inf. Crit.	1,104.582	1,201.201	1,047.917	1,167.839

Notes: $\dagger p < 0.10,^{*} p < 0.05,^{**} p < 0.01,^{***} p < 0.001$.

Table A3.4 **Logistic Regression on Binary Support Variable**

	Conventional (1)	(2)	Humanitarian (3)	(4)
		Dependent Variable: Probability of Support for Policy		
Control1	−0.117	−0.214		
	(0.218)	(0.229)		
OpposeCue1	−0.534***	−0.680***		
	(0.184)	(0.194)		
Male		−0.141		−0.103
		(0.157)		(0.147)
Congress		0.245***		0.344***
		(0.089)		(0.085)
Military		0.342***		−0.020
		(0.087)		(0.078)
Newspapers		0.153*		0.104
		(0.079)		(0.074)
Presidency		0.095		0.088
		(0.078)		(0.074)
Ideology		−0.076		−0.068
		(0.068)		(0.062)

News Interest		−0.128*		−0.144**
		(0.070)		(0.063)
Control2			−0.086	−0.119
			(0.210)	(0.217)
OpposeCue2			−0.467***	−0.488***
			(0.179)	(0.184)
Constant	−0.809***	−2.555***	−0.607***	−1.209***
	(0.154)	(0.517)	(0.152)	(0.462)
Observations	1,000	997	1,000	997
Log Likelihood	−549.291	−510.768	−597.601	−571.028
Akaike Inf. Crit.	1,104.582	1,041.536	1,201.201	1,162.056

Notes: †$p < 0.10$,* $p < 0.05$,** $p < 0.01$,*** $p < 0.001$.

Table A3.5 **Conventional Scenario, Percentage of Respondents in Support, by Demographic Group**

	Military Elite Cues				
	Support	Oppose	Approval Gap	N	p-value
Respondent Party ID					
Democrat	33.3%	19.9%	−13.5%*	348	0.022
Republican	36.1%	22.8%	−13.4%*	261	0.041
Ideology					
Liberal	23.4%	21.7%	−1.7%	231	0.811
Conservative	35.4%	21.9%	−13.5%*	243	0.048
Moderate	35.8%	20.0%	−15.8%*	252	0.018
World View					
Internationalist	47.3%	30.7%	−16.5%**	345	0.007
Isolationist	10.0%	15.5%	5.5%	192	0.299
Military Confidence					
High	40.2%	24.9%	−15.3%**	436	0.005
Low	16.7%	8.1%	−8.6%	104	0.268
Political Interest					
High	34.1%	23.8%	−10.3%†	376	0.079
Low	30.3%	18.8%	−11.5%*	380	0.024
Total	30.8%	20.7%	−10.1%**	792	.006

Notes: Significance levels refer to two-way t-tests of the difference between concurrent cues (support) and oppositional cues (oppose). †$p < 0.10$,* $p < 0.05$,** $p < 0.01$,*** $p < 0.001$.

Table A3.6 **Humanitarian Scenario, Percentage of Respondents in Support, by Demographic Group**

			Military Elite Cues		
	Support	Oppose	Approval Gap	N	p-value
Respondent Party ID					
Democrat	38.8%	27.9%	−10.9%†	343	0.071
Republican	32.3%	25.6%	−6.7%	272	0.311
Ideology					
Liberal	37.7%	29.2%	−8.5%	232	0.240
Conservative	34.9%	24.3%	−10.6%	248	0.124
Moderate	38.5%	25.0%	−13.5%†	248	0.076
World View					
Internationalist	43.8%	32.1%	−11.6%	351	0.065
Isolationist	27.5%	17.4%	−10.1%	189	0.160
Military Confidence					
High	39.5%	26.9%	−12.6%*	442	0.015
Low	21.1%	22.2%	1.2%	100	0.914
Political Interest					
High	37.9%	27.0%	−10.9%*	373	0.056
Low	33.3%	25.2%	−8.2%	377	0.154
Total	35.2%	25.4%	−9.8%*	787	0.012

Notes: Significance levels refer to two-way t-tests of the difference between concurrent cues (support) and oppositional cues (oppose). †$p < 0.10$,* $p < 0.05$,** $p < 0.01$,*** $p < 0.001$.

Questionnaire and Intervention Vignettes

Scenario-based Vignettes

Respondents were drawn from a nationally representative opt-in panel organized by YouGov in December 2016. Individuals were uniformly exposed to the following prompt outlining the scope of the experiment:

You are about to read two news stories depicting a potential US foreign policy decision. These situations and the persons mentioned within do not pertain to any particular real-life case, but reflect events that have happened in the past and may happen again. Please read the articles carefully and imagine your feelings regarding the situation. Afterwards, you will be asked a few questions about the stories.

Conventional Scenario

The respondent was then prompted with this baseline news story for the conventional scenario:

> **WASHINGTON (AP)**—Tense relations between Russia and a former Soviet state have moved closer to full-scale war. Russian military forces began small-scale bombings inside the country and increased its troop presence along the border. Russia claims it is supporting ethnic Russians within the country.
>
> Relations between the US and the small state have been historically positive, though no formal security agreement exists between them. The American president, after meeting with fellow [POTUSID] policy advisors, stated to the press that the US should strongly consider military intervention to deter further violence. [CUE]

The value for *POTUSID* was randomized between "Democratic" and "Republican." The value for *CUE* was randomized between the following:

- NULL, for *control* respondents.
- "A senior military commander for American forces stationed in the region, an Army general, expressed support for the proposed intervention in an article for a highly respected newspaper, stating that the policy would be wise," for *supportive cue* respondents.
- "However, a senior military commander for American forces stationed in the region, an Army general, expressed opposition to the proposed intervention in an article for a highly respected newspaper, stating that the policy would be unwise," for *opposition statement* respondents.
- "However, national media outlets recently obtained a leaked, classified internal memorandum. In the memo, a senior American military commander in the region, an Army general, expressed opposition to the proposed intervention, stating it would be an unwise decision," for *opposition leak* respondents.
- "However, a retired Army general, who previously served as senior military commander for American forces stationed in the region, expressed

opposition to the proposed intervention in an interview with television news, stating that the policy would be unwise," for *opposition retired* respondents.

Humanitarian Scenario

The respondent was then prompted with this baseline news story for the humanitarian scenario:

> **WASHINGTON (AP)**—The people of a small foreign country have engaged in a recent campaign of protests against a ruling dictator. This leader has committed major acts of violence against his citizens in the past and government forces have now violently clashed with protesters. The conflict has brought on a major humanitarian crisis, internally displacing many citizens and forcing many more to flee the country.
>
> One proposed policy being considered by US security officials is a military intervention to prevent a further humanitarian disaster. The US president, after speaking with fellow [POTUSID] advisers, stated to the press that the US should strongly consider a military intervention. [CUE]

The value for *POTUSID* was again randomized between "Democratic" and "Republican." The value for *CUE* was randomized between the following:

- NULL, for *control* respondents.
- "A senior military commander for American forces stationed in the region, an Army general, expressed support for the proposed intervention in an article for a highly respected newspaper, stating that the policy would be wise," for *supportive cue* respondents
- "However, a senior military commander for American forces stationed in the region, an Army general, expressed opposition to the proposed intervention in an article for a highly respected newspaper, stating that the policy would be unwise," for *opposition statement* respondents.
- "However, national media outlets recently obtained a leaked, classified internal memorandum. In the memo, a senior American military commander in the region, an Army general, expressed opposition to the proposed intervention, stating it would be an unwise decision," for *opposition leak* respondents.
- "However, a retired Army general, who previously served as senior military commander for American forces stationed in the region, expressed opposition to the proposed intervention in an interview with television news, stating that the policy would be unwise," for *opposition retired* respondents.

Chapter 4

Supplementary Wartime Reporting Statistics

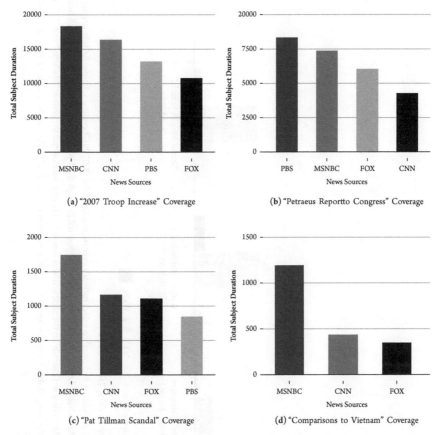

Figure A4.1 Media Coverage of Military News Stories by Source, 2007

Note: These figures display the total duration (in on-air seconds) devoted by each of the major television news sources to each of the indicated sub-storylines as coded and sampled by the 2007 Pew Research News Coverage Index (NCI) dataset. Total source broadcast time calculated by summing total on-air time spent on each sub-storyline across all segments in each source.

Pew Research News Coverage Index (NCI) Dataset

Dataset Methodology

Analysis of the selective exposure hypotheses conducted in the main body of the text draw extensively on media reporting data provided by the Pew Research News Coverage Index (NCI) Dataset, a sampling-based index of stories reported by major media outlets across television, the internet, radio, and

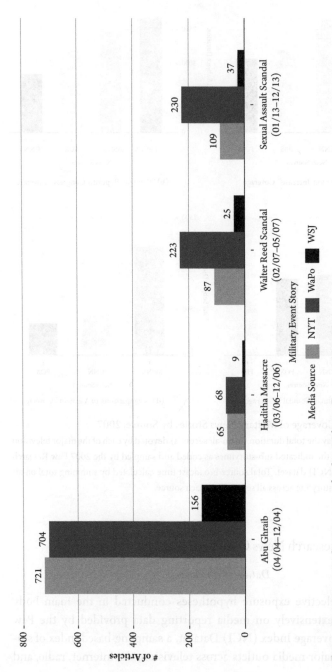

Figure A4.2 Print Media Coverage of Other Military Events, 2004–2013

Note: This figure depicts the number of print media articles per source dedicated to select military events outside of the 2007 NCI coding scheme. Article counts were obtained for the New York Times and Washington Post through the LexisNexis database and for the Wall Street Journal through the ProQuest database. Dates of search fields are included in parentheses. Abu Ghraib stories were those containing "Abu Ghraib/Ghuraib" in the article body; similarly, Haditha stories had to contain "Haditha" and "killing OR murder" in the body, to distinguish it from other combat events in the area; Walter Reed stories contained the name of the medical facility in the article body, and sexual assault stories contained both "military" and "sexual assault."

print newspapers. A full description of the dataset's methodology can be found on the Pew Research website.[1] However, for the purposes of this analysis, I provide an overview of the collection and coding schemes for the NCI dataset, as the selective exposure argument uses this data in 2007 to make the case for limited reporting across conservative outlets on Iraq Combat Events.

The population of data points captured by the dataset's sampling process produces an image of the media information environment per day, meant to be "illustrative but not strictly representative." This is to say that the dataset employs quasi-random sampling of news stories across the different media, weighting these observations based on the number of outlets per medium, the number of programs per outlet, and the volume of news to be collected during given periods of time. Coding the entire content of a news segment or newspaper is prohibitively time consuming. As a result, the collection process increases efficiency at the cost of completeness by focusing on the most prominent aspects of these segments, such as using the first 30 minutes of television news segments or the front page of print media sources in order to provide an accurate picture of the predominant stories during a given news cycle. While this means the image captured by the dataset is a sampled subset of prominent stories, this does not pose a serious threat to inference in the selective exposure argument discussed in the main body of the text. Lead stories and newspaper headlines are precisely the high-salience, high-exposure stories that this hypothesis is attempting to test for distribution and acceptance by the public; as a result, "D-block" television segments or non-front page, under-the-fold print stories are less important to our consideration.

Network Television News

The network television news medium includes morning and evening segments broadcast by the three major networks (ABC, CBS, and NBC) and the evening segments of PBS. The three primary networks typically air two daytime programs (such as the *Today Show* or *Good Morning America*) and one evening program, whereas PBS is typically captured in a sampling of *Newshour with Jim Lehrer*. Collection of story topics for these programs codes the substance of the first 30 minutes of one or two of the three programs, which typically focus on stories of national importance. Though this means that stories at the end of the broadcast are less likely to be collected, Pew Research asserts that "we have learned that the morning shows generally move away from the news of the day after the first 30 minutes." Evening news segments are collected in a similar fashion, with the entire 30 minutes of two of the three programs a day being sampled. Finally, the PBS *Newshour* broadcast rotates to be coded based on the first 30 minutes, followed by the second 30 minutes, followed by its non-collection.

All television programs, both network and cable news, are coded based on the entire 30-minutes time frame of collection, discounting inserts from local affiliates, advertisements, promotions, or weather reports. Furthermore, segments within programs will be coded in their entirety even if they run past the 30-minute time window (for instance, a three-minute segment that started at the 28-minute mark would be coded even though it concludes at the 31-minute mark). Removing local inserts, non-substantive information, and "teasers" of upcoming stories narrows the collected sample to the top stories of national importance. Therefore, despite the rotating sample scheme, the information collected is representative of the prevailing news stories of the day.

Cable Television News

Cable news focuses on particular sources in a similar fashion, utilizing the top three cable news distributors by audience reach (MSNBC, CNN, and FOX). Selection on these subsets precluded the inclusion of corporately related but unsampled news source like CNBC, or CNN Headline News. Because cable news broadcasts on a continuous basis, a different scheme of collection is adopted due to the indistinguishability of segments from the same network to a broad audience. Instead, Pew breaks the reporting day into four time periods: early morning, daytime, early evening, and primetime. Early morning segments are not collected due to the fact that they are not uniformly available to a national audience; east coast segments are broadcast too early for west coast audiences to consume. Daytime segments are collected in a manner similar to network news, with two 30-minute segments collected per day, rotating among the three networks.

Early evening and primetime, taken together, form a news block typically lasting from 6 PM to 11 PM on weekdays. Prior to 2009, CNN and FOX had three of their four cable news programs coded, with MSNBC having two of their four coded. This was done is reflection of the audience reach at the time, in which MSNBC had lower ratings than CNN and FOX. Since 2009, this has been amended to sample one or two segments from CNN, one or two segments from MSNBC, and two segments from FOX, for a total of between 30–60 minutes of coded substance per source per day, for a total of nearly 3.5 hours of coded substance per day.

For our purposes, the sampling scheme for collection of the news story data warrants several considerations. First, the rotating basis of the collection during the relevant time period of analysis (2007) means that liberal news source MSNBC would have had far fewer opportunities to be collected; as a result, the gap in reporting trends between conservative and liberal media outlets on Iraq Combat Events may actually be biased downward since more MSNBC

Below is the current list of evening cable programs included in our sample as of August 2011.

	CNN	Fox News	MSNBC
6 p.m.	Situation Room	Special Report w/Bret Baier	
7 p.m.	John King, USA	Fox Report w/ Shephard Smith	Hardball
8 p.m.	Anderson Cooper 360	The O'Reilly Factor	The Last Word
9 p.m.	—	Hannity	The Rachel Maddow Show
10 p.m.	—	—	The Ed show

Figure A4.3 Pew Research NCI Dataset, Cable News Sampling Scheme Post-2011
Note: This figure depicts the post-2011 collection scheme for cable news segments during the critical early evening-primetime joint period. This is an amendment from the collection scheme used for the main body's data from 2007 in that while CNN and FOX would have had three of their programs sampled, MSNBC would only have had two sampled. Figure reproduced with permission of Pew Research at http://www.journalism.org/news_index_methodology.

stories were not collected to this end. FOX and CNN would have been, on average, collected 50% more than the MSNBC segments; while this is reflective of differing audience reach, it also heightens the importance of reporting biases between sources as discussed in the main analysis. Second, the rotation scheme does not harm inference based on "% of newshole" dependent variable use. The graphically displayed reporting trends in Figure 3.1 utilize daily percentages of the Iraq Combat Event-related segments as a percentage of the collected outlet airtime. Because of the rotating collection scheme as it was conducted pre-2011, this means that day-to-day total time per outlet would have remained fixed, while segment length devoted to this story, our main variable of interest, was allowed to vary based on news source. These daily percentages were then plotted as individual pointed that the LOESS smoother could visually depict in a more substantively useful fashion.

Newspapers

Analysis of print media relied on collection of same-day delivery of electronic, full-text versions of the major newspapers through various providers available to Pew Research. The newspapers are organized on a three-tiered system of audience reach and level of distribution. As of 2007, when the substantive data used in the main analysis was collected, Tier 1 included the *New York Times*, *Wall Street Journal*, *LA Times*, *USA Today*, and the *Washington Post*, though the latter has since fallen to Tier 2 due to lower circulation. Tier 2 newspapers typically include regionalized print media with local audiences and non-national distribution, such as the *Atlanta Constitution-Journal*, while Tier 3 are more localized. Collection on a daily basis included coding two of the four Tier 1 papers per day. Since no Tier 2 or Tier 3 papers enter in our analysis, I leave discussion of that analysis scheme out.

Again, complete coding of the entire newspaper is cost prohibitive for minimal quantitative value. Two of the four Tier 1 papers are sampled each day, with the sampled newspapers being coded based on the stories which appear on page A1, both above and below the fold, and any substance continued inside the newspaper so long as it begins on the front page. The logic for consideration of these stories is that editors make a conscious choice to allocate finite column-inches to stories of particular import. Just as non-collection of local inserts or the last 30 minutes of network news increases efficiency with little loss of substance, so too does ignoring inside-the-fold stories that were not prominent or important enough to be placed on the front page. The purpose of the index, and its application for this study, is the frequency and location of specific story topics in the information environment; as such, study of headlines and lead stories is precisely where focus ought to be. This scheme results in about 20 newspaper stories collected and coded per day.

For this analysis, newspaper prominence was calculated using the NCI's five-point scale of story prominence, inverting the scale, and dividing the selected story by the sum of all stories from that paper per day. For example, a story about Iraq Combat Events featured on the front page of the *New York Times* that was coded as "Front Page/Second Prominent," would have been entered as 102 in the dataset, on the scale of 101 (Front Page/Most Prominent) to 105 (Front Page/Other, Below the Fold). I repurpose this measure into an inverse five-point scale of importance; the above story would be given a score of 4, just as a story that was 104: *Front Page/Other, Above the Fold* would have been given a 2. I sum the total prominence of stories reported by that source as divide it by the prominence of the observed story, in order to ascertain a proxy measure of the percentage of finite prominence the editor's devoted to the story. As argued here, this is a fair measure of the importance of the story to this source and its availability to its audience.

Radio

Because online news sources do not factor in my analysis, I also forgo discussion of their collection scheme. Radio sources, however, factor prominently in my analysis as a decidedly conservative-heavy transmission medium for information. Because of the wide variation in types of radio sources, Pew subsets the available radio outlets into one of three categories. First, *Public Radio* collects rotating 30-minute segments of National Public Radio's (NPR) *Morning Edition* and *All Things Considered*. The scheme of sampling rotates between the first 30 minutes of the former, the second 30 minutes of the former, the first 30 minutes of the latter, and the second 30 minutes of the latter. NPR broadcasts are typically two hours in length for either segment, with member stations picking which parts of that broadcast to incorporate into their own. The dataset includes additional 30-minute sampling of WFYI, the member station from which Pew collects NPR broadcasts.

The second category, *Talk Radio*, includes those outlets with a public affairs of news-oriented tone. Just as larger conservative audiences on cable news leads to a sampling scheme that favors FOX over MSNBC, the vastly larger conservative audience for talk radio favors *Hannity* and *Rush Limbaugh* over *Ed Schultz*; as of 2007, Schultz and Hannity were sampled every other day and Limbaugh was sampled everyday, with all coded based on the first 30 minutes of the broadcast. Again, this upweights the conservative outlets measured in the 2007 version of the dataset, with conservative media outlets collected more frequently in line with their larger audience reach. The third category is *Headline Feeds*, which are hourly news feeds from larger national outlets like CBS or CNN, but are of limited length and typically sum up national or international headlines from the parent news source. Pew NCI collects two Headline Feeds per day, at ABC and CBS Radio, each for five minutes in length for a total of 10 minutes per day.

This analysis calculated the length of the segment spent of specific topics (like Iraq Combat Events) as a percentage of the total length of the segment. Again, the total length of the recorded segment is fixed while the time spent on specific subjects is allowed to vary. One key consideration for this analysis is the large oversampling of conservative radio outlets compared to only five-minute headline feeds from more centrist or liberal news sources. In any given day, Hannity or Limbaugh have nearly 5–10 times more airtime to discuss high-salience news stories than the headline feeds. This imbalance biases the expected result of our analysis downward, making the gap in reporting trends even more stark. With less time to report on specific stories, headline feeds still spend more time talking about war events than conservative radio hosts, as seen in Figure 4.2(b).

Chapter 5

Sample Statistics and Supplementary Results

Table A5.1 **Randomization Checks and Covariate Balance**

Respondent Demographic	Control	Professionalism	Performance	Partisanship
Party Identification				
Democrat	37.5%	44.1%	34.7%	35.7%
Republican	20.8%	21.4%	22.1%	28.4%
Gender				
Male	44.1%	46.1%	40.0%	46.3%
Female	60.0%	54.0%	60.1%	53.6%

Table A5.1 **Continued**

Respondent Demographic	Control	Professionalism	Performance	Partisanship
Age				
25th Percentile	37	35.75	29	33
50th Percentile	50	47	46	48.5
75th Percentile	62	61	61	60
Race				
White	69.0%	67.5%	71.1%	65.4%
Non-white	31.0%	32.4%	28.8%	34.5%
Sample Size	245	256	253	246

Notes: Percentages reflect segment of survey population assigned to each experimental condition broken down by key demographic values. Subjects were assigned on a random basis to each of the four conditions.

Table A5.2 **Randomization Check: Logit Regression with Treatment Assignment as DV**

	Dependent Variable: Treatment Assignment			
	Control	Partisan	Professional	Performance
	(1)	(2)	(3)	(4)
Democrat	−0.069	−0.206	0.232	0.037
	(0.174)	(0.171)	(0.171)	(0.173)
Independent	0.212	−0.365*	−0.038	0.174
	(0.207)	(0.215)	(0.215)	(0.207)
Male	−0.024	0.132	0.125	−0.236
	(0.150)	(0.149)	(0.147)	(0.149)
Age	0.007	−0.002	0.001	−0.005
	(0.004)	(0.004)	(0.004)	(0.004)
White	0.002	−0.227	−0.024	0.250
	(0.165)	(0.162)	(0.161)	(0.165)
Constant	−1.459***	−0.757***	−1.241***	−0.958***
	(0.290)	(0.285)	(0.286)	(0.284)
Observations	1,000	1,000	1,000	1,000
Log Likelihood	−554.703	−555.304	−567.054	−562.331
Akaike Inf. Crit.	1,121.407	1,122.608	1,146.109	1,136.662

Notes: †$p < 0.10$,* $p < 0.05$,** $p < 0.01$,*** $p < 0.001$.

Questionnaire Design

Programming Instructions: Assign random integer from 1 to 4, record this integer as *assignment*. Assignment of this integer is recorded and dictates the value of [**Prompt1**], [**Prompt2**], and [**Text**].

Assigning Textual Prompt

The variable [**Text**] takes on the following values depending on integer assignment:

- *Assignment*=1, [**Text**]=*We are interested in how well certain news stories regarding US foreign policy can reach the public. The length of the "war on terror" and associated US military activities have created a large amount of information that can be hard to follow.*
- *Assignment*=2, 3, 4, [**Text**]=*We are interested in how well certain news stories regarding US foreign policy can reach the public. The length of the "war on terror" and associated US military activities have created a large amount of information that can be hard to follow. We want to ask about some stories that occurred and were reported to see if you happened to hear about them.*

Assigning News Vignette #1

The variable [**Prompt1**] takes on the following values depending on integer assignment:

- *Assignment*=1, [**Prompt1**]=*Would you say that you follow stories about US foreign policy in the news?*
- *Assignment*=2, [**Prompt1**]=*Story 1: The 2012 presidential election saw candidates Barack Obama and Mitt Romney receive many high-profile endorsements, several hundred of which coming from the military community. Among these were retired military officers General Wesley Clark, former Supreme Allied Commander in Europe, and General Tommy Franks, former commander of US forces in the Middle East, who publicly supported Obama and Romney, respectively.*
- *Assignment*=3, [**Prompt1**]=*Story 1: In 2009, several former Army soldiers received multiple life sentences for an event in 2006 where the men had participated in the rape and murder of a 14-year-old Iraqi girl. The soldiers, stationed near the town of Mahmudiyah at the time, were convicted of this crime along with the murder of the girl's mother, father, and younger sister.*
- *Assignment*=4, [**Prompt1**]=*Story 1: A British development aid worker named Linda Norgrove was captured by Taliban forces in eastern Afghanistan in late 2010. During an attempted raid to free the captured civilian, members of the Navy's*

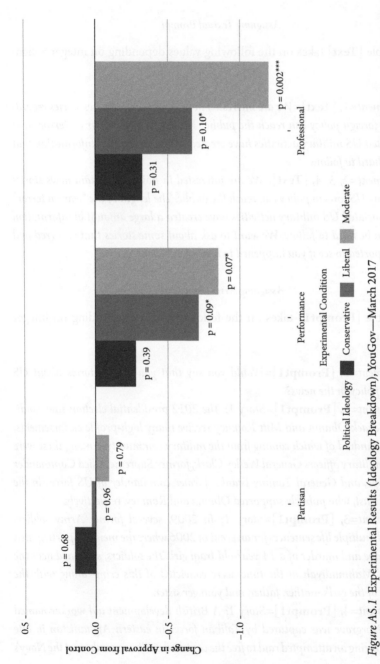

Figure A5.1 Experimental Results (Ideology Breakdown), YouGov—March 2017

Note: This figure depicts deviation in expressed confidence in the military institution as measured by the 11-pt scale in all experimental conditions. Respondent patterns broken down by identification into liberal, conservative, and moderate subsamples based on self-identification on five-point political ideology scale. Reported p-values reflect significance at 95% level for two-tailed t-test for difference in means between experimental and control subgroups. $N_{Total} = 907$

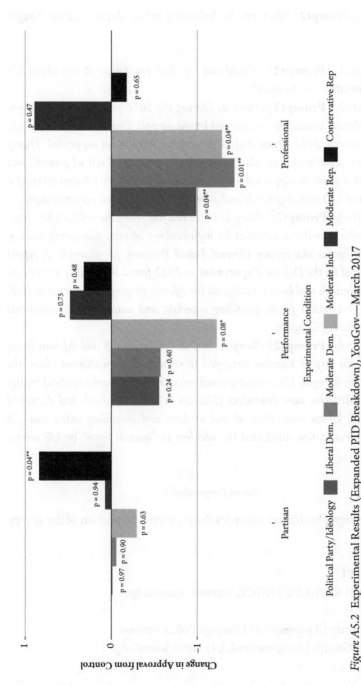

Figure AS.2 Experimental Results (Expanded PID Breakdown), YouGov—March 2017

Note: This figure depicts deviation in expressed confidence in the military institution as measured by the 11-pt scale in all experimental conditions. Respondent patterns broken down by identification into cross party-ideology subsamples based on self-identification on five-point political ideology scale and identification on the seven-point party ID scale (including leaners). Reported p-values reflect significance at 95% level for two-tailed t-test for difference in means between experimental and control subgroups. $N_{Total} = 678$

SEAL Team Six accidentally killed Norgrove when one of the sailors mistakenly threw a grenade into the area where she was hiding.

Assigning News Vignette #2

The variable [**Prompt2**] takes on the following values depending on integer assignment:

- *Assignment=1,* [**Prompt2**]=*Would you say that you follow stories about US military operations in the news?*
- *Assignment=2,* [**Prompt2**]=*Story 2: During the 2016 presidential campaign, both presidential candidates announced broad support from retired military officers like General Mike Flynn and General John Allen, who supported Trump and Clinton, respectively. Donald Trump released a list of 88 retired generals and admirals that publicly supported his candidacy, while Hillary Clinton released a similar list of 110 retired generals and admirals that supported her campaign.*
- *Assignment=3,* [**Prompt2**]=*Story 2: In the last few years, the military has experienced problems with misconduct by high-ranking officers, prompting the resignation of figures like former General David Petraeus, for example. A report commissioned by the Defense Department in 2012 found that nearly thirty generals and admirals had been investigated for offenses ranging from sexual assault, misuse of government funds, gambling scandals, and inappropriate statements about members of Congress.*
- *Assignment=4,* [**Prompt2**]=*Story 2: In October 2015, US and Afghan forces fighting in the city of Kunduz struggled to remove Taliban elements from the town. During the fight, US combat aircraft misidentified a nearby medical facility staffed by Médecins sans Frontières (Doctors Without Borders) and destroyed the hospital, killing more than 30 aid workers and wounding many more. A follow-up investigation attributed the accident to "human error" by US service members.*

Survey Progression

Standard demographic battery precedes the experimental portion of the survey.
[**TEXT**]

[**PROMPT1**]
Question 1: SINGLE CHOICE. Interest/Knowledge

- Control Group (*Assignment=1*) Foreign Policy Interest
- Treatment Groups (*Assignment=2,3,4*) News Knowledge 1

Did you hear this story?

• Yes/No

[PROMPT2]
Question 2: SINGLE CHOICE. Interest/Knowledge

• Control Group (*Assignment=1*) Foreign Policy Interest
• Treatment Groups (*Assignment=2,3,4*) News Knowledge 2

Did you hear this story?

• Yes/No

Question 3–5: DYNAMIC GRID. Institutional Confidence
On scale of 0–10 (with 0 being the least and 10 being the most), how much trust and confidence do you have in each of the following institutions?
Rows [randomized order]

• Congress
• The presidency
• The military

News Vignette Analogs

Each of the treatment conditions in this experimental design was exposed to news stories that were intended to provoke "top-of-the-head" thinking and introduce specific types of newly salient information regarding military misconduct of poor performance. In order to minimize deception and increase external validity, the stories used were actual cases of partisan, professional, and performance-based events reported in multiple news outlets. Below, I provide a short summary of each of the cases used for vignettes in this experiment and the relevant cites for these stories in the information environment.

Partisan Activity

The first partisan vignette included information about retired military elites, including General Wesley Clark and General Tommy Franks, providing high-profile endorsements to presidential candidate Mitt Romney and President Barack Obama in the 2012 presidential campaign. Clark, a retired Supreme Allied Commander of NATO Force Europe and former 2004 Democratic presidential candidate, was one of several prominent military officers to endorse the incumbent president; along with retired Major General Paul Eaton, these officers opposed Mitt Romney's take on foreign policy early in the campaign season and touted Obama's successful operation to kill Osama bin Laden.[2] Obama's campaign co-chairs included retired Admiral John Nathman, the former second-highest ranking officer in the Navy, who would go on to speak at the Democratic National Convention.[3] The endorsements for Mitt Romney were considerably more numerous; on the eve of the election, nearly 500 retired generals and admirals sponsored a full-page ad in the *Washington Times* endorsing Romney. The list involved five former Chairmen of the Joints Chiefs of Staff—including Clinton appointee General Hugh Shelton—and General Tommy Franks, the former Central Command (CENTCOM) commander in 2003 during the Iraq invasion under President Bush.[4]

In the second vignette, similar information is exposed to the respondent regarding endorsement in the 2016 president campaign, though in this election both candidates displayed both high-profile individual endorsements and large blocs of retired officers. Republican nominee Donald Trump released a letter in September 2016 with the endorsement of 88 retired generals and admirals, including former commander of US forces in Korea General Burwell Bell and former commander of the US Army's Delta Force, Lieutenant General Jerry Boykin. Trump's list boasted officers who were more advanced in age and had retired ten or more years previously, though most notable among his military endorsements was that of retired Lieutenant General Mike Flynn, a close adviser and former intelligence officer who would go on to speak at the Republican National Convention.[5] Democratic nominee Secretary Hillary Clinton responded with her own list of 110 retired officers' endorsements, including recent Afghanistan forces commander General John Allen and General Wesley Clark once again. Allen would go on to speak at the party nominating convention that year as well, with Clark leading a cadre of 15 officers who independently voiced their fears over a Trump presidency and the denigration of fellow veteran Senator John McCain that Trump has stated earlier.[6]

Professionalism Failures

In the second treatment condition, individuals were exposed instead to priming information regarding professional or ethical failures by military elites or the institution as a means for making such calculations salient to the respondent's calculation of confidence in the military. The intent in this treatment condition was to focus on events of singular or collective values violations in which the driving mechanism was not incompetence, but rather motivated harm or ethical faults. In the first vignette, respondents were exposed to a news story regarding the trial and conviction of several US soldiers in 2009 for an event which occurred in Mahmudiyah, Iraq, in 2006. A group of five soldiers led by Private

Steven Dale Green, raped a 14-year-old Iraqi girl before proceeding to kill both her and her family. Green's unit was serving in the famed Sunni "Triangle of Death" outside of Baghdad when the incident occurred, followed by his arrest and the arrest of four other soldiers who participated in the crime. The event was all the more damaging to the military's institutional reputation as Green had been arrested shortly before his enlistment, admitted to the Army on one of the many "moral waivers" the military had issued in an attempt to boost recruitment in the worst years of the Iraq War.[7]

In the second vignette, respondents were exposed to a news story that focused on the elite-level of the military institution and its misconduct. This involved the 2014 publication of the increasingly list of senior military officials relived of command or fired due to various forms of misconduct and professional failures. Citing the 2012 resignation of retired General David Petraeus from his post as Director of Central Intelligence due to an unknown affair as the impetus, Defense Secretary Leon Panetta commissioned a study of ethical standards for senior officers. Resulting media exposure captured misconduct ranging from sexual assault, sexual misconduct, forgery, public intoxication, bribery, unauthorized gift acceptance from foreign entities, and misuse of government funds.[8] In many cases, the hypocrisy of the violations was particularly egregious, from a South Carolina-based one-star general advocating "zero-tolerance for sexual harassment" while being investigated for assaulting his mistress, to the relief of a high-ranking nuclear commander for public drunkenness while with Russian military officials in Moscow.

Battlefield Performance Problems

In the third treatment condition, respondents were subjected to news stories regarding military failures of a standard variety: battlefield results. This included cases of incompetence, miscalculation, miscoordination, or tactical lack of proficiency designed to make salient the standard calculation of confidence in the military institution according the institutionalist theory. The first vignette detailed the failure of a 2010 mission by the Navy's SEAL Team Six to rescue Linda Norgrove, a British national and aid worker captured by elements of the Taliban. Norgrove was moved outside the compound in which the SEALs believed she was housed by her captors and one of the team's members accidentally killed Norgrove with a grenade believing her to be an enemy combatant.[9] In addition to drawing attention to a tactical failure by the military institution, it also invokes the popularly recognized SEAL Team Six, made famous from successful operations in anti-piracy off the coast of Somalia in 2009 and in Pakistan to killed Osama bin Laden in 2011. Using such an organization is meant to draw a stronger contrast in the miscalculation between expectation and newly salient information.

In the second vignette, respondents were exposed to a story detailing the accidental bombing of a Medecins sans Frontieres (Doctors Without Borders) clinic in Kunduz, Afghanistan, in 2015. The clinic's staff were administering to the increasing number of wounded created by Taliban resurgence in Kunduz. Part of coalition response to the increased violence included fire from a nearby AC-130 Spectre gunship, which despite initial reports was called in to support US efforts on the ground. In the subsequent investigation, it was clear that the location of the hospital was in dispute at numerous points, resulting in a nearly 30-minute barrage on the clinic that left 42 dead and dozens more wounded. President Obama apologized directly to the president of MSF, admitting US miscalculations in the incident.[10] In this case, miscalculations of targeting and tactical proficiency not only failed to produce a positive outcomes, but created a tangibly negative one in the destruction of a medical facility crewed largely by third-party nationals.

Chapter 6
Descriptive Statistics and Supplementary Results

Table A6.1 **Balance and Covariate Balance Statistics**

Respondent Demographic	Non-Partisan	Activist Left	Activist Right
Party Identification			
Democrat	39.60	37.46	39.11
Republican	27.63	23.63	26.47
Gender			
Male	45.58	50.14	50.29
Female	54.41	49.85	49.70
Age			
25th Percentile	33	29	30
50th Percentile	46	40	44
75th Percentile	59	58	59
Race			
White	68.66	73.19	64.70
Non-white	31.33	26.80	35.29

Notes: Percentages reflect segment of survey population assigned to each experimental condition broken down by key demographic values. Subjects were assigned on a random basis to each of the three conditions.

Table A6.2 **Randomization Check: Logit Regression on Dichotomous Assignment Variable**

	Dependent Variable: Treatment Condition Assignment		
	Non-Partisan	Activist Left	Activist Right
	(1)	(2)	(3)
Democrat	0.114	−0.178	0.067
	(0.155)	(0.153)	(0.155)
Republican	0.223	−0.281	0.057
	(0.172)	(0.173)	(0.173)
Male	−0.230*	0.128	0.104
	(0.136)	(0.135)	(0.136)
Age	−0.001	0.006	−0.005
	(0.011)	(0.011)	(0.011)
GenX	0.108	0.089	−0.203
	(0.272)	(0.279)	(0.276)
Millenial	−0.329	0.496	−0.171
	(0.429)	(0.431)	(0.430)
Constant	−0.535	−1.110	−0.452
	(0.724)	(0.728)	(0.726)
Observations	1,038	1,038	1,038
Log Likelihood	−658.491	−657.105	−655.712
Akaike Inf. Crit.	1,330.983	1,328.210	1,325.425

Notes: $^{*}p<0.1$; $^{**}p<0.05$; $^{***}p<0.01$.

Additional Survey Statistics

Table A6.3 **Mean Values for Endorser Credibility Metrics, Non-Partisan Treatment Condition (By Respondent Party ID)**

	Partisans			Strong Partisans	
	Democrats	Independents	Republicans	Democrats	Republicans
Knowledgeable	5.57	5.26	5.95	5.54	5.93
Experienced	5.72	5.48	5.97	5.56	6.00
Trustworthy	5.20	5.00	5.67	5.18	5.72
Reliable	5.38	5.04	5.60	5.36	5.64

Table A6.3 **Continued**

	Partisans			Strong Partisans	
	Democrats	*Independents*	*Republicans*	*Democrats*	*Republicans*
Expertise	11.30	10.74	11.93	11.11	11.93
Trustworthiness	10.58	10.05	11.27	10.55	11.37
Credibility	21.88	20.79	23.21	21.66	23.30
N	139	115	97	90	62

Notes: Reported figures depict mean values for measured endorser credibility metrics in the non-partisan condition. Columns 1–3 partisan categories represent respondents who identified as Democrat, Independent, or Republican on a three-point scale (PID3). Columns 4–5 strong partisan categories are those respondents who identified as "strong" Democrats and Republicans on the extended six-point scale (PID6). Rows 1–4 indicate items utilized for construction of additive measures on scale of 1–7; rows 5–6 indicate additive scores for expertise and trustworthiness, respectively, on a scale of 1–14. Row 7 depicts mean total credibility scores, on scale of 1–28.

Table A6.4 **Mean Values for Endorser Credibility Metrics, Activist Left Treatment Condition (By Respondent Party ID)**

	Partisans			Strong Partisans	
	Democrats	*Independents*	*Republicans*	*Democrats*	*Republicans*
Knowledgeable	5.89	5.24	4.76	5.86	4.71
Experienced	6.03	5.51	5.10	6.00	4.95
Trustworthy	5.64	4.84	4.20	5.64	4.17
Reliable	5.78	4.97	4.51	5.68	4.31
Expertise	11.93	10.76	9.87	11.86	9.66
Trustworthiness	11.43	9.82	8.71	11.32	8.48
Credibility	23.36	20.58	18.59	23.18	18.15
N	130	109	82	79	45

Notes: Reported figures depict mean values for measured endorser credibility metrics in the activist left condition. Columns 1–3 partisan categories represent respondents who identified as Democrat, Independent, or Republican on a three-point scale (PID3). Columns 4–5 strong partisan categories are those respondents who identified as "strong" Democrats and Republicans on the extended six-point scale (PID6). Rows 1–4 indicate items utilized for construction of additive measures on scale of 1–7; rows 5–6 indicate additive scores for expertise and trustworthiness, respectively, on a scale of 1–14. Row 7 depicts mean total credibility scores, on scale of 1–28.

Survey Experiment Supplementals
Questionnaire Design

Programming Instructions: Assign random integer from 1 to 3, record this integer as *assignment*. Assignment of this integer is recorded and dictates the value of [**Prompt1**], [**Prompt2**], and [**Image**].

Table A6.5 **Mean Values for Endorser Credibility Metrics, Activist Right Treatment Condition (By Respondent Party ID)**

	Partisans			Strong Partisans	
	Democrats	*Independents*	*Republicans*	*Democrats*	*Republicans*
Knowledgeable	4.55	4.93	6.01	4.61	6.27
Experienced	4.99	5.23	6.03	5.12	6.08
Trustworthy	4.17	4.25	5.74	4.13	5.97
Reliable	4.45	4.51	5.91	4.47	6.22
Expertise	9.54	10.16	12.04	9.73	12.35
Trustworthiness	8.63	8.76	11.65	8.61	12.20
Credibility	18.18	18.93	23.70	18.35	24.56
N	133	117	90	80	48

Notes: Reported figures depict mean values for measured endorser credibility metrics in the activist right condition. Columns 1–3 partisan categories represent respondents who identified as Democrat, Independent, or Republican on a three-point scale (PID3). Columns 4–5 strong partisan categories are those respondents who identified as "strong" Democrats and Republicans on the extended six-point scale (PID6). Rows 1–4 indicate items utilized for construction of additive measures on scale of 1–7; rows 5–6 indicate additive scores for expertise and trustworthiness, respectively, on a scale of 1–14. Row 7 depicts mean total credibility scores, on scale of 1–28.

Assigning Textual Prompt

The variable [**Image**] takes on the following values depending on integer assignment:

- *Assignment*=1, see Figure A8.1
- *Assignment*=2, see Figure A8.2
- *Assignment*=3, see Figure A8.3

The variable [**Prompt1**] takes on the following value:

- "General (Retired) Wilson has publicly written and spoken in support of the proposed strike, considering such a move to be necessary. In a recent interview, Wilson stated that "the risk posed by North Korea is too great; the US needs to take action.""

The variable [**Prompt2**] takes on the following value:

- "In several editorial articles and interviews, General (Retired) Wilson has argued against the reduction, calling instead for Congress to increase funding to the State Department and the US Agency for International Development (USAID)."

Morgan L. Wilson

Morgan Wilson retired from the United States Army after 36 years of service at the rank of four-star general. Wilson's long career includes the following:

- Multiple combat tours in command of soldiers in Iraq and Afghanistan, earning awards for both merit and valor.

- B.S, United States Military Academy, West Point; M.A, International Relations, University of Chicago.

- Following retirement, General (Retired) Wilson joined the non-partisan Council on Foreign Relations and is currently authoring a scholarly book on the history of US foreign policy.

- Wilson did not endorse a major party candidate in the 2016 general election.

- Wilson has appeared on National Public Radio in a discussion on US security policy during the Cold War.

Figure A8.1 Experimental Military Elite Profile (Non-Partisan)
Note: This figure represents the elite profile viewed in the non-partisan category, ASSIGNMENT=1.

Survey Progression

Standard demographic battery precedes the experimental portion of the survey.

This survey is being conducted by Qualtrics on behalf of researchers at varying organizations. The survey will ask you about a variety of topics, and the results will inform academic research and press releases. Your participation is voluntary and your responses will be held confidential. As specified by the online research panel which invited you to participate in this survey, you will receive an incentive for your participation. We have tested the survey and found that, on average it takes approximately 15 minutes to complete. This time may vary depending on factors such as your Internet connection speed and the answers you give. To indicate that you consent to participate in this research, please click on the "Next" button below.

Morgan L. Wilson

Morgan Wilson retired from the United States Army after 36 years of service at the rank of four-star general. Wilson's long career includes the following:

- Multiple combat tours in command of soldiers in Iraq and Afghanistan, earning awards for both merit and valor.

- B.S., United States Military Academy, West Point; M.A., International Relations, University of Chicago.

- Following retirement, General (Retired) Wilson joined the national security team for prominent Democratic primary candidates in both the 2012 and 2016 presidential elections.

- Wilson publicly endorsed Hillary Clinton during the 2016 general election.

- Wilson appears regularly on MSNBC and CNN as a vocal critic of President Trump's foreign and security policy.

Figure A8.2 Experimental Military Elite Profile (Non-Partisan)
Note: This figure represents the elite profile viewed in the activist-left category, ASSIGNMENT=2.

We are interested in public attitudes on different policy issues in American society. In the following short survey, you will be presented with a few short questions on several issues currently under debate, along with the opinion of one of many relevant voices on these subjects. We have included a brief summary of the qualifications and experience of the commentator as well. Please read all information carefully and offer your honest opinion on each of the questions.

Question 1: SINGLE CHOICE. Manipulation Check
Before considering your position, this is the profile for one of the voices that has offered their own opinion on the issue we'd like to ask you about.

Morgan L. Wilson

Morgan Wilson retired from the United States Army after 36 years of service at the rank of four-star general. Wilson's long career includes the following:

- Multiple combat tours in command of soldiers in Iraq and Afghanistan, earning awards for both merit and valor.

- B.S., United States Military Academy, West Point; M.A., International Relations, University of Chicago.

- Following retirement, General (Retired) Wilson joined the national security team for prominent Republican primary candidates in both the 2012 and 2016 presidential elections.

- Wilson publicly endorsed President Donald Trump during the 2016 general election.

- Wilson appears regularly on FOX News and talk radio as a vocal critic of President Obama's foreign and security policy.

Figure A8.3 Experimental Military Elite Profile (Non-Partisan)
Note: This figure represents the elite profile viewed in the activist-right category, ASSIGNMENT=3.

[**IMAGE**]
Before proceeding, we just want to make sure you have read the above information about this individual's background. Which media outlet did this individual appear on as a commentator?

- MSNBC
- National Public Radio
- FOX News

Question 2A-D: SLIDER. Individual Endorser Credibility
On a scale from 1–7, how would you rate General Wilson on the following characteristics?

Rows [randomized order]

- Knowledgeable
- Trustworthy
- Reliable
- Experienced

Columns [1–7]

Question 3A-D: SLIDER. Institutional Credibility

Please indicate to what extent you agree/disagree with these statements with regards to the following institution: **The military**

Rows [randomized order]

- The military is skilled at what they do.
- The military makes truthful claims.
- The military has a great amount of experience.
- I trust the military.

Columns

- 1 (Strongly Disagree)
- 2
- 3
- 4 (Neither Agree/Disagree)
- 5
- 6
- 7 (Strongly Agree)

Question 4: SINGLE CHOICE. North Korea Strike

North Korea

As you may know, there is a lot of debate over potential military action in North Korea. The North Korean regime has defied the international community and US warnings against developing and testing their nuclear weapons. One of the options being considered is a pre-emptive strike with conventional weapons on the North Korean military.

[PROMPT1]

What is your opinion on the proposal to pre-emptively strike North Korea?

Choices [random direction]

- Strongly oppose
- Somewhat oppose

- Neither support nor oppose
- Somewhat support
- Strongly support

Question 5: SINGLE CHOICE. Foreign Aid/Federal Budget
Federal Budget
Another issue being discussed is how to spend taxpayer money in the federal budget. One proposal has been to dramatically reduce funding to the State Department, the agency that manages US diplomatic efforts around the world, and to cut its spending on foreign and humanitarian aid to other countries.

[PROMPT2]
What is your opinion on the proposal to decrease funding to the State Department and foreign aid programs?
Choices [random direction]

- Strongly oppose
- Somewhat oppose
- Neither support nor oppose
- Somewhat support
- Strongly support

Military Elite Profile Analogs

As discussed in the main body of the analysis, the characteristics of the military elite profiles used in this experimental design encompassed six broad categories. The *overseas experience, academic qualification,* and *command responsibility* portions of each profile were kept fixed, with values representative of many high-ranking retired military elites. Overseas experience values reflect the current pool of retired elites, which include those with experience in the Vietnam War to those with more recent command tenures in Iraq, Afghanistan, and various peacekeeping missions. The composite profile developed here used recent overseas deployments, as this subset of retired officers is considerably larger and more politically active.

The information regarding academic qualifications and command responsibility was developed using the experiences of several high-profile military elites with both experience commanding large formations abroad and advanced degrees. These included H. R. McMaster, David Petraeus, David Barno, Stanley McChrystal, and James Stavridis, all retired elites with undergraduate degrees from the country's military service academies and graduate or post-graduate degrees in international relations, history, public policy, national security, or law and diplomacy. Most of these figures also commanded at the three- and four-star level during their military service, from regional combat headquarters elements such as the International Security Assistance Force (ISAF) in Afghanistan to major combatant commands such as Central Command (CENTCOM) and EUCOM (European Command). While command at these levels is not necessarily a common trait among politically active elites, nor is it a requisite for engagement in media commentary or partisan activism, setting the expertise at its highest realistic levels made all subsequent devaluing of that expertise based on partisan behavior easier to measure.

The remaining three characteristics, experimentally varied in the above design, were also drawn from the profiles of existing military elites. This was done in order to develop an ecologically realistic set of characteristics that was both rooted in realism while also allowing for the maximum contrast between partisan and non-partisan elites. I briefly detail some of the actual figures used to develop these categories below according to each of the experimental dimensions varied in the experimental design used for this analysis.

Media Presence

Perhaps one of the most visible methods by which military elites can engage in activism or partisan behavior is through media commentary, editorialism, or analysis. This avenue has few barriers to entry and can magnify the voices of even relatively junior elites by providing a larger, and potentially partisan audience. The *media presence* value was varied across treatment conditions in order to reflect the different outlets that military elites might appear on in order to broadcast information. I chose to have the non-partisan elite appear on National Public Radio, the activist-left elite on MSNBC, and the activist-right on FOX News, in order to attach decidedly partisan audiences to their messaging. While print media outlets would have been equally realistic in terms of an avenue that military elites often utilize for messaging, it is more difficult to draw strong liberal-conservative contrast using these outlets than to use cable new outlets with decidedly partisan followings, such as MSNBC, CNN, or FOX.[11] The current media environment makes it difficult to establish a truly non-partisan source for broad messaging. I chose the non-partisan elite to appear on National Public Radio, despite it appearing as left-leaning in some political circles; to mitigate this, I ensured that the elite's comments were infrequent (in that Wilson's media presence was low) and benign (in that they were observational rather than critical).

Some examples of military elites used to develop this profile include cable news analysts, media commentators, or print media editorial writers. Military elites such as former US Army Europe commander Lieutenant General (Ret.)

Mark Hertling, former Army Vice Chief of Staff General (Ret.) Jack Keane, former SOUTHCOM commander General (Ret.) Barry McCaffrey, and Medal of Honor recipient Colonel Jack Jacobs appeared regularly on cable news outlets CNN, FOX News, and MSNBC, respectively.[12] At the time of collection, Hertling and Jacobs had commented regularly on President Donald Trump's relationship with veteran familites, Keane on the state of national security policy and US military efforts in Iraq and Syria, and McCaffrey on the state of US-North Korea affairs.[13] These networks frequently included interviews or editorials with other retired military elites including former Guantanamo Bay military prosecutor Colonel Morris Davis, former Supreme Allied Commander for NATO Admiral (Ret.) James Stavridis, who both appeared on MSNBC, and Medal of Honor recipient Dakota Meyer, who appeared on FOX News. The strong contrast offered by appearance on these networks was incorporated into the experimental profiles by ensuring the partisan conditions made clear that media exposure was both frequent and politically charged; the substance of the manipulation check question also sought to embed this information more directly with the respondent. The ubiquitous appearance of these figures on cable news networks demonstrates their potential reach. However, the perception of a partisan slant to the elites themselves is not merely a product of their appearance through an outlet with established partisan audiences, but also in the substance of the commentary itself.

Political Activism and Advocacy

In addition to regular exposure to partisan audiences through outlets such as cable news, the tone and tenor of military elite activism is itself revealing of partisan sentiment. The previously mentioned cable news analysts often provide commentary which exceeds objective analysis, instead mounting an ardent defense of or attack on specific political leaders. However, certain elites engage in regular policy activism even if their media profile is comparably low. Former Katrina relief commander Lieutenant General (Ret.) Russel Honore became a staunch environmental activist after retirement and in 2017 was an outspoken critic of administration response to the devastation in Puerto Rico following Hurricane Maria; Honore made headlines by reprimanding the president directly during the crisis, stating "the mayor's living on a cot, and I hope the president has a good day at golf."[14] Former special operations commander Lieutenant General (Ret.) William Boykin engaged in a variety of evangelical activist groups upon retirement. He was removed from a speech at the United States Military Academy at West Point in 2012 due to a record of comments characterizing US military efforts in Iraq and Afghanistan as "Christian battle," denouncing Islam as a "totalitarian way of life," and offered that the religion should not protected under the First Amendment.[15]

Policy advocacy or criticism has also included security policy more directly. Major General (Ret.) Robert Scales denounced Obama administration efforts in managing the humanitarian crisis in Syria in 2013, describing them as "amatuerism."[16] As mentioned in the main body of the analysis, blocs of military officers have collectively denounced Trump administration policy on a host of issues, including its position on torture, relations with the media, climate change, immigration, and diplomatic efforts with North Korea. While a sizable bloc also opposed a Trump administration directive to ban transgender soldiers from openly serving in the military, 16 retired general and flag officers, including regular FOX News commentator Lieutenant General (Ret.) Thomas McInerney, penned a letter of support for the ban through Boykin's Family Research Council in 2017.[17] The partisan overtones of military activism, in some cases on both sides of an issue, were adapted into the design of the experimental profiles by ensuring that while the non-partisan profile contained no such policy advocacy, the partisan profiles had an established record of opposition or support to the agendas of specific political elites.

Partisan Endorsements

Finally, the experimental profiles drew on established actions of partisan support or endorsements to political candidates, a form of military elite activism that is occurring with increased frequency and visibility. Though the impact of these types of endorsements has been found to be relatively small, their significance to the perceived objectivity of military elites and the institution of the armed forces is potentially large.[18] This pattern was readily observable during the 2016 presidential campaign, in which retired general officers played a prominent role in both major party conventions and in public endorsements for the candidates. Despite Martin Dempsey's admonishment that "the military is not a political prize," nearly 200 former officers offered public endorsements of either Secretary Hilary Clinton or Donald Trump during the campaign. The majority of the four-star officers, the highest-ranking elites in the military, who offered endorsements supported Clinton, including former Democratic presidential candidate and Supreme Allied Commander for NATO General (Ret.) Wesley Clark. Female officers were also outspoken supporters of the Clinton campaign, including former intelligence chief Lieutenant General (Ret.) Claudia Kennedy. Trump's position on torture also drove elites such as Major General (Ret.) Antonio Taguba, the former Abu Ghraib investigator, into the Clinton camp as well. However, Trump drew support from evangelical activists like Boykin, as well as from McInerney, who made headlines in 2010 for supporting an Army officer who refused to deploy to Afghanistan because he believed President Barack Obama was not born in the United States.[19]

Both major party conventions included high-profile speeches by senior officers, with former Afghanistan commander General (Ret.) John Allen speaking at the Democratic Convention and former DIA commander Lieutenant General (Ret.) Michael Flynn speaking at the Republican Convention, actions which were decried by a host of civil-military theorists, political commentators, and retired officers such as Dempsey. Medal of Honor recipient and self-professed Republican Florent Groberg also spoke at the convention in support of Clinton's campaign. Again, while the magnitude of these endorsements is debatable, their increasing regularity has significant implications for the perceived credibility of the military and its representatives. Furthermore, the profiles included reference to these elites having advised campaigns in national security and foreign policy. Both Lieutenant General (Ret.) Keith Kellogg and Flynn served on the Trump campaign as security advisers and members of transition team.[20] Former CIA chief and CENTCOM commander General (Ret.) David Petraeus advised the Clinton campaign, while Stavridis was reported at the time to have been vetted as a possible vice presidential candidate.[21] As such, the experimental profiles used in this analysis incorporated similar endorsements for or services on the staffs of political candidates in the 2016 election. In addition to high media presence on partisan networks and open policy advocacy or criticism, the profiles were designed in this way to maximize contrast to the non-partisan category while remaining to the the form of actual military elites in the informational environment.

NOTES

Chapter 1

1. Ernest Hemingway. *The Sun Also Rises*. New York: Scribner, 1956, p. 109.
2. Mano Sundaresan and Amy Isackson. "Democracy is declining in the U.S. but it's not all bad news, a report finds." *National Public Radio* (December 1, 2021); *Autocratization Turns Viral: Democracy Report 2021*. Tech. rep. Varieties of Democracy, March 2021; Christopher Ingraham. "Analysis—the United States is backsliding into autocracy under Trump, scholars warn." *Washington Post* (September 18, 2020); *NEW REPORT: US Democracy Has Declined Significantly in the Past Decade, Reforms Urgently Needed*. March 22, 2021; Annabelle Timsit. " 'Very few' believe U.S. democracy sets a good example, global survey finds." *Washington Post* (November 2, 2021).
3. Maggie Astor. "Now in your inbox: political misinformation." *New York Times* (December 13, 2021); Francis Fukuyama. "Opinion—One single day. That's all it took for the world to look away from us." *New York Times* (January 5, 2022); Matthew S. Schwartz. "1 in 4 Americans say violence against the government is sometimes OK." *National Public Radio* (January 31, 2022); Amanda Seitz and Hannah Fingerhut. "Americans agree misinformation is a problem, poll shows." *Associated Press* (October 8, 2021).
4. Kori N. Schake and Jim Mattis, eds. *Warriors and Citizens: American Views of Our Military*. Stanford, CA: July 14, 2021 https://news.gallup.com/poll/352316/americans-confidence-major-institutions-dips.aspx Hoover Institution Press, 2016.
5. Megan Brenan. *Americans' Confidence in Major U.S. Institutions Dips*. https://news.gallup.com/poll/352316/americans-confidence-major-institutions-dips.aspx (July 14, 2021).
6. Peter D. Feaver. "The civil-military problematique: Huntington, Janowitz, and the question of civilian control." *Armed Forces & Society* 23.2 (1996), pp. 149–178.
7. Samuel P. Huntington. *The Soldier and the State: The Theory and Politics of Civil-Military Relations*. Cambridge: Belknap Press, 1957.
8. Huntington, *The Soldier and the State*, p. 84.
9. Bengt Abrahamsson and Morris Janowitz. *Military Professionalization and Political Power*. 1st edition. Beverly Hills, CA: SAGE Publications, Inc., 1972; Richard H. Kohn. "Out of control: the crisis in civil-military relations." *The National Interest* 35 (1994), pp. 3–17; Morris Janowitz. "Military elites and the study of war." *Conflict Resolution* 1.1 (1957), pp. 9–18; Peter D. Feaver. *Armed Servants: Agency, Oversight, and Civil-Military Relations*. Cambridge, MA; London: Harvard University Press, 2003; Eliot A. Cohen. *Supreme Command: Soldiers, Statesmen, and Leadership in Wartime*. Reprint edition. New York: Anchor, 2003; Rebecca Schiff. "Civil-military relations reconsidered: a theory of concordance." *Armed Forces & Society* 22.1 (1995), pp. 7–24.
10. Huntington, *The Soldier and the State*, pp. 2–3.
11. Jess Blankshain. "A primer on US civil–military relations for national security practitioners." *Wild Blue Yonder* (July 2020); Risa Brooks. "Paradoxes of professionalism: rethinking

civilmilitary relations in the United States." *International Security* 44.4 (Apr. 2020). Cambridge, MA: MIT Press, pp. 7–44; Richard D. Hooker, Jr. "Soldiers of the state: reconsidering American civil-military relations." *Parameters* 41.4 (2011), pp. 1–14; Hans Born. "Democratic control of armed forces: relevance, issues, and research agenda." *Handbook of the Sociology of the Military*. Ed. Giuseppe Caforio. New York: Springer, 2007, pp. 151–167.

12. Brooks, "Paradoxes of Professionalism."

13. Cohen, *Supreme Command*, p. 208.

14. Morris Janowitz. *The Professional Soldier: A Social and Political Portrait*. Reissue edition. Glencoe, IL: Free Press, 1960, p. 343.

15. Suzanne C. Nielsen. "Civil-military relations theory and military effectiveness." *Public Administration and Management* 10.2 (2005), pp. 61–84.

16. Pauline M. Shanks Kaurin. "An 'unprincipled principal': implications for civil-military relations." *Strategic Studies Quarterly* 15.2 (2021), pp. 50–68; Peter Kasurak. "Huntington in Canada: the triumph of subjective control." *Armed Forces & Society* Vol. 48, Iss 2. (2020), pp. 1–20.

17. Blankshain, "A primer on US civil–military relations for national security practitioners"; Peter Feaver. "Should senior military officers resign in protest if Obama disregards their advice?" *Foreign Policy*. https://foreignpolicy.com/2014/10/07/should-senior-military-officers-resign-in-protest-if-obama-disregards-their-advice/ (October 2014); Marybeth P. Ulrich. "Civil-military relations norms and democracy: what every citizen should know." *Reconsidering American Civil-Military Relations: The Military, Society, Politics, and Modern War*. Ed. Lionel Beehner, Risa A. Brooks, and Daniel Maurer. New York: Oxford University Press, 2020, pp. 41–62.

18. Alice Hunt Friend. Interview by *Critical Questions*. Center for Strategic and International Studies (CSIS), May 5, 2017. For additional commentary on the concept of politicization, with a focus on its application to the military, see Andrew Exum. "The dangerous politicization of the military", *The Atlantic* (July 24, 2017); Jim Golby and Mara Karlin, "The case for rethinking the politicization of the military." *Brookings* (June 12, 2020).

19. Heidi A. Urben. *Party, Politics, and the Post-9/11 Army*. Amherst NY: Cambria Press, 2021, pp. 2–3.

20. Aaron Blake. "Analysis—it's only 'politicizing' a tragedy if you disagree with the policy." *Washington Post* (November 1, 2017); Meghashyam Mali. "Norquist accuses Dems of politicizing Sandy Hook school shooting." *The Hill* (December 23, 2012); Grace Panetta. "Sen. Lindsey Graham accuses Biden of politicizing a violent insurrection intended to overturn the 2020 election." *Business Insider* (January 6, 2022).

21. Jennifer Szalai. "Why is 'politicization' so partisan?" *New York Times* (October 17, 2017).

22. James Golby. "Uncivil-military relations: politicization of the military in the Trump era." *Strategic Studies Quarterly* 15.2 (2021), pp. 149–174.

23. Jason Lyall. *Divided Armies: Inequality and Battlefield Performance in Modern War*. Princeton, NJ: Princeton University Press, 2020.

24. For various polling instruments that have found such attitudes see Peter Moore, "Could a coup really happen in the United States?" YouGov, Sept. 9, 2015, https://today.yougov.com/topics/politics/articles-reports/2015/09/09/could-coup-happen-in-united-states; German Feierhard, Noam Lupu, and Susan Stokes, "A significant minority of Americans say they could support a military takeover of the U.S. government." *Washington Post* (Feb. 16, 2018); Noam Lupu, Luke Plutowski, and Elizabeth J. Zechmeister, "Would Americans ever support a coup? 40 percent now say yes." *Washington Post* (Jan. 6, 2022).

25. Alan Feuer. "A retired colonel's unlikely role in pushing baseless election claims." *New York Times* (December 12, 2021).

26. Kori Schake and Michael Robinson. "Assessing civil-military relations and the January 6th Capitol insurrection." *Orbis* 65.3 (2021), pp. 532–544; Daniel Milton and Andrew Mines. *"This is War": Examining Military Experience among the Capitol Hill Siege Participants*. Tech. rep. West Point, NY: Combating Terrorism Center, United States Military Academy, April 12, 2021.

27. Anthony Downs. *An Economic Theory of Democracy*. 1st edition. Boston: Harper and Row, 1957; Paul M. Sniderman, Richard Brody, and Philip Tetlock. *Reasoning and Choice: Explorations in Political Psychology*. New York: Cambridge University Press, 1993.

28. Amy Zegart. "The three paradoxes disrupting American politics." *The Atlantic* (August 5, 2017).

29. Sniderman, Brody, and Tetlock, *Reasoning and Choice: Explorations in Political Psychology*; John R. Zaller. *The Nature and Origins of Mass Opinion*. New York: Cambridge University Press, 1992.

30. Alexandra Guisinger and Elizabeth N. Saunders. "Mapping the boundaries of elite cues: how elites shape mass opinion across international issues." *International Studies Quarterly* 61.2 (2017), pp. 425–441; Terrence L. Chapman. *Securing Approval: Domestic Politics and Multilateral Authorization for War*. Chicago: University of Chicago Press, 2011; Matt Guardino and Danny Hayes. "Foreign voices, party cues, and U.S. public opinion about military action." *International Journal of Public Opinion Research* Vol. 30, Iss 3 (May 2017); Stanley Feldman, Leonie Huddy, and George E. Marcus. *Going to War in Iraq: When Citizens and the Press Matter*. Reprint edition. Chicago: University of Chicago Press, 2015.

31. Arthur Lupia. "Shortcuts versus encyclopedias: information and voting behavior in California insurance reform elections." *American Political Science Review* 88.01 (1994), pp. 63–76; William J. McGuire. "The nature of attitudes and attitude change." *Handbook of Social Psychology*. Ed. G. Lindzey and E. Aronson. 2nd ed. Cambridge, MA: Addison-Wesley, 1969, pp. 135–214.

32. Arthur Lupia and Mathew D. McCubbins. *The Democratic Dilemma: Can Citizens Learn What They Need to Know?* Cambridge; New York: Cambridge University Press, 1998; Richard E. Petty and John T. Cacioppo. *Communication and Persuasion: Central and Peripheral Routes to Attitude Change*. New York: Springer, 1986.

33. Charles S. Taber and Milton Lodge. "Motivated skepticism in the evaluation of political beliefs." *American Journal of Political Science* 50.3 (2006), pp. 755–769.

34. Guisinger and Saunders, "Mapping the boundaries of elite cues: how elites shape mass opinion across international issues."

35. Julian E. Zelizer. "How the Tet Offensive undermined American faith in government." *The Atlantic* (January 15, 2018).

36. Risa Brooks and Michael A. Robinson. "Let the generals speak? Retired officer dissent and the June 2020 George Floyd protests." *War on the Rocks*. https://warontherocks.com/2020/10/let-the-generals-speak-retired-officer-dissent-and-the-june-2020-george-floyd-protests/ (October 9, 2020); Daniel Maurer. *The Generals' Constitution*. https://www.justsecurity.org/70674/the-generals-constitution/ (June 2020).

37. Respondents were asked which statements were closer to their own beliefs: "Modern wars are unwinnable," "Modern wars are winnable, but our military hasn't figured out how to win them," "Modern wars are winnable, but civilian policy decisions prevent the military from winning," and "Modern wars are winnable, and our military is winning them." After those responding "Don't Know" (28%), the next largest bloc of respondents believed that modern wars were "unwinnable" (19%) (Kori N. Schake and Jim Mattis, eds. *Warriors and Citizens: American Views of Our Military*. Stanford, CA: Hoover Institution Press, 2016).

38. Kenneth A. Schultz. "Perils of polarization for U.S. foreign policy." *Washington Quarterly* 40.4 (2018), pp. 7–28.

39. Quoted in Jim Gourley, "Where is the tipping point for trust in America's military? And are we near it?" *Foreign Policy* (Feb. 14, 2014).

40. Quoted in Mark Perry, "Are Trump's generals in over their heads?" *Politico* (Oct 25, 2017).

41. Jason K. Dempsey. *Our Army: Soldiers, Politics, and American Civil-Military Relations*. Princeton, NJ: Princeton University Press, 2009.

42. Quoted in Richard Sisk, "Former Joints Chief Chairman slams retired generals' political remarks." https://www.military.com/daily-news/2016/08/01/former-joint-chiefs-chairman-slams-retired-generals-remarks.html (Aug. 1, 2016).

43. Polina Beliakova. "Erosion by deference: civilian control and the military in policymaking." *Texas National Security Review* 4.3 (June 2021), pp. 55–75.

44. Peter D. Feaver and Richard H. Kohn. "Civil-military relations in the United States: what senior leaders need to know (and usually don't)." *Strategic Studies Quarterly* 15.2 (2021), pp. 12–37.

45. James Golby and Mara Karlin. "Why 'best military advice' is bad for the military—and worse for civilians." *Orbis* 62.1 (2018), pp. 137–153.

46. Andrew Exum. "The dangerous politicization of the military." *The Atlantic*. https://www.theat
lantic.com/politics/archive/2017/07/the-danger-of-turning-the-us-military-into-a-political-
actor/534624/ (July 24, 2017); Matthew Fay. *Persistently Politicizing the Military*. https://
www.niskanencenter.org/persistently-politicizing-military/ (July 2017).

47. Brooks and Robinson, "Let the generals speak?"; Schake and Robinson, "Assessing civil-
military relations and the January 6th Capitol insurrection"; Lindsay Cohn, Alice Friend, and
Jim Golby. "Analysis—this is what was so unusual about the U.S. Navy making Captain Brett
Crozier step down." *Washington Post* (April 5, 2020).

48. Jacob S. Hacker and Paul Pierson. *Let them Eat Tweets: How the Right Rules in an Age of Extreme
Inequality*. 1st edition. New York: Liveright, 2020; Ezra Klein. *Why We're Polarized*. Illustrated
edition. New York: Avid Reader Press / Simon & Schuster, 2020; Michael Albertus and Victor
Menaldo. "Opinion—why are so many democracies breaking down?" *New York Times* (May
8, 2018).

49. Philip Bump. "Perspective—the White House is increasingly—and worryingly—using the
military as a shield against criticism." *Washington Post* (October 20, 2017); Joe Gould. "Handful of hawkish US lawmakers urge military leaders to fight new CR." *Military Times* (December
2, 2017). H. R. McMaster and Gary D. Cohn. "America First doesn't mean America alone."
Wall Street Journal (May 30, 2017).

50. David A. Graham. "Are Trump's generals mounting a defense of democratic institutions?" *The
Atlantic* (January 31, 2017). Jonathan Stevenson. "Opinion—the generals can't save us from
Trump." *New York Times* (July 28, 2017).

51. Missy Ryan. "New disclosures show how Gen. Mark A. Milley tried to check Trump. They
could also further politicize the military." *Washington Post* (September 17, 2021); Alan Feuer,
Adam Goldman, and Katie Benner. "Oath Keepers founder is said to be investigated in Capitol
riot." *New York Times* (March 10, 2021); Feuer, "A retired colonel's unlikely role in pushing
baseless election claims."

Chapter 2

1. David T. Burbach. "Confidence without sacrifice: American public opinion and the US military." *Reconsidering American Civil-Military Relations: The Military, Society, Politics, and Modern
War*. Ed. Lionel Beehner, Risa Brooks, and Daniel Maurer. New York: Oxford University Press,
2021; David T. Burbach. "Gaining trust while losing wars: confidence in the U.S. military after
Iraq and Afghanistan." *Orbis* 61.2 (2017), pp. 154–171; Andrew A. Hill, Leonard Wong, and
Stephen J. Gerras. "Self-interest well understood: the origins & lessons of public confidence
in the military." *Daedalus* 142.2 (2013), pp. 49–64.

2. Megan Brenan. *Amid Pandemic, Confidence in Key U.S. Institutions Surges. Gallup* (Aug. 2020).
Brenan, *Americans' Confidence in Major U.S. Institutions Dips*.

3. Robert M. Bray et al. "Substance use and mental health trends among U.S. military active duty
personnel: key findings from the 2008 DoD health behavior survey." *Military Medicine* 175.6
(June 2010), pp. 390–399; John Darrell Sherwood. *Black Sailor, White Navy: Racial Unrest in
the Fleet during the Vietnam War Era*. New York: NYU Press, 2007.

4. Don M. Snider. "Will Army 2025 be a military profession?" *Parameters* 45.4 (2015), pp. 39–51.

5. Bo Rothstein and Dietlind Stolle. "The quality of government and social capital: a theory of
political institutions and generalized trust." *Comparative Politics* 40.4 (2008), pp. 441–459;
Marc Hetherington. "The political relevance of political trust." *American Political Science Review*
92.4 (1998), pp. 791–808; William Mishler and Richard Rose. "What are the origins of political trust? Testing institutional and cultural theories in post-communist societies." *Comparative
Political Studies* 34.1 (2001), pp. 30–62; John T. Williams. "Systemic influences on political
trust: the importance of perceived institutional performance." *Political Methodology* (1985),
pp. 125–142.

6. Ken Newton and Pippa Norris. "Confidence in public institutions." *Disaffected Democracies.
What's Troubling the Trilateral Countries*. Princeton, NJ: Princeton University Press, 2000),
p. 66.

7. Rosa Brooks. "Civil-military paradoxes." *Warriors & Citizens: American Views of Our Military*.
Ed. Kori N. Schake and Jim Mattis. Hoover Institution Press, 2016, pp. 21–68; Benjamin
Wittes and Cody Poplin. "Public opinion, military justice, and the fight against terrorism

overseas." *Warriors & Citizens: American Views of Our Military*. Ed. Kori N. Schake and Jim Mattis. Stanford, CA: Hoover Institution Press, 2016, pp. 143–159; James Golby, Lindsay Cohn, and Peter D. Feaver. "Thanks for your service: civilian and veteran attitudes after fifteen years of war." *Warriors and Citizens: American Views of Our Military*. Stanford, CA: Hoover Institution Press, 2016, pp. 69–96.

8. Burbach, "Gaining trust while losing wars"; Burbach, "Confidence without sacrifice: American public opinion and the US military."
9. Kaifeng Yang and Marc Holzer. "The performance-trust link: implications for performance measurement." *Public Administration Review* 66.1 (2006), pp. 114–126.
10. Paul Gronke and Peter D. Feaver. "Uncertain confidence: civilian and military attitudes and civil-military relations." *Soldiers and Civilians: The Civil-Military Gap and American National Security*. Ed. Richard H. Kohn and Peter D. Feaver. Cambridge, MA: MIT Press, 2001, p. 133.
11. John R. Hibbing and Elizabeth Theiss-Morse. *Congress as Public Enemy: Public Attitudes toward American Political Institutions*. 1st Ed. Cambridge; New York: Cambridge University Press, 1995; Gronke and Feaver, "Uncertain confidence", p. 133.
12. David C. King and Zachary Karabell. *The Generation of Trust: Public Confidence in the U.S. Military Since Vietnam*. Washington, DC: AEI Press, 2002.
13. *Military and National Defense*. September 15, 2007. Justin McCarthy, "About Half Say U.S. Military is No. 1 in the World." Gallup, March 2, 2022, https://news.gallup.com/poll/390356/half-say-military-no-world.aspx.
14. Burbach, "Confidence without sacrifice: American public opinion and the US military."
15. Rothstein and Stolle, "The quality of government and social capital."
16. David T. Burbach. "Partisan dimensions of confidence in the U.S. military, 1973–2016." *Armed Forces & Society* 45.2 (2019), pp. 211–233.
17. King and Karabell, *The Generation of Trust*.
18. Bray et al., "Substance use and mental health trends among U.S. military active duty personnel"; Sherwood, *Black Sailor, White Navy*.
19. Don Snider and Louis Yuengert. "Professionalism and the volunteer military." *Parameters* 45.4 (2015), pp. 39–64.
20. Seymour M. Hersh. "Torture at Abu Ghraib." *The New Yorker* (April 30, 2004).
21. Tom Bowman. "Walter Reed was Army's wake-up call in 2007." *National Public Radio* (August 31, 2011).
22. J. Taylor Rushing. "Group of senators begin push to remove sex assault cases from chain of command." *Stars and Stripes* (November 6, 2013).
23. Matt DeLong. "Pat Tillman's mother calls for McChrystal's removal from White House post." *Washington Post* (April 14, 2011).
24. Craig Whitlock. "Leaks, feasts and sex parties: how 'Fat Leonard' infiltrated the Navy's floating headquarters in Asia." *Washington Post* (January 31, 2018).
25. Ian Shapira. "He was America's most notorious war criminal, but Nixon helped him anyway." *Washington Post* (May 25, 2019).
26. Pew Research polled these attitudes about military officers alongside other "key institutional actors" including members of Congress, journalists, technology company leaders, police officers, religious leaders, and school principals. Military officers ranked lowest among those who were believed to act unethically "all" or "most of the time" (50%), compared to members of Congress (81%). They ranked highest among those most likely to "face serious consequences" for unethical behavior "all" or "most of the time" (57%), compared to members of Congress (71%).
27. Claire Gecewicz and Lee Rainie. *Why Americans Don't Fully Trust Many Who Hold Positions of Power and Responsibility*. Tech. rep. Pew Research Center, September 19, 2019.
28. Huntington, *The Soldier and the State*; Peter D. Feaver and Richard H. Kohn, eds. *Soldiers and Civilians* 1st edition. Cambridge, MA: the MIT Press, 2001; Brooks, "Paradoxes of professionalism."
29. Hill, Wong, and Gerras, " 'Self-interest well understood.' "
30. Burbach, David T. "Gaining trust while losing wars: confidence in the U.S. military after Iraq and Afghanistan." *Orbis* 61.2 (2017), pp. 154–171.

31. Dempsey, *Our Army*; Hugh Liebert and James Golby. "Midlife crisis? The all-volunteer force at 40." *Armed Forces & Society* 43.1 (2017), pp. 115–138.

32. David Evans. "Crowe endorsement of Clinton raises more than eyebrows." https://www.chicagotribune.com/news/ct-xpm-1992-09-25-9203270346-story.html (September 25, 1992).

33. Zachary Griffiths and Olivia Simon. "Not putting their money where their mouth is: retired flag officers and Presidential endorsements." *Armed Forces & Society* (December 9, 2019).

34. Peter Feaver. "Controversy over military partisan cheerleading continues." *Foreign Policy* (August 2, 2016).

35. Robert H. Scales. "U.S. military planners don't support war with Syria." *Washington Post* (Sept. 2013).

36. Brianna Kablack et al. "The military speaks out." *New America* (Jan. 2021); Maurer, *The Generals' Constitution*; Brooks and Robinson, "Let the Generals speak?"

37. Feaver and Kohn, "Civil-military relations in the United States: what senior leaders need to know (and usually don't)."

38. Quinta Jurecic. "Opinion—Did the 'adults in the room' make any difference with Trump?" *New York Times* (Aug. 2019).

39. Richard H. Kohn. "The erosion of civilian control of the military in the United States today." *Naval War College Review* 55.3 (2002), p. 9; James Golby and Peter D. Feaver. "Former military leaders criticized the election and the administration. That hurts the military's reputation." *Washington Post* (May 15, 2021).

40. Lilliana Mason. " "I disrespectfully agree": the differential effects of partisan sorting on social and issue polarization." *American Journal of Political Science* 59.1 (2015), pp. 128–145; Shanto Iyengar, Gaurav Sood, and Yphtach Lelkes. "Affect, not ideology." *Public Opinion Quarterly* 76.3 (2012), pp. 405–431; Shanto Iyengar and Sean J. Westwood. "Fear and loathing across Party lines: new evidence on group polarization." *American Journal of Political Science* 59.3 (2015), pp. 690–707; Shanto Iyengar and Kyu S. Hahn. "Red media, blue media: evidence of ideological selectivity in media use." *Journal of Communication* 59.1 (2009), pp. 19–39; Natalie Stroud. "Media use and political predispositions: revisiting the concept of selective exposure." *Political Behavior* 30.3 (2008), pp. 556–576; Kathleen Jamieson and Joseph Cappella. *Echo Chamber: Rush Limbaugh and the Conservative Media Establishment*. New York: Oxford University Press, 2008.

41. Lilliana Mason. *Uncivil Agreement: How Politics Became Our Identity*. Illustrated edition. Chicago; London: University of Chicago Press, 2018.

42. Klein, *Why We're Polarized*.

43. Marc Hetherington. "Putting polarization in perspective." *British Journal of Political Science* 39 (2009), pp. 413–448; Alan I. Abramowitz and Kyle L. Saunders. "Is polarization a myth?" *The Journal of Politics* 70.2 (2008). Chicago: University of Chicago Press, pp. 542–555; Yphtach Lelkes and Paul M. Sniderman. "The ideological asymmetry of the American Party system." *British Journal of Political Science* 46 (2014), pp. 825–844.

44. For information on the DW-Nominate roll-call voting ideological index, see Jeffrey B. Lewis et al. *Voteview: Congressional Roll-Call Votes Database*. Tech. rep. 2021; for the CF Score finance dataset and the Database on Ideology, Money in Politics, and Elections see Adam Bonica. *Database on Ideology, Money in Politics, and Elections: Public Version 2.0*. Computer file. Stanford, CA: Stanford University Library, 2016.

45. Morris P. Fiorina, Samuel J. Abrams, and Jeremy C. Pope. *Culture War? The Myth of a Polarized America*. 3rd edition. Boston, MA: Longman, 2010; Morris P. Fiorina, Samuel A. Abrams, and Jeremy C. Pope. "Polarization in the American public: misconceptions and misreadings." *Journal of Politics* 70.2 (2008), pp. 556–560.

46. Gary C. Jacobson. *A Divider, Not a Uniter: George W. Bush and the American People* 1st edition. New York: Longman, 2006; Abramowitz and Saunders, "Is polarization a myth?"

47. Daniel W. Drezner. "The end of the median voter theorem in presidential politics?" *Washington Post* (May 29, 2015).

48. David E. Broockman et al. "Why local party leaders don't support nominating centrists." *British Journal of Political Science* 51.2 (2021), pp. 724–749; Geoffrey Skelley. "Few Americans who identify as independent are actually independent. That's really bad for

politics." *FiveThirtyEight*. https://fivethirtyeight.com/features/few-americans-who-identify-as-independent-are-actually-independent-thats-really-bad-for-politics/ (April 15, 2021).

49. Klein, *Why We're Polarized*.

50. A March 2021 YouGov survey conducted in coordination with the University of Massachusetts surveyed 846 respondents and found that 59% of Trump voters did not agree that Joe Biden was the "legitimately elected and duly inaugurated President of the United States." UMass Amherst/YouGov poll, March 5–9 2021, https://polsci.umass.edu/sites/default/files/StateofStateBakerMarch2021Toplines.pdf.

51. Murat Somer and Jennifer McCoy. "Transformations through polarizations and global threats to democracy." *The ANNALS of the American Academy of Political and Social Science* 681.1 (2019), pp. 8–22.

52. Kevin Drum. "The real reason Americans are so damn angry all the time." *Mother Jones* (Oct. 2021) Daniel W. Drezner. "Perspective—Is Fox News to blame for American rage?" *Washington Post* (August 1, 2021).

53. Mason, " 'I disrespectfully agree'."

54. Iyengar, Sood, and Lelkes, "Affect, not ideology."

55. Mason, " 'I disrespectfully agree' "; Lilliana Mason. "A cross-cutting calm: how social sorting drives affective polarization." *Public Opinion Quarterly* 80.S1 (2016), pp. 351–377; Iyengar, Sood, and Lelkes, "Affect, not ideology"; Iyengar and Westwood, "Fear and loathing across Party lines: new evidence on group Polarization."

56. Thomas J. Rudolph and Marc Hetherington. "Affective polarization in political and nonpolitical settings." *International Journal of Public Opinion Research* Vol. 33, Iss 3 (Jan. 2021).

57. Anthony Salvanto et al. "Americans see democracy under threat—CBS News poll." *CBS News*. https://www.cbsnews.com/news/joe-biden-coronavirus-opinion-poll/ (January 17, 2021); Nate Cohn. "Why political sectarianism is a growing threat to American democracy." *New York Times*. https://www.nytimes.com/2021/04/19/us/democracy-gop-democrats-sectarianism.html (April 19, 2021).

58. Hetherington, "Putting polarization in perspective."

59. Lelkes and Sniderman, "The ideological asymmetry of the American Party system"; Drew Desilver. "The polarization in today's Congress has roots that go back decades." *Pew Research Center* (March 10, 2022).

60. Hacker and Pierson, *Let Them Eat Tweets*, p. 41.

61. Lee Drutman. "Why there are so few moderate Republicans left." *FiveThirtyEight*. https://fivethirtyeight.com/features/why-there-are-so-few-moderate-republicans-left/ (August 24, 2020).

62. Desilver, "The polarization in today's Congress has roots that go back decades."

63. Broockman et al., "Why local party leaders don't support nominating centrists."

64. Nathaniel Rakich. "Redistricting has maintained the status quo so far. That's good for Republicans." https://fivethirtyeight.com/features/redistricting-has-maintained-the-status-quo-so-far-thats-good-for-republicans/ (December 2, 2021); Reid J. Epstein and Nick Corasaniti. "Republicans gain heavy house edge in 2022 as Gerrymandered maps emerge." *New York Times* (November 15, 2021).

65. Pippa Norris. "Measuring populism worldwide." *Party Politics* 26.6 (2020), pp. 697–717.

66. Sahil Chinoy. "Opinion—What happened to America's political center of gravity?" *New York Times* (June 26, 2019).

67. Rothstein and Stolle, "The quality of government and social capital."

68. Brenan, *Americans' Confidence in Major U.S. Institutions Dips*; Dana Milbank. "Opinion—'Roe' is dead. The Roberts Court's 'stench' will live forever." *Washington Post* (December 1, 2021).

69. Kori Schake. "What is happening to our apolitical military?" *The Atlantic* (July 19, 2021).

70. O. R. Holsti. *Public Opinion and American Foreign Policy*. Ann Arbor: Michigan University Press, 2004; Ole R. Holsti. "A widening gap between the U.S. military and civilian society? Some evidence, 1976–96." *International Security* 23.3 (1998), p. 5; Dempsey, *Our Army*; Urben, *Party, Politics, and the Post-9/11 Army*; Heidi Urben. "Civil-military relations in a time of war." PhD thesis. Georgetown University, 2010.

71. James Golby and Mara Karlin. *The Case for Rethinking the Politicization of the Military*. Source: Brookings Institution. https://www.brookings.edu/blog/order-from-chaos/2020/06/12/the-case-for-rethinking-the-politicization-of-the-military/ (June 12, 2020).

72. Golby, "Uncivil-military relations: politicization of the military in the Trump era."

73. Carl von Clausewitz. *On War, Indexed Edition*. Trans. Michael Eliot Howard and Peter Paret. Reprint edition. Princeton, NJ: Princeton University Press, 1989; Cohen, *Supreme Command*; Brooks, "Paradoxes of professionalism"; Blankshain, "A primer on US civil–military relations for national security practitioners."

74. Following this logic, it would seem that "partisanization" may be more appropriate semantics over politicization; nonetheless, for sake of clarity and consistency with existing works, I choose politicization as the proper term.

75. Jim Lucas and Tereza Pultarova. "What is parallax?" *Space.com*. https://www.space.com/30417-parallax.html (January 11, 2022).

76. Phillip Carter. "Military Chiefs' reluctance to march." *Slate* (December 12, 2017).

77. Kohn, "The erosion of civilian control of the military in the United States today."

78. Dempsey, *Our Army*; Mackubin Thomas Owens. "Military officers: political without partisanship." *Strategic Studies Quarterly* 9.3 (2015); Heidi Urben. *Like, Comment, Retweet: The State of the Military's Nonpartisan Ethic*. Tech. rep. National Defense University, 2017; Hill, Wong, and Gerras, " 'Self-Interest Well Understood'. "

79. Risa Brooks. "Militaries and political activity in democracies." *American Civil-Military Relations: The Soldier and the State in a New Era*. Baltimore: Johns Hopkins University Press, 2009.

80. Griffiths and Simon, "Not putting their money where their mouth is"; Urben, "Civil-military relations in a time of war"; James Golby, Kyle Dropp, and Peter D. Feaver. *Military Campaigns: Veterans' Endorsements and Presidential Elections*. Tech. rep. Center for a New American Security, 2012; Kori N. Schake. "The line held: civil-military relations in the Trump administration." *Strategic Studies Quarterly* 15.2 (2021), pp. 38–49.

81. Military endorsements for major party political candidates expanded from indiviudal officers in the 1990s to bloc letters signed by hundreds of officers by the 2010s: David Evans, "Crowe endorsement of Clinton raises more than eyebrows." *Chicago Tribune* (Sept 25, 1992); Stephen Dinan, "Retired top brass push for Romney." *Washington Times* (Nov 4, 2012); Thomas E. Ricks, "We have a big problem with retired generals wading into partisanship." *Foreign Policy* (Sept. 12, 2016).

82. Jeremy M. Teigen. *Why Veterans Run: Military Service in American Presidential Elections, 1789–2016* 1st edition. Philadelphia: Temple University Press, 2018.

83. Mackubin Thomas Owens. *US Civil-Military Relations after 9/11: Renegotiating the Civil-Military Bargain*. 1st edition. New York: Bloomsbury Academic, 2011.

84. Kohn, "Out of control."

85. Schake, "The line held: civil-military relations in the Trump administration"; Golby, "Uncivil-military relations: politicization of the military in the Trump era."

86. For such examples of such externally politicizing actions see: Missy Ryan and Thomas Gibbons-Neff. "In inaugural Pentagon visit, Trump signs orders on immigration vetting, military strength." *New York Times* (Jan. 27, 2017); Ethan Weston, "Trump asks Navy crowd to call Congress about his budget." *Arizona Daily Sun* (July 23, 2017); Wesley Morgan, "Trump's Fourth of July extravaganza troubles former military leaders." *Politico* (July 2, 2019); Greg Sargent, "Trump: you wouldn't like my supporters in the military if they got angry." *Washington Post* (Mar. 14, 2019); Leo Shane, III, Meghan Myers, and Carl Prine, "Trump grants clemency to troops in three controversial war crimes cases." *Military Times* (Nov. 15, 2019).

87. Zachary Krislov and Jocelyn Kiley. "Partisans see opposing party as more ideologically extreme." *Pew Research Center* (August 23, 2016).

88. James Doubek. "Joint Chiefs denounce racism after Trump's comments." *National Public Radio* (August 17, 2017).

89. Andrew deGrandpre. "Trump's generals condemn Charlottesville racism—while trying not to offend the president." *Washington Post* (Aug. 2017); Dave Philipps. "Inspired by Charlottesville, Military Chiefs condemn racism." *New York Times* (August 16, 2017).

90. Secretary of the Air Force Public Affairs. *Resources Available for DAF Members, Families Affected by Local Laws.* https://www.af.mil/News/Article-Display/Article/2977048/resources-available-for-daf-members-families-affected-by-local-laws/ (March 24, 2022).

91. Soo Youn. "Air Force offers help to LGBTQ personnel, families hurt by state laws." *Washington Post* (April 16, 2022).

92. Lee Drutman. "The moderate middle is a myth." *FiveThirtyEight.* https://fivethirtyeight.com/features/the-moderate-middle-is-a-myth/ (September 24, 2019); Carroll Doherty, Jocelyn Kiley, and Bridget Johnson. "Political Independents: who they are, what they think." *Pew Research Center* (March 24, 2019).

93. Karin Zeitvogel. "Pentagon expresses 'revulsion' over Tucker Carlson's comments about women service members." *Stars and Stripes* (March 11, 2021); "Tucker Carlson: Pentagon rebukes Fox host for attacking 'feminine' military." *BBC News* (March 12, 2021); Missy Ryan. "Military brass denounced Tucker Carlson's remarks about a 'feminine' force. Women say barriers remain for pregnant troops." *Washington Post* (March 20 2021).

Chapter 3

1. Kenneth A. Schultz. *Democracy and Coercive Diplomacy.* New York: Cambridge University Press, 2001; Dan Reiter and Allan Stam. *Democracies at War.* Princeton, NJ: Princeton University Press, 2002; William Howell and Jon C. Pevehouse. *While Dangers Gather: Congressional Checks on Presdiential War Powers.* Princeton, NJ: Princeton University Press, 2007.

2. Adam J. Berinsky. "Assuming the costs of war: events, elites, and American public support for military conflict." *The Journal of Politics* 69.4 (2007), pp. 975–997; Guisinger and Saunders, "Mapping the boundaries of elite cues: how elites shape mass opinion across international issues"; Matthew A. Baum and Tim J. Groeling. *War Stories: The Causes and Consequences of Public Views of War.* Princeton, NJ: Princeton University Press, Jan. 2010; Feldman, Huddy, and Marcus, *Going to War in Iraq*; Terrence L. Chapman. "The United Nations Security Council and the rally 'round the flag effect." *Journal of Conflict Resolution* 48.6 (2004), pp. 886–909; Joseph M. Grieco et al. "Lets get a second opinion: international institutions and American public support for war." *International Studies Quarterly* 55.2 (2011), pp. 563–583; Guardino and Hayes, "Foreign voices, Party cues, and U.S. public opinion about military action"; Songying Fang. "The informational role of international institutions and domestic politics." *American Journal of Political Science* 52.2 (2008), pp. 304–321.

3. Matthew A. Baum and Tim J. Groeling. "Shot by the messenger: partisan cues and public opinion regarding national security and war." *Political Behavior* 31.2 (2009), pp. 157–186; John G. Bullock. "Elite influence on public opinion in an informed electorate." *American Political Science Review* 105.3 (2011), pp. 496–515; Zaller, *The Nature and Origins of Mass Opinion*; Lupia and McCubbins, *The Democratic Dilemma.*

4. James Golby, Peter D. Feaver, and Kyle Dropp. "Elite military cues and public opinion about the use of military force." *Armed Forces & Society* 44.1 (2017), pp. 44–71; Paul R. Brewer and Kimberly Gross. "Values, framing, and citizens' thoughts about policy issues: effects on content and quantity." *Political Psychology* 26.6 (2005), pp. 929–948.

5. Downs, *An Economic Theory of Democracy*; Zaller, *The Nature and Origins of Mass Opinion*; Lupia and McCubbins, *The Democratic Dilemma.*

6. Huntington, *The Soldier and the State*; Janowitz, *The Professional Soldier*; Peter D. Feaver. "Crisis as shirking: an agency theory explanation of the souring of American civil-military relations." *Armed Forces & Society* 24.3 (1998), pp. 407–434.

7. Elizabeth N. Saunders and Scott Wolford. "Elites, voters, and democracies at war." Paper for the George Washington University Institute for Security and Conflict Studies Workshop (2017).

8. Peter D. Feaver. "The right to be right: civil-military relations and the Iraq surge decision." *International Security* 35.4 (2011), pp. 87–125; Bob Woodward. *The War Within: A Secret White House History 2006–2008.* 1st edition. New York: Simon & Schuster, 2009, p. 288.

9. James Golby. "Duty, honor ... party? Ideology, institutions, and the use of military force." PhD dissertation. Stanford University, 2011.

10. Ronald R. Krebs, Robert Ralston, and Aaron Rapport. "No right to be wrong: what Americans think about civil-military relations." *Perspectives on Politics*. Cambridge: Cambridge University Press, 2021, pp. 1–19.

11. Dempsey, *Our Army*; Owens, "Military officers: political without partisanship"; Liebert and Golby, "Midlife crisis?"

12. Dempsey, *Our Army*; Owens, "Military officers: political without partisanship"; Golby, Feaver, and Dropp, "Elite military cues and public opinion about the use of military force."

13. Zaller, *The Nature and Origins of Mass Opinion*; Holsti, *Public Opinion and American Foreign Policy*; Sniderman, Brody, and Tetlock, *Reasoning and Choice: Explorations in Political Psychology*; James N. Druckman. "On the limits of framing effects: who can frame?" *Journal of Politics* 63.4 (2001), pp. 1041–1066.

14. Berinsky, "Assuming the costs of war"; Guisinger and Saunders, "Mapping the boundaries of elite cues: how elites shape mass opinion across international issues"; Grieco et al., "Let's get a second opinion"; Fang, "The informational role of international institutions and domestic politics"; Chapman, *Securing Approval*; Danielle Lupton and Clayton Webb. "Wither elites? The role of elite credibility and knowledge in public perceptions of foreign policy." Paper for American Political Science Association (APSA) annual conference. https://preprints. apsanet.org/engage/apsa/article-details/6026c66bed338ebf944d221f (February 16, 2021).

15. Petty and Cacioppo, *Communication and Persuasion*.

16. Golby, Feaver, and Dropp, "Elite military cues and public opinion about the use of military force"; Krebs, Ralston, and Rapport, "No right to be wrong."

17. Petty and Cacioppo, *Communication and Persuasion*.

18. Lupia and McCubbins, *The Democratic Dilemma*; Carl I. Hovland and Walter Weiss. "The influence of source credibility on communication effectiveness." *Public Opinion Quarterly* 14.4 (1951), pp. 635–650; Downs, *An Economic Theory of Democracy*; Zaller, *The Nature and Origins of Mass Opinion*.

19. Brooks, "Militaries and Political Activity in Democracies."

20. Brooks, "Militaries and Political Activity in Democracies."

21. Colin Powell, "U.S. Forces: Challenges Ahead" Foreign Affairs (Winter 1992/1993); "Why generals get nervous." *New York Times* (October 8, 1992); David H. Petraeus. "Battling for Iraq." *Washington Post* (September 26, 2004).

22. James Fallows. "Karmic justice: Gen. Eric Shinseki." *The Atlantic* (December 7, 2008).

23. Petraeus, "Battling for Iraq"; McMaster and Cohn, "America First doesn't mean America alone."

24. Grieco et al., "Let's get a second opinion"; Jonathan Chu. *Social Cues by International Organizations: NATO, the Security Council, and Public Support for Humanitarian Intervention*. SSRN Scholarly Paper 3977910. Rochester, NY: Social Science Research Network, October 4, 2019.

25. Colin Powell. *My American Journey*. 1st edition. New York: Ballantine Books, 2003.

26. Clark's comments were reported in the press as an indication that the air campaign was not succeeding. He was privately reprimanded by Secretary of Defense William Cohen and Chairman of the Joint Chiefs of Staff Hugh Shelton for knowingly using the public as a way to advance the ground invasion agenda. The service chiefs and key Clinton administration officials were "starkly unsupportive" of Clark's subsequent attempts to push the issue. Peter Boyer, "General Clark's battles," *The New Yorker* (Nov. 17, 2003).

27. Golby, Cohn, and Feaver, "Thanks for your service: civilian and veteran attitudes after fifteen years of war."

28. James Golby and Peter D. Feaver. "Biden inherits a challenging civil-military legacy." *War on the Rocks*. http://warontherocks.com/2021/01/biden-inherits-a-challenging-civil-military-legacy/ (January 1, 2021).

29. Rosa Brooks. *How Everything Became War and the Military Became Everything: Tales from the Pentagon* First Printing edition. New York: Simon & Schuster, 2016. pg. 313.

30. Controlled leaks have a long history that pre-dates modern technology for distribution. In January 1950, General Douglas MacArthur allowed the release of classified State Department briefing materials predicting an urgent threat to the island of Taiwan in response to the "appeasement" policy adopted by President Truman and Dean Acheson. While this was

seen by many as an attempt by MacArthur to support Republican allies in Congress and facilitate a future presidential run, the incident contributed to the increasingly confrontational relationship between Truman and MacArthur that would result in one of the most notable civil-military clashes in US history during the Korean War and MacArthur's relief from duty. Callum A. MacDonald, *Korea: The War before Vietnam*. London: MacMillan Press, Ltd, 1986, 21.

31. Golby, Dropp, and Feaver, *Military Campaigns: Veterans' Endorsements and Presidential Elections*; Maurer, *The Generals' Constitution*; Kablack et al., "The military speaks out"; Brooks and Robinson, "Let the generals speak?"

32. On Syria: Robert H. Scales. "U.S. military planners don't support war with Syria." *Washington Post* (Sept. 5, 2013). On Iraq: David Cloud and Eric Schmitt, "More retired generals call for Rumsfeld's resignation." *New York Times* (April 14, 2006). On North Korea: Anna Fifield. "Retired military leaders urge Trump to choose words, not action, to deal with North Korea." *Washington Post* (Dec. 13, 2017). On the federal budget: Dan Lamothe. "Retired generals cite past comments from Mattis while opposing Trump's proposed foreign aid cuts." *Washington Post* (Feb. 27, 2017). On media relations: Kristine Phillips. " 'Greatest threat to democracy': commander of bin Laden raid slams Trump's anti-media sentiment." *Washington Post* (Feb. 24, 2017). On torture: Michael D. Shear, Nicholas Fandos, and Jennifer Steinhauer. "Trump asks critic of vaccines to lead vaccine safety panel." *New York Times* (Jan. 10, 2017). On LGBT service policy: Chris Kenning. "Retired military officers slam Trump's proposed transgender ban." *Reuters* (Aug. 1, 2017) and John M. Shalikashvili. "Second thoughts on gays in the military." *New York Times* (Jan. 2, 2007).

33. Urben, *Like, Comment, Retweet: The State of the Military's Nonpartisan Ethic*.

34. Kohn, "The erosion of civilian control of the military in the United States today"; Dempsey, *Our Army*; Owens, "Military officers: political without partisanship"; Michael G. Mullen. "From the chairman: military must stay apolitical." *Joint Forces Quarterly* 3.50 (2008).

35. Phillip Carter et al. "Trump is surrounding himself with generals. That's dangerous." *Washington Post* (November 30, 2016); Peter White. "Trump may put 5 military officers in top posts. That's unprecedented." *Washington Post* (December 1, 2016).

36. Lupia and McCubbins, *The Democratic Dilemma*.

37. Baum and Groeling, "Shot by the messenger."

38. Golby, Feaver, and Dropp, "Elite military cues and public opinion about the use of military force"; Carrie A. Lee. "Polarization, casualty sensitivity, and military operations: evidence from a survey experiment." *International Politics* (Special Issue, March 2022); Lupton and Webb, "Wither Elites?"

39. A September 18–21, 2017, Washington Post/ABC News Poll probed public attitudes on a potential preemptive strike on North Korea by US military forces in response to escalating rhetoric over the North Korean nuclear program. When asked who they "trust to handle North Korea responsibly," 72% of respondents answered "US military leaders," compared to only 37% who answered President Donald Trump. Confidence in the president was highly divided along partisan lines; in addition, expressed confidence between the two entities was highly polarized, with 42% of respondents expressing no trust at all in the president and 43% trusting the military "a great deal." Scott Clement and Philip Rucker, "Poll: far more trust generals than Trump on N. Korea, while two-thirds oppose preemptive strike," *Washington Post* (Sept. 24, 2017).

40. Zaller, *The Nature and Origins of Mass Opinion*; Taber and Lodge, "Motivated skepticism in the evaluation of political beliefs."

41. The survey was conducted with the firm YouGov in December 2016 using online survey questionnaires to a optin survey panel of 1,000 respondents. Specific wording of the questionnaire and format of news articles can be found in the Appendix.

42. Specific information on the composition of the survey battery, to include individual-level characteristics and precise question wording can be found in the data appendix.

43. This question utilized Gallup's formulation of their "Confidence in Institutions" poll conducted annually. The question asked is "I am going to read you a list of institutions in American society. Please tell me how much confidence you, yourself, have in each

one—a great deal, quite a lot, some, very little, or none at all?" The most recent national response for confidence in the military institution in June 2016 was 73% in the top two blocks. The sample for this experiment was substantially lower at 55%, making this sample a "hard case" for recovering effects given the lower overall confidence in the military establishment *Gallup*, "Confidence in Institutions," http://www.gallup.com/poll/1597/confidence-institutions.aspx.

44. The significance of the treatment condition is reflected in the data appendix, which captures the results of a logistic regression model using a binary indicator variable for approval of the policy. The treatment condition for oppositional cuing remains substantively and statistically significant across base and fully specified models, which include controlling for respondent gender, education, partisan identification, political ideology, and the partisan identity of the president. The results are robust to an alternative model using ordered logistics regression and similar covariates.

45. Golby, Feaver, and Dropp, "Elite military cues and public opinion about the use of military force."

46. Frank Newport. *Americans' Conjidence in Institutions Edges Up.* http://news.gallup.com/poll/212840/americans-confidence-institutions-edges.aspx (June 26, 2017).

47. Amnon Cavari and Guy Freedman. "Partisan cues and opinion formation on foreign policy." *American Politics Research* 47.1 (Jan. 2019), pp. 29–57.

48. Taber and Lodge, "Motivated skepticism in the evaluation of political beliefs"; Iyengar and Westwood, "Fear and loathing across Party lines: new evidence on group polarization."

49. Golby, Feaver, and Dropp, "Elite military cues and public opinion about the use of military force."

50. Adam J. Berinsky. *In Time of War: Understanding American Public Opinion from World War II to Iraq.* 1st edition. Chicago: University of Chicago Press, 2009.

51. Grieco et al., "Let's get a second opinion"; Golby, Feaver, and Dropp, "Elite military cues and public opinion about the use of military force."

52. In their 2013 YouGov survey, Kori Schake and Jim Mattis asked respondents "Do you think people serving in the military are more likely to vote Democratic or Republican?," to which 42% replied "somewhat" or "much more" likely to vote Republican, compared to only 11% who replied the same for Democrat. This is unsurprising given both historical and recent works on the partisan identity of military service members, but confirms for our purposes that public perception often views the military not only as more conservative, but more Republican.

53. Krebs, Ralston, and Rapport, "No right to be wrong."

54. Peter D. Feaver and James Golby. "Opinion—The myth of 'war weary' Americans." *Wall Street Journal* (December 1, 2020).

55. Robin Toner and Jim Rutenberg. "Partisan Divide on Iraq Exceeds Split on Vietnam." *New York Times* (July 30, 2006).

56. George W. Bush. *Decision Points.* New York, NY, 2010, p. 92.

57. Brooks, "Militaries and political activity in democracies."

58. LtGen Newbold served as director of operations, J-3, for the Joint Staff at the Pentagon from 2000–2002. A key figure in the war-planning effort, Newbold shared similar misgivings about the wisdom of an Iraq invasion and the acceptable level of resource commitment for it to succeed. Finding Rumsfeld resistant to information that called the Iraq mission's feasibility into doubt, Newbold offered his premature resignation in 2002. Thomas Donnelly. "Testing the 'Fluornoy Hypothesis': civil military relations in the post-9/11 era." *Warriors and Citizens: American Views of Our Military*, ed. Kori Schake and Jim Mattis, Chapter within Schake and Mattis (2016). Hoover Institute Press, Stanford CA.

59. Greg Newbold. "Why Iraq was a mistake." *Time* (April 9, 2006).

60. Martin L. Cook. "Revolt of the generals: a case study in professional ethics." *Parameters* 38.1 (2008), p. 4; Cloud and Schmitt, "More retired Generals call for Rumsfeld's resignation."

61. Quoted in David Margolick, "The night of the Generals." *Vanity Fair* (March 5, 2007).

62. Thom Shanker and David S. Cloud. "Rumsfeld says calls for ouster 'will pass'." *New York Times* (April 18, 2006).

63. Though Rumsfeld had officially tendered his resignation before the election, President Bush did not announce this fact until the day after the election, which further heightened

partisan in-fighting among Republicans who believed control of the Senate could have been preserved had candidates been relieved of public scrutiny targeted at Rumsfeld. Kristin Roberts. "Rumsfeld resigned before election, letter shows." *Reuters* (Aug. 15, 2007).

64. Mackubin Thomas Owens. "Rumsfeld, the generals, and the state of US civil-military relations." *Naval War College Review* 59.4 (2006), p. 68.
65. Kohn, "The erosion of civilian control of the military in the United States today."
66. Dempsey, *Our Army.*
67. Bush, *Decision Points*, p. 93.
68. Feaver, "The right to be right."
69. Cook, "Revolt of the generals," p. 7.
70. Brooks, *How Everything Became War and the Military Became Everything*, pp. 311–312.
71. Sheryl Gay Stolberg. "Obama defends strategy in Afghanistan." *New York Times* (August 17, 2009).
72. Robert Haddick. "This week at war: the biden plan returns." *Foreign Policy* (October 22, 2010); Holly Bailey. "Joe Biden, White House Truth Teller." *Newsweek* (October 9, 2009).
73. Bob Woodward. *Obama's Wars*. Reprint edition. New York; Toronto: Simon & Schuster, 2011, p. 178. Rosa Brooks, "How Everything Became War and the Military Became Everything", p. 312.
74. Peter Baker. "How Obama came to plan for surge in Afghanistan." *New York Times* (December 5, 2009).
75. John F. Burns. "McChrystal rejects scaling down Afghan military aims." *New York Times* (Oct. 1, 2009).
76. Woodward, *Obama's Wars*, p. 196.
77. Peter D. Feaver. "Bob Woodward strikes again! (McChrystal assessment edition)." *Foreign Policy* (September 21, 2009).
78. Michael Hastings. "The runaway General: the profile that brought down McChrystal." *Rolling Stone* (June 22, 2010).
79. Brooks, *How Everything Became War and the Military Became Everything*, p. 314.
80. Baker, "How Obama came to plan for surge in Afghanistan."

Chapter 4

1. Huntington, *The Soldier and the State*; Michael C. Desch. "Explaining the gap: Vietnam, the Republicanization of the South, and the end of the mass army." *Soldiers and Civilians: The Civil-Military Gap and American National Security.* Cambridge, MA: MIT Press, 2001; Kohn, "Out of control"; Desch, "Explaining the gap: Vietnam, the Republicanization of the South, and the end of the mass army."
2. Berinsky, "Assuming the costs of war."
3. Downs, *An Economic Theory of Democracy*; Lupia and McCubbins, *The Democratic Dilemma*; Zaller, *The Nature and Origins of Mass Opinion.*
4. Iyengar and Hahn, "Red media, blue media"; Jamieson and Cappella, *Echo Chamber: Rush Limbaugh and the Conservative Media Establishment*; Stroud, "Media use and political predispositions: revisiting the concept of selective exposure."
5. Petty and Cacioppo, *Communication and Persuasion.*
6. Joseph Nye. "The media and declining confidence in government." *Harvard International Journal of Press/Politics* 2.3 (1997), pp. 4–9; Susan J. Pharr, Robert D. Putnam, and Russell J. Dalton. "A quarter-century of declining confidence." *Journal of Democracy* 11.2 (2000), pp. 5–25.
7. Abigail Post and T. S. Sechser. "Hidden norms in international relations: public opinion and the use of nuclear weapons." Paper for Peace Science Society annual meeting. October 20, 2016; Golby, Feaver, and Dropp, "Elite military cues and public opinion about the use of military force"; Andrew H. Sidman and Helmut Norpoth. "Fighting to win wartime morale in the American public." *Electoral Studies* 31.2 (2012), pp. 330–341.
8. Schake and Mattis, *Warriors and Citizens.*
9. Roberto Stefan Foa and Yascha Mounk. "The democratic disconnect." *Journal of Democracy* 27.3 (2016), pp. 5–17.

10. Gronke and Feaver, "Uncertain confidence: civilian and military attitudes and civil-military relations"; Hill, Wong, and Gerras, " 'Self-interest well understood'. "

11. Liebert and Golby, "Midlife Crisis?"; Burbach, "Confidence without sacrifice: American public opinion and the US military"; Burbach, "Partisan dimensions of confidence in the U.S. military, 1973–2016."

12. Rothstein and Stolle, "The quality of government and social capital."

13. Schultz, "Perils of polarization for U.S. foreign policy."

14. Golby, Feaver, and Dropp, "Elite military cues and public opinion about the use of military force"; Dempsey, Our Army; Kohn, "The erosion of civilian control of the military in the United States today."

15. Dempsey, Our Army; Urben, "Civil-military relations in a time of war"; Desch, "Explaining the gap: Vietnam, the Republicanization of the South, and the end of the mass army"; Golby, "Duty, honor . . . party? Ideology, institutions, and the use of military force"; Feaver and Kohn, Soldiers and Civilians; Schake and Mattis, Warriors and Citizens.

16. Kohn, "Out of control."

17. Powell, Colin, John Lehman, William Odom, Samuel Huntington, and Richard Kohn. "Out of control: The crisis in civil-military relations." The National Interest 36 (1994), pp. 23–31.

18. Golby, "Duty, honor . . . party? Ideology, institutions, and the use of military force"; Kohn, "The erosion of civilian control of the military in the United States today"; Eugene R. Wittkopf. Faces of Internationalism: Public Opinion and American Foreign Policy. Durham: Duke University Press Books, July 1990.

19. Holsti, "A widening gap between the U.S. military and civilian society?"; Desch, "Explaining the gap: Vietnam, the Republicanization of the South, and the end of the mass army."

20. Dempsey, Our Army.

21. Schake and Mattis, Warriors and Citizens, find that 58% of Republicans believed military servicemembers to be "more socially conservative" than the rest of society, compared with 9% of Democrats who believed servicemembers were "less socially conservative" than the rest of society. Additionally, 72% of Republicans believed military values to be "about the same" or "less progressive" than the rest of society, compared with 16% of Democrats would believed military values were "more progressive." This speaks to the perception that Republicans feel military veterans are "more like us" than Democrats or Independents. The survey finds that Republicans see the military as more meritocratic and that holding on to an "old-fashioned view of morality" is necessary for the institution. Compared to Democrats, Republicans are also more likely to believe that the military has "a great deal of respect for civilian society" and less likely to believe that civilian society possesses the same respect for the military in turn. https://www.hoover.org/warriors-and-citizens-crosstabs-1.

22. Ronald R. Krebs and Robert Ralston. "Patriotism or paychecks: who believes what about why soldiers serve." Armed Forces & Society 48.1 (Jan. 2022), pp. 25–48.

23. Urben, Party, Politics, and the Post-9/11 Army pp. 86, 113.

24. Danielle Lupton and Max Z. Margulies. "Analysis—Trump's election fraud allegations suggest military voters uniformly supported him. It's not so." Washington Post (November 18, 2020).

25. Nye, "The media and declining confidence in government."

26. Iyengar and Hahn, "Red media, blue media"; Taber and Lodge, "Motivated skepticism in the evaluation of political beliefs"; Abramowitz and Saunders, "Is polarization a myth?"; Mason, " 'I disrespectfully agree' "; Iyengar, Sood, and Lelkes, "Affect, not ideology."

27. Christina Lefevre-Gonzalez. "Restoring historical understandings of the 'public interest' standard of American broadcasting: an exploration of the fairness doctrine." International Journal of Communication 7 (2013), pp. 89–109.

28. Iyengar and Hahn, "Red media, blue media."

29. Matthew A. Baum and Tim J. Groeling. "New media and the polarization of American political discourse." Political Communication 25 (2008), pp. 345–365.

30. Iyengar and Hahn, "Red media, blue media"; Stroud, "Media use and political predispositions: revisiting the concept of selective exposure."

31. Lilliana Mason and Julie Wronski, "One Tribe to Bind Them All: How Our Social Group Attachments Strength Partisanship," Advances in Political Psychology Vol 39, Iss 1, 2018.

32. Melissa Bell. "Richard Nixon and Roger Ailes 1970s plan to put the GOP on TV." *Washington Post* (July 1, 2011).

33. Mark Jurkowitz et al. *U.S. Media Polarization and the 2020 Election: A Nation Divided*. Tech. rep. Pew Research Center (Jan. 2020).

34. John Gramlich. "5 facts about Fox News." *Pew Research Center*. https://www.pewresearch.org/fact-tank/2020/04/08/five-facts-about-fox-news/ (April 8, 2020).

35. Jurkowitz et al., *U.S. Media Polarization and the 2020 Election: A Nation Divided*.

36. Steven Kull, Clay Ramsay, and Evan Lewis. "Misperceptions, the media, and the Iraq War." *Political Science Quarterly* 118.4 (2003), pp. 569–598; Dana Blanton. *Fox News Poll: 24 Percent Believe Obama Not Born in U.S.* Publisher: Fox News (Mar. 2015); Andrey Simonov et al. *The persuasive effect of Fox News: non-compliance with social distancing during the Covid-19 pandemic*. Working Paper. National Bureau of Economic Research, May 2020.

37. Drezner, "Perspective—Is Fox News to blame for American rage?"; Drum, "The real reason Americans are so damn angry all the time."

38. Gramlich, "5 facts about Fox News."

39. Taylor Orth. "Which groups of Americans are most likely to believe conspiracy theories?" *YouGov*. https://today.yougov.com/topics/politics/articles-reports/2022/03/30/which-groups-americans-believe-conspiracies (March 30, 2022); Giovanni Russonello. "QAnon now as popular in U.S. as some major religions, poll suggests." *New York Times* (May 27, 2021).

40. Larry M. Bartels. "Beyond the running tally: partisan bias in political perceptions." *Political Behavior* 24.2 (2002), pp. 126.

41. Shanto Iyengar and Donald R. Kinder. *News That Matters: Television and American Opinion, Updated Edition*. Chicago: University of Chicago Press, 1989.

42. Nye, "The media and declining confidence in government"; Thomas Hanitzsch and Rosa Berganza. "Explaining journalists' trust in public institutions across 20 countries: media freedom, corruption, and ownership matter most: explaining journalists' public trust." *Journal of Communication* 62.5 (2012), pp. 794–814; Krista E. Wiegand and David L. Paletz. "The elite media and the military-civilian culture gap." *Armed Forces & Society* 27.2 (2001), pp. 183–204.

43. Liebert and Golby, "Midlife Crisis?"

44. Christopher H. Achen and Larry M. Bartels. *Democracy for Realists: Why Elections Do Not Produce Responsive Government*. Revised edition. Princeton, NJ: Princeton University Press, 2017, p. 268.

45. Jurkowitz et al., *U.S. Media Polarization and the 2020 Election: A Nation Divided*.

46. A 2014 report from the Pew Research center found that 47% of individuals identifying as "conservative" or "very conservative" obtained news on government and politics from a single source: FOX News. This compares to smaller outlet followings among political liberals, where MSNBC and CNN have followings of 12% and 15%, respectively. "Consistent" conservatives are also far more likely to actively distrust other media outlets than liberals; of the 36 media outlets surveyed, conservatives held more distrust than trust for 24 of them, compared to 8 out of 36 among liberals. "Political polarization and media habits: from Fox News to Facebook, how liberals and conservatives keep up with politics." Pew Research Center (Oct. 21, 2014).

47. Stroud, "Media use and political predispositions: revisiting the concept of selective exposure"; Iyengar and Hahn, "red media, blue media."

48. Andrew Dugan and Zac Auter. *Republicans', Democrats' Views of Media Accuracy Diverge*. Source: Gallup. http://news.gallup.com/poll/216320/republicans-democrats-views-media-accuracy-diverge.aspx (August 25, 2017).

49. Berinsky, "Assuming the costs of war."

50. Feldman, Huddy, and Marcus, *Going to War in Iraq*, p. 179.

51. Pew Research Center, News Coverage Index Methodology, www.pewresearch.org/journalism/news_index_methodology/.

52. For television and radio programs, I generate "% of Newshole" by calculating a daily total of duration (in on-air seconds) spent on the Iraq Combat Events (ICE) topic by each source, divided by the total number of on-air seconds sampled by the NCI database. This yields an estimate of the daily percentage of the on-air time devoted to Iraq Combat Event stories per day, per source. For print media, I reverse-coded the "prominence" variable from the NCI

dataset that rates all newspaper stories on a five-point scale based on location in the paper's print edition (most prominent, second most prominent, other-above the fold, etc...), taking the daily average of these to create a "Prominence Proportion" per day, per source.

53. Greg Wilesmith. *Reporting Afghanistan and Iraq: Media, Military, and Governments and How They Injluence Each Other.* Tech. rep. University of Oxford Reuters Institute for the Study of Journalism, 2011.

54. Feldman, Huddy, and Marcus, *Going to War in Iraq,* p. 174.

55. Jurkowitz et al., *U.S. Media Polarization and the 2020 Election: A Nation Divided.*

56. Our best picture of these percentages of conservative viewership is captured by Pew Research Center, October 21, 2014, "Political Polarization and Media Habits."

57. The Pew NCI dataset codes component sub-story lines that collectively compose broader or "big stories." For example, Iraq combat events are broadly coded together *(storyid=100),* but include more specific categorizations based on their nature as "Combat/violence/casualties" *(substoryline=100001),* "Iraqi refugees" *(substoryline=100010),* or "Evaluations of US troop surge" *(substoryline=100014).* Graphical depictions of outlet variation in reporting times is available in the Appendix.

58. Graphical depiction of print media reporting on these stories is available in Appendix.

59. David M. Blei, Andrew Y. Ng, and Michael I. Jordan. "Latent dirichlet allocation." *Journal of Machine Learning Research* (Jan. 3, 2003), pp. 993–1022; Margaret E. Roberts, Brandon M. Stewart, and Dustin Tingley. "stm: R package for Structural Topic Models." *Journal of Statistical Software* 91.2 (2019), pp. 1–40.

60. Roberts, Stewart, and Tingley, "stm: R package for Structural Topic Models."

61. "Interview with David Petraeus." *FOX News,* Chris Wallace (Dec. 23, 2007).

62. "Interview with Senators Graham/Levin." *FOX News,* Chris Wallace (Apr. 15, 2007); "Interview with House Minority Leader John Boehner." *FOX News,* Neil Cavuto (Mar. 21, 2007).

63. "New documentary on war has some up in arms." *FOX News,* Alan Colmes (Apr. 24, 2007); "Talking Points Memo and impact: who respects the troops." *FOX News,* Bill O'Reilly (Feb. 8, 2007); "Talking Points Memo and top story." *FOX News,* Bill O'Reilly (Apr. 24, 2007).

64. "Retired general Blasts Iraq War effort, media coverage." *FOX News,* Alan Colmes (Oct. 15, 2007).

65. Susan Moeller. *Packaging Terrorism: Co-opting the News for Politics and Profit.* Malden, MA: Wiley-Blackwell, 2009, p. 85.

66. Feldman, Huddy, and Marcus, *Going to War in Iraq,* p. 160.

67. Erik Peterson, Sharad Goel, and Shanto Iyengar. "Partisan selective exposure in online news consumption: evidence from the 2016 presidential campaign." *Political Science Research and Methods* 9.2 (2019), pp. 242–258; Erik Peterson and Shanto Iyengar. "Partisan gaps in political information and information-seeking behavior: motivating reasoning or cheerleading?" *American Journal of Political Science* 65.1 (2021), pp. 133–147.

68. Charles Creitz. *Ingraham: Biden Defense Chief Starting 'Ideological and Un-American Purge of the US Military'.* Source: Fox News. https://www.foxnews.com/media/laura-ingraham-biden-lloyd-austin-60-day-stand-down-extremism (February 4, 2021).

69. Newsmax. *Welcome to Biden's Woke Military: Dr. @SebGorka https://t.co/YsrGVDOVWZ.* Tweet. May 20, 2021.

70. Max Boot. "Opinion—Imagine if a Squad member called a general a stupid pig. Tucker Carlson just did." *Washington Post* (June 28, 2021); Lara Seligman and Connor O'Brien. "Conservatives lash out at the military over 'woke' policies." *POLITICO* (May 21, 2021); Oriana Pawlyk. *Air Force Takes First Step to Buy Maternity Flight Suits.* June 24, 2020.

71. Brendan Cole. "Tucker Carlson doubles down on Mark Milley criticism, brands comments 'race attack'." *Newsweek* (June 26, 2021); Kristina Wong. *Milley's Defense of CRT to Understand "White rage" Stokes Controversy.* June 24, 2021.

72. Mark Satter. *GOP ramps up attacks on teaching critical race theory to military.* Source: Roll Call. https://www.rollcall.com/2021/07/15/gop-ramps-up-attacks-on-teaching-critical-race-theory-to-military/ (July 15, 2021).

73. Brenan, *Americans' Confidence in Major U.S. Institutions Dips.*

74. Michael R. Gordon and Bernard E. Trainor. *The Endgame: The Inside Story of the Struggle for Iraq, from George W. Bush to Barack Obama.* Reprint edition. New York: Vintage, 2012.

75. Don Gonyea. "Anger over 'Betray Us' ad simmers on Hill." *National Public Radio* (September 22, 2007).
76. Andrew Kohut and Scott Keeter. *Petraeus' Proposals Favored, But No Lift in War Support.* Tech. rep. Pew Research Center, September 18, 2007.
77. *"Washington Post* Editorial Staff: Fact Checker—General Betray Us?" *Washington Post* (September 20, 2007).

Chapter 5

1. Williams, "Systemic influences on political trust."
2. Alan Gerber and Donald Green. "Misperceptions about perceptual bias." *Annual Review of Political Science* 2.1 (1999), p. 192.
3. Bartels, "Beyond the running tally: partisan bias in political perceptions."
4. Gerber and Green, "Misperceptions about Perceptual Bias."
5. Taber and Lodge, "Motivated skepticism in the evaluation of political beliefs"; Zaller, *The Nature and Origins of Mass Opinion.*
6. Schultz, "Perils of Polarization for U.S. Foreign Policy."
7. Golby, "Duty, honor . . . party? Ideology, institutions, and the use of military force"; Feaver and Kohn, *Soldiers and Civilians*; Holsti, "A widening gap between the U.S. military and civilian society?"; Urben, "Civil-military relations in a time of war"; Dempsey, *Our Army.*
8. Hetherington, "The political relevance of political trust."
9. Mishler and Rose, "What are the origins of political trust?"
10. Gronke and Feaver, "Uncertain confidence: civilian and military attitudes and civil-military relations"; King and Karabell, *The Generation of Trust*; Hill, Wong, and Gerras, " 'Self-interest well understood' "; Burbach, "Gaining trust while losing wars."
11. Maja Garb and Marjan Malesic. "The causes of trust and distrust in the military." *Defense & Security Analysis* 32.1 (2016), pp. 64–78; Yang and Holzer, "The performance–trust link."
12. Hill, Wong, and Gerras, " 'Self-interest well understood'. "
13. Mason, " 'I disrespectfully agree' "; Abramowitz and Saunders, "Is polarization a myth?"; Joseph Bafumi and Robert Y. Shapiro. "A new partisan voter." *The Journal of Politics* 71.1 (2009), pp. 1–24.
14. Bafumi and Shapiro, "A new partisan voter." p. 21.
15. Yphtach Lelkes and Paul M. Sniderman. "The ideological asymmetry of the American party system." *British Journal of Political Science* 46.04 (2016), pp. 825–844; Brendan Nyhan and Jason Reifler. "When corrections fail: the persistence of political misperceptions." *Political Behavior* 32.2 (2010), pp. 303–330; Taber and Lodge, "Motivated skepticism in the evaluation of political beliefs"; Leonie Huddy, Lilliana Mason, and Lene Aaroe. "Expressive partisanship: campaign involvement, political emotion, and partisan identity." *American Political Science Review* 109.1 (2015), pp. 1–17.
16. Krebs and Ralston, "Patriotism or Paychecks."
17. Gecewicz and Rainie, *Why Americans Don't Fully Trust Many Who Hold Positions of Power and Responsibility.*
18. Jonathan McDonald Ladd. "The neglected power of elite opinion leadership to produce antipathy toward the news media: evidence from a survey experiment." *Political Behavior* 32.1 (2010), pp. 29–50, using a formulation similar to Martin Gilens. "Political ignorance and collective policy preferences." *American Political Science Review* 95.2 (2001), pp. 379–396, where even though the question asks about awareness of the story, this is not the measurable variable of interest; because the experiment is probing negative attitudes, the intent is to merely bring the information to the top of the respondent's head without drawing attention to the treatment. My own design differs from Ladd's in several ways. First is the use of a more compact scale for measurement of trust (rather than the feeling thermometer employed by Ladd for measuring attitudes on the media). Second, the news stories are meant as priming information in themselves, whereas the Ladd study uses elite criticism of the media institution as priming information. I adopt a similar strategy for measuring the control condition, where the only measurable variable is whether the respondent heard the story.

19. Zaller, *The Nature and Origins of Mass Opinion*.

20. S. E. Taylor and Susan Fiske. "Salience, attention, and attribution: top of the head phenomena." *Advances in Experimental Social Psychology*. Vol. 11. New York: Academic Press, 1978, pp. 249–288; Dennis Chong and James N. Druckman. "A theory of framing and opinion formation in competitive elite environments." *Journal of Communication* 57.1 (2007), pp. 99–118.

21. News snippets reflected substantive information from actual news stories. Anthony Faiola, "British aid worker Norgrove killed accidentally by U.S. soldier, inquiry finds," *Washington Post Foreign Service* (Dec. 3, 2010); Barbara P. Usher, "Kunduz bombing: US attacked MSF clinic 'in error.' " *BBC News* (Nov. 25, 2015).

22. James Dao. "Ex-soldier gets life sentence for Iraq murders." *New York Times* (May 21, 2009); Craig Whitlock. "Military brass, behaving badly: files detail a spate of misconduct dogging armed forces." *Washington Post* (January 26, 2014).

23. Brian J. Gaines et al. "Same facts, different interpretations: partisan motivation and opinion on Iraq." *The Journal of Politics* 69.4 (2007), pp. 957–974; Gerber and Green, "Misperceptions about perceptual bias."

24. This general response pattern is largely robust to re-classification of respondents according to the five-point ideology scale, with liberals and moderates expressing clear disapproval of professionalism and performance categories and conservatives exhibiting statistically insignificant changes to expressed trust across all conditions. Similar patterns are also visible when re-coding partisan identity based on the seven-point scale, allowing "leaners" to be counted as part of a major party. In this setting, Democrats similarly maintain strong disapproval of both the professionalism and performance conditions and Republicans are similarly unmoved across all conditions. Independents, now classified as those who refused to identify even as a leaner to any party, expressed strong disapproval in the partisan condition (10.4% loss) and the professional condition (10.9% loss).

25. Nyhan and Reifler, "When corrections fail"; Chong and Druckman, "A theory of framing and opinion formation in competitive elite environments."

26. David P. Redlawsk. "Hot cognition or cool consideration? Testing the effects of motivated reasoning on political decision making." *The Journal of Politics* 64.4 (2002), pp. 1021–1044, p. 1021.

27. Nyhan and Reifler, "When corrections fail."

28. Iyengar, Sood, and Lelkes, "Affect, not ideology"; Mason, " 'I disrespectfully agree' "; Iyengar and Westwood, "Fear and loathing across Party lines: new evidence on group polarization."

29. Lilliana Mason and Julie Wronski. "One tribe to bind them all: how out social group attachments strengthen partisanship." *Advances in Political Psychology* 39.1 (2018), pp. 257–277; Lelkes and Sniderman, "The ideological asymmetry of the American Party system."

30. Gallup, "Confidence in institutions, June Wave Survey." Source: Gallup. https://news.gallup.com/poll/1597/confidenceinstitutions.aspx (2007).

31. The Pew Research Center for the People and the Press, "Little confidence in military or press depictions of Iraq." April 5, 2007.

32. Pew Research Center/Washington Post Survey, "Sexual assault in the military widely seen as important issues, but no agreement on solution." June 12, 2013.

33. Taber and Lodge, "Motivated skepticism in the evaluation of political beliefs." p. 757.

34. After removing outliers who took more than 1,000 seconds to complete the survey, I found that Republicans and Democrats in the *non-partisan* condition spent approximately 83 and 86 seconds on this portion of the survey instrument, respectively. In the *professionalism* condition, the same subgroups spent approximately 84 and 100 seconds, respectively, and 76 and 97 seconds, respectively, in the *performance* condition. The amounts to a 19% increase in Republican time expenditure in the former and a 27% increase in the latter.

35. Miles Hewstone, Mark Rubin, and Hazel Willis. "Intergroup bias." *Annual Review of Psychology* 53 (2002), pp. 575–604; Iyengar and Westwood, "Fear and loathing across Party lines: new evidence on group polarization."

36. Democratic trust in the mass media has remaining consistently high since 2001, with a nadir of 51% expressing "a great deal" or "fair amount" in 2016; however, Democrats expressed more traditionally high levels of trust in the media in 2017 at 72%, as Republican trust cratered to

14% in the same year. Art Swift. "Democrats' confidence in mass media rises sharply from 2016." *Gallup* (Sept. 21, 2017).

37. Peter Feaver. "The military revolt against Joe Biden." *Foreign Policy* (May 2021), pp. 25–26.

38. Risa Brooks. "Through the looking glass: Trump era civil-military relations in comparative perspective." *Strategic Studies Quarterly* 15.2 (2021), pp. 69–98; Schake, "The line held: civil-military relations in the Trump administration"; Golby and Feaver, "Biden inherits a challenging civil-military legacy"; Golby, "Uncivil-military relations: politicization of the military in the Trump era."

39. Kaurin, "An 'Unprincipled Principal': Implications for civil-military relations."

40. Michael R. Gordon. "Trump's mix of politics and military is faulted." *New York Times* (February 8, 2017).

41. Alexander Marlow. "Exclusive—Trump: Paul Ryan Blocked Subpoenas of Democrats." Source: Breitbart. https://www.breitbart.com/politics/2019/03/13/exclusive-president-donald-trump-paul-ryan-blocked-subpoenas-of-democrats/ (March 13, 2019).

42. Golby, "Uncivil-military relations: politicization of the military in the Trump era."

43. Tim Sullivan. "Trump tweet intimating military will fire on 'looters' in Minnesota sparks another warning from Twitter." *Military Times* (May 29, 2020).

44. Missy Ryan and Thomas Gibbons-Neff. "In inaugural Pentagon visit, Trump signs orders on immigrant vetting, military strength." *Washington Post* (January 27, 2017).

45. Schake, "The line held: civil-military relations in the Trump administration." p. 44.

46. Wesley Morgan. "Trump's Fourth of July extravaganza troubles former military leaders." *POLITICO* (July 2, 2019).

47. Golby, "Uncivil-military relations: politicization of the military in the Trump era"; Alice Hunt Friend. "Analysis—The Pentagon is moving money to pay for Trump's border wall. Here are the consequences." *Washington Post* (September 6, 2019).

48. Julie Hirschfeld Davis and Helene Cooper. "Trump says transgender people will not be allowed in the military." *New York Times* (July 26, 2017).

49. Michael A. Robinson. "Trump's pardon of two former Army officers has sparked new controversy. Here's why." *Washington Post* (November 17, 2019).

50. Dave Philipps. "Trump clears three service members in war crimes cases." *New York Times* (November 15, 2019).

51. Jared Keller. "Joint Chiefs to troops: Biden is your next commander-in-chief. Deal with it." *Task & Purpose* (January 12, 2021).

52. Helene Cooper et al. "As the D.C. police clear the Capitol grounds, the mayor extends a public emergency." *New York Times* (January 6, 2021).

53. Paul Szoldra. "Army lieutenant who called Joint Chiefs memo 'seditious' probably about to get a class on the UCMJ." *Task & Purpose* (January 31, 2021).

54. Chris Jackson. *Ipsos/Reuters Poll—The Big Lie.* poll. Washington, DC: Ipsos, May 21, 2021.

55. Rick Klein. "Trump said 'blame on both sides' in Charlottesville, now the anniversary puts him on the spot". Source: ABC News. https://abcnews.go.com/Politics/trump-blame-sides-charlottesville-now-anniversary-puts-spot/story?id=57141612 (August 12, 2018).

56. Scott Clement and David Nakamura. "Poll shows clear disapproval of how Trump responded to Charlottesville violence." *Washington Post* (August 21, 2017).

57. deGrandpre, "Trump's generals condemn Charlottesville racism—while trying not to offend the president"; Philipps, "Inspired by Charlottesville, military chiefs condemn racism"; Phil McCausland. *Military joint chiefs denounce Charlottesville racism.* Source: NBC News. https://www.nbcnews.com/news/us-news/military-joint-chiefs-denounce-charlottesville-racism-n793376 (August 16, 2017).

58. Feaver, "The military revolt against Joe Biden"; White, "Trump may put 5 military officers in top posts. That's unprecedented."

59. Mark Abadi. "Trump won't stop saying 'my generals'—and the military community isn't happy." *Business Insider* (October 25, 2017).

60. Rebecca Shabad. "How unusual is Trump's Cabinet of generals?" *CBS News* (December 9, 2016); Risa A. Brooks, Michael A. Robinson, and Heidi A. Urben. "Biden has picked a retired general for defense secretary. Here's why it matters." *Washington Post* (December 9, 2020); Michael A. Robinson, Risa A. Brooks, and Heidi A. Urben. "How Biden's pick for Defense

Secretary might shake up civil-military relations." *Political Violence at a Glance* (December 8, 2020).

61. David Barno and Nora Bensahel. "Why no general should serve as White House chief of staff." *War on the Rocks* (September 12, 2017).

62. Daniel W. Drezner. "Perspective—Is this the tipping point for trust in the U.S. military?" *Washington Post* (October 26, 2017).

63. Michael A. Robinson. "What the Mattis resignation tells us about how Trump is damaging the military's credibility." *Washington Post* (December 21, 2018); Nancy A. Youssef. "Trump, calling Mattis a Democrat, opens the door to his departure." *Wall Street Journal* (October 14, 2018).

64. Philip Rucker and Carol Leonnig. *A Very Stable Genius: Donald J. Trump's Testing of America*. New York, NY Books, 2020, p. 204.

65. Rucker and Leonnig, *A Very Stable Genius*, p. 234.

66. Alex Horton. "Army is investigating soldiers who appeared in Democratic convention video." *Washington Post* (August 19, 2020); Leo Shane, III. "Concerns about uniformed Marines on camera during Republican convention dismissed by White House, military officials." *Marine Corps Times* (August 26, 2020).

67. James Crowley. "Donald Trump Jr. says military 'politicized,' knocks stunt against Marjorie Taylor Greene." *Newsweek* (March 20, 2021).

68. Elliot Ackerman. "Opinion—Yes, they defended the Capitol. But should they be decorated?" *New York Times* (March 26, 2021).

Chapter 6

1. Urben, *Like, Comment, Retweet: The State of the Military's Nonpartisan Ethic*; Liebert and Golby, "Midlife crisis?"; Owens, "Military officers: political without partisanship"; Hill, Wong, and Gerras, " 'Self-interest well understood.' "

2. Newport, *Americans' Confidence in Institutions Edges Up*; Brenan, *Americans' Confidence in Major U.S. Institutions Dips*; Brenan, *Amid Pandemic, Confidence in Key U.S. Institutions Surges*.

3. Petty and Cacioppo, *Communication and Persuasion*.

4. Baum and Groeling, "Shot by the messenger"; Golby, Feaver, and Dropp, "Elite military cues and public opinion about the use of military force"; Guisinger and Saunders, "Mapping the boundaries of elite cues: how elites shape mass opinion across international issues"; Grieco et al., "Let's get a second opinion."

5. Hovland and Weiss, "The influence of source credibility on communication effectiveness"; Lupia and McCubbins, *The Democratic Dilemma*; McGuire, "The nature of attitudes and attitude change."

6. Marvin E. Goldberg and Jon Hartwick. "The effects of advertiser reputation and extremity of advertising claim on advertising effectiveness." *Journal of Consumer Research* 17 (1990), pp. 172–179.

7. Roobina Ohanian. "Construction and validation of a scale to measure celebrity endorsers' perceived expertise, trustworthiness, and attractiveness." *Journal of Advertising* 19.3 (1990), pp. 39–52; Hovland and Weiss, "The influence of source credibility on communication effectiveness"; Stephen J. Newell and Ronald E. Goldsmith. "The development of a scale to measure perceived corporate credibility." *Journal of Business Research* 52 (2001), pp. 235–247.

8. Newell and Goldsmith, "The development of a scale to measure perceived corporate credibility"; Barbara A. Lafferty and Ronald E. Goldsmith. "Corporate credibility's role in consumers' attitudes and purchase intentions when a high versus a low credibility endorser is used in the ad." *Journal of Business Research* 44 (1999), pp. 109–116.

9. Golby and Feaver, "Former military leaders criticized the election and the administration. That hurts the military's reputation."

10. Huntington, *The Soldier and the State*; Cohen, *Supreme Command*.

11. Clausewitz, *On War, Indexed Edition*, p. 605.

12. Brooks, "Paradoxes of professionalism.", pp. 17–18.

13. This is most pointedly captured by Department of Defense Direction (DoDD) 1344.10, which specifically enjoins servicemembers from serving in partisan clubs, engaging in public

endorsement or advocacy, perform duties for political campaigns, or display signs or posters on their vehicles or property if living on a military installation. The complete list of these banned activities can be found in paragraph 4.1.2 in DoDD 1344.10, "Political activity by members of the Armed Forces." *US Department of Defense*, Feb. 19, 2008.

14. Urban, *Like, Comment, Retweet: The State of the Military's Nonpartisan Ethic.*
15. Kohn, "The erosion of civilian control of the military in the United States today."
16. Dempsey, *Our Army.*
17. Quoted in Bryan Bender. "Twitter and Facebook are politicizing the military." *Politico* (Feb. 26, 2017).
18. Owens, "Military officers: political without partisanship."
19. Peter Moore. *YouGov*—"Could a coup really happen in the United States?" https://today.yougov.com/topics/politics/articles-reports/2015/09/09/could-coup-happen-in-united-states (September 9, 2015).
20. Foa and Mounk, "The democratic disconnect."
21. Analysis of the WVS data reveals that respondents under the age of 30 in the 2011 wave expressed 23% support for army rule. Foa and Mounk specifically draw attention to this trend among rich, younger Americans, whose expressed support for army rule was nearly 35%. These patterns match with a broader shift in acceptance for both technocratic rule and for leaders who don't have to "bother with parliament and elections."
22. The TISS and YouGov surveys included both elite and mass subsamples; this increase is among the non-veteran masses, the most salient subsample for our purposes, as it indicates a shift in attitudes about civil-military norms among those citizens with no military experience.
23. In response to the same question, the 2013 audience expressed much higher levels of approval for military officials retiring in protest or refusing to carry out the order at all compared to the TISS sample, Golby, Cohn, and Feaver, "Thanks for your service", 115.
24. For expanded discussion on WVS results, see Roberto Stefan Foa and Yascha Mounk. "The democratic disconnect." *Journal of Democracy* 27.3 (2016), pp. 5–17; on YouGov/TISS results, see Peter D. Feaver and Richard H. Kohn, eds. *Soldiers and Civilians.* 1st edition. Cambridge, MA: The MIT Press, 2001 and Schake and Mattis, *Warriors and Citizens.* YouGov findings in 2015 survey described in further detail: Peter Moore, "Could a coup really happen in the United States?." YouGov (Sept. 9, 2015).
25. Golby, Dropp, and Feaver, "Military campaigns: veterans' endorsements and presidential elections", 17.
26. On torture and the budget, these figures included former commander of US Special Operations Command Admiral William McRaven, former CENTCOM commanders General David Petraeus and General James Mattis, and nearly 100 other general and flag officers who co-signed the open letters to the administration. The transgender ban was opposed by former Afghanistan commander General John Allen and "revolt" figure Major General Paul Eaton, though was more remarkable in that it was also openly opposed by active military elites such as serving Coast Guard commandant Admiral Paul Zukunft. Dan Lamothe. "Retired generals cite past comments from Mattis while opposing Trump's proposed foreign aid cuts." *Washington Post* (Feb. 27, 2017); Kristine Phillips. " 'Greatest threat to democracy': commander of bin Laden raid slams Trump's anti-media sentiment." *Washington Post* (Feb. 24, 2017); Michael D. Shear, Nicholas Fandos, and Jennifer Steinhauer. "Trump asks critic of vaccines to lead vaccine safety panel." *New York Times* (Jan. 10, 2017); Chris Kenning. "Retired military officers slam Trump's proposed transgender ban." *Reuters* (Aug. 1, 2017).
27. Robert H. Scales. "U.S. military planners don't support war with Syria." *Washington Post* (Sept. 5, 2013); Michael G. Mullen. "I was on the National Security Council. Bannon doesn't belong there." *New York Times* (Feb. 6, 2017); Anna Fifield. "Retired military leaders urge Trump to choose words, not action, to deal with North Korea." *Washington Post* (Dec. 13, 2017).
28. Huntington, *The Soldier and the State*; Janowitz, *The Professional Soldier.*
29. Owens, "Military officers: political without partisanship"; Golby, Dropp, and Feaver, *Military Campaigns: Veterans' Endorsements and Presidential Elections*; Dempsey, *Our Army.*
30. Feaver and Kohn, *Soldiers and Civilians.*
31. Quoted in Jim Garamone. "Dempsey: political activity erodes trust in military." *Armed Forces Press Service* (Aug. 12, 2012).

32. Owens, "Military officers: political without partisanship"; Dempsey, *Our Army*; Golby, Dropp, and Feaver, *Military Campaigns: Veterans' Endorsements and Presidential Elections*; Urben, *Like, Comment, Retweet: The State of the Military's Nonpartisan Ethic*.

33. Golby, Feaver, and Dropp, "Elite military cues and public opinion about the use of military force.", p. 19.

34. Golby, Dropp, and Feaver, *Military Campaigns: Veterans' Endorsements and Presidential Elections*.

35. Golby, Dropp, and Feaver, *Military Campaigns: Veterans' Endorsements and Presidential Elections*.

36. Mason, " 'I disrespectfully agree' "; Mason, "A cross-cutting calm."

37. Iyengar and Westwood, "Fear and loathing across Party lines: new evidence on group polarization"; Iyengar, Sood, and Lelkes, "Affect, not ideology."

38. See Appendix for military elites used to compose the composite profiles used in the experimental conditions and basic logic for development of the experimental profiles.

39. Ronald E. Goldsmith, Barbara A. Lafferty, and Stephen J. Newell. "The impact of corporate credibility and celebrity credibility on consumer reaction to advertisements and brands." *Journal of Advertising* 29.3 (2000), pp. 43–54.

40. The scale as developed by Roobina Ohanian. "Construction and validation of a scale to measure celebrity endorsers' perceived expertise, trustworthiness, and attractiveness." *Journal of Advertising* 19.3 (1990), pp. 39–52, includes three scales for expertise, trustworthiness, and attractiveness, the last category being in accordance with William J. McGuire. "The nature of attitudes and attitude change." *Handbook of Social Psychology*. Ed. G. Lindzey and E. Aronson. 2nd edition. Cambridge, MA: Addison-Wesley, 1969, pp. 135–214, on the significance of source appearance on perceived credibility. The modified scale used by Ronald E. Goldsmith, Barbara A. Lafferty, and Stephen J. Newell. "The impact of corporate credibility and celebrity credibility on consumer reaction to advertisements and brands." *Journal of Advertising* 29.3 (2000), pp. 43–54, and others focuses more specifically on the expertise and trustworthiness dimensions, placing it closer in line with established political science theorization on the key components of elite credibility; Arthur Lupia and Mathew D. McCubbins. *The Democratic Dilemma: Can Citizens Learn What They Need to Know?* Cambridge; New York: Cambridge University Press, 1998.

41. Newell and Goldsmith, "The development of a scale to measure perceived corporate credibility."

42. Iyengar and Westwood, "Fear and loathing across Party lines: new evidence on group polarization."

43. Lafferty and Goldsmith, "Corporate credibility's role in consumers' attitudes and purchase intentions when a high versus a low credibility endorser is used in the ad.", p. 114.

44. Dempsey, *Our Army*.

45. John R. Zaller and Stanley Feldman. "A simple theory of the survey response: answering questions versus revealing preferences." *American Journal of Political Science* 36.3 (1992), pp. 579–616.

46. Ronald R. Krebs and Robert Ralston. "Civilian control of the military is a partisan issue." (July 14, 2020); Krebs, Ralston, and Rapport, "No right to be wrong."

47. James Golby and Peter Feaver. "Military prestige during a political crisis: use it and you'll lose it." *War on the Rocks* (June 5, 2020).

48. Jim Michaels. "What's at risk when retired generals plunge into partisan politics." *USA TODAY* (August 4, 2016); Feaver, "Controversy over military partisan cheerleading continues."

49. Dempsey, *Our Army*.

50. Urben, *Like, Comment, Retweet: The State of the Military's Nonpartisan Ethic*; Urben, *Party, Politics, and the Post-9/11 Army*.

51. Pablo Barbera. "Birds of the same feather Tweet together: Bayesian ideal point estimation using Twitter data." *Political Analysis* 23.1 (2015), pp. 76–91.

52. Keith T. Poole and Howard Rosenthal. *Ideology and Congress: A Political Economic History of Roll Call Voting*. 2nd edition. New Brunswick: Routledge, 2007; Adam Bonica. "Mapping the ideological marketplace." *American Journal of Political Science* 58 (2014), pp. 367–386.

53. These distributions were calculated using information gathered through the Twitter API, capturing the follower networks user identification numbers and similarly capturing the

CFScores for all political elites followed by the military elite follower network. The ideological distribution is based on the subset of followers who followed at least two politicians on Twitter (excluding Barack Obama). Extreme ideology values were coerced to maximum (1.5) or minimum (-1.5) for ease of observation, leaving a total number of 505,696 observations across all military elite profiles. Military elite accounts were chosen based on senior or elite status possessing at least 1,000 base followers, in order to examine those with the greatest audience reach and latent/practical influence.

54. For Honore critiques of Hurricane Maria relief, Jack Healy, Frances Robles, and Ron Nixon, "Aid is getting to Puerto Rico. Distributing it remains a challenge." *New York Times* (Oct. 3, 2017); for fallout from Boykin's remarks and his subsequent removal from a prepared speech at West Point, Erik Eckholm. "General withdraws from West Point talk." *New York Times* (Jan. 30, 2012).

55. Maggie Astor. "Michael Flynn suggested at a QAnon-affiliated event that a coup should happen in the U.S." *New York Times* (June 1, 2021).

56. Joe Uchill. "Former intel chief Hayden: think twice on a Trump job offer." *The Hill* (November 13, 2017).

57. "Dakota Meyer: Trump is following through on his promises to veterans." *FOX News Insider* (July 3, 2017); Miranda Green. "Medal of Honor recipient explains why he's a Republican voting for Clinton." DecodeDC (July 28, 2016).

58. Barbera, "Birds of the same feather Tweet together: Bayesian ideal point estimation using Twitter data."

59. Dempsey, *Our Army*, p. 191.

60. Heidi Urben. "Wearing politics on their sleeves? Levels of political activism of active duty Army officers." *Armed Forces & Society* 40.3 (July 1, 2014), pp. 568–591.

61. Golby, Dropp, and Feaver, *Military Campaigns: Veterans' Endorsements and Presidential Elections*; Griffiths and Simon, "Not putting their money where their mouth is."

62. Bryan Bender. " 'Disturbing and reckless': retired brass spread election lie in attack on Biden, Democrats." *POLITICO* (May 11, 2021); William H. McRaven. "Opinion—Our Republic is under attack from the president." *New York Times* (October 17, 2019); William H. McRaven. "Opinion—Trump is actively working to undermine the Postal Service—and every major U.S. institution." *Washington Post* (August 16, 2020).

63. Feaver, "The military revolt against Joe Biden."

64. Eleanor Watson and Robert Legare. "Over 80 of those charged in the January 6 investigation have ties to the military." *CBS News* (December 15, 2021).

65. Milton and Mines, *"This is war"*; Gina Harkins and Hope Hodge Seck. *Marines, Infantry Most Highly Represented among Veterans Arrested after Capitol Riot*. Source: Military.com. https://www.military.com/daily-news/2021/02/26/marines-infantry-most-highly-represented-among-veterans-arrested-after-capitol-riot.html (February 27, 2021). Arie Perlinger. *American Zealots: Inside Right-Wing Domestic Terrorism*. New York: Columbia University Press, 2020; Kathleen Belew. "Perspective—Militia groups were hiding in plain sight on Jan. 6. They're still dangerous." *Washington Post* (January 6, 2022).

66. Michael Robinson and Kori Schake. "Opinion—The military's extremism problem is our problem." *New York Times* (March 2, 2021); Schake and Robinson, "Assessing civil-military relations and the January 6th Capitol insurrection."

67. Elizabeth N. Saunders. "Analysis—Is Trump hurting the military?" *Washington Post* (June 2, 2020).

68. Meghann Myers. "Esper encourages governors to 'dominate the battlespace' to put down nationwide protests." *Military Times* (June 1, 2020).

69. Tom Cotton. "Opinion—Tom Cotton: Send In the Troops." *New York Times* (June 3, 2020).

70. Gordon Lubold and Nancy A. Youssef. "Top general apologizes for being at Trump church photo shoot—WSJ." *Wall Street Journal* (June 11, 2020).

71. Maurer, *The Generals' Constitution*.

72. Joseph Votel. "An apolitical military is essential to maintaining balance among American institutions." *Military Times* (June 8, 2020).

73. Vincent K. Brooks. *Dismay and Disappointment—A Breach of Sacred Trust*. Source: Belfer Center for Science and International Affairs, Harvard University. https://www.belfercenter.org/publication/dismay-and-disappointment-breach-sacred-trust (June 4, 2020).

74. Steve Inskeep. "Former Joint Chiefs Chairman condemns Trump's threat to use military at protests." *National Public Radio* (June 4, 2020); Daniel Villareal. "Former Joint Chiefs chairman breaks silence on Trump's leadership, says Trump shows 'disdain' for peaceful protests." *Newsweek* (June 2, 2020).
75. Maurer, *The Generals' Constitution.*
76. Fred Kaplan. "Military commanders are finally speaking out against Trump." *Slate Magazine* (June 3, 2020).
77. Kevin Breuninger. "Former Defense Secretary James Mattis says he'll 'speak out' about Trump policies 'when the time's right.'" Source: CNBC. https://www.cnbc.com/2019/09/03/mattis-says-hell-speak-out-about-trump-policies-when-time-is-right.html (September 3, 2019); Jeffrey Goldberg. "James Mattis Denounces President Trump, Describes Him as a Threat to the Constitution." *The Atlantic* (June 3, 2020).
78. Brooks and Robinson, "Let the generals speak?"; Breuninger, "Former Defense Secretary James Mattis says he'll 'speak out' about Trump policies 'when the time's right.'"

Chapter 7

1. Golby, "Uncivil-military relations: politicization of the military in the Trump era."
2. Kristina Wong. *Over 120 Retired Flag Officers Warn U.S. Under Assault from Socialism.* Source: Breitbart. https://www.breitbart.com/politics/2021/05/11/over-120-retired-flag-officers-warn-country-is-under-assault-from-socialism-and-marxism/ (May 11, 2021); Golby and Lee, "Analysis—The National Guard has been called out in Washington, D.C. Here's what you need to know."
3. Bender, " 'Disturbing and reckless'. "
4. "Oliver North: Repealing 'don't ask, don't tell' could be 'very detrimental' to military." Fox News (Mar. 2015); Emma Margolin. "Obama cements historic LGBT rights legacy." Source: NBC News. https://www.nbcnews.com/feature/nbc-out/transgender-military-ban-lifted-obama-cements-historic-lgbt-rights-legacy-n600541 (June 30, 2016); James A. Lyons. "How politicizing the military puts national security at risk." *Washington Times* (Octtober 13, 2016).
5. Brooke Singman. "Trump Pentagon likely to abandon social experiments for core mission under Mattis, say experts." Fox News (January 1, 2017); The Editorial Board. "Opinion—Uncle Sam no longer wants you." *New York Times* (July 27, 2017).
6. Nick Laughlin and Peyton Shelburne. "The Morning Consult COVID-19 Vaccine Dashboard." Source: Morning Consult. https://morningconsult.com/covid19-vaccine-dashboard/ (July 19, 2021); Justin McCarthy. "Roundup of Gallup COVID-19 Coverage." Source: Gallup. https://news.gallup.com/opinion/gallup/308126/roundup-gallup-covid-coverage.aspx (July 13, 2021).
7. Jennifer Steinhauer. "Younger military personnel reject vaccine, in warning for commanders and the nation." *New York Times* (February 27, 2021); Emily Jacobs. "GOP lawmakers split over mandating COVID vaccine for US military." *New York Post* (July 6, 2021); Alex Horton. "Marine Corps compliance with vaccine mandate on course to be military's worst." *Washington Post* (November 21, 2021).
8. Adam Liptak. "Supreme Court rules against Navy SEALs in vaccine mandate case." *New York Times* (March 25, 2022).
9. Andrew Jeong and Alex Horton. "Federal court denies Oklahoma Gov. Kevin Stitt's attempt to stop military vaccine mandate." *Washington Post* (December 29, 2021); Paul Mcleary. "Almost 50 Republicans back Navy SEAL lawsuit over vaccine mandate." *POLITICO* (December 20, 2021); Steve Beynon. " 'He is not your commander-in-chief:' texas governor promises guardsmen he'll fight biden over vaccine mandate—Military.com." *Military.com* (January 4, 2022).
10. Brooks, "Paradoxes of professionalism."
11. Lindsay Cohn, Max Z. Margulies, and Michael A. Robinson. "What discord follows: the divisive debate over military disobedience." *War on the Rocks* (August 2, 2019); Michael A. Robinson, Lindsay Cohn, and Max Z. Margulies. "Dissents and sensibility: conflicting loyalties, democracy, and civil-military relations." *Reconsidering American Civil-Military Relations: The Military, Society, Politics, and Modern War* Ed. Lionel Beehner, Risa Brooks, and Daniel Maurer. Oxford: Oxford University Press, 2020, pp. 63–82.

12. Mark J. Osiel. "Obeying orders: atrocity, military disciplines, and the law of war." *California Law Review* 86.5 (1998), pp. 939–941, 943–1129.
13. Lindsay Cohn. "Analysis—Yes, Trump can send the military to shut down protests. Here's what you need to know." *Washington Post* (June 2, 2020); Carrie A. Lee. "Analysis—Lt. Col. Vindman's retirement will hurt military effectiveness. This is why." *Washington Post* (July 9, 2020).
14. Robinson, Cohn, and Margulies, "Dissents and sensibility: conflicting loyalties, democracy, and civil-military relations."
15. Risa A. Brooks, Michael A. Robinson, and Heidi A. Urben. "What makes a military professional? Evaluating norm socialization in West Point cadets." *Armed Forces & Society* (June 2021); Kyle Cheney and Nicholas Wu. "Meadows Jan. 5 email indicated Guard on standby to 'protect pro Trump people,' investigators say." *POLITICO* (December 12, 2021).
16. Urben, *Party, Politics, and the Post-9/11 Army* p. 194.
17. Urben, *Party, Politics, and the Post-9/11 Army*, pp. 192–93.
18. Jason Schwartz. " 'We are fighting for information about war': Pentagon curbs media access." *POLITICO* (July 26, 2018); James Stavridis. "It's been over 300 days since a pentagon press briefing. that should concern everyone." *Time* (April 16, 2019).
19. Leo Shane, III, Meghann Myers, and Carl Prine. "Trump grants clemency to troops in three controversial war crimes cases." *Military Times* (November 22, 2019); Robinson, "Trump's pardon of two former Army officers has sparked new controversy. Here's why."
20. Pauline M. Shanks Kaurin and Bradley J. Strawser. "Disgraceful pardons: dishonoring our honorable." *War on the Rocks* (March 25, 2019).
21. Milton and Mines, "This is War.", p. 8.
22. Perlinger, *American Zealots: Inside Right-Wing Domestic Terrorism*; Robinson and Schake, "Opinion—The military's extremism problem is our problem."
23. David T. Burbach, Lindsay Cohn, and Danielle Lupton. "Analysis—What's happening in Portland could hurt civilian control of the military. Here's how." *Washington Post* (July 29, 2020); Danielle Lupton, David T. Burbach, and Lindsay Cohn. "Authoritarian tactics on US soil." *Political Violence at a Glance* (August 5, 2020).
24. Ty Seidule. "Opinion—What to rename the Army bases that honor Confederate soldiers." *Washington Post* (June 18, 2020); David Vergun. *Secretary Austin Announces Members of Base-Naming Commission.* Source: Navy.mil. https://www.navy.mil/DesktopModules/ArticleCS/Print.aspx?PortalId=1&ModuleId=523&Article=2503229 (February 12, 2021).
25. Urben, *Like, Comment, Retweet: The State of the Military's Nonpartisan Ethic*; Urben, *Party, Politics, and the Post-9/11 Army*.
26. James Golby and Peter D. Feaver. "Thank you for your lip service? Social pressure to support the troops." *War on the Rocks* (August 14, 2019).
27. Ronald R. Krebs and Robert Ralston, "Why conservatives turned on the U.S. military", *Foreign Affairs* (September 28, 2021).
28. Tucker Carlson. "Tucker Carlson: US military has gone full woke, waging war on those who disagree with them—Fox News." Source: Fox News. https://www.foxnews.com/opinion/tucker-carlson-military-gone-full-woke-pentagon-lloyd-austin (March 27, 2021); Creitz, Ingraham.
29. Brenan, *Americans' Confidence in Major U.S. Institutions Dips.*
30. Daniel W. Drezner. "Perspective—The erosion of American trust hits the U.S. military." *Washington Post* (February 16, 2022).
31. Cohn, Margulies, and Robinson, "What discord follows"; Brooks, "Paradoxes of professionalism"; Samuel Finer. *The Man on Horseback: The Role of the Military in Politics* New Brunswick, NJ: Routledge, 1962.
32. Brooks, "Through the looking glass: Trump era civil-military relations in comparative perspective."
33. Vincenzo Bove, Mauricio Rivera, and Chiara Ruffa. "Beyond coups: terrorism and military involvment in politics." *European Journal of International Relations* 26.1 (2020), pp. 263–288.
34. Manaswini Ramkumar. "The Scylla and Charybdis of duty discharge: military dilemma with undemocratic leaders." *War on the Rocks* (October 11, 2021).

35. Heidi Urben and James Golby. "A matter of trust: five pitfalls that could squander the American public's confidence in the military." *Reconsidering American Civil-Military Relations: The Military, Society, Politics, and Modern War* Ed. Lionel Beehner, Risa Brooks, and Daniel Maurer. New York: Oxford University Press, 2021, pp. 137–148.

36. Schultz, "Perils of polarization for U.S. foreign policy."

37. Burbach, "Confidence without sacrifice: American public opinion and the US military"; Golby and Feaver, "Thank you for your lip service?"

38. Jennifer Steinhauer. "Once in thrall of 'the generals,' Congress now gives the orders on military issues." *New York Times* (May 21, 2021).

39. Reid J. Epstein, "The G.O.P. delivers its 2020 platform. It's from 2016." *New York Times*, (August 25, 2020); Democratic Party Platform, https://democrats.org/where-we-stand/party-platform/renewing-american-leadership/, (August 5, 2020).

40. Bryan Bender. "Biden's reliance on retired military brass sets off alarm bells." *POLITICO* (December 7, 2020); Golby and Feaver, "Biden inherits a challenging civil-military legacy"; Daniel W. Drezner. "Perspective—Joe Biden bends a campaign pledge." *Washington Post* (December 8, 2020).

41. Teigen, *Why Veterans Run*; Jeremy M. Teigen. "Analysis—Do military veterans really win more elections? Only in 'purple' districts." *Washington Post* (July 20, 2017).

42. G. Lee Robinson et al. "Veterans and Bipartisanship." *Armed Forces & Society* 46.1 (2020), pp. 132–162.

43. Jess Blankshain. "Who has 'skin in the game'? The implications of an operational reserve for civil-military relations." *Reconsidering American Civil-Military Relations: The Military, Society, Politics, and Modern War* Ed. Lionel Beehner, Daniel Maurer, and Risa A. Brooks. New York: Oxford University Press, 2020, pp. 97–114; Thomas E. Ricks, Jess Blankshain, and Lindsay Cohn. "Some thoughts on the problem of politicians in the National Guard." *Foreign Policy*. https://foreignpolicy.com/2014/12/11/some-thoughts-on-the-problem-of-politicians-in-the-national-guard-joni-ernst/ (December 11, 2014).

44. Christianna Silva. "Gen. Mark Milley says the military plays 'no role' in elections." *National Public Radio* (October 11, 2020).

45. Lindsay Cohn and Steve Vladeck. "The election and the military." *Lawfare* (November 2, 2020).

46. Ryan, "New disclosures show how Gen. Mark A. Milley tried to check Trump. They could also further politicize the military."

47. Silva, "Gen. Mark Milley says the military plays 'no role' in elections"; Ryan, "New disclosures show how Gen. Mark A. Milley tried to check Trump. They could also further politicize the military."

48. Paul D. Eaton, Antonio M. Taguba, and Steven M. Anderson. "Opinion—3 retired generals: the military must prepare now for a 2024 insurrection." *Washington Post* (December 17, 2021); Michael Hayden, James Clapper, Stanley McChrystal, Douglas Lute, and Mark Hertling, "We fought to defend democracy. This new threat to America now keeps us awake at night." USA Today, June 22, 2022, https://www.usatoday.com/story/opinion/contributors/2022/06/22/american-democracy-former-cia-director/7685947001/.

49. Golby and Lee, "Analysis—The National Guard has been called out in Washington, D.C. Here's what you need to know."

50. Milton and Mines, "This is War"; Belew, "Perspective—Militia groups were hiding in plain sight on Jan. 6. They're still dangerous."

51. Feuer, Goldman, and Benner, "Oath Keepers founder is said to be investigated in Capitol riot"; Abbie Shull. "20 active-duty troops signed up for the extremist Oath Keepers militia—many with their military emails." *Business Insider* (January 21, 2022); Rina Torchinsky. "1 in 5 Patriot Front applicants say they have ties to the military." *National Public Radio* (February 9, 2022).

52. Peter W. Singer and Eric B. Johnson. "the need to inoculate military servicemembers against information threats: the case for digital literacy training for the force." *War on the Rocks* (February 1, 2021).

53. Carol E. Lee. "Some of the U.S. military elite share QAnon, 2020 lies, racism on-line". Source: NBC News. https://www.nbcnews.com/news/military/secret-facebook-groups-america-s-best-warriors-share-racist-jabs-n1263985 (April 16, 2021); Steinhauer, "Younger military personnel reject vaccine, in warning for commanders and the nation."

54. Schake and Robinson, "Assessing civil-military relations and the January 6th Capitol insurrection"; Milton and Mines, "This is War"; Urben, *Party, Politics, and the Post-9/11 Army*; Golby and Lee, "Analysis—The National Guard has been called out in Washington, D.C. Here's what you need to know."

55. Carrie A. Lee and Celestino Perez, Jr. "Education against extremism: suggestions for a smarter Stand-down." *War on the Rocks* (July 16, 2021).

56. Belew, "Perspective—Militia groups were hiding in plain sight on Jan. 6. They're still dangerous"; Milton and Mines, "This is War."

Appendix

1. Pew Research Center Journalism and Media, News Coverage Index Methodology, http://www.journalism.org/news_index_methodology, accessed Oct. 18, 2017.

2. Nia-Malika Henderson. "Gen. Wes Clark set to pound Romney on foreign policy." *Washington Post* (Nov. 21, 2011).

3. Byron Tau. "Obama campaign announces co-chairs." Politico44 Blog (Feb. 22, 2012).

4. Stephan Dinan. "Retired top military brass push for Romney." *Washington Times* (Nov. 4, 2012).

5. David Wright, Ryan Browne, and Naomi Lin. "88 former military leaders write letter backing Donald Trump for president." *CNN* (Sept. 6, 2016).

6. Dianna Cahn. "Former admirals and generals warn Trump is 'dangerous' to military and country." *Stars and Stripes* (Sept. 21, 2016); Dan Merica. "Clinton to Trump: my military endorsements are bigger than yours." *CNN* (Sept. 9, 2016).

7. Jim Dwyer and Robert F. Worth. "Accused G.I. was troubled long before iraq." *New York Times* (July 14, 2006).

8. Craig Whitlock. "Military brass, behaving badly: files detail a spate of misconduct dogging armed forces." *Washington Post* (Jan. 26, 2014).

9. Anthony Faiola. "British aid worker Norgrove killed accidentally by U.S. soldier, inquiry finds." *Washington Post Foreign Service* (Dec. 3, 2010).

10. "Obama apologises to MSF president for Kunduz bombing." *BBC News* (Oct. 7, 2015). Obama's apology was also given amidst increasing rumors that the attack was a deliberate move by the US to dislodge Taliban fighters "holed up" in the clinic, though this was eventually denied by both the US and MSF.

11. These outlets have both large audience followings and stark partisan divergence on trustworthiness. In 2014, 52% of those classified as consistent liberals expressed trust in MSNBC as a news source, against 9% who distrusted it. The same category of liberals contained only 6% who trusted FOX News, compared to 81% who distrusted it, by comparison. Consistent conservatives included 7% trusting MSNBC against 75% distrust, and 88% trust for FOX News over 3% distrust. "Political polarization and media habits: from Fox News to Facebook, how liberals and conservatives keep up with politics." Pew Research Center (Oct. 21, 2014).

12. "Lt. Gen. Mark Hertling: military analyst." CNN, http://www.cnn.com/profiles/ mark-hertling-profile; "Col. Jack Jacobs: MSNBC military analyst." MSNBC (Dec. 14, 2007); "Jack Keane: retired army four-star general." FOX News, http://www.foxnews.com/person/k/jack-keane.html; "Gen. Barry R. McCaffrey, USA (Ret.)." MSNBC (Jan. 17, 2008). All accessed Dec. 21, 2017.

13. "Col. Jack Jacobs: Trump Gold Star Family remarks 'almost obscene.' " Video clip, *NBC Nightly News with Lester Holt* (Oct. 17, 2017); Hertling quoted in Stephen Collinson. "Trump has repeatedly politicized military service and sacrifice." CNN.com (Oct. 18, 2017); "Trump's national security strategy a departure from the past." Video clip, FOX News (Dec. 19, 2017);

"Gen. Barry McCaffrey: Trump could lead U.S. to war with N. Korea." Video clip, *The 11th Hour with Brian Williams*, MNSBC (Oct. 13, 2017).

14. Quoted in Brandon Carter. "General who oversaw Katrina response slams Trump for Puerto Rico attacks." *The Hill* (Sept. 30, 2017).

15. Erik Eckholm. "General withdraws from West Point talk." *New York Times* (Jan. 30, 2012).

16. Robert H. Scales. "U.S. military planners don't support war with Syria." *Washington Post* (Sept. 5, 2013).

17. Letter enclosed in Peter LaBarbera. "Retired generals praise Trump's 'courageous' transgender military ban." LifeSiteNews (Aug. 1, 2017).

18. Golby, Dropp, and Feaver, *Military Campaigns: Veterans' Endorsements and Presidential Elections.*

19. Eric Schmitt, "Clinton and Trump each lay claim to military brass." *New York Times* (Sept. 7, 2016).

20. Michael Crowley. "Trump's foreign policy team baffles GOP experts." Politico (Mar. 21, 2016).

21. Gabriel DeBenedetti. "Clinton to convene meeting with Petraeus, other national security experts." Politico (Sept. 8, 2016).

BIBLIOGRAPHY

Abadi, Mark. "Trump won't stop saying 'my generals'—and the military community isn't happy." *Business Insider* (October 25, 2017).

Abrahamsson, Bengt and Morris Janowitz. *Military Professionalization and Political Power*. 1st edition. Beverly Hills, CA: SAGE Publications, Inc., 1972.

Abramowitz, Alan I. and Kyle L. Saunders. "Is polarization a myth?" *The Journal of Politics* 70.2 (2008), pp. 542–555.

Achen, Christopher H. "Social psychology, demographic variables, and linear regression: breaking the iron triangle in voting research." *Political Behavior* 14.3 (1992), pp. 195–211.

Achen, Christopher H. and Larry M. Bartels. *Democracy for Realists: Why Elections Do Not Produce Responsive Government*. Revised edition. Princeton, NJ: Princeton University Press, 2017.

Ackerman, Elliot. "Opinion—Yes, they defended the capitol. But should they be decorated?" *New York Times* (March 26, 2021).

Air Force Public Affairs, Secretary of the. "Resources available for DAF members, families affected by local laws." March 24, 2022 https://www.af.mil/News/Article-Display/Article/2977048/resources-available-for-daf-members-families-affected-by-local-laws/.

Albertus, Michael and Victor Menaldo. "Opinion—Why are so many democracies breaking down?" *New York Times* (May 8, 2018).

Ali, Lorraine. "Our democratic crisis is a media crisis. And the mainstream press is losing." *Los Angeles Times* (December 22, 2021).

Almond, Gabriel Abraham and Sidney Verba. *The Civic Culture: Political Attitudes and Democracy in Five Nations*. Princeton, NJ: Princeton University Press, 1963.

Althaus, Scott L., Brittany H. Bramlett, and James G. Gimpel. "When war hits home the geography of military losses and support for war in time and space." *Journal of Conflict Resolution* 56.3 (2012), pp. 382–412.

Astor, Maggie. "Michael Flynn suggested at a QAnon-affiliated event that a coup should happen in the U.S." *New York Times* (June 1, 2021).

Astor, Maggie. "Now in your inbox: political misinformation." *New York Times* (December 13, 2021).

"Autocratization turns viral: democracy report 2021." Tech. rep. Varieties of Democracy, March 2021.

Avant, Deborah D. *Political Institutions and Military Change: Lessons from Peripheral Wars*. 1st edition. Ithaca: Cornell University Press, 1994.

Bafumi, Joseph and Robert Y. Shapiro. "A new partisan voter." *The Journal of Politics* 71.1 (2009), pp. 1–24.

Bailey, Holly. "Joe Biden, White House truth teller." *Newsweek* (October 9, 2009).

Baker, Peter. "How Obama came to plan for surge in Afghanistan." *New York Times* (December 5, 2009).

Barbera, Pablo. "Birds of the same feather Tweet together: Bayesian ideal point estimation using Twitter data." *Political Analysis* 23.1 (2015), pp. 76–91.

Barno, David and Nora Bensahel. "Why no general should serve as White House Chief of Staff." *War on the Rocks* (September 12, 2017).

Bartels, Larry M. "Beyond the running tally: partisan bias in political perceptions." *Political Behavior* 24.2 (2002), pp. 117–150.

Baum, Matthew A. and Tim J. Groeling. "New media and the polarization of American political discourse." *Political Communication* 25 (2008), pp. 345–365.

Baum, Matthew A. and Tim J. Groeling. "Shot by the messenger: partisan cues and public opinion regarding national security and war." *Political Behavior* 31.2 (2009), pp. 157–186.

Baum, Matthew A. and Tim J. Groeling. *War Stories: The Causes and Consequences of Public Views of War*. Princeton, NJ: Princeton University Press, 2010.

BBC News. "EU referendum: ex-military officers fighting for EU exit." *British Broadcasting Corporation* (May 25, 2016).

Beehner, Lionel, Risa Brooks, and Daniel Maurer, eds. *Reconsidering American Civil-Military Relations: The Military, Society, Politics, and Modern War*. Oxford; New York: Oxford University Press, 2020.

Belew, Kathleen. "Perspective—Militia groups were hiding in plain sight on Jan. 6. They're still dangerous." *Washington Post* (January 6, 2022).

Beliakova, Polina. "Erosion by deference: civilian control and the military in policymaking." *Texas National Security Review* 4.3 (2021), pp. 55–75.

Bell, Melissa. "Richard Nixon and Roger Ailes 1970s plan to put the GOP on TV." *Washington Post* (July 1, 2011).

Bender, Bryan. "'Disturbing and reckless': retired brass spread election lie in attack on Biden, Democrats." *POLITICO* (May 11, 2021).

Bender, Bryan. "Biden's reliance on retired military brass sets off alarm bells." *POLITICO* (December 7, 2020).

Bender, Bryan. "Twitter and Facebook are politicizing the military." *POLITICO* (February 26, 2017).

Berelson, Bernard R., Paul F. Lazarsfeld, and William N. McPhee. *Voting: A Study of Opinion Formation in a Presidential Campaign*. Reprint edition. Chicago: University of Chicago Press, 1986.

Berinsky, Adam J. "Assuming the costs of war: events, elites, and American public support for military conflict." *The Journal of Politics* 69.4 (2007), pp. 975–997.

Berinsky, Adam J. *In Time of War: Understanding American Public Opinion from World War II to Iraq*. 1st edition. Chicago: University of Chicago Press, 2009.

Berinsky, Adam J., G. A. Huber, and G. S. Lenz. "Evaluating online labor markets for experimental research: Amazon.com's mechanical Turk." *Political Analysis* 20.3 (2012), pp. 351–368.

Betros, Lance. "Political partisanship and the military ethic in America." *Armed Forces & Society* 27.4 (2001), pp. 501–523.

Beynon, Steve. "'He is not your Commander-in-Chief:' Texas governor promises Guardsmen he'll fight Biden over vaccine mandate—Military.com." *Military.com* (January 4, 2022).

Blake, Aaron. "Analysis—It's only 'politicizing' a tragedy if you disagree with the policy." *Washington Post* (November 1, 2017).

Blankshain, Jess. "A primer on US civil–military relations for national security practitioners." *Wild Blue Yonder* (July 2020).

Blankshain, Jess. "Who Has 'skin in the game'? The implications of an operational reserve for civil-military relations." *Reconsidering American Civil-Military Relations: The Military, Society, Politics, and Modern War*. Ed. Lionel Beehner, Daniel Maurer, and Risa A. Brooks. New York: Oxford University Press, 2020, pp. 97–114.

Blanton, Dana. "Fox News poll: 24 Percent believe Obama not born in US." Fox News. March 27, 2015.

Blei, David M., Andrew Y. Ng, and Michael I. Jordan. "Latent dirichlet allocation." *Journal of Machine Learning Research* 3 (2003), pp. 993–1022.

Board, The Editorial. "Opinion—Uncle Sam no longer wants you." *New York Times* (July 27, 2017).

Bonica, Adam. *Database on Ideology, Money in Politics, and Elections: Public Version 2.0.* Computer file. Stanford, CA: Stanford University Library, 2016.

Bonica, Adam. "Ideology and interests in the political marketplace." *American Journal of Political Science* 57.2 (2013), pp. 294–311.

Bonica, Adam. "Mapping the ideological marketplace." *American Journal of Political Science* 58 (2014), pp. 367–386.

Boot, Max. "Opinion—Imagine if a Squad member called a general a stupid pig. Tucker Carlson just did." *Washington Post* (June 28, 2021).

Born, Hans. "Democratic control of armed forces: relevance, issues, and research agenda." *Handbook of the Sociology of the Military*. Ed. Giuseppe Caforio. New York: Springer, 2007, pp. 151–167.

Bove, Vincenzo, Mauricio Rivera, and Chiara Ruffa. "Beyond coups: terrorism and military involvement in politics." *European Journal of International Relations* 26.1 (2020), pp. 263–288.

Bowman, Tom. "Walter Reed was Army's wake-up call in 2007." *National Public Radio* (August 31, 2011).

Boyer, Peter J. "General Clark's battles." *The New Yorker* (November 17, 2003).

Braniff, William, Ellen Gustafson, and Joe Plenzler. "Fighting falsehoods: veterans coalition aims to battle extremism with truth." *Military Times* (December 3, 2021).

Bray, Robert M. et al. "Substance use and mental health trends among U.S. military active duty personnel: key findings from the 2008 DoD health behavior survey." *Military Medicine* 175.6 (2010), pp. 390–399.

Brehm, John and Wendy Rahn. "Individual-level evidence for the causes and consequences of social capital." *American Journal of Political Science* 41.3 (1997), pp. 999–1023.

Brenan, Megan. "Americans' confidence in major U.S. institutions dips." Gallup (July 14, 2021).

Brenan, Megan. "Amid pandemic, confidence in key U.S. institutions surges." Gallup (August 12, 2020).

Breuninger, Kevin. "Former Defense Secretary James Mattis says he'll 'speak out' about Trump policies 'when the time's right.'" CNBC September 3, 2019 https://www.cnbc.com/2019/09/03/mattis-says-hell-speak-out-about-trump-policies-when-time-is-right.html.

Brewer, Paul R. and Kimberly Gross. "Values, framing, and citizens' thoughts about policy issues: effects on content and quantity." *Political Psychology* 26.6 (2005), pp. 929–948.

Broockman, David E. and Christopher Skovron. "Bias in perceptions of public opinion among political elites." *American Political Science Review* 112.3 (2018), pp. 542–563.

Broockman, David E. et al. "Why local Party leaders don't support nominating centrists." *British Journal of Political Science* 51.2 (2021), pp. 724–749.

Brooks, Risa. "Militaries and political activity in democracies." *American Civil-Military Relations: The Soldier and the State in a New Era*. Baltimore, MD: Johns Hopkins University Press, 2009.

Brooks, Risa. "Paradoxes of professionalism: rethinking civil-military relations in the United States." *International Security* 44.4 (2020), pp. 7–44.

Brooks, Risa. "Through the looking glass: Trump era civil-military relations in comparative perspective." *Strategic Studies Quarterly* 15.2 (2021), pp. 69–98.

Brooks, Risa A., Michael A. Robinson, and Heidi A. Urben. "Biden has picked a retired general for defense secretary. Here's why it matters." *Washington Post* (December 9, 2020).

Brooks, Risa A., Michael A. Robinson, and Heidi A. Urben. "What makes a military professional? Evaluating norm socialization in West Point cadets." *Armed Forces & Society* (June 2021).

Brooks, Risa, Jim Golby, and Heidi Urben. "Crisis of command." *Foreign Affairs* May/June 2021 (April 29, 2021).

Brooks, Risa and Michael A. Robinson. "Let the generals speak? Retired officer dissent and the June 2020 George Floyd protests." *War on the Rocks* (October 9, 2020).

Brooks, Rosa. "Are US civil-military relations in crisis?" *Parameters* 51.1 (2021), pp. 51–63.

Brooks, Rosa. "Civil-military paradoxes." *Warriors & Citizens: American Views of Our Military*. Ed. Kori N. Schake and Jim Mattis. Stanford, CA: Hoover Institution Press, 2016, pp. 21–68.

Brooks, Rosa. *How Everything Became War and the Military Became Everything: Tales from the Pentagon*. First printing edition. New York: Simon & Schuster, 2016.

Brooks, Vincent K. *Dismay and Disappointment—A Breach of Sacred Trust*. Belfer Center for Science and International Politics. June 4, 2020 https://www.belfercenter.org/publication/dismay-and-disappointment-breach-sacred-trust.

Bullock, John G. "Elite influence on public opinion in an informed electorate." *American Political Science Review* 105.3 (2011), pp. 496–515.

Bump, Philip. "Analysis—'When do we get to use the guns?': the ongoing danger of false fraud claims." *Washington Post* (October 27, 2021).

Bump, Philip. "Perspective—The White House is increasingly—and worryingly—using the military as a shield against criticism." *Washington Post* (October 20, 2017).

Burbach, David T. "Confidence without sacrifice: american public opinion and the US military." *Reconsidering American Civil-Military Relations: The Military, Society, Politics, and Modern War*. Ed. by Lionel Beehner, Risa Brooks, and Daniel Maurer. New York: Oxford University Press, 2021.

Burbach, David T. "Gaining trust while losing wars: confidence in the U.S. military after Iraq and Afghanistan." *Orbis* 61.2 (2017), pp. 154–171.

Burbach, David T. "Partisan dimensions of confidence in the U.S. military, 1973–2016." *Armed Forces & Society* 45.2 (2019), pp. 211–233.

Burbach, David T., Lindsay Cohn, and Danielle Lupton. "Analysis—What's happening in Portland could hurt civilian control of the military. Here's how." *Washington Post* (July 29, 2020).

Burns, John F. "McChrystal rejects scaling down Afghan military aims." *New York Times* (October 1, 2009).

Bush, George W. *Decision Points*. Crown (New York, NY), 2010.

Caforio, Giuseppe, ed. *Handbook of the Sociology of the Military*. New York: Springer, 2007.

Cahn, Dianna. "Former admirals and generals warn Trump is 'dangerous' to military and country." *Stars and Stripes* (September 21, 2016).

Campbell, Angus et al. *The American Voter*. Chicago: University of Chicago Press, 1980.

Carlson, Tucker. "Tucker Carlson: US military has gone full woke, waging war on those who disagree with them—Fox News" March 27, 2021.

Carter, Brandon. "General who oversaw Katrina response slams Trump for Puerto Rico attacks." Text. The Hill, September 30, 2017 http://thehill.com/blogs/blog-briefing-room/news/353239-general-who-oversaw-katrina-response-slams-trump-for-puerto

Carter, Phillip. "Military chiefs' reluctance to march." *Slate* (December 12, 2017).

Carter, Phillip and Loren DeJonge Schulman. "Trump is surrounding himself with generals. That's dangerous." *Washington Post* (November 30, 2016).

Cavari, Amnon and Guy Freedman. "Partisan cues and opinion formation on foreign policy." *American Politics Research* 47.1 (2019), pp. 29–57.

Caverley, Jonathan D. "When an immovable object meets an irresistible force: military popularity and affective partisanship." *Reconsidering American Civil-Military Relations: The Military, Society, Politics, and Modern War*. Ed. Lionel Beehner, Risa Brooks, and Daniel Maurer. New York: Oxford University Press, 2021.

Chapman, Terrence L. "Audience beliefs and international organization legitimacy." *International Organization* 63.04 (2009), p. 733.

Chapman, Terrence L. "International security institutions, domestic politics, and institutional legitimacy." *Journal of Conflict Resolution* 51.1 (2007), pp. 134–166.

Chapman, Terrence L. *Securing Approval: Domestic Politics and Multilateral Authorization for War*. Chicago: University of Chicago Press, 2011.

Chapman, Terrence L. "The United Nations Security Council and the rally 'round the flag effect." *Journal of Conflict Resolution* 48.6 (2004), pp. 886–909.

Cheney, Kyle and Nicholas Wu. "Meadows Jan. 5 email indicated Guard on standby to 'protect pro Trump people,' investigators say." *POLITICO* (December 12, 2021).

Chinoy, Sahil. "Opinion—What happened to America's political center of gravity?" *New York Times* (June 26, 2019).

Chong, Dennis and James N. Druckman. "A theory of framing and opinion formation in competitive elite environments." *Journal of Communication* 57.1 (2007), pp. 99–118.

Chu, Jonathan. *Social Cues by International Organizations: NATO, the Security Council, and Public Support for Humanitarian Intervention.* SSRN Scholarly Paper 3977910. Rochester, NY: Social Science Research Network, 2019.

Citrin, Jack. "Comment: the political relevance of trust in government." *American Political Science Review* 68.03 (1974), pp. 973–988.

Clausewitz, Carl von. *On War, Indexed Edition.* Trans. Michael Eliot Howard and Peter Paret. Reprint edition. Princeton, NJ: Princeton University Press, 1989.

Clement, Scott and Philip Rucker, "Poll: far more trust generals than Trump on N. Korea, while two-thirds oppose preemptive strike," *Washington Post* (Sept. 24, 2017).

Clement, Scott and David Nakamura. "Poll shows clear disapproval of how Trump responded to Charlottesville violence." *Washington Post* (August 21, 2017).

Cloud, David S. and Eric Schmitt. "More retired generals call for Rumsfeld's resignation." *New York Times* (April 14, 2006).

Cohen, Eliot A. "Are U.S. forces overstretched? Civil-military relations." *Orbis* 41.2 (1997), pp. 175–176.

Cohen, Eliot A. *Supreme Command: Soldiers, Statesmen, and Leadership in Wartime.* Reprint edition. New York: Anchor, 2003.

Cohn, Lindsay. "Analysis—Yes, Trump can send the military to shut down protests. Here's what you need to know." *Washington Post* (June 2, 2020).

Cohn, Lindsay, Alice Friend, and Jim Golby. "Analysis—This is what was so unusual about the U.S. Navy making Captain Brett Crozier step down." *Washington Post* (April 5, 2020).

Cohn, Lindsay, Max Z. Margulies, and Michael A. Robinson. "What discord follows: the divisive debate over military disobedience." *War on the Rocks* (August 2, 2019).

Cohn, Lindsay and Steve Vladeck. "The election and the military." *Lawfare* (November 2, 2020).

Cohn, Nate. "Why political sectarianism is a growing threat to American democracy." *New York Times* (April 19, 2021).

Cole, Brendan. "Tucker Carlson doubles down on Mark Milley criticism, brands comments 'race attack.'" *Newsweek* (June 26, 2021).

Converse, Philip E. "Information flow and the stability of partisan attitudes." *Public Opinion Quarterly* 26 (1962), pp. 578–599.

Cook, Martin L. "Revolt of the generals: a case study in professional ethics." *Parameters* 38.1 (2008), p. 4.

Copleovitch, Mark. "The asymmetry of the 'asymmetric polarization' is so asymmetric that the very concept & term obscures the important reality: one party has collapsed into far right authoritarianism, and the other one remains a replacement-level center-left pro-democracy party." *https://t.co/RQqIRj0QHg.* Tweet. November 23, 2021.

Cooper, Helene, Julian E. Barnes, Eric Schmitt, Jonathan Martin, Maggie Haberman, and Mike Ives. "As the D.C. police clear the Capitol grounds, the mayor extends a public emergency." *New York Times* (January 6, 2021).

Cotton, Tom. "And, if necessary, the 10th Mountain, 82nd Airborne, 1st Cav, 3rd Infantry—whatever it takes to restore order. No quarter for insurrectionists, anarchists, rioters, and looters." Tweet. June 1, 2020.

Cotton, Tom. "Opinion—Tom Cotton: send in the troops." *New York Times* (June 3, 2020).

Cox, Daniel A. "After the ballots are counted: Conspiracies, political violence, and American exceptionalism." Tech. rep. Washington, DC: American Enterprise Institute, Feb. 2021.

Creitz, Charles. "Ingraham: Biden defense chief starting 'ideological and un-American purge of the US military.'" Fox News February 4, 2021 https://www.foxnews.com/media/laura-ingraham-biden-lloyd-austin-60-day-stand-down-extremism.

Crowley, James. "Donald Trump Jr. says military 'politicized,' knocks stunt against Marjorie Taylor Greene." Newsweek (March 20, 2021).

Crozier, Michel, Samuel P. Huntington, and Joji Watanuki. Crisis of Democracy: Report on the Governability of Democracies to the Trilateral Commission. New York: New York University Press, 1975.

Dao, James. "Ex-soldier gets life sentence for Iraq murders." New York Times (May 21, 2009).

Davidson, Janine. "The contemporary presidency: civil-military friction and presidential decision making: explaining the broken dialogue." Presidential Studies Quarterly 43.1 (2013), pp. 129–145.

Davis, Julie Hirschfeld and Helene Cooper. "Trump says transgender people will not be allowed in the military." New York Times (July 26, 2017).

De Waal, James. "Britain needs to take a page from American civil-military relations." Foreign Policy (November 21, 2013). https://foreignpolicy.com/2013/11/21/britain-needs-to-take-a-page-from-american-civil-military-relations/

deGrandpre, Andrew. "Trump's generals condemn Charlottesville racism—while trying not to offend the president." Washington Post (August 16, 2017).

Delli Carpini, Michael X., ed. Political Decision-Making, Deliberation and Participation. 1st edition Research in Micropolitics 6. Amsterdam: Jai, 2002.

DeLong, Matt. "Pat Tillman's mother calls for McChrystal's removal from White House post." Washington Post (April 14, 2011).

"Democratic Party Platform 2020." https://democrats.org/where-we-stand/party-platform/ (August 5, 2020).

Dempsey, Jason K. Our Army: Soldiers, Politics, and American Civil-Military Relations. Princeton, NJ: Princeton University Press, 2009.

Dempsey, Martin. "Gen. Dempsey to fellow officers: stay off the political battlefield." National Public Radio (August 3, 2016).

Desch, Michael. "Why have the wars in Iraq and Afghanistan been so corrosive of civil-military relations?" Foreign Policy (October 18, 2010). https://foreignpolicy.com/2010/10/18/why-have-the-wars-in-iraq-and-afghanistan-been-so-corrosive-of-civil-military-relations/

Desch, Michael C. Civilian Control of the Military: The Changing Security Environment. Baltimore, MD: Johns Hopkins University Press, 2001.

Desch, Michael C. "Explaining the gap: Vietnam, the Republicanization of the South, and the end of the mass army." Soldiers and Civilians: The Civil-Military Gap and American National Security. Cambridge, MA: MIT Press, 2001.

Desilver, Drew. "The polarization in today's Congress has roots that go back decades." Pew Research Center (March 10, 2022).

Desjardins, Lisa. "How Republicans responded to Mattis' criticism of Trump." PBS News June 4, 2020 https://www.pbs.org/newshour/politics/how-republicans-responded-to-mattis-criticism-of-trump.

Dinan, Stephen. "Retired top military brass push for Romney." Washington Times (November 4, 2012).

Doherty, Carroll, Jocelyn Kiley, and Bridget Jameson. "Views of parties' positions on issues, ideologies." Tech. rep. Pew Research Center, June 22, 2016.

Doherty, Carroll, Jocelyn Kiley, and Bridget Johnson. "Political Independents: who they are, what they think." Pew Research Center (March 14, 2019).

Donnelly, Thomas. "Testing the Fluornoy hypothesis: civil military relations in the post-9/11 Era." Warriors and Citizens: American Views of Our Military. Ed. Kori N. Schake and Jim Mattis. Stanford, CA: Hoover Institution Press, 2016.

Doubek, James. "Joint Chiefs denounce racism after Trump's comments." National Public Radio (August 17, 2017).

Downs, Anthony. *An Economic Theory of Democracy*. 1st edition. Boston: Harper and Row, 1957.

Drezner, Daniel W. "Perspective—Is Fox News to blame for American rage?" *Washington Post* (August 1, 2021).

Drezner, Daniel W. "Perspective—Is this the tipping point for trust in the U.S. military?" *Washington Post* (October 26, 2017).

Drezner, Daniel W. "Perspective—Joe Biden bends a campaign pledge." *Washington Post* (December 8, 2020).

Drezner, Daniel W. "Perspective—The erosion of American trust hits the U.S. military." *Washington Post* (February 16, 2022).

Drezner, Daniel W. "The end of the median voter theorem in presidential politics?" *Washington Post* (May 29, 2015).

Druckman, James N. "On the limits of framing effects: who can frame?" *Journal of Politics* 63.4 (2001), pp. 1041–1066.

Druckman, James N., Matthew S. Levendusky, and Audrey Mclain. "No need to watch: how the effects of partisan media can spread via interpersonal discussions." *American Journal of Political Science* 62.1 (2018), pp. 99–112.

Druckman, James N. and Arthur Lupia. "Preference formation." *Annual Review of Political Science* 3.1 (2000), pp. 1–24.

Druckman, James N., Erik Peterson, and Rune Slothuus. "How elite partisan polarization affects public opinion formation." *American Political Science Review* 107.01 (2013), pp. 57–79.

Druckman, James N. et al. *Cambridge Handbook of Experimental Political Science*. Cambridge: Cambridge University Press, 2011.

Druckman, James N. et al. "Competing rhetoric over time: frames versus cues." *The Journal of Politics* 72.1 (2010), pp. 136–148.

Drum, Kevin. "The real reason Americans are so damn angry all the time." *Mother Jones* (September/October 2021).

Drutman, Lee. "The moderate middle is a myth." *FiveThirtyEight* September 24, 2019 https://fivethirtyeight.com/features/the-moderate-middle-is-a-myth/.

Drutman, Lee. "Why there are so few moderate Republicans left." *FiveThirtyEight* August 24, 2020 https://fivethirtyeight.com/features/why-there-are-so-few-moderate-republicans-left/.

Dugan, Andrew and Zac Auter. "Republicans', Democrats' views of media accuracy diverge." Gallup August 25, 2017 http://news.gallup.com/poll/216320/republicans-democrats-views-media-accuracy-diverge.aspx.

Dwyer, Jim and Robert F. Worth. "Accused G.I. was troubled long before Iraq." *New York Times* (July 14, 2006).

Eaton, Paul D., Antonio M. Taguba, and Steven M. Anderson. "Opinion—3 retired generals: the military must prepare now for a 2024 insurrection." *Washington Post* (December 17, 2021).

Eckholm, Erik. "Lt. Gen. William Boykin, known for anti-Muslim remarks, cancels West Point talk." *New York Times* (January 30, 2012).

England, Zach, Kyle Rempfer, Geoff Ziezulewicz, and Diana Stancy Correll. "Top military leaders speak out about racism in wake of George Floyd's death in police custody." *Military Times* (June 3, 2020).

Epstein, Reid J. "The G.O.P. delivers its 2020 platform. It's from 2016." *New York Times* (August 25, 2020).

Epstein, Reid J. and Nick Corasaniti. "Republicans gain heavy House edge in 2022 as gerrymandered maps emerge." *New York Times* (November 15, 2021).

Evans, David. "Crowe endorsement of Clinton raises more than eye-brows." *chicagotribune.com* September 25, 1992 https://www.chicagotribune.com/news/ct-xpm-1992-09-25-9203270346-story.html.

Exum, Andrew. "The dangerous politicization of the military." *The Atlantic* July 24, 2017 https://www.theatlantic.com/politics/archive/2017/07/the-danger-of-turning-the-us-military-into-a-political-actor/534624/.

Faiola, Anthony. "British aid worker Norgrove killed accidentally by U.S. soldier, inquiry finds." *Washington Post* (December 3, 2010).

Fallows, James. "Karmic justice: Gen. Eric Shinseki." *The Atlantic* (December 7, 2008).

Fang, Songying. "The informational role of international institutions and domestic politics." *American Journal of Political Science* 52.2 (2008), pp. 304–321.

Farley, Robert. "Over the horizon: warning signs in U.S. civil-military relations." *World Politics Review* (October 20, 2010).

Fay, Matthew. *Persistently Politicizing the Military*. https://www.niskanencenter.org/persistently-politicizing-military/ (July 2017).

Feaver, Peter. "Controversy over military partisan cheerleading continues." *Foreign Policy* August 2, 2016 https://foreignpolicy.com/2016/08/02/controversy-over-military-partisan-cheerleading-continues/.

Feaver, Peter. "Should senior military officers resign in protest if Obama disregards their advice?" *Foreign Policy* October 7, 2014 https://foreignpolicy.com/2014/10/07/should-senior-military-officers-resign-in-protest-if-obama-disregards-their-advice/.

Feaver, Peter. "The military revolt against Joe Biden." *Foreign Policy* May 12, 2021 https://foreignpolicy.com/2021/05/12/joe-biden-military-revolt-liz-cheney/.

Feaver, Peter D. *Armed Servants: Agency, Oversight, and Civil-Military Relations* Cambridge, MA; London: Harvard University Press, 2003.

Feaver, Peter D. "Bob Woodward strikes again! (McChrystal assessment edition)." *Foreign Policy* September 21, 2009 https://foreignpolicy.com/2009/09/21/bob-woodward-strikes-again-mcchrystal-assessment-edition/.

Feaver, Peter D. "Civil-military relations." *Annual Review of Political Science* 2.1 (1999), pp. 211–241.

Feaver, Peter D. "Crisis as shirking: an agency theory explanation of the souring of American civil-military relations." *Armed Forces & Society* 24.3 (1998), pp. 407–434.

Feaver, Peter D. "The civil-military problematique: Huntington, Janowitz, and the question of civilian Control." *Armed Forces & Society* 23.2 (1996), pp. 149–178.

Feaver, Peter D. "The right to be right: civil-military relations and the Iraq surge decision." *International Security* 35.4 (2011), pp. 87–125.

Feaver, Peter D. and James Golby. "Opinion—The myth of 'war weary' Americans." *Wall Street Journal* (December 1, 2020).

Feaver, Peter D. and Richard H. Kohn. "Civil-military relations in the United States: what senior leaders need to know (and usually don't)." *Strategic Studies Quarterly* 15.2 (2021), pp. 12–37.

Feaver, Peter D. and Richard H. Kohn. eds. *Soldiers and Civilians*. 1st edition. Cambridge, MA: MIT Press, 2001.

Feiger, Leah and Kathy Gilsinan. "Will the generals ever crack?" *The Atlantic* (November 11, 2019).

Feldman, Stanley, Leonie Huddy, and George E. Marcus. *Going to War in Iraq: When Citizens and the Press Matter*. Reprint edition. Chicago: University of Chicago Press, 2015.

Fernandez, Marisa. "John Kelly unloads on Trump's foreign policy toward Ukraine, North Korea." February 13, 2020 Axios https://www.axios.com/john-kelly-criticizes-trump-35c9138b-4abb-4756-b773-dc3a2c6a65c9.html.

Feuer, Alan. "A retired colonel's unlikely role in pushing baseless election claims." *New York Times* (December 12, 2021).

Feuer, Alan, Adam Goldman, and Katie Benner. "Oath Keepers founder is said to be investigated in Capitol Riot." *New York Times* (March 10, 2021).

Fifield, Anna. "Retired military leaders urge Trump to choose words, not action, to deal with North Korea." *Washington Post* (December 13, 2017).

Finer, Samuel. *The Man on Horseback: The Role of the Military in Politics*. New Brunswick, NJ: Routledge, 1962.

Fiorina, Morris P., Samuel A. Abrams, and Jeremy C. Pope. "Polarization in the American public: misconceptions and misreadings." *Journal of Politics* 70.2 (2008), pp. 556–560.

Fiorina, Morris P., Samuel J. Abrams, and Jeremy C. Pope. *Culture War? The Myth of a Polarized America*. 3rd edition. Boston, MA: Longman, 2010.

Foa, Roberto Stefan and Yascha Mounk. "The democratic disconnect." *Journal of Democracy* 27.3 (2016), pp. 5–17.

Foster, Chase and Jeffry Frieden. "Crisis of trust: socio-economic determinants of Europeans' confidence in government." *European Union Politics* (Augugst 10, 2017).

Friend, Alice Hunt. "Analysis—The Pentagon is moving money to pay for Trump's border wall. Here are the consequences." *Washington Post* (September 6, 2019).

Friend, Alice Hunt. *Military Politicization*. May 5, 2017 https://www.csis.org/analysis/military-politicization.

Friend, Alice Hunt and Daniel E. White. "American 'battlespace': the military's reckoning with racism and politicization." *World Politics Review* (June 16, 2021).

Fritze David Jackson and John, Gregory Korte. "John Kelly, hired to restore order for President Donald Trump, is out as chief of staff." *USA TODAY* December 8, 2019 https://www.usatoday.com/story/news/politics/2018/12/08/john-kelly-out-donald-trump-chief-staff/339220002/.

Fukuyama, Francis. "Opinion—One single day. That's all it took for the world to look away from us." *New York Times* (January 5, 2022).

Fukuyama, Francis. *Trust: The Social Virtues and the Creation of Prosperity*. New York: Free Press, 1995.

Gabbay, Michael. "A dynamical systems model of small group decision making." *Diplomacy Games*. Ed. Rudolf Avenhaus and I. William Zartman. Berlin; Heidelberg: Springer, 2007, pp. 99–121.

Gaines, Brian J. et al. "Same facts, different interpretations: partisan motivation and opinion on Iraq." *The Journal of Politics* 69.4 (2007), pp. 957–974.

Garamone, Jim. "Dempsey: political activity erodes public trust in military." *Armed Forces Press Service* (August 22, 2012).

Garb, Maja and Marjan Malesic. "The causes of trust and distrust in the military." *Defense & Security Analysis* 32.1 (2016), pp. 64–78.

Gartner, Scott Sigmund and Gary M. Segura. "All politics are still local: the Iraq War and the 2006 midterm elections." *PS: Political Science & Politics* Vo. 41 Iss 1 (January 2008).

Gass, Nick. "Obama: 'We're not going to do an Iraq-style invasion of Iraq or Syria.' " *POLITICO* (December 3, 2015).

Gecewicz, Claire and Lee Rainie. "Why Americans don't fully trust many who hold positions of power and responsibility." Tech. rep. Pew Research Center, September 19, 2019.

Gerber, Alan and Donald Green. "Misperceptions about perceptual bias." *Annual Review of Political Science* 2.1 (1999), pp. 189–210.

Gilens, Martin. "Political ignorance and collective policy preferences." *American Political Science Review* 95.2 (2001), pp. 379–396.

Gilens, Martin and Naomi Murakawa. "Elite cues and political decision making." *Political Decision Making, Deliberation, and Participation* 6 (2002), pp. 15–49.

Gilliam, Ben. "TN lawmaker files to 'reprimand' the Associated Press." *WJHL—Tri-Cities News & Weather* (January 22, 2022).

Golby, James. "Duty, honor . . . party? Ideology, institutions, and the use of military force." PhD dissertation. Stanford University, 2011.

Golby, James. "Uncivil-military relations: politicization of the military in the Trump era." *Strategic Studies Quarterly* 15.2 (2021), pp. 149–174.

Golby, James, Lindsay Cohn, and Peter D. Feaver. "Thanks for your service: civilian and veteran attitudes after fifteen years of war." *Warriors and Citizens: American Views of Our Military*. Stanford, CA: Hoover Institution Press, 2016, pp. 69–96.

Golby, James, Kyle Dropp, and Peter D. Feaver. "Military campaigns: veterans' endorsements and presidential elections." Tech. rep. Center for a New American Security, 2012.

Golby, James and Peter Feaver. "Military prestige during a political crisis: use it and you'll lose it." *War on the Rocks* (June 5, 2020).

Golby, James and Peter D. Feaver. "Biden inherits a challenging civil-military legacy." *War on the Rocks* (January 1, 2021).

Golby, James and Peter D. Feaver. "Former military leaders criticized the election and the administration. That hurts the military's reputation." *Washington Post* (May 15, 2021).

Golby, James and Peter D. Feaver. "Thank you for your lip service? Social pressure to support the troops." *War on the Rocks* (August 14, 2019).

Golby, James, Peter D. Feaver, and Kyle Dropp. "Elite military cues and public opinion about the use of military force." *Armed Forces & Society* 44.1 (2017).

Golby, James and Mara Karlin. "The case for rethinking the politicization of the military." Online Article Brookings Institution June 12, 2020 https://www.brookings.edu/blog/order-from-chaos/2020/06/12/the-case-for-rethinking-the-politicization-of-the-military/.

Golby, James and Mara Karlin. "Why 'Best military advice' is bad for the military—and worse for Civilians." *Orbis* 62.1 (2018), pp. 137–153.

Golby, Jim and Carrie A. Lee. "Analysis—The National Guard has been called out in Washington, D.C. Here's what you need to know." *Washington Post* (January 7, 2021).

Goldberg, Jeffrey. "James Mattis denounces President Trump, describes him as a threat to the constitution." *The Atlantic* (June 3, 2020).

Goldberg, Marvin E. and Jon Hartwick. "The effects of advertiser reputation and extremity of advertising claim on advertising effectiveness." *Journal of Consumer Research* 17 (1990), pp. 172–179.

Goldsmith, Ronald E., Barbara A. Lafferty, and Stephen J. Newell. "The impact of corporate credibility and celebrity credibility on consumer reaction to advertisements and brands." *Journal of Advertising* 29.3 (2000), pp. 43–54.

Gonyea, Don. "Anger over 'Betray Us' ad simmers on Hill." *National Public Radio* (September 22, 2007).

Gordon, Michael R. "Trump's mix of politics and military is faulted." *New York Times* (February 8, 2017).

Gordon, Michael R. and Bernard E. Trainor. *The Endgame: The Inside Story of the Struggle for Iraq, from George W. Bush to Barack Obama*. Reprint edition. New York: Vintage, 2012.

Gould, Joe. "Handful of hawkish US lawmakers urge military leaders to fight new CR." *Military Times* (December 2, 2017).

Gourley, Jim and Thomas Ricks. "Where is the tipping point for America's trust in the military? And are we near it?" *Foreign Policy* (February 14, 2014).

Graham, David A. "Are Trump's generals mounting a defense of democratic institutions?" *The Atlantic* (January 31, 2017).

Gramlich, John. "5 facts about Fox News." Pew Research Center April 8, 2020 https://www.pewresearch.org/fact-tank/2020/04/08/five-facts-about-fox-news/.

Green, Miranda. "Medal of Honor recipient explains why he's a Republican voting for Clinton." *DecodeDC* (July 28, 2016).

Grieco, Joseph M. et al. "Lets get a second opinion: international institutions and American public support for war." *International Studies Quarterly* 55.2 (2011), pp. 563–583.

Griffiths, Zachary and Olivia Simon. "Not putting their money where their mouth is: retired flag officers and presidential endorsements." *Armed Forces & Society* (December 9, 2019).

Gronke, Paul and Peter D. Feaver. "Uncertain confidence: civilian and military attitudes and civil-military relations." *Soldiers and Civilians: The Civil-Military Gap and American National Security*. Ed. Richard H. Kohn and Peter D. Feaver. Cambridge, MA: MIT Press, 2001.

Gross, K., P. R. Brewer, and S. Aday. "Confidence in government and emotional responses to terrorism after September 11, 2001." *American Politics Research* 37.1 (2009), pp. 107–128.

Guardino, Matt and Danny Hayes. "Foreign voices, Party cues, and U.S. public opinion about military action." *International Journal of Public Opinion* 30.3 (Autumn 2018).

Guisinger, Alexandra and Elizabeth N. Saunders. "Mapping the boundaries of elite cues: how elites shape mass opinion across international issues." *International Studies Quarterly* 61.2 (2017), pp. 425–441.

Hacker, Jacob S. and Paul Pierson. *Let Them Eat Tweets: How the Right Rules in an Age of Extreme Inequality.* 1st edition. New York: Liveright, 2020.

Haddick, Robert. "This week at war: the Biden plan returns." *Foreign Policy* October 22, 2010 https://foreignpolicy.com/2010/10/22/this-week-at-war-the-biden-plan-returns/.

Hanitzsch, Thomas and Rosa Berganza. "Explaining journalists' trust in public institutions across 20 countries: media freedom, corruption, and ownership matter most: explaining journalists' public trust." *Journal of Communication* 62.5 (2012), pp. 794–814.

Harkins, Gina and Hope Hodge Seck. "Marines, infantry most highly represented among veterans arrested after Capitol Riot." February 27, 2021 Military.com https://www. military.com/daily-news/2021/02/26/marines-infantry-most-highly-represented-among-veterans-arrested-after-capitol-riot.html.

Hartman, Todd K. and Christopher R. Weber. "Who said what? The effects of source cues in issue frames." *Political Behavior* 31.4 (2009), pp. 537–558.

Hastings, Michael. "The runaway general: the profile that brought down McChrystal." *Rolling Stone* (June 22, 2010).

Hayes, Danny and Matt Guardino. "The influence of foreign voices on U.S. public opinion: foreign voices and U.S. public opinion." *American Journal of Political Science* 55.4 (2011), pp. 831–851.

Hayden, Michael, James Clapper, Stanley McChrystal, Douglas Lute, and Mark Hertling, "We fought to defend democracy. This new threat to America now keeps us awake at night." *USA Today*, June 22, 2022, https://www.usatoday.com/story/opinion/contributors/2022/06/22/american-democracy-former-cia-director/7685947001/.

Healy, Jack, Frances Robles, and Ron Nixon. "Aid is getting to Puerto Rico. Distributing it remains a challenge." *New York Times* (October 3, 2017).

Hemingway, Ernest. *The Sun Also Rises.* New York: Scribner, 1956.

Henderson, Nia-Malika. "Gen. Wes Clark set to pound Romney on foreign policy." *Washington Post* (Nov. 2011).

Henning, Christian, Volker Saggau, and Johannes Hedtrich. "Elite networks, political belief formation and government performance: an agent-based approach to a general political economy equilibrium." May 17, 2010 https://opensiuc.lib.siu.edu/pnconfs_2010/36/.

Hersh, Seymour M. "Torture at Abu Ghraib." *The New Yorker* (April 30, 2004).

Hetherington, Marc. "Putting polarization in perspective." *British Journal of Political Science* 39 (2009), pp. 413–448.

Hetherington, Marc. "The political relevance of political trust." *American Political Science Review* 92.4 (1998), pp. 791–808.

Hetherington, Marc and Elizabeth Suhay. "Authoritarianism, threat, and Americans support for the War on Terror." *American Journal of Political Science* 55.3 (2011), pp. 546–560.

Hewstone, Miles, Mark Rubin, and Hazel Willis. "Intergroup bias." *Annual Review of Psychology* 53 (2002), pp. 575–604.

Hibbing, John R. and Elizabeth Theiss-Morse. *Congress as Public Enemy: Public Attitudes toward American Political Institutions.* 1st edition. Cambridge; New York: Cambridge University Press, 1995.

Hill, Andrew A., Leonard Wong, and Stephen J. Gerras. "Self-interest well understood: the origins & lessons of public confidence in the military." *Daedalus* 142.2 (2013), pp. 49–64.

Hlavac, Marek. *Stargazer: Well-Formatted Regression and Summary Statistics Tables.* Bratislava, Slovakia, 2022.

Holsti, O. R. *Public Opinion and American Foreign Policy*. Ann Arbor: Michigan University Press, 2004.

Holsti, Ole R. "A widening gap between the U.S. military and civilian society? Some evidence, 1976–96." *International Security* 23.3 (1998), p. 5.

Holsti, Ole R. "Politicization of the United States military: crisis or tempest in a teapot?" *International Journal* 57.1 (2001), pp. 1–18.

Hooker, Jr., Richard D. "Soldiers of the state: reconsidering American civil-military relations." *Parameters* 41.4 (2011), pp. 1–14.

Horton, Alex. "Army is investigating soldiers who appeared in Democratic convention video." *Washington Post* (August 19, 2020).

Horton, Alex. "Marine Corps compliance with vaccine mandate on course to be military's worst." *Washington Post* (November 21, 2021).

Hovland, Carl I. and Walter Weiss. "The influence of source credibility on communication effectiveness." *Public Opinion Quarterly* 14.4 (1951), pp. 635–650.

Howell, William and Jon C. Pevehouse. *While Dangers Gather: Congressional Checks on Presidential War Powers*. Princeton, NJ: Princeton University Press, 2007.

Huddy, Leonie, Lilliana Mason, and Lene Aarøe. "Expressive partisanship: campaign involvement, political emotion, and partisan identity." *American Political Science Review* 109.1 (2015), pp. 1–17.

Huntington, Samuel P. *The Soldier and the State: The Theory and Politics of Civil-Military Relations*. Cambridge: Belknap Press, 1957.

Ignatius, David. "Opinion—Trump and his supporters are discovering how hard it is to sabotage election results." *Washington Post* (November 17, 2020).

Imai, Kosuke, Luke Keele, Dustin Tingley, and Teppei Yamamoto. "Unpacking the black box of causality: learning about causal mechanisms from experimental and observational studies." *American Political Science Review* 105.04 (November 2011), pp. 765–789.

Ingraham, Christopher. "Analysis—The United States is backsliding into autocracy under Trump, scholars warn." *Washington Post* (September 18, 2020).

Inskeep, Steve. "Former Joint Chiefs Chairman condemns Trump's threat to use military at protests." *National Public Radio* (June 4, 2020).

Iyengar, Shanto and Kyu S. Hahn. "Red media, blue media: evidence of ideological selectivity in media use." *Journal of Communication* 59.1 (2009), pp. 19–39.

Iyengar, Shanto and Donald R. Kinder. *News That Matters: Television and American Opinion*. Updated edition. Chicago: University of Chicago Press, 1989.

Iyengar, Shanto, Gaurav Sood, and Yphtach Lelkes. "Affect, not ideology." *Public Opinion Quarterly* 76.3 (2012), pp. 405–431.

Iyengar, Shanto and Sean J. Westwood. "Fear and loathing across Party lines: new evidence on group polarization." *American Journal of Political Science* 59.3 (2015), pp. 690–707.

Iyengar Shanto, Yptach Lelkes, Matthew Levendusky, Neil Mahotra, and Sean J. Westwood. "The origins and consequences of affective polarization in the United States." *Annual Review of Political Science* 22.1 (2019), pp. 129–146.

Jackman, Simon and Paul M. Sniderman. "The limits of deliberative discussion: a model of everyday political arguments." *Journal of Politics* 68.2 (2006), pp. 272–283.

Jackson, Chris. *Ipsos/Reuters Poll—The Big Lie*. Poll. Washington, DC: Ipsos, May 21, 2021.

Jacobs, Emily. "GOP lawmakers split over mandating COVID vaccine for US military." *New York Post* (July 6, 2021).

Jacobson, Gary C. *A Divider, Not a Uniter: George W. Bush and the American People*, 1st edition. New York: Longman, 2006.

Jamieson, Kathleen and Joseph Cappella. *Echo Chamber: Rush Limbaugh and the Conservative Media Establishment*. New York: Oxford University Press, 2008.

Janowitz, Morris. "Military elites and the study of war." *Conflict Resolution* 1.1 (1957), pp. 9–18.

Janowitz, Morris. *The Professional Soldier: A Social and Political Portrait*. Reissue edition. New York: Free Press, 1960.

Jeong, Andrew and Alex Horton. "Federal court denies Oklahoma Gov. Kevin Stitt's attempt to stop military vaccine mandate." *Washington Post* (December 29, 2021).

Jurecic, Quinta. "Opinion—Did the 'adults in the room' make any difference with Trump?" *New York Times* (August 29, 2019).

Jurkowitz, Mark et al. "U.S. media polarization and the 2020 election: a nation divided." Tech. rep. Pew Research Center, January 24, 2020.

Kablack, Brianna et al. "The military speaks out." *New America* (January 19, 2021).

Kaplan, Fred. "Military commanders are finally speaking out against Trump." *Slate Magazine* (June 3, 2020).

Karol, David and Edward Miguel. "The electoral cost of war: Iraq casualties and the 2004 US presidential election." *Journal of Politics* 69.3 (2007), pp. 633–648.

Kasurak, Peter. "Huntington in Canada: the triumph of subjective control." *Armed Forces & Society* 48.2 (November 24, 2020), pp. 1–20.

Kaurin, Pauline M. Shanks. "An 'unprincipled principal': implications for civil-military relations." *Strategic Studies Quarterly* 15.2 (2021), pp. 50–68.

Kaurin, Pauline M. Shanks and Bradley J. Strawser. "Disgraceful pardons: dishonoring our honorable." *War on the Rocks* (March 25, 2019).

Keller, Jared. "Joint Chiefs to troops: Biden is your next commander-in-chief. Deal with it." *Task & Purpose* (January 12, 2021).

Kenning, Chris. "Retired military officers slam Trump's proposed transgender ban." *Reuters* (August 1, 2017).

Kertzer, Joshua D. and Thomas Zeitzoff. "A bottom-up theory of public opinion about foreign policy." *American Journal of Political Science* 61.3 (July 2017).

Kheel, Rebecca. "Top Republican: 'outrageous' to extend National Guard deployment at Capitol." The Hill March 4, 2021 https://thehill.com/policy/defense/541707-top-republican-it-would-be-outrageous-to-extend-national-guard-deployment-at.

King, David C. and Zachary Karabell. *The Generation of Trust: Public Confidence in the U.S. Military Since Vietnam*. Washington, DC: AEI Press, 2002.

Klein, Ezra. *Why We're Polarized*. Illustrated edition. New York: Avid Reader Press / Simon & Schuster, 2020.

Klein, Rick. "Trump said 'blame on both sides' in Charlottesville, now the anniversary puts him on the spot." ABC News August 12, 2018 https://abcnews.go.com/Politics/trump-blame-sides-charlottesville-now-anniversary-puts-spot/story?id=57141612.

Kohn, Richard H. "How democracies control the military." *Journal of Democracy* 8.4 (1997), pp. 139–153.

Kohn, Richard H. "Out of control: the crisis in civil-military relations." *The National Interest* 35 (1994), pp. 3–17.

Kohn, Richard H. "Richard Kohn fires a warning flare about a Joint Force Quarterly article." Foreign Policy September 29, 2010 https://foreignpolicy.com/2010/09/29/richard-kohn-fires-a-warning-flare-about-a-joint-force-quarterly-article/.

Kohn, Richard H. "The erosion of civilian control of the military in the United States today." *Naval War College Review* 55.3 (2002), p. 9.

Kohn, Richard H. et al. "An exchange on civil-military relations." *The National Interest* 36 (1994), pp. 23–31.

Kohut, Andrew and Scott Keeter. "Petraeus' proposals favored, but no lift in war support." Tech. rep. Pew Research Center, September 18, 2007.

Kollman, Ken. *Outside Lobbying*. Princeton, NJ: Princeton University Press, 1998.

Krebs, Ronald R. and Robert Ralston. "Civilian control of the military is a partisan issue." July 14, 2020 https://www.foreignaffairs.com/articles/united-states/2020-07-14/civilian-control-military-partisan-issue.

Krebs, Ronald R. and Robert Ralston. "Patriotism or paychecks: who believes what about why soldiers serve." *Armed Forces & Society* 48.1 (2022), pp. 25–48.

Krebs, Ronald R. and Robert Ralston, "Why conservatives turned on the U.S. military", *Foreign Affairs* (September 28, 2021).

Krebs, Ronald R., Robert Ralston, and Aaron Rapport. "No right to be wrong: what Americans think about civil-military relations." *Perspectives on Politics* (2021). New York: Cambridge University Press, pp. 1–19.

Krebs, Ronald R., Robert Ralston, and Aaron Rapport. "Why they fight: how perceived motivations for military service shape support for the use of force." *International Studies Quarterly* 65.4 (2021), pp. 1012–1026.

Kriner, Douglas and William Howell. "Political elites and public support for war." In L. Dodd and B. Oppenheimer (eds), *Congress Reconsidered*, Vol 10. Congressional Quarterly Press, 2013.

Krislov, Zachary and Jocelyn Kiley. "Partisans see opposing party as more ideologically extreme." Pew Research Center (August 23, 2016).

Kuklinski, James H. and Norman L. Hurley. "On hearing and interpreting political messages: a cautionary tale of citizen cue-taking." *The Journal of Politics* 56.3 (1994), pp. 729–751.

Kuklinski, James H. et al. "Misinformation and the currency of democratic citizenship." *The Journal of Politics* 62.3 (2000), pp. 790–816.

Kull, Steven, Clay Ramsay, and Evan Lewis. "Misperceptions, the media, and the Iraq War." *Political Science Quarterly* 118.4 (2003), pp. 569–598.

Ladd, Jonathan McDonald. "The neglected power of elite opinion leadership to produce antipathy toward the news media: evidence from a survey experiment." *Political Behavior* 32.1 (2010), pp. 29–50.

Lafferty, Barbara A. and Ronald E. Goldsmith. "Corporate credibility's role in consumers' attitudes and purchase intentions when a high versus a low credibility endorser is used in the ad." *Journal of Business Research* 44 (1999), pp. 109–116.

Lamothe, Dan. "Marine's court-martial highlights the military straining to deal with partisan politics." *Washington Post* (October 16, 2021).

Lamothe, Dan. "Retired generals cite past comments from Mattis while opposing Trump's proposed foreign aid cuts." *Washington Post* (February 27, 2017).

Lau, Richard R. and David P. Redlawsk. "Advantages and disadvantages of cognitive heuristics in political decision making." *American Journal of Political Science* (2001), pp. 951–971.

Laughlin, Nick and Peyton Shelburne. "The Morning Consult COVID-19 Vaccine Dashboard." Morning Consult July 19, 2021 https://morningconsult.com/covid19-vaccine-dashboard/.

Lee, Carol E. "Some of the U.S. military elite share QAnon, 2020 lies, racism on-line." NBC News April 16, 2021 https://www.nbcnews.com/news/military/secret-facebook-groups-america-s-best-warriors-share-racist-jabs-n1263985.

Lee, Carrie A. "Analysis—Lt. Col. Vindman's retirement will hurt military effectiveness. This is why." *Washington Post* (July 9, 2020).

Lee, Carrie A. "Analysis—Trump overrode the Navy's plans to discipline a SEAL. That wasn't as troubling as some think." *Washington Post* (December 10, 2019).

Lee, Carrie A. "Polarization, casualty sensitivity, and military operations: evidence from a survey experiment." *International Politics* (March 2022).

Lee, Carrie A. and Celestino Perez, Jr. "Education against extremism: suggestions for a smarter stand-down." *War on the Rocks* (July 16, 2021).

Lefevre-Gonzalez, Christina. "Restoring historical understandings of the 'public interest' standard of American broadcasting: an exploration of the Fairness Doctrine." *International Journal of Communication* 7 (2013), pp. 89–109.

Lelkes, Yphtach and Paul M. Sniderman. "The ideological asymmetry of the American Party system." *British Journal of Political Science* 46 (2014), pp. 825–844.

Levitsky, Steven and Daniel Ziblatt. *How Democracies Die*. Reprint edition. New York: Crown, 2019.

Lewis, Jeffrey B., Keith T. Poole, Howard Rosenthal, Adam Boche, Aaron Rudkin, and Luke Sonnet. "Voteview: Congressional roll call votes database." Tech. rep. 2021.

Liebert, Hugh and James Golby. "Midlife crisis? The all-volunteer force at 40." *Armed Forces & Society* 43.1 (2017), pp. 115–138.

Lindberg, Tod. "The very liberal view of the US military." *Warriors and Citizens: American Views of Our Military*. Stanford, CA: Hoover Institution Press, 2016.

Line, United Members of the Long Gray. "A letter to the West Point class of 2020, from fellow members of the Long Gray Line." *Medium* (June 24, 2020).

Lipset, Seymour Martin and William Schneider. "The decline of confidence in American institutions." *Political Science Quarterly* 98.3 (1983), p. 379.

Liptak, Adam. "Supreme Court rules against Navy SEALs in vaccine mandate case." *New York Times* (March 25, 2022).

Lodge, Milton and Charles S. Taber. "Three steps toward a theory of motivated political reasoning." *Elements of Reason: Understanding and Expanding the Limits of Political Rationality*. Cambridge: Cambridge University Press, 2000.

Loewen, Peter John and Daniel Rubenson. "Canadian war deaths in Afghanistan: costly policies and support for incumbents." Tech. rep. Working paper, 2010 http://individual.utoronto.ca/loewen/Research_files/war_deaths_vfinal%20.pdf.

Lubold, Gordon and Nancy A. Youssef. "Top general apologizes for being at trump Church photo shoot—WSJ." *The Wall Street Journal* (June 11, 2020).

Lucas, Jim and Tereza Pultarova. "What is parallax?" *Space.com* January 11, 2022 https://www.space.com/30417-parallax.

Lupia, Arthur. "Shortcuts versus encyclopedias: information and voting behavior in California insurance reform elections." *American Political Science Review* 88.01 (1994), pp. 63–76.

Lupia, Arthur and Mathew D. McCubbins. *The Democratic Dilemma: Can Citizens Learn What They Need to Know?* Cambridge; New York: Cambridge University Press, 1998.

Lupton, Danielle L. "Analysis—Having fewer veterans in Congress makes it less likely to restrain the president's use of force." *Washington Post* (November 10, 2017).

Lupton, Danielle L. "Out of the service, into the House: military experience and congressional war oversight." *Political Research Quarterly* 70.2 (2017), pp. 327–339.

Lupton, Danielle, David T. Burbach, and Lindsay Cohn. "Authoritarian tactics on US soil." *Political Violence at a Glance* (August 5, 2020).

Lupton, Danielle and Max Z. Margulies. "Analysis—Trump's election fraud allegations suggest military voters uniformly supported him. It's not so." *Washington Post* (November 18, 2020).

Lupton, Danielle and Clayton Webb. "Wither elites? The role of elite credibility and knowledge in public perceptions of foreign policy." Paper for American Political Science Association annual conference February 16, 2021 https://preprints.apsanet.org/engage/apsa/article-details/6026c66bed338ebf944d221f.

Lupu, Noam, Luke Plutowski, and Elizabeth J. Zechmeister. "Analysis—Would Americans ever support a coup? 40 percent now say yes." *Washington Post* (January 6, 2022).

Lyall, Jason. *Divided Armies: Inequality and Battlefield Performance in Modern War*. Princeton, NJ: Princeton University Press, 2020.

Lyons, James A. "How politicizing the military puts national security at risk." *Washington Times* (October 13, 2016).

Macdonald, Callum A. *Korea: The War before Vietnam*. New York: Free Press, 1986.

Mali, Meghashyam. "Norquist accuses Dems of politicizing Sandy Hook school shooting." *The Hill* (December 23, 2012).

Margolick, David. "The night of the generals." *Vanity Fair* (March 5, 2007). https://www.vanityfair.com/news/2007/04/iraqgenerals200704

Margolin, Emma. "Obama cements historic LGBT rights legacy." June 30, 2016.

Marlow, Alexander. "Exclusive—Trump: Paul Ryan blocked subpoenas of Democrats." *Breitbart* (March 13, 2019). https://www.breitbart.com/politics/2019/03/13/exclusive-president-donald-trump-paul-ryan-blocked-subpoenas-of-democrats/

Marsden, Peter V. and James D. Wright, eds. *Handbook of Survey Research*. 2nd edition. Bingley: Emerald, 2010.

Marsh, K. P. "The intersection of war and politics: the Iraq War troop surge and bureaucratic politics." *Armed Forces & Society* 38.3 (2012).

Mason, Lilliana. "'I disrespectfully agree': the differential effects of partisan sorting on social and issue polarization." *American Journal of Political Science* 59.1 (2015), pp. 128–145.

Mason, Lilliana. "A cross-cutting calm: how social sorting drives affective polarization." *Public Opinion Quarterly* 80.S1 (2016), pp. 351–377.

Mason, Lilliana. *Uncivil Agreement: How Politics Became Our Identity*. Illustrated edition. Chicago: University of Chicago Press, 2018.

Mason, Lilliana and Julie Wronski. "One tribe to bind them all: how out social group attachments strengthen partisanship." *Advances in Political Psychology* 39.1 (2018), pp. 257–277.

Maurer, Daniel. "The Generals' Constitution." https://www.justsecurity.org/70674/the-generals-constitution/ (June 2020).

Mazzetti, Mark and Eric Schmitt. "Obama's 'boots on the ground': U.S. special forces are sent to tackle global threats." *New York Times* (December 27, 2015).

McCarthy, Justin. "Roundup of Gallup COVID-19 coverage." Gallup July 13, 2021 https://news.gallup.com/opinion/gallup/308126/roundup-gallup-covid-coverage.aspx

McCarthy, Justin. "U.S. confidence in organized religion remains low." Gallup, July 13, 2019. https://news.gallup.com/poll/259964/confidence-organized-religion-remains-low.aspx.

McCarthy, Justin. "About Half Say U.S. Military is No. 1 in the World," Gallup, March 2, 2022, https://news.gallup.com/poll/390356/half-say-military-no-world.aspx.

McCausland, Phil. "Military joint chiefs denounce Charlottesville racism." NBC News August 16, 2017 https://www.nbcnews.com/news/us-news/military-joint-chiefs-denounce-charlottesville-racism-n793376.

McCubbins, Mathew D., Roger G. Noll, and Barry R. Weingast. "Structure and process, politics and policy: administrative arrangements and the political control of agencies." *Virginia Law Review* (1989), pp. 431–482.

McGuire, William J. "The nature of attitudes and attitude change." *Hand-book of Social Psychology*. Ed. G. Lindzey and E. Aronson. 2nd edition. Cambridge, MA: Addison-Wesley, 1969, pp. 135–214.

Mcleary, Paul. "Almost 50 Republicans back Navy SEAL lawsuit over vaccine mandate." *POLITICO* (December 20, 2021).

McMaster, H. R. and Gary D. Cohn. "America first doesn't mean america alone." *Wall Street Journal* (May 30, 2017).

McRaven, William H. "Opinion—Our Republic is under attack from the president." *New York Times* (October 17, 2019).

McRaven, William H. "Opinion—Trump is actively working to undermine the Postal Service—and every major U.S. institution." *Washington Post* (August 16, 2020).

Mearsheimer, John J. *The Tragedy of Great Power Politics*. 1st edition. New York: W. W. Norton & Company, 2014.

Merica, Dan. "Clinton to Trump: My military endorsements are bigger than yours." CNN September 9, 2016 https://www.cnn.com/2016/09/09/politics/hillary-clinton-donald-trump-military-endorsements/index.html.

Metz, Steven and John R. Martin. *Decisionmaking in Operation Iraqi Freedom: The Strategic Shift of 2007*. Operation Iraqi Freedom key decisions monograph series vol. 2. Carlisle, PA: Strategic Studies Institute, U.S. Army War College, 2010.

Michaels, Jim. "What's at risk when retired generals plunge into partisan politics." *USA TODAY* (August 4, 2016).

Milbank, Dana. "Opinion—'Roe' is dead. The Roberts Court's 'stench' will live forever." *Washington Post* (December 1, 2021).

Milburn, Andrew R. "Breaking ranks: dissent and the military professional." Tech. rep. DTIC Document, 2010.

"Military and national defense." Gallup September 14, 2007 https://news.gallup.com/poll/1666/Military-National-Defense.aspx.

Miller, Arthur. "Political issues and trust in government: 1964–1970." *American Political Science Review* 68.3 (1974), pp. 951–972.

Miller, Arthur. "Rejoinder to 'Comment' by Jack Citr political discontent or ritualism?" *American Political Science Review* 68.3 (1974), pp. 989–1001.

Milton, Daniel and Andrew Mines. "'This is war': examining military experience among the Capitol hill siege participants." Tech. rep. West Point, NY: Combating Terrorism Center, United States Military Academy, Apr. 2021.

Mishler, William and Richard Rose. "What are the origins of political trust? Testing institutional and cultural theories in post-communist societies." *Comparative Political Studies* 34.1 (2001), pp. 30–62.

Mitchell, Amy and Rachel Weisel. "Political polarization and media habits: from Fox News to Facebook, how liberals and conservatives keep up with politics." Tech. rep. Pew Research Center, October 21, 2014.

Moeller, Susan. *Packaging Terrorism: Co-opting the News for Politics and Profit* Malden, MA: Wiley-Blackwell, 2009.

Montanaro, Domenico, "Here's Just How Little Confidence Ameircans Have in Political Institutions", NPR, January 17, 2018.

Moore, Peter. "YouGov—Could a coup really happen in the United States?" September 9, 2015 https://today.yougov.com/topics/politics/articles-reports/2015/09/09/could-coup-happen-in-united-states.

Moore, Peter. "YouGov—Poll results: civil service." December 7, 2016 https://today.yougov.com/topics/politics/articles-reports/2016/12/07/poll-results-civil-service.

Morgan, Wesley. "Trump's Fourth of July extravaganza troubles former military leaders." *POLITICO* (July 2, 2019).

Mounk, Yascha and Roberto Stefan Foa. "Opinion—Yes, people really are turning away from democracy." *Washington Post* (December 8, 2016).

Mullen, Michael G. "From the Chairman: military must stay apolitical." *Joint Forces Quarterly* 3.50 (2008).

Mullen, Michael G. "I was on the National Security Council. Bannon doesn't belong there." *New York Times* (February 6, 2017).

Murdie, Amanda. "The bad, the good, and the ugly: the curvilinear effects of civil–military conflict on international crisis outcome." *Armed Forces & Society* 39.2 (2013), pp. 233–254.

Myers, Meghann. "Esper encourages governors to 'dominate the battlespace' to put down nation-wide protests." *Military Times* (June 1, 2020).

Navarre, Brianna. "Study classifies U.S. democracy as 'backsliding' for the first time—best countries—US news." *U.S. News & World Report* (November 24, 2021).

"New report: US democracy has declined significantly in the past decade, reforms urgently needed." Freedom House March 22, 2021 https://freedomhouse.org/article/new-report-us-democracy-has-declined-significantly-past-decade-reforms-urgently-needed.

Newbold, Greg. "Why Iraq was a mistake." *Time* (April 9, 2006).

Newell, Stephen J. and Ronald E. Goldsmith. "The development of a scale to measure perceived corporate credibility." *Journal of Business Research* 52 (2001), pp. 235–247.

Newport, Frank. "Americans' confidence in institutions edges up." June 26, 2017 http://news.gallup.com/poll/212840/americans-confidence-institutions-edges.aspx.

Newsmax. "Welcome to Biden's woke military: Dr. @SebGorka https://t.co/YsrGVDOVWZ." Tweet. May 20, 2021.

Newton, Ken and Pippa Norris. "Confidence in public institutions." *Disaffected Democracies. What's Troubling the Trilateral Countries*. Princeton, NJ: Princeton University Press, 2000).

Nguyen, Daisy. "Appeals court: Trump wrongly diverted $2.5 billion in military construction funds for border wall." *Military Times* June 29, 2020 https://www.militarytimes.com/news/your-military/2020/06/26/appeals-court-trump-wrongly-diverted-25-billion-in-milcon-funds-for-border-wall/.

Nicholson, Stephen P. "Dominating cues and the limits of elite influence." *The Journal of Politics* 73.4 (2011), pp. 1165–1177.

Nielsen, Suzanne C. "Civil-military relations theory and military effectiveness." *Public Administration and Management* 10.2 (2005), pp. 61–84.

Nielsen, Suzanne C. and Hugh Liebert. "The continuing relevance of Morris Janowitz's 'The Professional Soldier' for the education of officers." *Armed Forces & Society* 47.4 (2021), pp. 732–749.

Nix, Dayne E. "American civil-military relations." *Naval War College Review* 65.2 (Spring 2012).

Norris, Pippa. "Measuring populism worldwide." *Party Politics* 26.6 (2020), pp. 697–717.

Nye, Joseph. "The media and declining confidence in government." *Harvard International Journal of Press/Politics* 2.3 (1997), pp. 4–9.

Nyhan, Brendan and Jason Reifler. "When corrections fail: the persistence of political misperceptions." *Political Behavior* 32.2 (2010), pp. 303–330.

"Obama apologises to MSF president." *BBC News* October 7, 2015 http://www.bbc.com/news/world-us-canada-34467631.

Ohanian, Roobina. "Construction and validation of a scale to measure celebrity endorsers' perceived expertise, trustworthiness, and attractiveness." *Journal of Advertising* 19.3 (1990), pp. 39–52.

Oliphant, James and Chris Kahn. "Half of Republicans believe false accounts of deadly U.S. Capitol riot—Reuters/Ipsos poll." *Reuters* April 5, 2021 https://www.reuters.com/article/us-usa-politics-disinformation-idUSKBN2BS0RZ.

"Oliver North: repealing 'don't ask, don't tell' could be 'very detrimental' to military." Fox February 4, 2010 https://www.foxnews.com/transcript/oliver-north-repealing-dont-ask-dont-tell-could-be-very-detrimental-to-military.

Orth, Taylor. "Which groups of Americans are most likely to believe conspiracy theories?—YouGov." March 30, 2022 https://today.yougov.com/topics/politics/articles-reports/2022/03/30/which-groups-americans-believe-conspiracies.

Osiel, Mark J. "Obeying orders: atrocity, military disciplines, and the law of war." *California Law Review* 86.5 (1998), pp. 939–941, 943–1129.

Owens, Mackubin Thomas. "Mac Owens on the forgotten dimensions of American civil-military relations." *Foreign Policy* (August 6, 2012).

Owens, Mackubin Thomas. "Maximum toxicity: civil-military relations in the Trump era." *Strategic Studies Quarterly* 15.2 (2021), pp. 99–119.

Owens, Mackubin Thomas. "Military officers: political without partisanship." *Strategic Studies Quarterly* 9.3 (2015).

Owens, Mackubin Thomas. "Rumsfeld, the generals, and the state of US civil-military relations." *Naval War College Review* 59.4 (2006), p. 68.

Owens, Mackubin Thomas. *US Civil-Military Relations after 9/11: Renegotiating the Civil-Military Bargain*. 1st edition. New York: Bloomsbury Academic, 2011.

Panetta, Grace. "Sen. Lindsey Graham accuses Biden of politicizing a violent insurrection intended to overturn the 2020 election." *Business Insider* (January 6, 2022).

Pawlyk, Oriana. "Air Force takes first step to buy maternity flight suits." June 24, 2020.

Perlinger, Arie. *American Zealots: Inside Right-Wing Domestic Terrorism*. New York: Columbia University Press, 2020.

Perry, Mark. "Are Trump's generals in over their heads?" *POLITICO* (October 25, 2017).

Peterson, Erik, Sharad Goel, and Shanto Iyengar. "Partisan selective exposure in online news consumption: evidence from the 2016 presidential campaign." *Political Science Research and Methods* 9.2 (2019), pp. 242–258.

Peterson, Erik and Shanto Iyengar. "Partisan gaps in political information and information-seeking behavior: motivating reasoning or cheerleading?" *American Journal of Political Science* 65.1 (2021), pp. 133–147.

Petraeus, David H. "Battling for Iraq." *Washington Post* (September 26, 2004).

Petrocik, John R., William L. Benoit, and Glenn J. Hansen. "Issue ownership and presidential campaigning, 1952–2000." *Political Science Quarterly* 118.4 (2003), pp. 599–626.

Petty, Richard E. and John T. Cacioppo. *Communication and Persuasion: Central and Peripheral Routes to Attitude Change*. New York: Springer, 1986.

Pew Research Center for Journalism and Media, News Content Index Methodology, https://www.pewresearch.org/journalism/news_index_methodology/, accessed October 18, 2017.

Pharr, Susan J., Robert D. Putnam, and Russell J. Dalton. "A quarter-century of declining confidence." *Journal of Democracy* 11.2 (2000), pp. 5–25.

Philipps, Dave. "Inspired by Charlottesville, military chiefs condemn racism." *New York Times* (August 16, 2017).

Philipps, Dave. "Trump clears three service members in war crimes cases." *New York Times* (November 15, 2019).

Phillips, Kristine. "Greatest threat to democracy: commander of bin Laden raid slams Trump's anti-media sentiment." *Washington Post* (February 24, 2017).

Poole, Keith T. and Howard Rosenthal. *Ideology and Congress: A Political Economic History of Roll Call Voting*. 2nd edition. New Brunswick: Routledge, 2007.

Post, Abigail and T. S. Sechser. "Hidden norms in international relations: public opinion and the use of nuclear weapons." University of Notre Dame, South Bend, IN, 2016.

Powell, Colin. *My American Journey*. 1st edition. New York: Ballantine Books, 2003.

Powell, Colin L. "U.S. forces: challenges ahead." *Foreign Affairs* (Dec. 1992).

Powell, Colin L. "Why generals get nervous." *New York Times* (October 8, 1992).

Putnam, Robert D. *Making Democracy Work: Civic Traditions in Modern Italy* Princeton, NJ: Princeton University Press, 1993.

Rakich, Nathaniel. "Redistricting has maintained the status quo so far. That's good for Republicans." *FiveThirtyEight* December 2, 2021 https://fivethirtyeight.com/features/redistricting-has-maintained-the-status-quo-so-far-thats-good-for-republicans/.

Ramkumar, Manaswini. "The Scylla and Charybdis of duty discharge: military dilemma with undemocratic leaders." *War on the Rocks* (October 11, 2021).

Redlawsk, David P. "Hot cognition or cool consideration? Testing the effects of motivated reasoning on political decision making." *The Journal of Politics* 64.4 (2002), pp. 1021–1044.

Reiter, Dan and Allan Stam. *Democracies at War*. Princeton, NJ: Princeton University Press, 2002.

Rhodes, Ben. "Has the myth of the 'good war' done us lasting harm?" *New York Times* (December 1, 2021).

Ricks, Thomas E. "I think this is the fundamental problem in U.S. civil-military relations these days" Foreign Policy April 21, 2014 https://foreignpolicy.com/2014/04/21/i-think-this-is-the-fundamental-problem-in-u-s-civil-military-relations-these-days/.

Ricks, Thomas E. "We have a big problem with retired generals wading into partisanship." *Foreign Policy* (September 9, 2016).

Ricks, Thomas E., Jess Blankshain, and Lindsay Cohn. "Some thoughts on the problem of politicians in the National Guard." *Foreign Policy* (December 11, 2014).

Rizvi, Arshad Javed. "Civil-military relations: a comparative study of Pakistan: from barracks to corporate culture (paths toward re-democratization: theoretical and comparative considerations."

Roberts, Kristin. "Rumsfeld resigned before election, letter shows." *Reuters* (August 15, 2007).

Roberts, Margaret E., Brandon M. Stewart, and Dustin Tingley. "stm: R package for Structural Topic Models." *Journal of Statistical Software* 91.2 (2019), pp. 1–40.

Robinson, G. Lee et al. "Veterans and bipartisanship." *Armed Forces & Society* 46.1 (2020), pp. 132–162.

Robinson, Linda. *Masters of Chaos: The Secret History of the Special Forces*. New York: PublicAffairs, 2005.

Robinson, Michael A. "Danger Close: Military Politicization and Elite Credibility", Ph.D. dissertation, Stanford University, 2018.

Robinson, Michael A. "Trump's pardon of two former Army officers has sparked new controversy. Here's why." *Washington Post* (November 17, 2019).

Robinson, Michael A. "What the Mattis resignation tells us about how Trump is damaging the military's credibility." *Washington Post* (December 21, 2018).

Robinson, Michael A., Risa A. Brooks, and Heidi A. Urben. "How Biden's pick for Defense Secretary might shake up civil-military relations." *Political Violence at a Glance* (December 8, 2020).

Robinson, Michael A., Lindsay Cohn, and Max Z. Margulies. "Dissents and sensibility: conflicting loyalties, democracy, and civil-military relations." *Reconsidering American Civil-Military Relations: The Military, Society, Politics, and Modern War*. Ed. Lionel Beehner, Risa Brooks, and Daniel Maurer. New York: Oxford University Press, 2020, pp. 63–82.

Robinson, Michael and Kori Schake. "Opinion—The military's extremism problem is our problem." *New York Times* (March 2, 2021).

Romano, Andrew. "Poll: 73% of Republicans blame 'left-wing protesters' for Jan. 6 attack. Just 23% blame Trump." May 27, 2021 https://news.yahoo.com/poll-73-percent-of-republicans-blame-left-wing-protesters-for-jan-6-attack-just-23-percent-blame-trump-191520343.html.

Romo, Vanessa. "Charlottesville jury convicts 'Unite The Right' protester who killed woman." *National Public Radio* December 7, 2018 https://www.npr.org/2018/12/07/674672922/james-alex-fields-unite-the-right-protester-who-killed-heather-heyer-found-guilt.

Rothstein, Bo and Dietlind Stolle. "The quality of government and social capital: a theory of political institutions and generalized trust." *Comparative Politics* 40.4 (2008), pp. 441–459.

Rowlatt, Justin. "Kunduz bombing: US attacked MSF clinic 'in error.'" *BBC News* November 25, 2015 http://www.bbc.com/news/world-asia-34925237.

Rubin, Jennifer. "Opinion—It's not 'polarization.' We suffer from Republican radicalization." *Washington Post* (November 18, 2021).

Rucker, Philip and Carol Leonnig. *A Very Stable Genius: Donald J. Trump's Testing of America*. New York: Penguin Books, 2020.

Rudolph, Thomas J. and Marc Hetherington. "Affective polarization in political and nonpolitical settings." *International Journal of Public Opinion Research* 33.3 (August 2021).

Rushing, J. Taylor. "Group of senators begin push to remove sex assault cases from chain of command." *Stars and Stripes* November 6, 2013 https://www.stripes.com/news/group-of-senators-begin-push-to-remove-sex-assault-cases-from-chain-of-command-1.251408.

Russonello, Giovanni. "QAnon now as popular in U.S. as some major religions, poll suggests." *New York Times* (May 27, 2021).

Ryan, Missy. "Military brass denounced Tucker Carlson's remarks about a 'feminine' force. Women say barriers remain for pregnant troops." *Washington Post* (March 20, 2021).

Ryan, Missy. "New disclosures show how Gen. Mark A. Milley tried to check Trump. They could also further politicize the military." *Washington Post* (September 17, 2021).

Ryan, Missy and Thomas Gibbons-Neff. "In inaugural Pentagon visit, Trump signs orders on immigrant vetting, military strength." *Washington Post* (January 27, 2017).

Saletan, William. "Americans are dangerously divided on the insurrection." *Slate Magazine* (June 9, 2021).

Salvanto, Anthony et al. "Americans see democracy under threat—CBS News poll." *CBS News* https://www.cbsnews.com/news/joe-biden-coronavirus-opinion-poll/ January 17, 2021.

Sargent, Greg. "Opinion—Trump: you wouldn't like my supporters in the military if they got angry." *Washington Post* (March 14, 2019).

Satter, Mark. "GOP ramps up attacks on teaching critical race theory to military." Roll Call July 15, 2021 https://www.rollcall.com/2021/07/15/gop-ramps-up-attacks-on-teaching-critical-race-theory-to-military/.

Saunders, Elizabeth N. "Analysis—Is Trump hurting the military?" *Washington Post* (June 2, 2020).

Saunders, Elizabeth N. and Scott Wolford. "Elites, voters, and democracies at war." Unpublished manuscript. Paper for the George Washington University Institute for Security and Conflict Studies Workshop (2017).

Scales, Robert H. "U.S. military planners don't support war with Syria." *Washington Post* (September 5, 2013).

Schake, Kori. "What is happening to our apolitical military?" *The Atlantic* (July 19, 2021).

Schake, Kori N. "The line held: civil-military Relations in the Trump administration." *Strategic Studies Quarterly* 15.2 (2021), pp. 38–49.

Schake, Kori N. and Jim Mattis, eds. *Warriors and Citizens: American Views of Our Military.* Stanford, CA: Hoover Institution Press, 2016.

Schake, Kori and Michael Robinson. "Assessing civil-military relations and the January 6th Capitol Insurrection." *Orbis* 65.3 (2021), pp. 532–544.

Schake, Kori, Peter Feaver, Risa Brooks, Jim Golby, and Heidi Urben. "Masters and commanders." *Foreign Affairs* August 25, 2021 https://www.foreignaffairs.com/articles/united-states/2021-08-24/masters-and-commanders.

Schiff, Rebecca. "Civil-military relations reconsidered: a theory of concordance." *Armed Forces & Society* 22.1 (1995), pp. 7–24.

Schmitt, Eric. "Clinton and Trump each lay claim to military brass." *New York Times* (September 7, 2016).

Schorr, Daniel. "Rumsfeld, a man with a plan." *National Public Radio* April 17, 2006 https://www.npr.org/templates/story/story.php?storyId=5346780.

Schultz, Kenneth A. *Democracy and Coercive Diplomacy.* New York: Cambridge University Press, 2001.

Schultz, Kenneth A. "Perils of polarization for U.S. foreign policy." *Washington Quarterly* 40.4 (2018), pp. 7–28.

Schwartz, Jason. " 'We are fighting for information about war': Pentagon curbs media access." *POLITICO* July 26, 2018 https://politi.co/2AcVZnd.

Schwartz, Matthew S. "1 in 4 Americans say violence against the government is sometimes OK." *National Public Radio* January 31, 2022 https://www.npr.org/2022/01/31/1076873172/one-in-four-americans-say-violence-against-the-government-is-sometimes-okay.

Seidule, Ty. "Opinion—What to rename the Army bases that honor Confederate soldiers." *Washington Post* (June 18, 2020).

Seitz, Amanda and Hannah Fingerhut. "Americans agree misinformation is a problem, poll shows." *Associated Press* (October 8, 2021).

Seligman, Lara and Connor O'Brien. "Conservatives lash out at the military over 'woke' policies." *POLITICO* (May 21, 2021).

Shabad, Rebecca. "How unusual is Trump's Cabinet of generals?" *CBS News* December 9, 2016 https://www.cbsnews.com/news/how-unusual-is-trumps-cabinet-of-generals/.

Shalikashvili, John M. "Opinion—Second thoughts on gays in the military." *New York Times* (January 2, 2007).

Shane, III, Leo. "Concerns about uniformed Marines on camera during Republican convention dismissed by White House, military officials." *Marine Corps Times* (August 26, 2020).

Shane, III, Leo. "Retired generals keep pushing their politics; some say it's getting uncomfortable." *Military Times* (August 6, 2016).

Shane, III, Leo. "Trump pardons former Rep. Duncan Hunter and four Iraq war vets convicted in Blackwater shooting." *Military Times* (December 22, 2020).

Shane, III, Leo, Meghann Myers, and Carl Prine. "Trump grants clemency to troops in three controversial war crimes cases." *Military Times* (November 22, 2019).

Shane, III, Leo and Kyle Rempfer. "Army investigating soldiers' appearance during Democratic convention over concerns of rule violations." *Military Times* (August 19, 2020).

Shanker, Thom and David S. Cloud. "Rumsfeld says calls for ouster 'will pass.'" *New York Times* (April 18, 2006).

Shapira, Ian. "He was America's most notorious war criminal, but Nixon helped him anyway." *Washington Post* (May 25, 2019).

Shear, Michael D., Nicholas Fandos, and Jennifer Steinhauer. "Trump asks critic of vaccines to lead vaccine safety panel." *New York Times* (Jan. 10, 2017).

Shear, Michael D. and Maggie Haberman. "Trump defends initial remarks on Charlottesville; again blames 'both sides.'" *New York Times* (August 15, 2017).

Sherwood, John Darrell. *Black Sailor, White Navy: Racial Unrest in the Fleet during the Vietnam War Era.* New York: NYU Press, 2007.

Shull, Abbie. "20 active-duty troops signed up for the extremist Oath Keepers militia—many with their military emails." *Business Insider* (January 21, 2022).

Sidman, Andrew H. and Helmut Norpoth. "Fighting to win: wartime morale in the American public." *Electoral Studies* 31.2 (2012), pp. 330–341.

Silva, Christianna. "Gen. Mark Milley says the military plays 'no role' in elections." *National Public Radio* (October 11, 2020).

Simonov Andrey, Szymon Sacher, Jean Pierre Dube, and Shirsho Biswas. "The persuasive effect of Fox News: non-compliance with social distancing during the COVID-19 pandemic." Working Paper. National Bureau of Economic Research, 2020.

Singer, Peter W. and Eric B. Johnson. "The need to inoculate military servicemembers against information threats: the case for digital literacy training for the force." *War on the Rocks* (February 1, 2021).

Singman, Brooke. "Trump Pentagon likely to abandon social experiments for core mission under Mattis, say experts." Fox News. January 1, 2017 https://www.foxnews.com/politics/trump-pentagon-likely-to-abandon-social-experiments-for-core-mission-under-mattis-say-experts.

Sisk, Richard. "Former Joint Chiefs chairman slams retired generals' political remarks." August 1, 2016.

Sisk, Richard. "General tries to avoid political firestorm over Puerto Rico relief." October 2, 2017.

Skelley, Geoffrey. "Few Americans who identify as Independent are actually Independent. That's really bad for politics." *FiveThirtyEight* April 15, 2021 https://fivethirtyeight.com/features/few-americans-who-identify-as-independent-are-actually-independent-thats-really-bad-for-politics/.

Snider, Don M. "Will Army 2025 be a military profession?" *Parameters* 45.4 (2015), pp. 39–51.

Snider, Don and Louis Yuengert. "Professionalism and the volunteer military." *Parameters* 45.4 (2015), pp. 39–64.

Sniderman, Paul M., Richard Brody, and Philip Tetlock. *Reasoning and Choice: Explorations in Political Psychology*. New York: Cambridge University Press, 1993.

Sniderman, Paul M. and Sean M. Theriault. "The structure of political argument and the logic of issue framing." *Studies in Public Opinion: Attitudes, Nonattitudes, Measurement Error, and Change* (2004), pp. 133–65.

Somer, Murat and Jennifer McCoy. "Transformations through polarizations and global threats to democracy." *The ANNALS of the American Academy of Political and Social Science* 681.1 (2019), pp. 8–22.

Sowers, Thomas S. "Beyond the soldier and the state: contemporary operations and variance in principal-agent relationships." *Armed Forces & Society* 31.3 (2005), pp. 385–409.

Stavridis, James. "It's been over 300 days since a pentagon press briefing. That should Concern everyone." *Time* (April 16, 2019).

Steinhauer, Jennifer. "As military addresses diversity, Republicans see culture war target." *New York Times* (June 10, 2021).

Steinhauer, Jennifer. "Once in thrall of 'the generals,' Congress now gives the orders on military issues." *New York Times* (May 21, 2021).

Steinhauer, Jennifer. "Younger military personnel reject vaccine, in warning for commanders and the nation." *New York Times* (February 27, 2021).

Stevenson, Jonathan. "Opinion—The generals can't save us from Trump." *New York Times* (July 28, 2017).

Stewart, Brandon M. and Yuri M. Zhukov. "Use of force and civil–military relations in Russia: an automated content analysis." *Small Wars & Insurgencies* 20.2 (2009), pp. 319–343.

Stolberg, Sheryl Gay. "Obama defends strategy in Afghanistan." *New York Times* (August 17, 2009).

Stroud, Natalie. "Media use and political predispositions: revisiting the concept of selective exposure." *Political Behavior* 30.3 (2008), pp. 556–576.

Sullivan, Tim. "Trump tweet intimating military will fire on 'looters' in Minnesota sparks another warning from Twitter." *Military Times* (May 29, 2020).

Sundaresan, Mano and Amy Isackson. "Democracy is declining in the U.S. but it's not all bad news, a report finds." *National Public Radio* (December 1, 2021).

Szalai, Jennifer. "Why is 'politicization' so partisan?" *New York Times* (October 17, 2017).

Szayna, Thomas S. et al., eds. *The Civil-Military Gap in the United States: Does It Exist, Why, and Does It matter?* Santa Monica, CA: RAND Corp, 2007.

Szoldra, Paul. "Army lieutenant who called Joint Chiefs memo 'seditious' probably about to get a class on the UCMJ." *Task & Purpose* (January 31, 2021).

Taber, Charles S. and Milton Lodge. "Motivated skepticism in the evaluation of political beliefs." *American Journal of Political Science* 50.3 (2006), pp. 755–769.

Tau, Byron. "Obama campaign announces co-chairs." *POLITICO* (February 22, 2012).

Taylor, S. E. and Susan Fiske. "Salience, attention, and attribution: top of the head phenomena." *Advances in Experimental Social Psychology*. Vol. 11. New York: Academic Press, 1978, pp. 249–288.

Teigen, Jeremy M. "Analysis—Do military veterans really win more elections? Only in 'purple' districts." *Washington Post* (July 20, 2017).

Teigen, Jeremy M. *Why Veterans Run: Military Service in American Presidential Elections, 1789–2016.* 1st edition. Philadelphia: Temple University Press, 2018.

The Economist. "Democracy index 2016: revenge of the deplorables." Tech. rep. 2017.

Thomsen, Danielle M. *Opting Out of Congress: Partisan Polarization and the Decline of Moderate Candidates.* Cambridge: Cambridge University Press, 2017.

Timsit, Annabelle. "'Very few' believe U.S. democracy sets a good example, global survey finds." *Washington Post* (November, 2021).

Tomz, Michael. "Domestic audience costs in international relations: an experimental approach." *International Organization* 61.04 (2007), pp. 821–840.

Toner, Robin and Jim Rutenberg. "Partisan divide on Iraq exceeds split on Vietnam." *New York Times* (July 30, 2006).

Torcal, Mariano. "The decline of political trust in Spain and Portugal: economic performance or political responsiveness?" *American Behavioral Scientist* 58.12 (2014), pp. 1542–1567.

Torchinsky, Rina. "1 in 5 Patriot Front applicants say they have ties to the military." *National Public Radio* (February 9, 2022).

"Tucker Carlson: Pentagon rebukes Fox host for attacking 'feminine' military." *BBC News* March 12, 2021 https://www.bbc.com/news/world-us-canada-56368679.

Uchill, Joe. "Former intel chief Hayden: think twice on a Trump job offer." *The Hill* (November 13, 2017).

Ulrich, Marybeth P. "Civil-military relations norms and democracy: what every citizen should know." *Reconsidering American Civil-Military Relations: The Military, Society, Politics, and Modern War.* Ed. Lionel Beehner, Risa A. Brooks, and Daniel Maurer. New York: Oxford University Press, 2020, pp. 41–62.

Urben, Heidi. "Civil-military relations in a time of war." PhD thesis. Georgetown University, 2010.

Urben, Heidi. "Like, comment, retweet: the state of the military's nonpartisan ethic." Tech. rep. National Defense University, 2017.

Urben, Heidi. "Wearing politics on their sleeves? Levels of political activism of active duty army officers." *Armed Forces & Society* 40.3 (2014), pp. 568–591.

Urben, Heidi A. *Party, Politics, and the Post-9/11 Army.* Amherst, NY: Cambria Press, 2021.

Urben, Heidi and James Golby. "A matter of trust: five pitfalls that could squander the American public's confidence in the military." *Reconsidering American Civil-Military Relations: The Military, Society, Politics, and Modern War.* Ed. Lionel Beehner, Risa Brooks, and Daniel Maurer. New York: Oxford University Press, 2021, pp. 137–148.

Usher, Barbara. "US bombed Kunduz clinic 'in error.'" *BBC News* November 25, 2011 http://www.bbc.com/news/world-asia-34925237.

Vergun, David. "Secretary Austin announces members of base-naming commission." Navy.mil February 12, 2021 https://www.navy.mil/DesktopModules/ArticleCS/Print.aspx?PortalId=1&ModuleId=523&Article=2503229.

Villareal, Daniel. "Former Joint Chiefs chairman breaks silence on Trump's leadership, says Trump shows 'disdain' for peaceful protests." *Newsweek* (June 2, 2020).

Votel, Joseph. "An apolitical military is essential to maintaining balance among American institutions." *Military Times* (June 8, 2020).

Warren, Mark E., ed. *Democracy and Trust*. Cambridge; New York: Cambridge University Press, 1999.

"Washington Post Editorial Staff: Fact Checker—General Betray Us?" *Washington Post* (September 20, 2007).

Watson, Eleanor and Robert Legare. "Over 80 of those charged in the January 6 investigation have ties to the military." *CBS News* December 15, 2021 CBS News https://www.cbsnews.com/news/capitol-riot-january-6-military-ties/.

White, Peter. "Trump may put 5 military officers in top posts. That's unprecedented." *Washington Post* (December 1, 2016).

Whitlock, Craig. "Leaks, feasts and sex parties: how 'Fat Leonard' infiltrated the Navy's floating headquarters in Asia." *Washington Post* (January 31, 2018).

Whitlock, Craig. "Military brass, behaving badly: files detail a spate of misconduct dogging armed forces." *Washington Post* (January 26, 2014).

Wickham, Hadley. *ggplot2: Elegant Graphics for Data Analysis*. New York: Spring-Verlag, 2016.

Wiegand, Krista E. and David L. Paletz. "The elite media and the military-civilian culture gap." *Armed Forces & Society* 27.2 (2001), pp. 183–204.

Wilesmith, Greg. "Reporting Afghanistan and Iraq: media, military, and governments and how they influence each other." Tech. rep. University of Oxford Reuters Institute for the Study of Journalism, 2011.

Wilke, Claus O. January 6, 2021 https://cran.r-project.org/web/packages/ggridges/vignettes/introduction.html.

Williams, John T. "Systemic influences on political trust: the importance of perceived institutional performance." *Political Methodology* (1985), pp. 125–142.

Wittes, Benjamin and Cody Poplin. "Public opinion, military justice, and the fight against terrorism overseas." *Warriors & Citizens: American Views of Out Military*. Ed. Kori N. Schake and Jim Mattis. Stanford, CA: Hoover Institution Press, 2016, pp. 143–159.

Wittkopf, Eugene R. *Faces of Internationalism: Public Opinion and American Foreign Policy*. Durham: Duke University Press Books, 1990.

Wong, Kristina. "Milley's defense of CRT to understand 'white rage' stokes controversy." Brietbart June 24, 2021 https://www.breitbart.com/politics/2021/06/24/top-u-s-military-officers-defense-of-critical-race-theory-to-understand-white-rage-stokes-controversy/.

Wong, Kristina. "Over 120 retired flag officers warn U.S. under assault from Socialism." May 11, 2021 https://www.breitbart.com/politics/2021/05/11/over-120-retired-flag-officers-warn-country-is-under-assault-from-socialism-and-marxism/.

Woodward, Bob. *Obama's Wars*. Reprint edition. New York; Toronto: Simon & Schuster, 2011.

Woodward, Bob. *The War With A Secret White House History 2006–2008*. 1st edition. New York: Simon & Schuster, May 2009.

Wright, David, Ryan Browne, and Naomi Lim. "88 former military leaders write letter backing Donald Trump for president." CNN September 6, 2016 https://www.cnn.com/2016/09/06/politics/donald-trump-military-leaders-endorsement-letter/index.html.

Yang, Kaifeng and Marc Holzer. "The performance-trust link: implications for performance measurement." *Public Administration Review* 66.1 (2006), pp. 114–126.

Youn, Soo. "Air Force offers help to LGBTQ personnel, families hurt by state laws." *Washington Post* (April 16, 2022).

Youssef, Nancy A. "Trump, calling Mattis a Democrat, opens the door to his departure." *Wall Street Journal* (October 14, 2018).

Zaller, John R. *The Nature and Origins of Mass Opinion*. New York: Cambridge University Press, 1992.

Zaller, John R. and Stanley Feldman. "A simple theory of the survey response: answering questions versus revealing preferences." *American Journal of Political Science* 36.3 (1992), pp. 579–616.

Zegart, Amy. "The three paradoxes disrupting American politics." *The Atlantic* (August 5, 2017).

Zeisberg, Mariah. *War Powers: The Politics of Constitutional Authority*. Princeton, NJ: Princeton University Press, 2013.

Zeitvogel, Karin. "Pentagon expresses 'revulsion' over Tucker Carlson's comments about women service members." *Stars and Stripes* (March 11, 2021).

Zelizer, Julian E. "How the Tet Offensive undermined American faith in government." *The Atlantic* (January 15, 2018).

INDEX

Note: Tables are indicated by a *t*, Figures are indicated by a *f*.

individual ideology and 33
information acquired and 79, 85, 90, 91
information for opinions formation 79
loss of credibility for military activism
by 153–54, 154*f*
loss of credibility for military institution
and 155–56, 156*f*
media influence on military performance 12
military positive affect from social function
of 19
political violence and 1
public and 8
public confidence in military and 118
public politics division from 19
partisan institutions
military public perception by 83
politicized military by 6
partisan media
credibility gap and 86–91
information consumption acquired 91
polarization and 33
selective information exposure 88–91
partisan military perceptions, cognitive bias
and 110–35
partisan politics 1
civilian leader interest in 6
civilian leaders damaged by 12
debate on 19
in-group members 111, 112
military elite endorsements 28, 162, 225–26,
234n80
military inclusion in 2–3, 11
polarization 2, 30–32, 31*f*
politicized institution for gain in 6
retired military elite and 14, 17, 28–29
Schultz on foreign policy and 12
violence 9
partisan public
active politicization of 165–66
battlefield performance measurement
116, 126, 136
partisan public response, to military
credibility 137, 138, 166, 167
H4E partisan public and elite source 70*t*,
148–49, 152, 153
H4F partisan public and institution 70*t*, 149
partisanship
hyperpartisanship 9, 11, 83, 114
military non-partisanship struggle 1, 13
public confidence in military and 16, 81–82,
82*f*, 92, 105, 113*f*
Rothstein and Stolle on co- 36
Supreme Court 37
partisan sorting
Fiorina on 33
political and social polarization from 83
of Republican Party ideology 34–35

passive politicization 16–17, 111
Don't Ask, Don't Tell and 173
of military 7, 15, 39, 42–43
of public and civilian leaders 7
Trump and 44–45, 129–33, 170
PCA. *See* principal component analysis
Perez, Celestino, Jr. 189
performance theories
battlefield performance 23, 110, 115–16, 126,
136, 213
Gronke and Feaver on 23
King and Karabell on 24
for military public esteem 13–14, 23–25, 24*f*,
27
Reagan and military image 24
Petraeus, David (general)
aspect politicization attack on 107–8
MoveOn.org anti-war advertisement on 107–8
Petty, Richard 50
Pew Research Center NCI dataset 92–93, 94*f*,
199–201, 200*f*, 203*f*, 242n57
PIE. *See* partisan behavior, institutional
endorsement, and electoral influence
Pierson, Paul 35
polarization
civil-military relationship and 8–10
Fiorina on 32–33
in military 9
military institution growing trend of 80
partisan media and 33
Somer and McCoy on 33
polarization in politics 6, 36, 173
Abramowitz and Jacobsen on 33
affective form of 32, 34, 35, 111, 117
asymmetrical trend in 34–35, 88
Civil Rights era and 30
Congressional distributions and 30–32,
31*f*, 186
in-group and out-group animus 34
Mason on 30
partisan politics and 2, 30–32, 31*f*
policy disagreements and 33
social function of 32
policy. *See also* foreign policy
civil-military relationship and
recommendations 17–19
credible information and preference of 10
information leaks shaping of 54–55, 74–75,
236n30
military elite cues on 49
military elite shaping of 15, 28–29
polarization in politics and disagreements in 33
retired military elite shaping of 15, 28–29
political activity, military credibility and
138–39
political appointments, of retired military
elite 160